THE CONSTRUCTION LAW LIBRARY FROM WILEY LAW PUBLICATIONS

ALTERNATIVE CLAUSES TO STANDARD CONSTRUCTION CONTRACTS
James E. Stephenson, Editor

ALTERNATIVE DISPUTE RESOLUTION IN THE CONSTRUCTION INDUSTRY
Robert F. Cushman, G. Christian Hedemann, and Avram S. Tucker, Editors

ARBITRATION OF CONSTRUCTION DISPUTES
Michael T. Callahan, Barry B. Bramble, and Paul M. Lurie

ARCHITECT AND ENGINEER LIABILITY: CLAIMS AGAINST DESIGN PROFESSIONALS
Robert F. Cushman and Thomas G. Bottum, Editors

CALCULATING CONSTRUCTION DAMAGES
William Schwartzkopf, John J. McNamara, and Julian F. Hoffar

CALIFORNIA CONSTRUCTION DEFECT LITIGATION: RESIDENTIAL AND COMMERCIAL
Thomas E. Miller

CALIFORNIA CONSTRUCTION LAW (FIFTEENTH EDITION)
Kenneth C. Gibbs and Gordon Hunt

CONSTRUCTION AND ENVIRONMENTAL INSURANCE CASE DIGESTS
Wiley Law Publications, Editors

CONSTRUCTION BIDDING LAW
Robert F. Cushman and William J. Doyle, Editors

CONSTRUCTION CLAIMS AND LIABILITY
Michael S. Simon

CONSTRUCTION CLAIMS ORGANIZATION SYSTEM
Robert S. Brams and Christopher Lerner

CONSTRUCTION CONTRACTING ALERT NEWSLETTER
Smith, Currie & Hancock

CONSTRUCTION CONTRACTOR'S HANDBOOK OF BUSINESS AND LAW
Robert F. Cushman, G. Christian Hedemann, and Peter J. King, Editors

CONSTRUCTION DELAY CLAIMS (SECOND EDITION)
Barry B. Bramble and Michael T. Callahan

CONSTRUCTION DOCUMENTATION (SECOND EDITION)
John A. Ricchini and James J. O'Brien

CONSTRUCTION ENGINEERING EVIDENCE
Loren W. Peters

CONSTRUCTION INDUSTRY CONTRACTS: LEGAL CITATOR AND CASE DIGEST
Wiley Law Publications Editorial Staff

CONSTRUCTION INDUSTRY FORMS (TWO VOLUMES)
Robert F. Cushman and George L. Blick, Editors

CONSTRUCTION INDUSTRY INSURANCE HANDBOOK
Deutsch, Kerrigan & Stiles

Construction Joint Ventures: Forms and Practice Guide
Mitchell W. Becker and Robert F. Cushman, Editors

Construction Litigation Formbook
David M. Buoncristiani, John D. Carter, and Robert F. Cushman

Construction Litigation: Representing the Contractor (second edition)
John D. Carter, Robert F. Cushman, and William J. Palmer, Editors

Construction Litigation: Representing the Owner (second edition)
Robert F. Cushman, Kenneth M. Cushman, and Stephen B. Cook, Editors

Construction Litigation: Strategies and Techniques
Barry B. Bramble and Albert E. Phillips, Editors

Construction Renovation Formbook
Robert F. Cushman and John W. DiNicola, Editors

Construction Scheduling: Preparation, Liability, and Claims
Jon M. Wickwire, Thomas J. Driscoll, and Stephen B. Hurlbut, Editors

Construction Subcontracting: A Legal Guide for Industry Professionals
Overton A. Currie, Neal J. Sweeney, and Randall F. Hafer, Editors

Construction Surety and Bonding Handbook
Gorden Hunt

Design-Build Contracting Handbook
Robert F. Cushman and Kathy Sperling Taub, Editors

Design Professional's Handbook of Business and Law
Robert F. Cushman and James C. Dobbs, Editors

Differing Site Condition Claims
Robert F. Cushman and David Tortorello, Editors

Federal Construction Contracting
James F. Nagle

Fifty State Construction Lien and Bond Law (two volumes)
Robert F. Cushman, Editor

Legal Guide to AIA Documents (third edition)
Werner Sabo

1992 Wiley Construction Law Update
Overton A. Currie and Neal J. Sweeney, Editors

Proving and Pricing Construction Claims
Robert F. Cushman and David A. Carpenter, Editors

Sweet on Construction Industry Contracts (second edition)
Justin Sweet

Troubled Construction Loans: Law and Practice
Stanley P. Sklar, Editor

CONSTRUCTION JOINT VENTURES: FORMS AND PRACTICE GUIDE

SUBSCRIPTION NOTICE

This Wiley product is updated on a periodic basis with supplements to reflect important changes in the subject matter. If you purchased this product directly from John Wiley & Sons, Inc., we have already recorded your subscription for this update service.

If, however, you purchased this product from a bookstore and wish to receive (1) the current update at no additional charge, and (2) future updates and revised or related volumes billed separately with a 30-day examination review, please send your name, company name (if applicable), address, and the title of the product to:

Supplement Department
John Wiley & Sons, Inc.
One Wiley Drive
Somerset, NJ 08875
1-800-225-5945

CONSTRUCTION JOINT VENTURES: FORMS AND PRACTICE GUIDE

MITCHELL W. BECKER

ROBERT F. CUSHMAN

Editors

Wiley Law Publications

JOHN WILEY & SONS, INC.

New York • Chichester • Brisbane • Toronto • Singapore

Library of Congress Cataloging-in-Publication Data

Construction industry joint venture formbook / Mitchell Becker, Robert F. Cushman, editors.
p. cm. — (Construction law library)
Published simultaneously in Canada.
ISBN 0-471-55638-6 (alk. paper)
1. Construction contracts—United States—Forms. 2. Joint ventures—United States—Forms. 3. Construction industry—Law and legislation—United States—Forms. I. Becker, Mitchell. II. Cushman, Robert Frank, 1931- . III. Series.
KF902.A3C6555 1992
343.73'07869'0269—dc20
[347.30378690269] 92-30756
CIP

Printed in the United States of America

10 9 8 7 6 5 4 3 2 1

PREFACE

> Working together and sometimes independently, [the Six Companies partners which joint ventured the construction of the Boulder Dam] were responsible for construction of the Moffat Tunnel in Colorado, Gray's Harbor in Washington and the Grand Coulee, Parker and Bonneville Dams.
>
> * * *
>
> Although the Six Companies partners would occasionally again build together, as they had at Boulder, in the future their partnership was often largely financial. One partner would find a project, then phone up the others, explaining how much capital was required and asking how much they were willing to invest. No lawyers were involved, and no contracts, and in the end, profits were simply divided in proportion to the capital each partner had put in.[1]

The use of a joint venture as a convenient and flexible vehicle to achieve a variety of objectives on construction projects, both in the United States and internationally, is becoming increasingly common. This book provides a single reference source for contractors, specialty contractors, suppliers, owners, operators, developers, design professionals and their attorneys, accountants, and insurance advisors who want to understand the structure and dynamics of the relationship between joint venture parties. Also discussed are the scope of the parties' relationship; the rights, duties, and contribution factors; the applicable tax liability and indemnification issues, as well as the dispute resolution ramifications. Readers who have hungered for up-to-date information pertaining to the state-of-the-art techniques and practical advice addressing these issues will find just that in this volume. Also at their fingertips are the right joint venture forms to use for a particular type of construction project and alternative forms for specific situations on a given project.

Compiling this information could be accomplished only through the collaboration of well-qualified specialists. As editors, we have mobilized the energies of recognized construction specialists who possess the qualifications and expertise to address these and other issues pertaining to construction joint venturing. The sample forms, which are subject-specific rather than generic or boilerplate, cover:

Commercial Projects
Industrial Projects

[1] L. McCartney, Friends in High Places, The Bechtel Story, 43–44 (1988).

Energy/Cogeneration/Sewage/Water Treatment Projects
Highways, Bridges, Airports, and Transit Projects
Telecommunication Projects
Health Care Projects
International Projects
Hazardous Waste and Cleanup Projects.

The writers have produced teaming/pre-bid and joint venture documents applicable to the type of project addressed in their chapter, highlighting and analyzing what they believe to be the most important contract provisions. These sample forms can be used as is or customized to suit the reader's specific needs. Readers will find the forms and explanatory text invaluable as they seek guidelines on structuring joint ventures. Other specific joint venture forms and important insurance information are also provided.

We have chosen our experts wisely and well and know that through the generous efforts and skills of these distinguished authors, we have in this formbook an outstanding reference work that could never have existed without cooperative effort.

August 1992

MITCHELL W. BECKER
New York, New York

ROBERT F. CUSHMAN
Philadelphia, Pennsylvania

ABOUT THE EDITORS

Mitchell W. Becker is senior vice president and general counsel for Morse Diesel International in New York, New York. Mr. Becker received a B.S. in civil engineering from Ohio State University, a master's degree in construction management/business from Ohio State University, and a Law Degree from New England School of Law. His employment experience in both the engineering and legal professions includes employment with large manufacturing concerns as well as construction firms. His previous responsibilities as a planning engineer, cost engineer, contracts analyst and legal counsel enable him to provide management direction in the areas of contract administration and legal matters. Mr. Becker is a member of the panel of arbitrators of the American Arbitration Association and a member of the Pennsylvania Bar Association. He has authored articles in the fields of manufactured quality assurance programs and contract administration.

Robert F. Cushman is a partner in the international law firm of Pepper, Hamilton & Scheetz and a recognized specialist and lecturer on all phases of construction and real estate law. He serves as legal counsel to numerous trade associations and construction, development, and bonding companies. Mr. Cushman is editor and coauthor of several books about construction, including the following John Wiley publications: *Construction Litigation: Representing the Contractor; Construction Litigation: Representing the Owner* (2d ed.); *Architect and Engineer Liability; Claims Against Design Professionals; Construction Defaults: Rights, Duties, and Liabilities; Construction Failures;* and *Proving and Pricing Construction Claims.* A member of the Pennsylvania bar, he is admitted to practice before the United States Supreme Court and the court of appeals for the Federal Circuit. Mr. Cushman has served as executive vice president and general counsel to the Construction Industry Foundation, as counsel to the American Construction Owners Association, and as regional chairman of the Public Contract Law Section of the American Bar Association. He is permanent chairman of the Andrews Conference Group's Construction Litigation and Hazardous Waste superconferences. Mr. Cushman is a charter member of the American College of Construction Attorneys.

SUMMARY CONTENTS

DETAILED CONTENTS

PART I

PRINCIPLES OF JOINT VENTURE AGREEMENTS

CHAPTER 1

OVERVIEW OF CONSTRUCTION JOINT VENTURING

Mitchell W. Becker
Peter F. Herzog

Mitchell W. Becker is senior vice president and general counsel for Morse Diesel International in New York, New York. Mr. Becker received a B.S. in civil engineering from Ohio State University, a master's degree in construction management business from Ohio State University, and a law degree from New England School of Law. His employment experience in both the engineering and legal professions includes employment with large manufacturing concerns as well as construction firms. His previous responsibilities as a planning engineer, cost engineer, contracts analyst, and legal counsel enable him to provide management direction in the areas of contract administration and legal matters. Mr. Becker is a member of the panel of arbitrators of the American Arbitration Association and a member of the Pennsylvania Bar Association. He has authored articles in the fields of manufactured quality assurance programs and contract administration.

Peter F. Herzog is associate general counsel of Morse Diesel International. He holds a bachelor of science degree in construction administration from the University of Wisconsin, and a J.D. from Illinois Institute of Technology-Chicago/Kent College of Law. He is a member of the Construction Law Institute and chairman of the Chicago Bar Association, YLS Construction Law Committee. Mr. Herzog has negotiated, drafted, and administered countless joint venture agreements of numerous types, and he has lectured extensively on joint venturing and construction contract negotiating.

§ 1.1 Introduction

The key to surviving and prospering in today's ever-changing construction marketplace is to be flexible enough to provide competitive construction services regardless of the scope or geographical location of the project.

This chapter discusses the need for joint ventures and the opportunities that can be created by them. It addresses the advantages and disadvantages of forming joint ventures, the methods of joint venturing, and some of the differences between joint ventures and other forms of "partnering." Finally, it provides a checklist, by category, of those generic terms and conditions found in most joint ventures.

Some of the following chapters focus the reader on the unique requirements of different industries. The chapters have been written by individuals with expertise in their respective industries. The chapter authors have provided the reader with agreement forms relative to their specific industry. The reader will find the commentaries accompanying the forms to be helpful in understanding the rationale for the specific terms and conditions suggested in the forms.

§ 1.2 Need for Joint Ventures

A formal and legalistic definition from *Black's Law Dictionary* (5th ed.) of a *joint venture* is "an association of persons jointly undertaking some commercial enterprise. It requires a community of interest in the performance of the subject matter, a right to direct and govern the policy in connection therewith, and duty, which may be altered by agreement to share in both profit and losses."

The construction industry in the United States is turning to the joint venture with increasing frequency in order to fill the need for a particular type of business entity to perform a particular type of function. The joint venture provides an ideal vehicle by which two or more entities can join forces, capital, knowledge, and/or expertise to form a single business entity with the particular resources, personnel, and capabilities required for the project at hand.

As construction projects have grown larger in size and more complex in scope, constructors and design professionals have found it increasingly necessary to expand their personnel and resources in order to meet the demands of these larger projects. Hiring entire staffs and investing in expensive capital improvements, however, may be cost-prohibitive in a selective, competitive bid scenario. Moreover, possessing the necessary staff and resources may even be a prerequisite for selection to the bid list, which prevents smaller contractors from staffing up only after being awarded the contract. The simplest solution to this dilemma is for two or more of the prospective bidders to combine their individual firms' strengths through a joint venture to create an organization large enough to manage the complex project properly.

A joint venture approach increases not only the staffing and resources of the resulting entity but also its financial strength, insurance capabilities, and bonding capacity. In a financially recessed construction market where more efforts are focused on larger-scale public projects funded by county, state, and federal dollars, the requisite bonding capacity is a competitive tool for survival.

Joint ventures are well-suited to accommodate the Affirmative Action and Disadvantaged Business Enterprise (DBE) participation programs, which are associated with publicly funded projects and most large private projects. In order to meet the required participation goals, a joint venture can be formed between a DBE and a non-DBE. In this way the DBE enjoys greater participation than if it were competitively bidding a smaller portion of the project on its own. The non-DBE can augment its work force with additional talent while partially or totally fulfilling the project's DBE participation requirements. On those projects requiring a payment and performance surety bond, a joint venture with a bondable coventurer may be the only means by which an unbonded DBE can participate. The joint venture can be structured to reward the coventurer supplying the bonds with a larger portion of the profits of the joint venture in exchange for its greater share of the risk. Even for construction projects not requiring bonded contractors, a joint venture may be the most efficient method of maximizing the participation of DBEs. The Equal Employment Opportunity and Affirmative Action programs required on most projects will fully recognize the participation of the DBE partner and credit the joint venture with compliance to the extent of the DBE's participation, even though the DBE may have less than a majority interest in the joint venture.

§ 1.3 Sharing the Risk

Joint ventures provide a means to share the project's potential risk and exposure among more participants. The types of risk and financial consequences to contractors are expanding constantly. These days, in addition to traditional risks such as weather delays, subcontractor bankruptcy, and labor strikes, contractors are being directed by owners and their lenders to assume new types of risk, including: discovery of contaminated soils, asbestos, concealed and subsurface conditions, loss of facility use, and loss of profits, as well as other consequential damages. It is not unusual to see liquidated damages for delays assessed at thousands of dollars per hour or, in some cases, per minute. A single day of delay can cost the contractor hundreds of thousands of dollars. Rather than assume all of the risk inherent in such projects, contractors have sought out joint venturers in order to share the risk in exchange for a share of the potential profits. Although members of a joint venture are generally jointly and severally liable for liabilities arising under the joint venture enterprise, the joint venture can be drafted by the parties to distribute the liability (risk) among the coventurers in either proportionate or disproportionate shares. It is this flexibility and adaptability that make the joint venture such a popular method of spreading the project risks over a broader and more financially responsive group of participants.

§ 1.4 Building a Technical Team

The more technically complex the scope of a construction project, the fewer the contractors qualified or experienced enough to build it. Whether the project involves the construction of processing facilities, control systems, clean rooms, or so-called smart buildings, an owner may choose to award a single general contract as opposed to multiple prime contracts in order to take advantage of a single point of responsibility and to avoid the possibility of getting caught in the middle of claims filed by separate prime contractors. By forming a joint venture with contractors who possess the technical skills and expertise required, a general contractor can select the technical team necessary to perform the project and thereby respond to the needs of the project owner.

§ 1.5 Creating Opportunities

In addition to merely filling some of the needs of owners and their projects, joint venturing can be useful in creating opportunities for contractors and other participants in the construction industry. By joining forces, coventurers can open doors that would otherwise remain closed to them individually.

One of the most popular reasons for joint venturing in the United States construction industry is to pair two or more contractors together in order to exploit the knowledge and experience of one of them with the dissimilar, yet required, strengths (such as financial and bonding) of the other. The unique knowledge and experience of the more technically qualified coventurer may benefit either the type of construction project or the geographic region in which it is located, or both.

§ 1.6 Vertical and Horizontal Integration

A construction joint venture entity can be structured either vertically or horizontally. As the terms suggest, *vertical integration* involves joining two or more parties who are positioned upstream and downstream from each other in the construction process. Generally, the parties will have different capabilities and resources. *Horizontal integration* joins two or more parties generally engaged in the same type of enterprise and therefore usually possessing similar expertise and capabilities.

One of the most common examples of vertical integration is a joint venture of a product manufacturer and a contractor who installs the product. By integrating or teaming with the manufacturer of the construction component, the contractor has the opportunity to accomplish certain goals because of the coventurer. For example, by making the manufacturer a member of the team that shares the team's profits and losses, the contractor can be assured that the manufacturer will devote a sufficient amount of effort to the production of the team's products. Second, the contractor can corner the market in a particular construction trade category by locking up a desirable manufacturer through an exclusive joint venture. Also, a smaller contractor can orchestrate a much larger purchase and installation package by joint venturing with the manufacturer rather than buying the product. This eliminates the need to use the contractor's line of credit.

Another example of vertical integration is the joint venture of a contractor and a design professional for design-build projects. Unlike traditionally structured projects in which an owner contracts separately for the services of a design professional and a contractor, an owner on a design-build project may choose to contract with one entity both to design and to construct the project. The owner could simply hire the contractor alone, who in turn would subcontract the design services to a design professional, but an alternative method allows the owner to contract with a joint venture consisting of the contractor and design professional. By doing so, the owner contracts with a single responsible entity and avoids the possibility of being caught in the middle of a dispute between its contractor and design professional, but maintains the benefits of privity of contract with both. In fact, because of the joint and several liability imposed on joint venture partners, the owner enjoys the security of being able to seek recovery of its damages from either or both of the coventurers, regardless of which of them is at fault. Even if the coventurer causing the owner's damages is judgment-proof, the owner could effect recovery from the surviving coventurer.

Probably the most common example of a horizontally integrated joint venture is when two or more coventurers join forces in order to construct a large project that would not otherwise be possible because of the size, complexity, geographical location, or risk involved. Usually, technical expertise is not an issue for either firm. The coventurers may be engaged in precisely the same type of enterprise and could be direct competitors. However, a horizontally integrated joint venture can produce a team whose value is far in excess of the sum of the parts.

§ 1.7 Alternatives to Joint Venturing

When making a decision to unite two business entities, the joint venture structure is just one of several methods available. The more popular alternatives to a joint venture include:

1. Corporation
2. Partnerships
3. Agency
4. Merger.

A *corporation* is defined in *Black's Law Dictionary* (5th ed.) as

> an artificial legal entity created under the laws of a state . . . ordinarily consisting of an association of numerous individuals. Such entity subsists as a body politic under a special denomination, which is regarded in law as having a personality and existence distinct from that of its several members, and which is . . . rested with the capacity of continuous succession, irrespective of changes in its membership . . . and of acting as a unit or single individual in matters relating to the common purpose of the association within the scope of the powers and authorities conferred . . . by law.

The key difference between a corporation and a joint venture is the concept that a corporation has a continuous and separate existence in perpetuity regardless of the continued existence of its individual members. In contrast, the joint venture exists only as long as its members exist.

The definition of a partnership is quite similar to that of a joint venture. A *partnership* is generally defined as an association of two or more persons or entities conducting themselves as co-owners of an enterprise for profit. However, one significant difference is that unlike joint venturers, partners are generally required to share the partnership losses among each of the partners, subject only to the limitations afforded limited partners under the locally adopted versions of the Uniform Partnership Act. Conversely, a joint venture allows the parties the freedom, under the laws of most states, to negotiate an agreement that excludes one or more of the parties from participating in the losses of the joint venture.

An *agency/principal agreement* is defined as a relationship between two parties wherein one party (the agent) is authorized to act on behalf of or represent the interests of the other party (the principal) subject to the limitations provided in the agreement. The obvious difference between a joint venture and an agency is that a joint venture is generally a mutual relationship. In other words, unlike an agency, which revolves around a principal and its representation by an agent, a joint venture traditionally represents mutual agreement between the parties so that each member may be empowered and authorized to represent the joint venture entity.

Finally, another common alternative to a joint venture is a merger or acquisition of one party by another. As simple as it sounds, a merger or acquisition is a highly regulated, complex, and time-consuming undertaking when compared to the relative ease involved with executing a joint venture agreement. Moreover, a merger or acquisition is intended to be permanent. A joint venture is intended to exist only as long as the parties intend for it to exist. They may design the joint venture to self-destruct in the event a contract is not awarded to the team. On the other hand, if awarded the contract, they may design the joint venture to exist through the completion of the project and any winding down period the parties deem necessary.

§ 1.8 Joint Venture Agreement Terms and Conditions

Any joint venture agreement, regardless of the type of project it applies to, needs to contain certain generic concepts. In the subsequent chapters, the individual authors address with specificity their concerns as to what should be contained in these individual clauses, giving the reader examples of specific contract language to meet certain needs.

The list in **§ 1.9** contains the issues that usually need to be addressed in some manner within any joint venture agreement. Appearing in outline form, it will be helpful to the reader as a general checklist. Cross-references indicate where to find specific discussion of these issues in subsequent chapters. Although not every item is addressed in the text, appropriate clauses can be found in the sample forms.

§ 1.9 Joint Venture Agreement Checklist

A. Management Considerations (see **§§ 2.20, 3.5, 4.4, 4.9, 7.4, 8.5, 10.12, 11.3**)

- **1.** Designating a Joint Venture Management Committee
  - **(a)** Representatives/Chairman
  - **(b)** Authority of committee/representatives
  - **(c)** Percentage required to approve
  - **(d)** Replacement of representatives
  - **(e)** Meeting frequency
- **2.** Establishing General Supervision/Management
  - **(a)** Project Manager
    - **1)** authority/control/responsibility
  - **(b)** Project Document Retention

B. Financial Considerations (see **§§ 2.21, 2.24, 2.32–2.34, 3.2–3.4, 4.4–4.5, 4.7, 4.10–4.12, 7.2, 7.6, 8.7, 10.10, 10.12, 10.13**)

- **1.** Initial Capitalization
  - **(a)** Subsequent capitalization
  - **(b)** Failure to contribute

2. Establishment of Joint Venture Bank Accounts
   (a) Where?
   (b) Signatory authority
3. Borrowing/Pledging Against Joint Venture Funds
4. Distribution of Profits/Advances Returned
5. Costs Chargeable to the Joint Venture
   (a) Defining nonchargeable costs
6. Audits/Tax Returns
   (a) Prepared by whom?
   (b) When/how often?
7. Means of Disposal of Equipment/Material
8. Establishment of Joint Venture Books of Accounts
   (a) Who maintains?
   (b) Access by other parties

C. Dispute Resolution (see §§ **2.35, 3.12, 4.19, 6.8, 7.15, 8.13, 10.15, 11.11**)
1. Forum
2. Timing
3. Nonunanimous Settlement Considerations

D. Insurance/Bonds (see § **4.13, Chapter 5**)

E. Tax Considerations (see §§ **2.13, 3.7, 4.11, 8.8, 10.3–10.6, 11.8**)

F. Scope of Services (see §§ **3.6, 4.6, 6.2, 6.5, 6.6, 7.5, 8.6, 11.2**)
1. Defining the Individual Venturer's Scope of Services
2. Minority Participation Requirements

G. Proprietary Information/Business Secrets (see §§ **2.27–2.28, 4.2, 7.9**)
1. Antitrust Considerations
2. Learning and Sharing Each Other's "Secrets"

H. Termination/Default (see §§ **3.9, 4.15–4.18, 7.11–7.14, 8.10–8.12, 10.16, 11.10**)
1. Termination
   (a) For convenience of owner
   (b) By death of one venturer
   (c) By bankruptcy/insolvency of one venturer
2. Default Issues
3. Rights/Obligations of Defaulting Party
4. Rights/Obligations of Nondefaulting Party
5. Project Guarantees/Defects

I. Risk Allocation (see §§ **2.25, 3.8, 4.12–4.14, 6.2, 7.8, 7.10, 8.9, 10.14, 11.2, 11.9**)

  1. Declaration of Profit/Loss Percentages
  2. Managing Venturer Fee
  3. Indemnifications
  4. Joint and Several Liability to Owner

J. General Boilerplate Terms

  1. Limitation and Purpose of Joint Venture (see §§ **2.17, 4.4**)
    (a) Description of project/projects
  2. Assignment of Rights and Obligations (see § **4.20**)
  3. Legal Jurisdiction for Dispute Resolution (see § **2.35**)
  4. Notice Provisions (see § **3.15**)
  5. Term of Agreement (see § **2.31**)
  6. Joint Venture Name (see §§ **2.16, 4.4**)
  7. Antitrust Considerations (see §§ **2.14, 8.3, 9.3–9.7**)
  8. Rights of Third-Party Beneficiaries (see §§ **5.10, 8.15**)
  9. Names, Addresses, Identification of Business Form of Each Member (see § **4.20**)
  10. Acquisition of Licenses (see § **4.2**)

CHAPTER 2

DRAFTING CONSTRUCTION JOINT VENTURES

G. Christian Hedemann
Mark S. Strukelj*

G. Christian Hedemann is vice president and general counsel of Fluor Daniel, Inc., Irvine, California, one of the leading engineering, construction, operations, and maintenance companies in the world. He previously worked for Bechtel, Stone & Webster, and in private practice where he was a litigator. He received his B.A. and J.D. degrees from the University of Colorado at Boulder.

Mark S. Strukelj is senior counsel in the law department of Fluor Daniel, Inc., Irvine, California, an international engineering and construction company. He advises Fluor Daniel in all aspects of engineering and construction contract law, project financed transactions, and related matters. Mr. Strukelj previously practiced general business law, primarily in the areas of tax and real estate. He obtained his undergraduate degrees at Loyola Marymount University and his law degree at Loyola Law School. Mr. Strukelj is a member of the California Bar Association.

FORMING THE ENTERPRISE

§ 2.1 Nature of Joint Venture or Consortium

The joint venture and consortium have always played important roles in the construction industry, and their use as convenient, flexible vehicles to achieve varied objectives in diverse contexts, both in the United States and internationally, is common. The consortium also has been used as a mechanism to facilitate cooperative efforts among multiple parties. Although many times the terms "joint venture" and "consortium" are used interchangeably, there are differences between the two entities.

Joint Venture

This chapter broadly uses the term *joint venture* to mean a business alliance of limited duration formed by two or more unrelated businesses or professional entities for the purpose of furnishing engineering, consulting, procurement, construction, and construction management services by consolidating the skills and resources of the participants.[1] The definition also includes the joint venture of a longer duration formed with the purpose of developing expertise or sales in a prospective, attractive market without being tied to a specific project.

A joint venture often has the legal attributes of a partnership, although the participants frequently provide in their agreement that for legal purposes a partnership is not being formed. Clearly, the main inspiration for the attempt to avoid acquiring partnership status is an aversion to assuming joint liability for each of the other participants' acts. Although it is possible to bind a client in a contract to the notion that joint liability does not exist, thus requiring the client to seek redress from each of the individual joint venturers, the joint venturers' exposure to third parties is commonly, and probably unavoidably, on a joint and several basis. For this reason, the legal distinction between partnerships and joint ventures is rarely made. The "*incidents* of both relationships are in all important respects the same, and courts freely apply the provisions of the Uniform Partnership Act [to joint ventures] where they are appropriate."[2]

A joint venture is sometimes distinguished from a partnership in a nonlegal way in that a joint venture is thought to be formed for a specific project while a partnership is intended to be formed to pursue a general or continuing business enterprise. In this sense, the phrase "joint venture" may be more appropriate for a construction project because the alliance typically dissolves after the project is completed. When dealing with the United States government in a joint venture, each participant may use its own approved accounting system rather than have the joint venture accounting system separately approved, as is the case with a true legal partnership.[3]

---

[1] The word *participant* is used to refer to an entity planning to form a joint venture or consortium with another entity.

[2] *See* Witkin, *Partnerships, in* Summary of California Law, ch. XIII, § 17 (9th ed. 1989).

[3] *See* A. Paul Ingrao, *Joint Ventures: Their Use in Federal Government Contracting,* 20 Pub. Contract L.J. 3 (1991) [hereinafter Ingrao]; *see also* Matanuska Valley Bank v. Arnold, 223 F.2d 728 (9th Cir. 1955).

Consortium

The term *consortium* connotes to nonlawyers a business relationship in which the participants desire to combine their efforts and skills without the opportunity to share in the profits and losses or economic gain and loss of the enterprise and without the risks associated with a joint enterprise. This often requires discrete scopes of work with no overlap or interrelation of functions. It also requires the client to agree to deal with each of the participants individually (that is, several, but not joint, liability), which many clients are unwilling to do. To avoid third-party liability, subcontracts and purchase orders would be entered into in the name of the responsible participant, not in the name of the consortium.

A consortium is not an entity but is a contractual relationship between the consortium members. Like a joint venture, a consortium is established to execute a specific project. However, the consortium is distinguished from a joint venture in that the consortium members generally do not have a joint interest in the subject matter of the venture (for example, the project to be constructed), do not share in the profits or losses of the venture, and do not undertake any fiduciary duty toward each other unless expressly agreed to under the consortium agreement.[4]

§ 2.2 Selecting a Venture Partner

The factors brought to bear in selecting a joint venture or consortium partner are legion. Clearly, experience and judgment play predominant roles. In selecting a partner, however, the initial enthusiasm must be tempered with sober awareness of the need to interact compatibly throughout the term of the alliance and to weather the day-to-day challenges of the operations and changing conditions of the participants. Often one of the participants will have a more dominant bargaining position than the others; in such cases experience suggests that flexibility and forbearance in the use of that bargaining power assist in securing a workable relationship in the long term.

Often, participants choose each other on the basis of earlier experiences in which favorable impressions were formed. The concern that a potential partner will gain an advantage or will be trained as a competitor in an area in which the partner does not presently compete is balanced against the advantages of

---

[4] *See* Milton, *International Consortium: Definition, Purpose and the Consortium Agreement,* 3 Fordham Int'l L.J. 121 (1979–80). Milton defines an *international consortium* as "a temporary contractual relationship of two or more business entities of different nationalities, formed for the purpose of executing, jointly and severally, a specific contract, usually involving complex civil engineering, for the supply of goods and/or services." *Id.*

working together, acquiring experience in areas in which each partner may lack the requisite strengths.

Loosely speaking, the selection of partners in joint ventures may even encompass a prime contractor-subcontractor relationship. "Teaming," in United States government parlance, often entails a prime contractor-subcontractor structure.

§ 2.3 Reasons to Form Enterprise

Although engineering and construction companies decide to form a joint venture or consortium for reasons that often are unique, some factors in addition to the acquisition of experience and strength recurringly bear on this decision.

§ 2.4 —Pooling Resources and Sharing Risks

A fundamental reason for teaming with other participants is the need to bring together the technical resources to enable the team to furnish the kind and magnitude of services which each participant would not be able to provide individually. It also allows the participants to share and allocate among themselves extraordinary risks that may be involved.[5] A notable example is the consortium of companies formed several decades ago to build the Hoover Dam. Through a joint venture, the performance of services and risks associated with that performance can be allocated to the participant with the technical expertise to perform those services and manage such risks.

Sometimes the complete shifting of risks is not desired. For example, one participant may have primary responsibility to engineer a facility with the other participant having the responsibility to construct it. Although duties have been specifically assigned to each participant, the parties can agree to share the risks that may arise from the provision of those services.

In a consortium, although the participants typically allocate risks based upon the individual scopes of work of the participants, if gaps arise after the project is initially allocated among the participants, the consortium agreement could require a proportionate sharing of the costs of any items not anticipated during that initial allocation.

When participants perform services as a joint venture on United States government projects, government regulatory requirements also must be considered in establishing and operating the joint venture.[6]

---

[5] *See* Segal, *Joint Adventures—The Sharing of Losses Dilemma,* 181 U. Miami L. Rev. 429 (1963–1964).

[6] *See* Ingrao at 3.

§ 2.5 —Meeting Legal Requirements

Many countries have enacted laws that require engineering and construction companies (among others) to form a joint venture or consortium, which might not otherwise be necessary, on the basis of strictly technological or business judgment. In an international context, such laws require foreign engineering and construction companies to enter into associations with one or more local firms to maximize utilization of often underemployed local talent (or some protected class) and to provide an incentive (or compulsion) for foreign firms to impart their technology and know-how to local firms in order to decrease the country's dependence on foreign expertise in the future.[7] The regulations governing United States work, requiring contractors to utilize minority, small, or women-owned contractors in performing such services, have a similar objective.

§ 2.6 —Business or Political Judgment

Aside from the need to form a joint venture or consortium to consolidate technical or financial resources, or to comply with applicable laws, engineering and construction companies may decide, on the basis of business or political judgment, that it would be advantageous from a marketing standpoint to form an association of some sort. For instance, one of the participants may be a sales representative or a source of knowledge of local business and political conditions.

§ 2.7 —Financing and Materials Supply

With the significant role that financing plays in many major projects, joint proposals may offer a substantive financing component. In such cases, financing institutions ordinarily are constrained by banking regulations and business risk factors to avoid being deemed as a joint venturer with either the borrower or the engineer/contractor. Moreover, laws in the United States that govern investment advisers may prohibit licensed financial advisers from forming a joint venture with unlicensed partners. When the proposal calls for the manufacture and supply of materials for incorporation into the project, a manufacturer of some of the materials may be a member of the joint venture

---

[7] *See* Franko, *International Joint Ventures in Developing Countries: Mystique and Reality,* 6 Law & Pol. Int'l Bus. 315 (1974); *Contractors Fight Forced Joint Ventures,* 196 ENR 49 (Feb. 12, 1976).

offering a turnkey package. In fact, such a manufacturer of materials also may be instrumental in obtaining financing for the project.[8]

§ 2.8 Form of Enterprise

The joint venture and consortium often are legally based on a written agreement between participants setting forth the terms on which participants agree to work together, including the participants' respective obligations, rights, and liabilities. Unlike the often cumbersome formality of the corporation, the joint venture/consortium agreement may be amended quite simply to accommodate the developing needs of the participants and to reflect changes in the project or the client's wishes.

§ 2.9 —Liability Considerations

In recent years, as the magnitude of construction projects has increased and the associated legal liability has reached menacing proportions, companies in the engineering and construction industries have attempted to limit their liability to minimize the risks to which they are exposed. Because under partnership law each of the participants may be liable for the acts of each of the other participants, and because one or more of the participants may be a company with substantial assets and significant activities unrelated to the joint venture, this concern is real and bears upon the choice of the legal form of the joint venture.[9]

Typically the joint venture/consortium agreement expressly excludes such joint liability. Nevertheless, a third party looking at the enterprise from the outside may not perceive or be on notice that liability is several. Furthermore, joint venturers may not desire to share the risks of the joint venture equally. Although a participant may be willing to share in the profits (or losses) generated by the joint venture, that participant's appetite may not be the same for other types of risks. For example, most participants will not accept the liability arising from a participant's unauthorized acts. Therefore, whether operating in a joint venture or a consortium form, the participants

---

[8] *See* United States v. Penn-Olin Chem. Co., 378 U.S. 158, 84 S. Ct. 1710 (1964), *on remand,* 246 F. Supp. 917 (D. Del. 1965), *aff'd per curiam,* 389 U.S. 308, 88 S. Ct. 502 (1967) (describing further reasons for which joint ventures are formed).

[9] *See* Ingrao at 3. In the context of United States government contracting, provisions of suspension and disbarment apply equally to all participants when fraud, criminal activity, or other improper conduct is imputed if the conduct is on behalf of a joint venture or with the knowledge of the participants.

often limit their liability through appropriate cross-indemnification from their coparticipants.[10]

§ 2.10 —Subsidiary Corporation as Participant

One response to the joint liability problem inherent in a joint venture/consortium is the formation by each of the participants of a subsidiary corporation whose sole purpose is to carry out the participants' activities in the venture. In such a case, the venture would consist of the subsidiaries, which would operate according to the terms of the joint venture/consortium agreement as though the parents had been the participants, with the goal that the subsidiaries would protect the parents from liability. Of course, a subsidiary of any company should always observe the corporate niceties of separateness and independence to avoid exposing its parent to liability for the subsidiary's acts, thereby defeating the purpose of forming the subsidiary.

§ 2.11 —Corporation

The participants may conclude for liability considerations that it is best to form a corporation, the stock of which is held by the participant/shareholders, which would have the effect of isolating the shareholders from liability arising out of the project. As a further insulation, the newly formed corporation, possessing minimal assets and capabilities, might execute subcontracts for substantially all of its project services to individual participant/shareholders so that each of the subcontractors would be liable only for its own actions. However, as discussed in **§ 2.13**, classification as a corporation may give rise to a double tax—a tax at the corporate entity level and a tax at the participant level. Some states have enacted legislation to allow participants to operate as a "limited liability company" (LLC), which provides a participant with limited liability (equal to its capital investment) with the income pass-through and special allocation attributes of a partnership.[11]

---

[10] See **§ 2.29** for further discussion of cross-indemnification among participants.

[11] For a more complete discussion of the elements of a limited liability company and a comparison of existing statutes, see Keatinge et al., *The Limited Liability Company: A Study of the Emerging Entity,* 47 Bus. Law. 378 (Feb. 1992); Wirtz & Harris, *The Emerging Use of the Limited Liability Company,* Taxes 377 (June 1992); Sakai & Ho, *The Limited Liability Company: A New Form of Business Organization,* Haw. B.J. 22 (May 1992). *See also* Burke & Sessions, *The Wyoming Limited Liability Company: An Alternative to Sub S and Limited Partnerships?,* 50 J. Tax'n 232 (1981); Johnson, *The Limited Liability Act,* 11 Fla. St. U. L. Rev. 387 (1983); Ribstein, *Limited Liability and Theories of the Corporation,* 50 Md. L. Rev. 80 (1991).

Although there may be advantages to the use of an LLC (for example, partnership status for United States tax purposes with treatment as a corporation in a foreign country), the LLC has important drawbacks, such as unclear status at the state level, limitations on transferability of interests, and limited duration. Clearly, choosing this form of doing business will depend upon the needs of the participant and the facts and circumstances of the particular transaction.

In a foreign context, it is worth noting that some countries are less than punctilious in viewing a subsidiary as separate from its parent. In a United States setting, establishing a corporation in which the percentage of ownership precludes consolidation on the parent's books may attract additional taxation at the subsidiary level.[12]

Shareholders' agreement and voting trusts. When a corporation or its equivalent is used, a shareholders' agreement or voting trust is often executed, defining the rights and obligations of the participant/shareholders and setting forth the bases upon which the company will be operated and the project managed. Such an agreement would be in addition to, but should complement, the legal mechanisms built into the articles of incorporation and bylaws of the company, and would contain project-related details similar to those usually found in joint venture/consortium agreements.

Restrictions on use of shareholders' agreements and voting trusts. Many countries and states have laws that restrict the enforceability of shareholders' agreements or voting trusts, particularly when the agreement confers upon one of the shareholders a degree of control and management that is disproportionate to its actual ownership of the corporation, or dispossesses some of the shareholders of their rights at law. In addition, some jurisdictions have laws that render unenforceable any agreement that attempts to give irrevocable authority to manage a corporation to persons other than officers or directors. The laws restricting use of shareholders' agreements or voting trusts naturally also apply to provisions in the articles of incorporation and bylaws having a similar effect. This may be problematic when management and control of the project is important to one of the participants providing most of the expertise, reputation, or financial resources to the joint venture and when that participant does not or cannot legally own a controlling interest of the stock. Such a participant may wish to maintain final authority with respect to project management decisions, and in such cases the provisions of the shareholders' agreement must be drafted with a view toward those laws. In some countries, there may be comparable restrictions on the enforceability of some control provisions set forth in partnership-type agreements.

---

[12] *See generally* Crestol, Hennesay & Rua, The Consolidated Tax Return (1988).

§ 2.12 Scope of Fiduciary Duties

Participants must be aware of the fiduciary relationship that is created between themselves and the joint venture/consortium, to a greater or lesser degree depending on the form of the alliance and applicable law. As discussed in **§ 2.1**, a consortium relationship generally does not in and of itself create a fiduciary responsibility among the consortium participants. However, the terms of the consortium agreement may contractually give rise to such a relationship.

Generally, when a fiduciary relationship exists, each participant may have a duty to disclose all information within the participant's knowledge relating to the business of the joint venture/consortium. To mitigate this duty, the participants can specify the nature of the information to be disclosed to the other participants and provide that all other types of information are not subject to disclosure.

Participants also may have an obligation not to self-deal to the detriment of the joint venture/consortium participants. Even if the joint venture agreement is silent on the subject, all dealings with the joint enterprise by any participant may have to be kept at arm's length to avoid a claim by the other participants that the self-dealing participant obtained an unfair competitive advantage.

Finally, participants may be constrained legally to offer business opportunities arising out of the joint venture's activities to the joint venture and not take personal advantage of those opportunities. To mitigate this duty, participants can specify in the joint venture agreement the scope of the business opportunities each participant must make available.[13]

§ 2.13 Tax Considerations

A joint venture may be treated for tax purposes as a partnership if it has partnership traits.[14] Tax law defines a *partnership* as "a syndicate, group, pool, joint venture, or other unincorporated organization through or by means of which any business, financial operation, or venture is carried on, and which is not, within the meaning of [The Internal Revenue Code], a corporation or a trust or estate."[15]

---

[13] *See* Design Professional's Handbook of Business and Law, ch. 4 (R. Cushman & J. Dobbs eds., John Wiley & Sons 1991); Witkin, *Partnerships, in* Summary of California Law, ch. XIII, §§ 18–21 (9th ed. 1989); Meinhard v. Salmon, 249 N.Y. 458, 164 N.E. 545 (1928); J. Carter, R. Cushman & C. Hartz, The Handbook of Joint Venturing, ch. 2, at 37 (1988).

[14] Under certain circumstances, for example in the co-ownership of property, a partnership is not necessarily created. *See* Treas. Reg. §§ 1.761-1(a) (as amended in 1972) and 301.7701-3(a) (1960). However, for purposes of discussing the tax consequences of a joint venture and because joint ventures are classified as partnerships under the tax law, the term "partnership" is used for clarity.

[15] *See* I.R.C. § 761(a) (codified at 26 U.S.C.). For cases defining joint ventures, see Tompkins v. Commissioner, 97 F.2d 396 (4th Cir. 1938); S&M Plumbing Co. v. Commissioner, 55 T.C. 702 (1971); Podell v. Commissioner, 55 T.C. 429 (1970).

Partnerships accordingly are defined in the negative. In making a determination, the court considers all of the facts and circumstances surrounding the relationship that evidence the parties' business purpose when joining together to conduct business.[16] A conclusory statement in the agreement that the relationship is not a partnership is not dispositive.

Various factors are considered to determine whether a business entity is a partnership: the intent to share in profits or losses or both, joint ownership of capital, joint participation in management, joint contribution of services, existence of a partnership (joint venture) agreement, and the filing of partnership tax returns. In any event, an objective to carry on business for profit is typically an essential characteristic of a partnership.[17]

A consortium in the engineering and construction industry is usually set up to avoid having the legal characteristics of partnership status. One participant may provide the consortium engineering services or equipment supply, while the other party provides construction (that is, each participant's scope of work is discrete). Each participant can agree to perform its services individually or provide equipment, earn the profit related to that task, and accept the associated risk attributable to that individual scope of work. Although the parties are working together to complete a common project, their interests on the project and other interests are separate and distinct. The end result is that each party receives its allocable share of the project profits based on its allocable share of the overall scope of work and each party would bear the burden of its individual profits for tax purposes. In addition, liability, to the extent possible, is several, but not joint.

Partnership Not Taxable in United States

In the United States, a partnership ordinarily does not constitute a taxable entity separate and apart from the participants, although it usually must file an information return. On the return, income or loss is computed as if the partnership were an individual taxpayer, disregarding various personal exemptions and deductions.[18] Accordingly, in most cases profits, losses, deductions, special allocation items, credits, and tax preferences directly pass through to the individual participants and, subject to certain limitations, must be declared for tax purposes (in the taxable year in which the taxable year of the partnership ends) on the respective participant's income tax returns, whether or not cash or other property is distributed or losses are covered by contributions.[19] Each

---

[16] *See* Carriage Square, Inc. v. Commissioner, 69 T.C. 119 (1977).

[17] *See* Rev. Rul. 55-606, 1955-2 C.B. 489. *Cf.* Brannen v. Commissioner, 78 T.C. 471, *aff'd,* 722 F.2d 695 (11th Cir. 1984) (in which profit motive was not determinative).

[18] *See* I.R.C. § 703(a). Regarding the treatment of limited liability companies as partnerships for tax purposes, see Rev. Rul. 88-76, 1988-38 I.R.B.14; Priv. Ltr. Rul. 89-37-010 (June 16, 1989); Priv. Ltr. Rul. 90-30-013 (Apr. 25, 1990); Priv. Ltr. Rul. 90-52-039 (Oct. 1, 1990); Priv. Ltr. Rul. 91-190-029 (Feb. 7, 1991).

[19] *See* I.R.C. §§ 702(a)-(b), 706(a); Temp. Treas. Reg. § 1.704-1T (1988).

participant's share of profits, losses, deductions, credits, and tax preferences is reflected in that individual's return and is consistent with the treatment of those items in the partnership return.[20]

Corporation Status

Potential participants in a joint venture should be aware of the possibility that the venture will be treated for tax purposes as a corporation. Treasury Regulations delineate six characteristics of a business enterprise that distinguish corporations from other entities recognized by the Internal Revenue Code:

1. Associates
2. An objective to carry on a business enterprise and share in its profits
3. Continuity of life
4. Centralization of management
5. Limited liability
6. Free transferability of interest.[21]

Because "associates" and "an objective to carry on a business enterprise and share profits" are common characteristics for both corporations and partnerships, only the remaining four characteristics are evaluated for purposes of business entity classification. Equal weight is given to each characteristic.[22] So long as the joint venture enterprise lacks at least two of the four remaining characteristics, it will be classified as a partnership.[23]

Characterization for United States Tax Purposes

There are innumerable foreign variants of business entities other than the corporation or partnership, and the United States will characterize those entities for tax purposes according to its own criteria, not according to the law of the place in which the entity is formed. For instance, the *limitada* may be taxable in the United States as a corporation notwithstanding its partnership attributes in the country of its formation.[24] In many countries (for example, Argentina and

---

[20] *See* I.R.C. §§ 702(b), 6222; Treas. Reg. § 1.702-1(a) (as amended in 1991); Bell, Leola v. Commissioner, 219 F.2d 442 (5th Cir. 1955).

[21] *See* Treas. Reg. § 301.7701-2(a)(1) (as amended in 1983).

[22] *See* Rev. Rul. 88-76, 1988-2 C.B. 360.

[23] *See* Treas. Reg. § 301.7701-2(a)(3) (as amended in 1983).

[24] *See* Abbott Lab. Int'l Co. v. United States, 160 F. Supp. 321 (N.D. Ill. 1958), *aff'd per curiam,* 267 F.2d 940 (7th Cir. 1959). *See also* Aramo-Stiftung v. Commissioner, 172 F.2d 896 (2d Cir. 1949).

Colombia), the limitada is not a corporation, and its members are taxed in the same manner as members of a partnership are taxed in the United States. However, because that entity has the attributes of a corporation under United States tax law, it is treated as a corporation for United States tax purposes.

Partnership May Be Taxable Outside the United States

In many countries other than the United States, a partnership is often a taxable entity, thus potentially giving rise to double taxation of the partnership, and possibly a withholding tax on profit remittances paid to the participant. In such situations, the participants may decide that this lack of tax benefit makes the limited liability aspects of a corporation more attractive than the traditional (in the United States) partnership form.

Foreign Taxation Checklist

The following is a checklist of some of the tax issues that may be involved in the selection of a joint venture form outside the United States:

____ The differences, if any, in tax rates applicable to locally formed companies and those applicable to domestically qualified branches of foreign corporations

____ The differences in tax rates, if any, on dividends payable by a local company to its foreign parent (often withheld by the payor subsidiary and sometimes exigible whether or not payment is actually made or legally permissible) and the tax rates on remittances of profits by branches to the home office

____ The need for a United States participant in a domestic joint venture corporation doing business abroad to have a part of the subsidiary joint venture's earnings included on its parent's consolidated tax return

____ The effect of any applicable tax treaties on the rate of taxation of the joint venture

____ The creditability of foreign taxes paid by the participants, considering especially the individual needs of the participants regarding the timing of the use of foreign tax credits[25]

____ The "controlled foreign corporation," subpart F, and foreign personal holding company provisions of the Internal Revenue Code[26]

---

[25] *See* Pugh & Thomas, *Income Tax Aspects of Joint Ventures Abroad, in* Private Investors Abroad—Problems and Solutions in International Business in 1975, at 275 (1976) [hereinafter Pugh & Thomas].

[26] I.R.C. §§ 951–972; Pugh & Thomas at 289–96.

____ The potential effect of laws that disallow deduction of certain kinds of expenses for purposes of calculating net income

____ Tax holidays or incentives that may be available

____ The effect of withholding taxes that may be levied on payments made by the joint venture to the participants for subcontracted services or profit remittance, and whether this is an expense to be borne by the joint venture or the participant.

The scope of **Chapter 2** does not permit a more extensive treatment of the tax issues (for example, tax basis of partnership assets, the individual partner's tax basis of its partnership interest, special allocations, and capital accounts) as they relate to a partnership structure. Although the partnership structure offers flexible structuring to fit the particular needs of the participants, the nuances of partnership taxation should be considered carefully by any prospective participant before venturing down the partnership road.[27]

§ 2.14 Antitrust Considerations

Although antitrust enforcement activity in the restraint of trade area in the United States has diminished in recent years, any participant entering a joint venture or consortium should consider the potential antitrust impact of the laws of any country with which the contemplated venture is connected.

In the United States, it has been clear for many years that the joint venture and the consortium fall within the purview of the antitrust laws.[28] In this connection, the engineering and construction industry has come under the scrutiny of antitrust enforcement agencies in a number of contexts.[29] This complex

---

[27] For a more complete treatment, see I.R.C. §§ 701–761; McKee, Nelson & Whitmore, Federal Taxation of Partnerships and Partners (2d ed. 1990); Wigner, *Joint Venture with Corporate Participants Including Questions on Characterization as an Association,* 22 N.Y.U. Tax. Inst. 611 (1964); Pugh & Thomas at 275.

[28] *See* United States v. Penn-Olin Chem. Co., 378 U.S. 158 (1964). Landes, *Harm to Competition: Cartels, Mergers, and Joint Ventures,* 52 Antitrust L.J. 625 (1983); Handler, *Emerging Antitrust Issues: Reciprocity and Joint Ventures,* 49 Va. L. Rev. 433 (1963); Pitofsky, *Joint Ventures Under the Antitrust Laws: Some Reflections on the Significance of* Penn-Olin, 82 Harv. L. Rev. 1007 (1969); Backman, *Joint Ventures and the Antitrust Laws,* 40 N.Y.U. L. Rev. 651 (1965); Bradley, *The Legal Status of Joint Ventures Under the Antitrust Laws: A Summary Assessment,* 21 Antitrust Bull. 453 (1976); Ingrao at 3. *See generally* Von Kalinowski, 10 Antitrust L. & Trade Reg. § 71 (1975); U.S. Dep't of Justice, Antitrust Guide Concerning Research Joint Ventures (1980).

[29] *Cf.* United States v. Halliburton Corp., No. 73-1806 (S.D.N.Y. June 30, 1976); United States v. Bechtel, No. C-76-99 (N.D. Cal. Jan. 5, 1979); Collusive Bidding and Related Practices, 2 Trade Reg. Rep. (CCH) § 4680; *Trustbusters Widen the War on Contractors,* Bus. Wk., Oct. 25, 1982, at 37 (regarding bid rigging). *See* U.S. Justice Dep't Antitrust Division, *Case C: Joint Bidding, in* Antitrust Guide for International Operations (1977).

subject is further complicated by the fact that the scope of United States laws governing anticompetitive abuses often extends into international transactions.[30]

In addition to being cognizant of United States law, participants in a joint venture or consortium also must be mindful of international laws that may restrict anticompetitive activities. For instance, with the elimination of European Economic Community (EEC) borders, joint cooperating enterprises may find they are subject to EEC competition law, which focuses on practices that restrict competition or abuse a "dominant" position within the EEC.[31] The EEC competition law is in addition to other applicable law and regulations in the particular member states.

Although antitrust issues are rarely a concern for the vast majority of joint enterprises in the engineering and construction industry, the following are a number of preliminary United States antitrust considerations applicable to the joint venture and consortium.[32] No attempt has been made to be comprehensive.

Eliminating a competitor. A joint venture or consortium is evaluated for restraint of trade purposes according to the standards applicable to mergers. Because each enterprise often is formed by agreements between competitors, one operative factor in an antitrust analysis is whether the participants would have been able or willing to perform the object of the joint enterprise alone.[33] If they could have individually competed for the project, it may be argued that competition is restrained by the fact that a competitive factor in the market has been eliminated. Alternatively, the combined forces of the participants may be said to give the new joint enterprise a dominance in the market that it has not gained by superior skill and industry, thus unfairly damaging other competitors without this advantage.

---

[30] *See* Kellison, *Joint Ventures Abroad and Per Se Antitrust Violations,* 1 Cal. W. Int'l L.J. 95 (1970); Joelson & Griffin, *Multinational Joint Ventures and the U.S. Antitrust Law,* 15 Va. J. Int'l L. 487 (1975).

[31] *See* Riggs & Giustini, *Joint Ventures under EEC Competition Law,* 46 Bus. Law. No. 3 (May 1991).

[32] In the rare case in which a proposed joint venture or consortium has attributes that may give rise to an antitrust concern, potential participants may request the United States Justice Department to review in advance the proposed joint enterprise and render an opinion as to the Justice Department's present enforcement intention under the United States antitrust laws. *See* 28 C.F.R. pt. 50.6; *see, e.g.,* Bus. Rev. Letter No. 57 (1972), Chicago Bridge & Iron & Gen. Elec. Co., 1976 Trade Reg. Rep. (CCH) ¶ 50,194 (concerning a joint venture to fabricate nuclear reactor pressure vessels).

[33] *See* United States v. Penn-Olin Chem. Co., 378 U.S. 158 (1964). *See also* United States v. National Elec. Ass'n, 1956 Trade Cas. (CCH) ¶ 68,534; Commonwealth Edison v. Federal Pac. Elec. Co., 1962 Trade Cas. (CCH) ¶ 70,488; United Nuclear Corp. v. Combustion Eng'g Inc., 302 F. Supp. 539, 555 (E.D. Pa. 1969). *See generally Merger Guidelines of the Department of Justice—1982,* 2 Trade Reg. Rep. (CCH) ¶ 4500.

Discouraging new entrants. The size of one or more of the participants in the relevant geographical or product market is considered in antitrust analysis in determining whether the merger might discourage other potential competitors from entering that relevant market.

Territorial divisions, exclusivity, and covenants not to compete. It may be important for the participants to agree contractually that they will not compete with the joint enterprise in a geographical or product area in which the joint enterprise will operate. In addition, participants often desire to cooperate on any exclusive basis through the joint venture or consortium. Care should be used in drafting such provisions to assure consistency with antitrust laws.[34]

Illegal tying and patent abuse. Antitrust law generally prohibits the practice of conditioning the sale of one product, on which the seller has a patent or a distinct competitive advantage, to the concurrent sale of another product, over which the seller has no advantage, thereby giving the seller an unfair competitive advantage in the market for the second product.[35] This principle may apply to the situation in which one of the participants is furnishing financing, patented process technology, or materials for a project, which are either unavailable in the open market, or which are offered at terms that are substantially better than those available in the open market, and the purchase of those services is tied to the sale of the nonunique services offered by the joint enterprise.

SUGGESTIONS FOR DRAFTING THE AGREEMENT

§ 2.15 General Considerations

Numerous issues must be raised and resolved when drafting joint venture and consortium agreements. Obviously, resolution of those issues and the formal structure established will be based in each case on the particular variables involved, including the country or state in which the project is located or the work is to be performed.

---

[34] *See* Continental T.V., Inc. v. GTE-Sylvania, 433 U.S. 36, 97 S. Ct. 2549 (1977), *on remand,* 461 F. Supp. 1046 (N.D. Cal. 1978), *aff'd,* 694 F.2d 1132 (9th Cir. 1982); United States v. Arnold Schwinn & Co., 388 U.S. 365, 87 S. Ct. 1856 (1967), *on remand,* 291 F. Supp. 567 (N.D. Ill. 1968), *dismissed,* 442 F. Supp. 1366 (N.D. Ill. 1977), *overruled by* Continental T.V., Inc., 433 U.S. 36; White Motor Co. v. United States, 372 U.S. 253, 83 S. Ct. 696 (1963).

[35] *See Patent Licensing Practices—Antitrust Division Reappraisal,* 1981-5 Trade Reg. Rep. (CCH) ¶ 50,434; Fortner Enters. v. United States Steel Corp., 394 U.S. 495, 89 S. Ct. 1252 (1969); United States Steel Corp. v. Fortner Enters., 429 U.S. 610 (1977).

In any event, it will probably be necessary to draft at least one agreement setting forth the participants' expectations regarding the joint enterprise, and the methods by which the project itself will be managed, including the obligations and rights of each of the participants. When submitting a proposal, it is often convenient to execute a brief statement of understanding (sometimes called a "Heads of Agreement Protocol," "Statement of Principles," "Memorandum of Understanding," and the like) that contains the basic outline of the important deal points, deferring the execution of a more extensive agreement until the proposal is accepted. If the corporate form or its equivalent is used, the participant/shareholders' agreement should relate directly to the formal mechanisms built into the articles of incorporation and bylaws. If services are to be performed in more than one country (for example, home office engineering and on-site construction work), two or more separate agreements with the client might be embodied in the overall agreement. If the services provided by the individual participants are to be functionally isolated from those of the others, having a master agreement containing general provisions, with subsidiary agreements with individual participants, may be helpful. **Sections 2.16** to **2.35** describe some of the features often found in joint venture and consortium agreements.[36]

§ 2.16 Limitation on Use of Names

The agreement may provide that the right to use the name of the participants is limited to the joint venture/consortium and that, upon termination of the joint venture/consortium, the right also terminates. In the event one of the participants withdraws or is expelled, provision should be made regarding continued use of the joint venture/consortium name. Those provisions may be fortified by a "mutual hold harmless" provision by which each party indemnifies the other against damages caused by unauthorized use of the individual participant's name. In countries in which trade name protection is not adequate, consideration might be given to liquidated damages, or the execution of a separate license agreement with the joint venture/consortium that would govern use of the name.

§ 2.17 Specification of Purpose

The agreement should specify the purpose for which the joint enterprise is being formed. It is usually prudent to specify with some precision the perimeters of the effort to distinguish the joint venture/consortium activities from

---

[36] *See generally* Note, *Joint Venture Corporations: Drafting the Corporate Papers,* 78 Harv. L. Rev. 393 (1964); Birrell, *International Joint Ventures, in* Private Investors Abroad—Problems and Solutions in International Business 241 (1976).

other activities of the participants on their own behalf. A number of contingencies to the validity of the joint venture/consortium should be listed, such as continued approval by government or client and approval by all parties of the terms negotiated into the prime contract.

§ 2.18 Obligations of Participants

The obligations of the participants should be set forth clearly. In this regard, the proposal or contract for the project in some cases may be made a part of the agreement. The agreement also should clarify whether the venture itself will hire personnel to perform the services or whether the participants will be required to furnish such personnel, either by way of a seconding agreement or subcontract. Any special obligations to disclose and utilize patents or secret processes should be spelled out.

§ 2.19 Restrictions on Use of Assets

Generally, assets are neither contributed to nor jointly owned by the participants in a consortium. In the case of a joint venture or if assets are owned by a consortium, however, the agreement should generally restrict the use of assets to the specified purposes of the joint venture/consortium. Similar restrictions might be placed on the ability of the participants to individually use the assets of the other participants other than as authorized in the joint venture/consortium agreement. The method of receiving and distributing funds should be set forth.

§ 2.20 Mechanism for Management and Control

One of the most important and potentially controversial features of the agreement is the mechanism for management and control of the joint enterprise and of the project in which the joint venture/consortium is involved. The procedure is dealt with in many different ways, but often involves the following pattern.

Board decides policy. A board or managing committee composed of representatives of the participants may be given responsibility for policy and broad-based management decisions, and this board would in turn appoint management personnel. The procedures by which the board meets and decides issues should be set forth, including the place, time, and notice requirements of the meetings and, in a multinational setting, the language of deliberation. The scope of the matters that must be submitted to the board, or that require unanimous consent, generally depends on the degree of responsibility and authority that the participants are willing to confer on the executive personnel carrying out the board's decisions.

Sponsoring participant. One of the participants may be designated as sponsor for purposes of maintaining overall project direction and implementing the decisions of the board. To ensure a mechanism for comprehensive project management and coordination, the agreement may refer in general terms to the methods by which decisions regarding staffing the project team will be made. Those matters can be specifically delegated to the sponsoring participant or left to the decision of the board.

Impasse breaking. The agreement may provide that in the event of an impasse regarding a decision affecting the project, one of the participants may act without the consent of the other in certain specified areas. For instance, in the interest of continuity the sponsor could be authorized to take certain actions relating to the project without the consent of the board. The danger of paralysis caused by a deadlock should be balanced against the efficiency of having one of the participants proceed to complete the project.

§ 2.21 Interests and Contributions

In the case of the joint venture, the percentage of the participation interest in and contribution to the joint venture by each of the participants should be stated. This statement should include the methods by which working capital, including funds to cover losses, will be originally and subsequently required to be contributed by the participants. The joint venture agreement may provide that profits and losses be shared in proportion to the participation percentages of the participants or on some other basis, if so agreed. It should be noted that distributions disproportionate to a participant's ownership interest may give rise to adverse tax consequences. Special tax-saving clauses might be introduced to avoid those results. Often, the percentage of joint venture interests is made subject to adjustment to reflect a level of effort by each participant that varies from the original allocation of interests.

The participants may wish to place some limit on the amount of working capital they may be obligated to contribute. In cases in which contributions involve more than one currency, the value of the contributions should be clarified in the agreement, and if the participants agree that noncash capital contributions may be made, such as the value of services or patents and processes, a limitation (for instance, a minimum cash requirement) might be appropriate. Ordinarily, the participants restrict the right to transfer interests in the joint venture, and specify the degree, if any, by which a participant may subcontract its obligations. Finally, the agreement should state whether the fee will be divided according to a predetermined rate or on some other basis.

§ 2.22 Basis of Compensation

If one of the participants will individually perform services or furnish some of its employees, or if, in the case of a joint venture, contributions to the capital of the joint venture are to be made in part by the value of the services of one of the participants, then the commercial basis on which such services will be performed should be specified.[37] When one of the participants will perform services to the joint venture or consortium by way of a subcontract, on a cost basis, it is necessary to clarify whether part of the fee, as contrasted to reimbursable costs, will be passed along to that participant. Considerable detail should be devoted to the description of compensation terms because the potential for disputes is great. All customary charges for overhead and special rates and surcharges should be described clearly. In long-term arrangements, rates should be subject to adjustment when increased costs can be substantiated.

§ 2.23 Distributions of Cash

A joint venture agreement should specify the time at which distributions of cash available from the joint venture to the participants will be made. If several contingent liabilities are involved, the participants may wish to defer cash distributions until those liabilities are discharged. If one of the participants has a unique need with regard to the timing or place of a distribution for tax purposes, or if potential currency conversion problems exist, it may be advisable to specify the timing, place, and currency of such distributions.

§ 2.24 Methods of Calculating Profit

In joint ventures, ambiguities in defining profit may arise over the appropriateness of special deductions, including contingency reserves, allocation for business development expenses, insurance premiums, employee benefits, and programs to be maintained individually by the participants' project support services (such as data processing, soils analyses, in-house economic analysis, and the services of the legal, insurance, and finance departments). Losses from prior years naturally should be recouped before any profit in the current year is deemed to exist. If the applicable tax laws allow special accounting methods that cause a different definition of profit than would result using generally accepted accounting principles, then the selected method should be stated.

---

[37] *See* I.R.C. §§ 61, 721 *et seq.;* Treas. Reg. § 1.721-1(b)(i) (1956) (regarding the tax treatment of such services).

§ 2.25 Limitation of Liability

Under a joint venture form, the liability of each participant in a joint venture is generally joint. Joint venture agreements usually set forth provisions limiting liability between the participants similar to the provisions contained in agreements with the clients of the participants. Frequently, a joint venture agreement provides that each of the participants indemnifies the other participants for any liability arising out of activities of the participants that are unrelated to the joint venture (for example, floating liens against one of the participants that encumber joint venture assets). When one of the participants brings specialized services to the joint venture, such as patented process technology or materials or financing services, it may be appropriate, on the one hand, for the participant supplying the specialized service or product to limit its liability to the other participants. On the other hand, the other participants may require that the participant furnishing such services hold the other participants harmless against liability arising out of these special activities. Use of an indemnity agreement also may be beneficial in the consortium setting, depending on the circumstances and the relative risks taken on by the participants without that indemnity. In any event, the usefulness of an indemnification by a participant is only as good as the financial strength of that participant.

§ 2.26 Right to Follow-Up Business and to Competition

Participants in a joint venture or consortium often feel that each participant should be prohibited from competing individually against the joint venture/consortium or the other participants with respect to business that is a follow-up to the project that is the object of the venture, or at least that some sort of right of first refusal should be allowed.

One of the practical disadvantages with such a restriction is that a particular client may find one of the participants unacceptable for some reason, thus foreclosing the project involved to all of the other participants. But in another context, if one of the participants has proprietary data or processes that are disclosed to the other participants on the project, it may be unfair to allow the other participants thereafter to bid individually on other jobs that utilize those data or processes.

A provision restricting follow-up business may cut both ways. For instance, during the course of construction, the client may perceive that one of the participants is making more significant contributions to the project than the other participants and may ask that participant to bid individually on follow-up work closely allied to the original project, without involving the other participants. If a contractual provision forbidding such activity exists, the participant having superior skill and industry may be unable to free itself from the association of a participant who does not contribute. Nevertheless, the participant who does in fact contribute to the success of the project and who may have played a role in developing new techniques, but whose role may not be known to the client, would have no protection of its rights in the business opportunity that developed in part as a result of its efforts.

Even in the absence of contractual provisions, as noted in **§ 2.12**, a fiduciary obligation may be imposed by law or under an agreement on each of the participants, prohibiting one of the participants from individually participating in business opportunities that were developed through the efforts of the joint venture or consortium.[38]

§ 2.27 Inventions and Secrecy

The right of the participants to inventions developed during the course of performing the project services must be addressed. This right is a matter of negotiation, and, unless one of the participants has a strong proprietary position in information to which the invention relates, it may be resolved by sharing ownership according to the participation percentages of the participants or by giving each a royalty-free license, with or without the right to sublicense. Additionally, participants often wish to provide that each will keep the proprietary information of the others confidential.

§ 2.28 Confidentiality of Information

Participants often disclose confidential or proprietary information to coparticipants at the inception or during the term of the joint venture or consortium. Typically, the contributing participant desires to maintain the confidentiality of that information. Accordingly, the joint venture or consortium agreement should contain a confidentiality provision that obligates each participant and the joint enterprise to maintain the confidentiality of the information and to return the information upon termination of the venture.

The confidentiality provision should describe the nature of the information to be maintained in confidence. The confidentiality provision should extend to the officers and employees of each participant. Also, the contributing participant should consider whether the duration of the confidentiality restrictions should continue throughout the term of the joint enterprise/consortium, or whether the duration should be longer or shorter than that term.

---

[38] *Cf.* Meinhard v. Salmon, 249 N.Y. 458, 164 N.E. 545 (1928).

§ 2.29 Methods of Conduct

When legal or ethical conflicts may exist, some benefit may come from stating that certain specified norms will be observed, particularly regarding such matters as public disclosure of policies and payments to agents. To attempt to protect other participants from the illegal or unethical activities of one participant, the agreement should contain language emphasizing that all laws will be obeyed and the highest ethical standards observed. In addition, a cross-indemnity should be considered and labor relations policies should be clarified.

§ 2.30 Contracting Methods

The participants may have individual contractual policies that potentially conflict. For instance, one of the participants may be willing to accept more liability for a project than the other participant. Alternatively, although one participant may require the client to provide advance funds and mobilization payments, the other participant may be willing to use its own funds until payment is received from the client. In short, contractual policies differ among companies as do business policies, and in the interest of good client relations, it is often advisable to decide in advance on certain fundamental contractual issues so the joint venture or consortium may deal with the client through a consistent approach.

In an international joint venture or consortium, services related to a project frequently are performed in more than one country, but the joint venture or consortium participates only in the country where the project is located. This scenario may be the case when a project is located in a less-developed country and one of the participants is a national of the country. If the enterprise anticipates that a participant will individually perform services directly for the client, such as worldwide procurement or home office engineering, without the participation of the other participants, this fact, together with division of fee implementation, should be considered.

§ 2.31 Duration and Termination

The joint venture or consortium ordinarily exists for the term of the project unless otherwise terminated by mutual agreement or by the withdrawal or expulsion of one of the participants. If one of the participants becomes insolvent, or breaches the joint venture/consortium agreement, or for other valid factors becomes unacceptable as a participant, the other participants may wish to have the right to take action necessary to ensure the continued success of the project in the name of the joint venture or consortium without the insolvent or breaching participant's consent. Such action may include replacing the unacceptable participant with another capable substitute (specifying the basis of compensation, if any) and ceasing all further distributions to the breaching participant. Obviously, any withdrawal has an impact on the ability of the joint venture or consortium to perform and, from the client's point of view, a change in the complexion of the joint venture or consortium may be a material change justifying termination or other damages. Also, the agreement should specify which provisions, if any, survive termination of the agreement.

§ 2.32 Preformation Expenses

The participants likely will incur expenses in advance of or collateral to the formation of the joint enterprise, such as costs for business development and legal efforts. The participants either agree to bear those expenses themselves—even though the expenses may directly contribute to the fortunes of the joint venture—or, in the case of a joint venture, agree that the expenses form a part of the capital contribution of the participants if the project is awarded.

§ 2.33 Accounting and Auditing

Each participant of a joint venture should have the right to audit the records of the joint venture as well as the records of the participants as they relate to services performed for the joint venture. Generally, such audit rights are not necessary for a consortium, although in a cost reimbursable setting the client typically will want audit rights. Participants may agree that a certified public accountant firm unrelated to the participants will prepare, keep, and audit such books and records, or one of the participants may perform one or more of those functions. In any case, the agreement should designate where the bank accounts will be located, who will be authorized to receive and disburse funds, and where the books of account will be stored. In the multinational setting, the currencies to be maintained should be stated specifically.

§ 2.34 Handling Taxes

If the joint venture is a partnership for tax purposes, responsibility for the preparation and filing of the joint venture's tax forms should be described clearly. Also, the participants should consider whether a "tax matters partner" should be designated.[39] Each participant may wish to retain certain notice and

[39] *See* I.R.C. § 6231. Generally, all partnerships must designate a "tax matters partner." However, a *small partnership* (defined as a partnership with 10 or fewer partners that has no

participation rights concerning any anticipated or ongoing tax dispute. In the event a tax matters partner is designated, that partner receives tax notices on behalf of the other partners, keeps all partners informed of administrative and judicial proceedings at the partnership level, and has certain rights relating to the audit of and settlement of adjustments to the partnership tax return.

§ 2.35 Governing Law and Arbitration

Increasingly, multinational joint venture and consortium agreements specify the law that governs interpretations of the applicable agreements and resulting disputes and agree to submit all disputes to arbitration. This practice may be problematic if the involvement of any third parties is desired, such as the client who is not a party to such an agreement and who would therefore be beyond the reach of the arbitration tribunal. On the other hand, the confidential, relatively informal nature of arbitration proceedings may be attractive for both the multinational and the domestic joint venture and consortium. When arbitration is chosen by participants in an international setting, and one of the participants is a national of the country where the project or client is located, it is important to ascertain whether that country has laws that enforce agreements to arbitrate outside that country. Arbitration in a neutral country is appropriate and often is considered fair.

The governing law and applicable rules for arbitration (if appropriate) should be stated. If the laws of the country where the project is located may not uphold key management or other provisions of the agreement, then a law that would validate those provisions should be selected.

---

special allocations among the partners) is excluded unless that partnership elects to be treated as a partnership for purposes of I.R.C. § 6231.

CHAPTER 3

COMMERCIAL CONSTRUCTION PROJECTS

Brendan J. McCarthy
K. Morgan Varner III

Brendan J. McCarthy is an associate with the Atlanta, Georgia, law firm of Varner, Stephens, Wingfield & Humphries. Concentrating in contract drafting, negotiation, and litigation, he routinely represents general contractors, architects, owners, and subcontractors in a variety of construction matters. Mr. McCarthy received his B.A. from The College of William and Mary in Williamsburg, Virginia, and his J.D. from the college's Marshall-Wythe School of Law.

K. Morgan Varner III is a senior partner in the Atlanta, Georgia, law firm of Varner, Stephens, Wingfield, & Humphries, which represents general contractors, subcontractors, owners, architects, engineers, and sureties in construction matters. A member of the American Bar Association Forum Committee on the Construction Industry, Mr. Varner specializes in all aspects of construction law, from contract negotiation to dispute resolution. He received his A.B. from Princeton University in Princeton, New Jersey, and his J.D. from Duke Law School in Durham, North Carolina. During his 24 years of practice, Mr. Varner has authored numerous articles and presented a number of seminars on construction law and contract matters.

---

§ 3.1 General Considerations

Broadly defined, the designation "commercial construction projects" includes all projects between heavy and industrial construction at one end of the spectrum and residential construction at the other. Although this chapter is relevant to all such commercial construction, many of the comments and provisions are more directly applicable to projects commonly thought of in the industry as pure "commercial construction," such as office buildings, hotels, retail, and mixed-use facilities.

In contemporary commercial construction the *joint venture* is a contractual combination of two or more independent companies that have formed an alliance for the purpose of entering into a single business transaction. In some instances, because of liability considerations, the parties may choose to create this alliance by forming a corporation. As shareholders, the joint venturing companies would be insulated from much of the liability arising in connection with the construction project. Additional insulation could be obtained if the joint venture subcontracted the actual construction work to the participants, thereby protecting each participant from any liability that might arise from the activities of the other participants.

Usually, however, the corporate form is too cumbersome from an organizational standpoint and the tax consequences are too unfavorable. Therefore, most joint ventures follow the nature of a partnership created by an agreement between the parties. Because of its predominance, the following discussion focuses primarily on this latter type of joint venture.

The fundamental goal the participants hope to achieve by forming a joint venture is the capability to obtain and perform jointly a particular construction project that none could have accomplished separately. The most common reasons for the formation of a joint venture are the need to combine the joint venturers' expertise and financial resources and to share risks. For example: a particular project may be too large for any joint venturer to bond separately or perform without risking capital beyond its capacity; the complexity of the project may make it necessary for the joint venturers to pool their technical skills; or one joint venturer may have greater financial strength and another superior knowledge of local conditions in the project area, including unusual construction conditions and risks, local business and political conditions, or the quality, reliability, and method of operation of local subcontractors and suppliers.

Regardless of the reason for entering into a joint venture arrangement, the relationship should be documented by a written agreement setting forth the terms of their cooperative efforts as well as each party's rights, obligations, and liabilities. If the corporate form is used, this agreement would be in the form of a shareholders' agreement, complemented by tailored language in the standard corporate documents (articles of incorporation, bylaws, and so on). When the joint venture follows the nature of a partnership, the agreement is very similar to a partnership agreement.

§ 3.2 Pre-Bid Agreement

In addition to a joint venture agreement as such, prospective joint venturers often enter into a *pre-bid* or *teaming agreement* to form a joint venture if they are awarded the contract for the project's construction. There is usually no reason to devote the time and effort or incur the expense involved in negotiating the specifics of the joint venture relationship until the prospective joint venture is awarded the contract.

The pre-bid agreement is vital, however. It cannot be merely an "agreement to agree." It must be a legally enforceable document that protects each party from being forced to participate in a joint venture or construct a project lacking the characteristics desired by such party. For example, the pre-bid agreement should provide that each party has the right to approve the terms of the bid to be submitted and the contract documents by which the project will be built. Similarly, it should contain provisions facilitating each party's ability to obtain sufficient information to make an informed decision regarding the acceptability of its overall exposure to liability arising out of participation in the joint venture and construction of the project. The agreement should provide for the exchange of information addressing each party's capability to fulfill its respective obligations as a joint venturer, specifically including construction experience and expertise and financial stability.

Payment of bid costs should also be addressed. It is desirable for the joint venturers to agree as to whether such costs will be shared, and if so, in what proportion. Moreover, the venturers should determine whether they would like those costs to be included in the construction work costs under the contract for the construction of the project; often the owner's consent must be obtained for that provision. The precise language to be used will depend on the characteristics of the project and the participating venturers.

Additionally, most pre-bid agreements reference, by attached exhibit or otherwise, the general type of joint venture agreement the parties anticipate executing in the event the construction contract is awarded to them. Although it would defeat the purpose of having a pre-bid agreement if the joint venture agreement were completely agreed to prior to the contract award, the eventual formation of the venture is facilitated by a thorough pre-bid exchange and review by all parties of the joint venture agreement each would desire to execute.

Each joint venture agreement must be fashioned to accommodate the characteristics of the project and participating venturers. Nevertheless, certain fundamental issues and provisions must be considered in drafting each such agreement. These are discussed in §§ **3.3** through **3.11**.

§ 3.3 Funding and Capitalization

Two types of joint venture funding issues must be examined. First, the more routine consideration involves the provision of financing to meet the initial and continuing funding requirements of the joint venture. The joint venture agreement should specify the initial contributions of each venturer and should set forth the method by which future contributions may be determined. Both initial and additional contributions are normally proportionate to each venturer's interest in the venture.

In most cases the joint venturers anticipate that the initial contributions plus the revenues generated during the construction of the project will be sufficient to sustain the venture's operation. However, the agreement should include a requirement that the parties make additional contributions if necessary for either the proper functioning of the joint venture or the funding of losses incurred. If a joint venturer is unable or unwilling to make such additional contributions, the agreement should provide that the other venturer or venturers may make the required contributions and receive an increased interest in the venture proportionate to their increased participation. Later, if there are any proceeds to be distributed to the delinquent venturer, it is customary for the venturer who made the contribution in place of the delinquent venturer to be repaid such contribution with interest from the proceeds that would otherwise have been distributed to the delinquent venturer. Often, such repayment does not affect the previously adjusted participation with regard to profits and assets. In other words, the venturer who contributed in place of the delinquent venturer maintains the increased interest in the joint venture regarding profits and assets. Responsibility for liabilities usually remains in accordance with the original proportions, however.

The second type of funding issue is far less common. It concerns those projects involving an owner who wishes to contract with a single entity to provide the construction and financing of the project (and in such cases usually the design and development as well). Particular care must be taken in the joint venture agreement regarding the allocation of risks that could arise from the obligation to provide financing. Due to the governmental regulation of the banking industry, financial institutions are generally prohibited from being a joint venturer. Consequently, unless one of the joint venturers is able to provide the necessary financing internally, the joint venture would need to raise the required funds from external sources. If raised from equity sources, the joint venture would be subject to federal and state securities laws. If raised from debt sources, the joint venture would be required to enter into a loan agreement with a lender. In either case, the potential liability of the joint venture, and hence each joint venturer, is significantly increased. Since in all likelihood a particular joint venturer (probably the developer/venturer) has the responsibility for obtaining the financing, the joint venture agreement should provide that such venturer bears all liability arising out of such obligation. This issue is discussed further in **§ 3.8**.

In addition to financing the venture, the participants will certainly be interested in withdrawing funds. The agreement should, therefore, be clear as to the timing and conditions of payment. If distributions are to be made only from profits, both the definition of "profits" (are deductions to be allowed for contingency reserves? employee benefits? contingent liabilities?) and the method of accounting (for example, "percentage of completion" or "completed contracts method") must be agreed upon and articulated in the agreement.

If distributions are to be made only subsequent to the completion of the project, profit calculations are somewhat easier in that most revenues and expenses will be known. A primary safeguard, namely, a provision dealing with unanticipated expenses that arise after disbursement, should be included. This obligates the venturers to pay their proportionate share of such additional expenses, and any other adjustments necessary, without regard to prior distributions.

In the event the participants wish to make distributions from sources other than profits or before the completion of the project, care must be taken to recognize and accommodate the additional potential risk. For example, such distributions could result in a need for later, additional contributions in order to complete the project. If any participant is unable to make such contribution, the remaining participants would be required to complete the project and the defaulting participant's contribution.

§ 3.4 Organization, Management, and Control

In creating a joint venture relationship, often one of the most difficult obstacles to overcome is establishing the mechanism for the venture's management and control. Because each participant faces potential exposure to financial loss if the venture is not successful, no venturer desires to be without a voice in the conduct of the venture's operation. This difficulty may not be as great when one of the participants is clearly the dominant party; nevertheless, certain decisions are of such importance that each joint venturer would like the right to participate.

Obviously, if no party has the ultimate right to make the final decision, there is the potential for an impasse. Any impasse that results in the inability of the joint venture to function in a timely manner could be extremely detrimental to both the joint venture and the construction project. Consequently, the joint venture agreement should include a provision for the resolution of deadlocks or impasses.

The most common mechanism for management and control consists of a management committee (composed of representatives of the participants) combined with a managing or sponsoring venturer. The *management committee* has the authority to make policy and management decisions for the joint venture and selects the person who will manage the venture's day-to-day activities (often referred to as *project manager*). The *sponsoring venturer* is authorized to act without the consent of the other venturers in certain designated areas, such as implementing actions necessary to avoid damage to the project if the management committee becomes entangled in an impasse.

The joint venture agreement should unambiguously and carefully articulate the definitions and limitations of the various levels of authority and responsibility. The project manager should be able to ascertain clearly both allowable actions and those requiring the approval of the management committee. Similarly, the management committee must have a precise understanding of their policy and management powers as well as the authority of the sponsoring venturer. The sponsoring venturer as well must be able to understand the actions it is authorized to take without the express authorization of the management committee and the conditions under which such actions are allowed. The fact that these provisions are often difficult to agree upon does not lessen their importance. It merely indicates the need for additional effort and reasonableness by the joint venturers in negotiating the agreement.

§ 3.5 Scope of Services Provided by Participants

Each joint venturer must have a definite understanding of both its obligations to the joint venture and the respective obligations of the other participants. It is advisable for the joint venture agreement to set forth in detail each joint venturer's duties, obligations, and responsibilities with regard to both the joint venture and the project. Because these roles often develop as the venturers gain knowledge of the project, they may not have been delineated when the venturers negotiated the other provisions of the agreement. In such instances a detailed statement of such duties, obligations, and responsibilities is added in an exhibit that is incorporated by reference in the agreement.

In fulfilling their obligations to the joint venture and the project, the venturers normally provide equipment and personnel. The agreement should be clear regarding the arrangement through which such assets are furnished. For example, if equipment is to be leased to the venture by one of the participants, guidelines and limitations for the terms of such leases should be stated.

With regard to personnel, the decisions might become more complicated. The agreement should specify whether personnel necessary to perform the joint venture services will be employed directly by the joint venture or furnished by the venturers pursuant to a subcontract, seconding agreement, or other arrangement. Employees generally should not terminate their employment with a venturer in order to become a direct employee of the joint venture. Among other things, these employees could forfeit accrued but nonvested benefits under the pension and profit-sharing plan of the company employing them. The venturers may ameliorate these consequences by amending the plan to cover persons indirectly employed by the company sponsoring the plan, thereby including those employed by the joint venture. Such amendments often create administrative and other difficulties, however, and many joint venture agreements provide that employees furnished to the joint venture remain employees of the participant.

If a venturer furnishes or contributes items other than equipment and/or personnel, the agreement should identify such assets and address how they are to be handled by the joint venture arrangement. For example, if a venturer furnishes a patent or secret process, the agreement should explain the return that venturer will receive. Similarly, the measures necessary to protect the respective interests in the asset of both the contributing venturer and the joint venture should be delineated, including any subsequent use or disclosure of a process, patent, or secret. The agreement should also provide for the distribution at the completion of the project of equipment purchased by the joint venture.

§ 3.6 Tax Issues

From the taxation perspective, joint ventures are combinations of two or more legal entities that have formed an alliance for the purpose of entering into a specific business transaction in order to make a profit. Such combinations generally fall into the income tax definition of a partnership and must file a partnership tax return. This is merely an information return, however, because a partnership is not taxed as a separate entity. Instead, the taxable income (or loss) is passed through to the partners who report it on their respective returns. Therefore, most joint ventures incur no separate tax, and the income or loss generated by the venture's activities is included in the tax return of the separate venturers. Avoiding double taxation in this way is usually the goal of joint venture participants.[1]

A joint venture can, however, have certain characteristics that will cause it to be classified as an "association" for tax purposes and taxed as a corporation rather than a partnership. Because corporations are taxed as a legal entity separate from their shareholders (unless subchapter S tax treatment is elected, which is not feasible in the case of a joint venture), double taxation would be imposed. Consequently, most joint venture participants wish to avoid being taxed as an association.

---

[1] For more discussion of taxation of joint ventures, see J. Morris, Joint Ventures: An Accounting, Tax, and Administrative Guide (John Wiley & Sons 1987). See also **Ch. 2**.

The general rule is that a partnership will not be classified as an association unless it has more corporate than noncorporate characteristics. Four characteristics distinguish a corporation from a partnership:

1. Continuity of life
2. Centralized management
3. Limited liability
4. Free assignability of interests.

A joint venture will not be taxed as a corporation unless it has three of these four aspects. Although the presence or absence of these characteristics is determined by federal income tax law, the legal relationships that govern them are determined by local law. Whether such characteristics exist in any given set of circumstances should not be assumed or inferred based on the intent of the parties or the apparent purpose of the venture.

Continuity of life. Under the Treasury Regulations, continuity of life is not absent simply because the venture is not organized to exist in perpetuity.[2] Rather, there may be continuity of life even though the organization will continue for only a specified length of time, unless the agreement provides that some event, such as the death, bankruptcy, incapacity, retirement, or expulsion of a participant, would cause a dissolution of the organization. Note that it is the dissolution of the organization that negates continuity of life, not merely the termination and liquidation of the organization's business and property. Under federal tax law, *dissolution* means an alteration of the identity of an organization by reason of a change in the relationship between its members. Local law determines whether there has been a change in the members' relationship that alters the identity of the organization.

Centralized management. The Treasury Regulations provide that an organization has the corporate characteristic of centralized management if any representative or representatives have the continuing exclusive authority to make the management decisions necessary to conduct the business for which the organization was formed.[3] Thus, the management committee of a joint venture would seem to provide centralized management. This is not necessarily correct, however. The Regulations also provide that centralized management does not exist if the centralized authority is merely to provide ministerial acts as the agent of the beneficial owners and management decisions are made by a vote of a majority of such beneficial owners.[4] Consequently, if the joint venture's management committee consists of representatives of the various beneficial owners and each

[2] Treas. Reg. § 301.7701-2(b)(1).

[3] *Id.* § 301.7701-2(c)(1).

[4] *Id.* § 301.7701-2(c)(3).

representative votes and otherwise acts as directed by his principal, it may be that centralized management does not exist.

Limited liability. According to the Regulations, the corporate characteristic of limited liability exists if under local law no member is personally liable for the debts of or claims against the organization.[5] Because each participant is normally responsible for such debts and claims, joint ventures generally do not have this characteristic; however, some concern may be justified if all participants are "shell" corporations having no substantial assets. In such case the Internal Revenue Service could argue that there was no one to whom creditors and claimants of the venture could look for recovery and, therefore, each venturer's liability was, in fact, limited to its interest in the joint venture.

Free assignability of interest. Commercial construction joint ventures normally involve an arrangement among parties whereby each participant relies on the other participants' providing services, knowledge, expertise, financial capacity, or other assets peculiar to such other participants. Therefore, the joint venture agreement usually prohibits any venturer from assigning or transferring its interest in the venture without the consent of the other venturers. Because the Treasury Regulations provide that in order for there to be free transferability of interest, venturers owning substantially all the interest in the joint venture must be able to substitute others for themselves without the consent of the other venturers,[6] normally construction joint ventures do not have the corporate characteristic of free transferability of interest.

§ 3.7 Liability, Risk Allocation, and Indemnity

Every prospective joint venture participant must critically analyze its potential exposure to risk. The type and magnitude of the liabilities that could be incurred must be identified, evaluated, and compared to potential benefits. Possible methods to minimize risk must be ascertained and utilized. Because liability to joint venturers may arise from more than one source, the agreement should contain provisions that delineate the respective liabilities of the participants, limit the liability between them, and require appropriate indemnities.

Generally, the risks arise from two principal sources—those inherent in the construction project itself, and those created by participating in the joint venture form of business organization. With regard to the project-related risks, the evaluation should be the same as would be done by each participant without regard to the existence of the joint venture. The routine questions must be satisfactorily answered. For example, will the project produce satisfactory cash

---

[5] *Id.* § 301.7701-2(d)(1).

[6] *Id.* § 301.7701-2(e)(1).

flow and ultimate profit? Are there any unusual features of the construction that could cause abnormal expenses or risk, such as concealed conditions, high-risk existing site conditions (for example, networks of fibre optic communication lines or subsurface water), or design requirements?

Certainly, the insurable risks should be handled as if there were no joint venture, including obtaining the same types of insurance coverage the participants would procure as individual general contractors. Further, each joint venturer should maintain its normal individual coverages. A review of existing policies is advisable, however, because some policies may contain an exclusion for joint venture participants.

Liability arising from the operation of the joint venture is generally allocated in accordance with the respective interests of the parties in the venture. However, when such liability results from a specialized service or product contributed to the joint venture by a particular venturer, the agreement should normally provide for the allocation of that liability entirely to the contributing venturer. For example, a participant contributing design expertise, financing services, or patented processes or materials should normally be responsible for all liability resulting from such services or products. The converse may also be appropriate. If the total participation of the venturer contributing such specialized services or products is limited to the contribution, the agreement could provide that the liability of the contributing venturer is limited to that arising from the contribution.

Although there is some potential liability to joint venturers due to fundamental characteristics of the joint venture as a form of business organization (for example, the potential violation of antitrust laws), the most common additional liability created by participating in a joint venture arises because each participant is exposed to liability not only for its own actions but also for the acts and omissions of the other participants. Therefore, the agreement should require each party to indemnify the other members from all losses and damages resulting from a breach of the agreement or misrepresentation by such party.

Of course, provisions in the joint venture agreement do not govern the liability of venturers to anyone except the other venturers. Most joint venture agreements, therefore, provide that if any participant becomes liable for more than its proper share under the terms of the agreement, the other participants will indemnify it as to such excess. In some cases the obligation to indemnify from liability to third parties not due to the acts or omissions of any particular venturer is limited by each indemnitor's respective interest in the joint venture.

Such indemnity provisions are valuable, however, only to the extent that the indemnitors have the financial strength to fulfill the indemnification obligation. It is, therefore, very important that each joint venturer be satisfied with the financial soundness of the other venturers. The pre-bid agreement should contain a provision requiring the exchange of financial information before the joint venture is formed. The joint venture agreement should contain a similar provision requiring an updating of such information either periodically or upon reasonable request of any venturer.

The indemnity provision in the joint venture agreement should also cover the obligation of each participant to indemnify the other participants from any liability resulting from activities of the indemnifying participant not related to the joint venture. Perhaps the most common example of the need for this type of provision arises when a creditor of one venturer encumbers a joint venture asset.

§ 3.8 Warranty and Guaranty

Upon entering into a construction contract as a contractor, the joint venture has the same warranty and guaranty obligations as would any other form of business organization under such contract. Because each joint venturer is severally responsible to the other contracting party (the owner) for the performance of the joint venture, each venturer is individually responsible for the fulfillment of the warranty and guaranty obligations required by the contract. For this reason, each participant should have a continuing interest in assuring that the joint venture fulfill those obligations from joint venture resources. Therefore, many joint venture agreements contain a *warranty reserve* provision stipulating that a monetary reserve will be established at the completion of the project and maintained until the expiration of the project's warranty period. The purpose of the reserve is to ensure there are joint venture funds to pay for all warranty work.

§ 3.9 Default

The consequences of a joint venturer's defaulting on its obligation to make a capital contribution as required by the agreement are discussed in **§ 3.4**. A participant could also fail to provide the services required by the joint venture agreement or otherwise breach the agreement. In such event, the agreement should grant the other participants the right to take the actions necessary to ensure the success of the project without the defaulting participant's consent. These actions should include the right either to perform the defaulting venturer's obligations for the proper consideration and or perhaps to replace such venturer.

§ 3.10 Duration and Termination

Ordinarily, the joint venture's existence is coextensive with the term of the obligations created by the governing construction contract. This term normally extends through the warranty periods set forth in the contract. There may, however, be reasons for early termination. If one of the venturers becomes unable (for example, by becoming insolvent) or unwilling to perform its obligations under the joint venture agreement, it may be appropriate for the other participants to have the right to terminate the venture.

The venturers must also consider that certain events will cause the joint venture to be automatically terminated and dissolved as a matter of law. Additionally, in some jurisdictions, upon the occurrence of certain events, the courts have broad powers to dissolve the venture upon the application of any member. Therefore, in addition to specifying the events that require or allow termination, the joint venture agreement should designate the party or parties who have the authority to wind up the affairs of the venture following termination, and provide guidelines for post-termination activities. Depending on the circumstances of termination, these activities could include continuation of the business of the joint venture, paying the debts of the venture, collecting monies owed to the venture, liquidation of assets and distribution of proceeds, and otherwise settling accounts between the joint venturers.

§ 3.11 Dispute Resolution

Any dispute that results in the inability of the joint venture to function in a timely manner could be extremely detrimental to both the joint venture and the construction project, and great care should be taken to avoid such deadlocks through proper management controls. See **§ 3.5**. Regardless of such controls, however, disputes will arise and must be resolved even if there is no impasse regarding the ability of the venture to operate. A decision-making mechanism that allows the continued operation of the venture in spite of a dispute does not necessarily resolve the dispute. It is advisable, therefore, for the joint venture agreement to contain a dispute resolution provision.

Perhaps the most common dispute resolution procedure is an agreement to arbitrate. The provision should state clearly whether all disputes or just certain types shall be arbitrated. The procedural rules should be specified (the Construction Industry Arbitration Rules of the American Arbitration Association are often used) and the place of arbitration and method of selecting the arbitrator or arbitrators should be designated. It may also be appropriate to state that the arbitrators have specific powers, such as the power to grant injunctive relief, and it is usually advisable to provide that a judgment may be obtained on the arbitrators' decision in any appropriate court having jurisdiction.

§ 3.12 Forms

The sample forms in **§§ 3.13** and **3.14** are designed to be generic for commercial construction projects. Although including provisions that generally implement the recommendations of this chapter, the forms should be used only as guidelines. Alternative language may be supplied, but many other possible situations are not addressed. The purpose of the forms is to provide fundamental information concerning substance and format, but each joint venture agreement must be tailored to accommodate the characteristics of the project and the participating venturers.

§ 3.13 Sample Pre-Bid Agreement

SAMPLE PRE-BID AGREEMENT

TABLE OF CONTENTS

This Pre-Bid Agreement is made and entered into this ________ day of __________, 19____, by and between __________, a __________ corporation, having its principal place of business at __________, hereinafter referred to as "A Corp." or "venturer" and __________, a __________ corporation, having its principal place of business at __________, hereinafter referred to as "B Corp." or "venturer" (A Corp. and B Corp., hereinafter sometimes collectively referred to as "venturers"), as follows:

WITNESSETH

WHEREAS, the venturers desire to prepare and submit a joint proposal for the contract to be awarded by __________ ("Owner") for the construction of the __________ (the "Project") pursuant to invitation dated __________, 19____, said contract bearing number ______, along with all other Contract Documents as defined in that agreement, known as "Invitation to Bid" are hereinafter collectively referred to as the "Construction Contract," and the work to be done by the General Contractor under the Construction Contract is hereinafter referred to as the "Construction Work," and

WHEREAS, the venturers desire for the joint proposal to be in an amount and on the terms mutually agreed upon between the venturers prior to submission, and

WHEREAS, in the event the joint proposal is accepted by the Owner, the venturers desire to enter into an agreement to form a joint venture ("Joint Venture Agreement") which shall enter into the Construction Contract with the Owner for the construction of the Project;

NOW, THEREFORE, the venturers, in consideration of the premises and mutual covenants and promises contained herein and other good and valuable consideration, the receipt and sufficiency of which are hereby acknowledged, hereby agree to submit a joint proposal for the purpose of bidding on the Construction Contract. To carry out this joint bid, the venturers mutually agree as follows:

1. Bid.

The venturers agree to prepare and submit a bid or proposal as a joint venture for the Construction Contract in an amount and on terms mutually agreed upon between the venturers prior to its submission. Each venturer shall have the right to approve the contract documents by which the Project will be built prior to the execution of the Construction Contract.

2. Withdrawal.

The venturers expressly acknowledge that at any time prior to the actual submission of the bid, either venturer may withdraw and be under no further obligation to the other venturer. The withdrawal of a venturer shall be effective upon the delivery of a written notice of withdrawal to the other party at the following addresses:

A Corp.:	B Corp.:
______________________	______________________
______________________	______________________
with a copy to	
(A Corp.'s attorneys)	(B Corp.'s attorneys)
______________________	______________________
______________________	______________________

In the event of a withdrawal by a venturer, the other venturer may submit a bid alone or with others, without any obligation to the withdrawing venturer.

3. Bid Filing.

No bid shall be filed under the joint names of the venturers unless:

a. Necessary commitments for performance and payment bonds have been obtained in advance of the bid;

b. Proper arrangements have been made for submission of a certified check in the amount of $______ payable to __________ (Owner), the same to be filed with the bid as required by the bidding documents;

c. Each venturer has provided proof reasonably satisfactory to the other venturer of the submitting venturer's financial substance and each venturer has agreed to keep confidential the financial information provided;

d. The venturers have agreed on the bid prices inserted in the bidding documents;

e. The venturers have agreed on the terms of the contract documents by which the Project will be constructed;

f. Each venturer is satisfied with the other venturer's ability and expertise to fulfill its respective obligations as a venturer under the terms of the Joint Venture Agreement.

4. Bonds.

If awarded the Construction Contract, the venturers shall jointly and severally execute the same and all bonds which may be required by the Construction

Contract and shall cause the execution and delivery of pertinent indemnity agreements required by the bonds.

5. Negotiations.

Any negotiations between the venturers and the Owner or between the venturers and the sureties, if any, subsequent to the submission of the bid and prior to the award, shall be conducted by the venturers jointly.

6. Bid Costs.

[All costs in connection with the bidding up to the date of the awarded contract shall be the individual charge of the venturer incurring the same and shall not be considered a cost of the Construction Work under the Construction Contract.]

[OR]

[The venturers agree to divide the costs incurred with bidding the contract in the following proportions:

A Corp. ___________, B Corp. ___________ .]

[OR]

[The Joint Venture shall reimburse each venturer, to the extent the Owner reimburses the Joint Venture, for all costs incurred prior to the award of the Construction Contract.]

7. Joint Venture Agreement.

If awarded the Construction Contract, the venturers shall execute a joint venture agreement in substantially the same form as Exhibit "A" annexed hereto, and the rights and obligations of the venturers arising out of this joint venture shall be stated in the Joint Venture Agreement.

IN WITNESS WHEREOF, the venturers have duly set their hands and seals the day and year first above written.

ATTEST:	A CORP.
______________________________	BY: ______________________________
SECRETARY	ITS: ______________________________
[CORPORATE SEAL]	
ATTEST:	B CORP.
______________________________	BY: ______________________________
SECRETARY	ITS: ______________________________
[CORPORATE SEAL]	

§ 3.14 Sample Joint Venture Agreement

SAMPLE JOINT VENTURE AGREEMENT

TABLE OF CONTENTS

This Joint Venture Agreement made and entered into this ________ day of __________, 19___, by and between __________, a __________ corporation with its principal place of business at __________, hereinafter referred to as "A Corp." or "venturer" and __________, a __________ corporation having its principal place of business at __________, hereinafter referred to as "B Corp." or "venturer" (A Corp. and B Corp., hereinafter sometimes collectively referred to as the "venturers"), as follows:

WITNESSETH

WHEREAS, the venturers desire to associate themselves for the purpose of entering into a contract for the performance of certain construction work identified as follows: ____
(the "Project"), which contract and all change orders, modifications, amendments, and supplements thereto, are hereinafter referred to as the "Construction Contract" and the work to be done by the General Contractor under such Construction Contract is hereinafter referred to as the "Construction Work"; and

WHEREAS, the venturers upon their joint proposal anticipate being awarded the Construction Contract by __________ ("Owner"), pursuant to invitation dated __________, 19____, said Contract bearing number ______; and

WHEREAS, the venturers hereto desire to undertake the performance of the Construction Contract as joint venturers, and their interest in the services to be rendered and the work to be done under the Construction Contract and any profits derived therefrom, and any liability for losses arising out of the performance thereof, be defined by an agreement in writing;

NOW, THEREFORE, said venturers, in consideration of the premises and mutual covenants, promises, representations, and warranties contained herein and other good and valuable consideration, the receipt and sufficiency of which are hereby acknowledged, hereby constitute themselves as joint venturers of a joint venture (the "Joint Venture") for the purpose of performing and completing the Construction Contract, but not for any other purpose, it being expressly understood that this Agreement contemplates only the furnishing and the performance of the Construction Work and other activities, labor, and materials necessary to the completion of the Construction Contract, and that the venturers are not making any permanent partnership agreement or permanent joint venture agreement to bid for, or undertake, any contract other than the Construction Contract, and nothing in this Agreement shall be construed as a limitation of the powers or rights of any venturer to carry on its separate business for its sole benefit except, however, the venturers shall cooperate with each other according to the terms and spirit thereof in the performance of the Construction Contract.

To carry out the Joint Venture, the venturers mutually agree to the terms, provisions, and conditions hereinafter set forth:

1. *Name Registration and Principal Office.* The Construction Contract shall be negotiated, agreed to, and entered into by both A Corp. and B Corp., as joint venturers, and the Joint Venture shall be known as the __________ Joint Venture and shall be named as Contractor in the Construction Contract. The venturers, for ease of reference, shall, to the extent they desire, use the words __________ and as and between the venturers and as to third persons, it shall be understood that the names so used shall have the same effect as if the full corporate names of the parties were used in place of said __________. For the purpose of the Joint Venture Agreement, the logo shall be as follows: ____________________________.
The Joint Venture shall be registered as required by any state, county, or other governmental authority having jurisdiction over the Joint Venture or the Project. The principal office of the Joint Venture shall be at __________.

2. *Management Committee.* The methods and manner of performance of the Construction Contract and the management of the Joint Venture shall be determined by the Management Committee, which shall consist of one representative appointed by each venturer. Each representative shall have full and complete authority to act on behalf of the venturer represented with regard to any matters or things in connection with, arising out of, or relative to said Joint Venture, and to act for, and bind, the respective venturer appointing such representative in any and all matters or things involving the performance of the Construction Contract, including, but not limited to, the execution of contracts with third persons.

A Corp. appoints ________ as its representative, and ________ as its alternate.

B Corp. appoints ________ as its representative, and ________ as its alternate.

Either venturer may at any time, and from time to time, change its representative by filing with the representative of the other venturer a written notice of appointment of a new representative or alternate, but until the filing of the written notice, the actions of the representative hereby appointed shall be conclusively binding on such venturer.

Unless expressly delegated in writing, the Management Committee shall have the sole authority to:

a) negotiate and execute the Construction Contract;

b) execute any amendments to the Construction Contract;

c) approve and execute all subcontracts, change orders, purchase orders, and rental agreements;

d) appoint, remove, and replace the Project Manager;

e) negotiate any settlements with the Owner or any other parties regarding the Construction Contract or the Project;

f) approve any changes to the schedule or progress of the Construction Work;

g) distribute any funds or profits in accordance with the terms of this Agreement.

Actions of the Management Committee shall be by unanimous vote and shall, as to any and all matters having to do with the Joint Venture, the Project, the Construction Contract, the performance thereof, or as to the interpretation of this Agreement, or as to any claim or dispute thereunder, be final, conclusive, and binding on the venturers with the same force and effect as if each venturer had actually taken such action or made such decision; provided, however, that neither venturer is prohibited from disputing decisions of the Management Committee as provided in this Agreement. If either venturer holds the majority interest in the Joint Venture as set forth in Paragraph 3, and as adjusted in accordance with the provisions of Paragraph 4, such venturer shall be designated the Sponsoring Venturer. **[In the event of disputes between the members of the Management Committee regarding the performance of the Construction Contract, the venturers agree that the decision of the Sponsoring Venturer shall become the decision on behalf of the Management Committee; provided, however, that the non-sponsoring venturer is not prohibited from submitting such disputes to arbitration pursuant to Paragraph 31 below.]**

[OR]

[In the event of disputes between members of the Management Committee such that a unanimous decision cannot be reached regarding the following issues, the

decision of the Sponsoring Venturer shall control the action of the Joint Venture; provided, however, that the non-sponsoring venturer shall not be prevented from submitting such dispute to arbitration pursuant to Paragraph 31 below:

a) action, if any, necessary to prevent damage to the Project;

b) action, if any, necessary to prevent a breach of any contract between the Joint Venture and any other party;

c) action, if any, necessary to prevent an increase in the cost of the Project;

d) action, if any, necessary to avoid a delay in the completion date of the Construction Work.]

[OR]

[In the event of disputes between members of the Management Committee such that a unanimous decision cannot be reached, the Sponsoring Venturer may act on behalf of the Management Committee if the Sponsoring Venturer reasonably believes:

a) that action is necessary to avoid damage to the Project;

b) that action is necessary to avoid a potential loss to the Joint Venture; or,

c) that action is necessary to protect the construction quality or schedule of the Construction Work.

Provided, however, that the non-sponsoring venturer shall not be prohibited from submitting such dispute to arbitration pursuant to Paragraph 31 below.]

[OR]

[If there is no Sponsoring Venturer and the Management Committee is unable to reach a unanimous decision regarding a material issue of performance of the Construction Contract, then [A Corp. or B Corp.] shall decide the issue; provided, however, that [A Corp. or B Corp., whichever did not decide the issue] shall not be prohibited from submitting such dispute to arbitration pursuant to Paragraph 31 below.]

[OR]

[If there is no Sponsoring Venturer and the Management Committee is unable to reach a unanimous decision regarding a material issue of performance of the Construction Contract or the interpretation of this Agreement, then either venturer may submit the issue to ____________, who shall decide the issue; provided, however, that either venturer shall not be prevented from submitting such dispute to arbitration pursuant to Paragraph 31 below.]

[OR]

[If there is no Sponsoring Venturer and the Management Committee is unable to reach a unanimous decision regarding a material issue of performance of the Construction Contract or the interpretation of this Agreement, then either venturer may submit the issue to arbitration pursuant to Paragraph 31 below.]

At all regular meetings of the Management Committee, each of the venturers either shall be represented in person or shall notify the representative of the other venturer in writing prior to the meeting of the name of another alternate or a waiver of its right to be present and its acceptance of any decisions that the representative of the venturer present shall make at said meeting. A representative or its alternate may participate in any meeting through the use of any means of communication by which all participants may simultaneously hear each other during the meeting. A representative participating in a meeting by this means shall be deemed present at such meeting. Provided reasonable notice of the date, time, place, and agenda to be discussed has been given with regard to such meeting, failure to participate in a meeting or to send an alternate shall be considered as an express concurrence by such venturer in and with the decisions, actions, and matters taken at such meeting. The actions and decisions of the Management Committee shall be binding on both of the venturers in connection with any action or thing involved with the Work called for by the Construction Contract or any action or matter arising under, or in connection with, the terms and provisions of this Agreement. Any representative not present shall be fully and promptly advised of any action taken. Neither representative, nor his successor, shall be personally liable to the Joint Venture or to either venturer by reason of his acts in accordance with this Agreement, except in the case of his gross negligence, or actual fraudulent or dishonest conduct.

3. *Share of Profits and Losses.* The venturers' interest in the Construction Contract, and all property and equipment acquired in connection with the performance thereof, and in any and all monies which may be derived from the performance thereof, and the obligations and liabilities of each of the venturers as among themselves in connection with the Construction Contract and with respect to any and all losses or liabilities in connection therewith, shall be in the following proportions (except as otherwise provided in Paragraph 4, in the event either venturer does not furnish its proportionate share of working capital):

A Corp. ___________ B Corp. ___________

4. *Capital Investment.* All necessary working capital, when and as required, shall be furnished by A Corp. and B Corp. in accordance with the percentages set forth in Paragraph 3 above. A bank account shall be opened in such bank as the venturers may determine, in which all funds advanced for the performance of the Construction Contract, as well as the funds received on account, shall be deposited. Said sums may be withdrawn by check, draft, or other instrument in such form and with such signatories by each venturer as the Management Committee may from time to time direct. Within five days after the execution of this Agreement, A Corp. and B Corp. shall each advance and pay into the bank account the following initial sums:

A Corp. ___________ B Corp. ___________

The need for working capital, in addition to the initial amounts required to be deposited by each venturer, shall be determined by the Management Committee and contributed as follows: Within fifteen days after the Management Committee determines any additional sums are required for the performance of the Construction Contract, both venturers shall deposit in the bank account their proportionate amounts as set forth in Paragraph 3 hereof.

In case either of the venturers is unable, or fails, or neglects, to advance or to contribute its proportionate share of the working capital required in the performance of the Construction Contract, then the other venturer may, but is not obligated to, advance such deficiency or any part thereof, and the venturer so advancing the sum shall be entitled to its adjusted proportionate share of the profits of the Joint Venture, so that the profits shall be allocated among the venturers in proportions in which the venturers shall have actually advanced working capital, even though, at a later date, the venturer in default shall have offered to make good or shall have made good its default in advancing working capital. Any venturer failing to advance its share of working capital shall not be relieved of its obligation to share the loss in the Joint Venture in the proportion set forth in Paragraph 3 above. Any venturer failing to advance its share of working capital may, at the election of the venturer not so in default, cease to have any representation on the Management Committee. The nondefaulting venturer shall be repaid all working capital advanced by the non-defaulting venturer because of the defaulting venturer's failure to pay, plus interest at the rate of ______ per annum, prior to the distribution of any profit as hereinafter provided.

The foregoing provision shall be deemed in addition to, and not in substitution for, any and all other rights or remedies the nondefaulting venturer shall have against the defaulting venturer.

No part of any funds advanced by the venturers to the Joint Venture shall be returned to either of the venturers until the completion of the Project and final settlement of all claims and liabilities in connection therewith, except as provided in Paragraph 16 below or as may otherwise be unanimously agreed upon in writing by the Management Committee and consented to, in writing, by the sureties of the Joint Venture.

5. *Project Manager.* **[Subject to the direction, control, and authority of the Management Committee, the Project Manager shall be responsible for:**

a) the direction and management of the Construction Work in accordance with the policies and procedures established by the Management Committee;

b) coordination of the Construction Work; and

c) coordination of all contacts with the Owner, the subcontractors, material suppliers, laborers, and any of their duly authorized representatives.]

[OR]

[The general supervision and management of the Work called for by the Construction Contract and any and all matters relating thereto shall be under the general charge and control of the Project Manager subject only to the control of the Management Committee. The Project Manager shall have the power, in the name of the Joint Venture, to execute and deliver purchase orders, rental agreements, subcontracts, and other agreements subject to prior review and approval by the Management Committee.]

The Project Manager shall be given such specific powers, in addition to the foregoing, as the Management Committee may from time to time delegate. The Project Manager shall be appointed by the unanimous agreement of the Management Committee and shall serve as such until either of the venturers shall reasonably require the Project Manager's removal, at which time, the Project Manager shall be removed. The Management Committee shall then immediately agree upon the Project Manager's replacement. If such agreement cannot be reached within forty-eight (48) hours following the removal, **[then the Sponsoring Venturer shall appoint a temporary Project Manager to serve until the Management Committee can agree on a replacement or the issue is resolved through arbitration.]**

[OR]

[then (A Corp. or B Corp.) shall appoint a temporary Project Manager to serve until the Management Committee can agree on a replacement or the issue is resolved through arbitration.]

This removal and replacement procedure shall also be applicable to the superintendents and other Project personnel.

6. *Limitation of Liability of Project Manager.* The Project Manager shall not be personally liable to the Joint Venture or to any of the venturers by reason of any action by the Project Manager in the capacity as Project Manager except for gross negligence, willful misconduct, fraudulent conduct, or dishonesty. This provision shall not alter the responsibility or obligation of either venturer to the other venturer or to the Joint Venture.

7. *Services.* Each venturer agrees to provide specific services, labor, equipment, and expertise in the performance of the Construction Contract as set forth in Exhibit "A" attached hereto and incorporated herein by reference.

8. *Construction Costs.* For the purposes of determining costs to the venturers of the Joint Venture, the costs of construction shall consist of the costs of the Construction Work as defined in the Construction Contract, and shall include, but not be limited to, costs incurred in connection with all subcontracts, labor, management, supervision, material, plant, equipment purchased or rented, bonds, insurance, taxes on labor and materials, imports, charges, legal fees, losses, expenses, liabilities not compensated by insurance, and all other expenses and obligations incurred or suffered in and about the performance of said Project of the nature which are properly chargeable as the costs of the performance of the Project under standard construction accounting practices. Said costs shall not include any charges against the Joint Venture for any overhead expenses or charges of the main or branch offices of the venturers, or for the time which may be expended in connection with the Construction Work by any of the venturers or their officers or employees, except as may be approved by the Management Committee, or except to the extent that such charges may be reimbursable to the Joint Venture by the Owner under the Construction Contract. Any in-house services provided to the Joint Venture by either venturer must be consented to by the other venturer. Any equipment rented from either venturer must be consented to by the other and be charged as a construction cost at a rate equalling ______% of the rates established in the most current edition of the "Compilation of Rental Rates for Construction Equipment" by the Association of Equipment Distributors.

9. *Books and Accounting.* Separate books of account for the performance of the Construction Contract and all matters pertaining thereto shall be kept and maintained at the main office of the Joint Venture. All records of the Joint Venture

shall be open for inspection by either venturer at all reasonable times. The books of the Joint Venture shall be maintained on a "percentage of completion" method and the tax returns of the Joint Venture shall be prepared in accordance with the provisions and regulations of § 460 of the Internal Revenue Code of 1986, as the same may be amended from time to time. The Project Manager shall furnish monthly to the Management Committee such statements and reports relating to the progress of the performance of the Construction Contract and to the financial condition of the Joint Venture as the Management Committee may reasonably request. At the completion of the Contract, and at such intervals as the Management Committee may agree upon, each venturer shall be furnished with the complete account of the receipts and disbursements of the Joint Venture. The Project Manager shall prepare and submit periodically, as the Management Committee may require, trial balances, balance sheets, and profit and loss statements. Not later than March 15 of each year during the existence of the Joint Venture, the Project Manager shall furnish to the venturers a Form 1065 and all tax return information of the Joint Venture. On December 31 of each year during the existence of the Joint Venture and at the completion of the Contract, if requested by either venturer, the accounts of the Joint Venture shall be audited by an independent certified public accountant selected by the Management Committee. Each such audit shall be performed in a manner which will permit the accountants to express an unqualified accountant's opinion with respect to the financial statements of the Joint Venture, if the existing facts warrant such an unqualified opinion. The cost of each such audit shall be borne by the Joint Venture.

To the extent that said records must be kept subsequent to the completion of the Construction Contract pursuant to a provision of the Construction Contract or as required by law, the records shall be kept at such place or places as the Management Committee may from time to time determine, and the costs thereof shall be borne by the venturers in the proportions stated in Paragraph 3.

10. *Ownership of Equipment.* Each venturer shall own its proportionate share, as set forth in Paragraphs 3 and 4 hereof, of all equipment, machines, materials, supplies, and other property purchased by the Joint Venture or charged to the account of the Joint Venture. At the completion of the Construction Contract, or sooner if such property is no longer required for the performance of the Construction Contract, such property shall be divided between the parties in a manner agreed upon by the Management Committee. If the Management Committee is unable to agree on such a division of some or all of such property, then such property shall be sold and each venturer shall be paid its share of the proceeds in the proportions set forth in Paragraphs 3 and 4 hereof. All funds and property acquired by the Joint Venture shall be held in the name of the Joint Venture.

11. *Labor and Employees.* Unless otherwise mutually agreed, the Joint Venture shall have no employees, and all personnel rendering services to the Joint Venture shall remain the employees of the respective venturers. All necessary personnel shall be provided from the staffs of the venturers. New personnel, employed specifically for work on the Project, will become employees of one of the venturers by mutual agreement at the time of the employment, with distribution of new persons as agreed upon between the venturers. The provision of the labor for the Project by the venturers shall be in compliance with the terms of any applicable collective

bargaining agreements to which either A Corp. or B Corp., or both, may be a party. Each venturer shall be reimbursed for all expenses incurred in providing said labor, including, but not limited to, salaries, insurance, employee benefits, workers' compensation insurance, public liability insurance, federal and social security taxes, state unemployment taxes, and any other taxes levied by the federal, state, or local authorities; provided, however, that if such items are reimbursable to the Joint Venture from the Owner under the Construction Contract, then the reimbursement to the venturers for such items shall not exceed the reimbursement received by the Joint Venture from the Owner. The receipt of such payments shall in no way affect or limit the venturer's interests in the Joint Venture as specified in Paragraphs 3 and 4 hereof. Each venturer shall invoice the Joint Venture monthly for the costs of providing such labor.

12. *Insurance.* The Joint Venture will acquire and maintain insurance to protect itself and the venturers from claims arising out of the Joint Venture's activities. The Joint Venture shall acquire all necessary payment bonds, performance bonds, fidelity bonds, completed operations insurance, commercial general liability insurance, workers' compensation insurance, automobile liability insurance, all-risk builder's risk insurance, and all in such amounts as the Management Committee believes reasonably necessary to protect the Joint Venture and the venturers. The premiums for such bonds and insurance shall be paid by the Joint Venture. To the extent that any venturer provides these coverages for the Joint Venture, that venturer shall be reimbursed for its costs of obtaining same, which payment shall not affect or limit that venturer's interest in the Joint Venture.

13. *Insolvency of a Venturer.* The venturers agree that if either venturer commits any act of bankruptcy or takes advantage of any state or federal insolvency, bankruptcy, reorganization, composition, or arrangement statute, or liquidation or receivership, or makes a general assignment for the benefit of creditors, such event or events could impair or frustrate the performance of the Joint Venture. The venturers accordingly agree that upon the occurrence of any such event, the Joint Venture shall be entitled to request of that venturer (the "insolvent venturer"), or its successor, adequate assurances of future performance. Failure to comply with such a request within ten (10) days of the delivery of the request shall entitle the noninsolvent venturer to declare that the insolvent venturer shall cease to have any say or voice in the management of this Project or any interest in the performance of the Construction Contract thereafter, or in the Joint Venture or in any of the Joint Venture's assets, and its delegation of authority to its representative to the Management Committee pursuant to Paragraph 2 hereof shall be deemed canceled. The representative to the Management Committee designated by the noninsolvent venturer shall have the full power and authority previously delegated to insolvent venturer's representative, and whenever it is provided in this Agreement that the act, consent, or decision of the venturers or the Management Committee is required, it shall be deemed to mean the act, consent, or decision of the noninsolvent venturer, excluding the insolvent venturer. The insolvent venturer, however, shall remain liable for its share of any losses as provided in this Agreement and shall be entitled to receive its share of the profits, if any, as provided in this Agreement, to be paid at the time and in the manner set forth in this Agreement. The representatives of the insolvent venturer shall be entitled to the monies advanced by the

insolvent venturer, plus such insolvent venturer's share of the profits, less such venturer's share of the losses, resulting from the performance of the Construction Contract to the date the insolvent venturer ceased to have any interest in the performance of the Construction Contract or in the Joint Venture or in any of its assets; provided, however, that the profit or loss computed as of such date shall be in the same proportion to the whole profit or loss resulting from the performance of the Construction Contract as the amount of Construction Work done thereunder as of such date bears to all Construction Work done thereunder. Such share in any profits or monies advanced shall not be payable to the bankrupt, insolvent, or liquidated venturer before the completion of the Construction Contract, the collection of all receipts, and the payment of all liabilities. In the event the share of the losses charged to the insolvent venturer exceeds the sum advanced by such insolvent venturer, the representatives of the insolvent venturer shall promptly pay to the noninsolvent venturer any such excess. The certified books of the Joint Venture, subject to standard construction accounting procedures, shall be conclusive in establishing whether a profit is realized or a loss sustained, the amount thereof, and the proportionate amount of Work done as of any such time or date.

14. *Assignment.* Neither venturer may assign, pledge, transfer, or hypothecate its obligations pursuant to, or interest in, this Agreement or any monies belonging to, or which may accrue to, the Joint Venture in connection with the Construction Contract or any interest in the Joint Venture account or in any property, real or personal, loaned or belonging to, or employed by, the Joint Venture, except with the prior written consent of the other venturer.

15. *Legal Counsel.* The Joint Venture may retain, as and when necessary, legal counsel to be mutually agreed upon by the Management Committee for use in connection with any matters of concern to the Joint Venture which may require legal counsel or assistance. The costs and fees incurred as a result of the retention of such legal counsel shall be promptly paid when due from the assets of the Joint Venture.

16. *Distributions.* Upon the completion of the Project, after providing for and paying all costs incurred in connection with the performance of the Construction Contract and this Agreement, and after paying or providing for any and all of the costs and charges ordinarily and usually charged as costs of performance of such a contract, including payment of any and all claims not compensated by insurance, and after providing proper reserves for any claims which either have been, or may be reasonably anticipated to be, brought against the Joint Venture or the venturers, and after repaying all sums advanced by any venturer for working capital, any profits (not losses) thereafter remaining, resulting from the performance of the Construction Contract, shall be distributed and divided between the venturers in accordance with their respective proportion as set forth in Paragraph 3 hereof, and as modified in accordance with Paragraph 4 hereof. When no longer required, any reserves, established in accordance with this Paragraph, shall be similarly distributed.

[By mutual agreement of the Management Committee and with the written consent of the Joint Venture's sureties and when adequate reserves have been established pursuant to this Paragraph, working capital deposited by the venturers and anticipated profits may be distributed to the venturers prior to the completion

of the Construction Contract in proportion to their respective interests as set forth in Paragraphs 3 and 4.]

[OR]

[Provided, however, that after the Construction Contract has reached a completion state of _____ percent or more (as computed by the Management Committee), and further provided that the Management Committee unanimously agrees the need for operating capital has diminished, the Joint Venture may distribute to the venturers their respective proportionate share of the anticipated profits and a proportionate return of capital contributions in such proportions as set forth in Paragraph 3 and amended in Paragraph 4, all in such amounts as the Management Committee unanimously agrees.]

Nothing contained in this Paragraph shall invalidate the obligation of the venturers to furnish additional capital as provided for in Paragraph 4 hereof should additional capital be determined necessary by the Management Committee at any time before or after any distribution. Likewise, regardless of any distribution which may have been made, if the performance of the Construction Contract shall result in a loss, the venturers shall be obligated in proportionate amounts as set forth in Paragraph 3 hereof (irrespective of the fact that a venturer may have advanced more than its respective share of working capital as provided in Paragraph 4), and the liability of the venturers for the bearing of losses shall continue against any claims which, at any time either before or after the performance of the Construction Contract, shall be made against them or any of them by reason of carrying out this Joint Venture or any matter or thing in connection therewith. In the event that, following disbursement as set out above, the Joint Venture incurs any loss, damage, expense, or other liability in connection with the performance of the Work, including, without limitations, such loss, damage, cost, expense, or other liability arising out of or resulting from defective or nonconforming Work, or other alleged failure to comply with the Contract Documents, or from third party claims, the venturers shall be responsible for such loss, damage, cost, expense, or other liability in the proportions as set forth in Paragraph 3 above.

Notwithstanding any other provisions of this Agreement, there shall be no distribution to either venturer of Joint Venture funds in excess of costs incurred by the venturers which are costs properly chargeable to the Joint Venture pursuant to Paragraph 8 hereof, prior to the completion of the Project without the written approval of the surety or sureties providing the Joint Venture's performance, payment, or other guaranty bonds executed in connection with the Work of the Construction Contract. The venturers agree, however, that they shall request annually the surety's or sureties' approval of the distribution of the amount or amounts necessary to pay state and federal income taxes assessed against each venturer due to Joint Venture profits for each fiscal year of the venturers which ends during the period the Project is being constructed.

17. *Relationship Between Venturers.* The relationship between the venturers shall be limited to the performance of the Construction Contract in accordance with the terms of this Agreement. This Agreement shall be construed and deemed to be a Joint Venture for the carrying out of the Construction Contract. Except to the extent necessary for performance of the Construction Contract, nothing herein

contained shall be considered to constitute the venturers as partners or constitute any venturer the general agent of the other venturer or to permit either venturer to bid for, or undertake, any other contracts for the other venturer.

18. *Completion and Termination.* Upon completion of the performance of the Construction Contract, including the fulfillment of all warranty obligations, the venturers shall settle and adjust all accounts, obligations, and liabilities incurred in connection with this Joint Venture, and after payment or settlement of all obligations and liabilities, shall return all working capital and other cash funds to the venturer or venturers having contributed such funds, and thereupon make full and final settlement with each other in such manner so that each party shall receive all the funds it contributed to the Joint Venture plus its percentage of all profits, or less that percentage of loss as the case may be, arising from the performance of the Construction Contract, as provided for in this Agreement, whereupon this Agreement shall terminate. Upon the termination of the Joint Venture, **[the Sponsoring Venturer]**

[OR]

[A Corp. or B Corp.]
shall have the authority to manage the affairs of the Joint Venture including:

a) continuing the business of the Joint Venture, if necessary to complete the Construction Contract;

b) paying the outstanding debts, obligations, and liabilities of the Joint Venture;

c) collecting the amounts owed to the Joint Venture arising from the Construction Contract or the Construction Work;

d) managing the distribution of the assets of the Joint Venture in accordance with the terms of this Agreement; and,

e) doing or performing all other things necessary to wind up the affairs of the Joint Venture.

19. *Choice of Law.* Any and all questions relative to the execution, validity, interpretation, and performance of this Agreement shall be governed by the laws of ____________.

20. *Cooperation.* Except as otherwise provided herein, each venturer shall make available for the Project such of its personnel, facilities, experience, and records as may be reasonably necessary or desirable to the end that the Project may be promptly and successfully completed.

21. *Financial Statements.* Within 15 days of the execution of this Agreement, each venturer shall provide to the other venturer proof reasonably satisfactory to the other venturer of the submitting venturer's financial substance. In addition to the proof originally provided in compliance with the preceding sentence, each venturer shall have the right to require the other venturer to submit from time to time current evidence of continuing financial substance. Each venturer agrees to keep confidential the financial information provided by the other venturer as far as is reasonably practicable.

22. *Binding Agreement.* This Agreement shall be binding upon and inure to the benefit of the venturers, their heirs, successors, and assigns.

23. *Representations and Warranties.*

A. In order to induce B Corp. to enter into this Agreement, A Corp. hereby makes the following representations and warranties and does hereby indemnify and hold B Corp. harmless from any and all loss, expense, or liability B Corp. may suffer as the result of any inaccuracy as of the date hereof in such representations and warranties:

(1) The execution of this Agreement has been duly authorized pursuant to the articles or charters by which A Corp. was created and is regulated, and this Agreement constitutes the legal, valid, and binding obligation of A Corp., which is, so far as A Corp. is aware, enforceable in accordance with the terms hereto.

(2) There is currently no claim, litigation, proceeding, or governmental investigation pending, or, so far as is known to A Corp., threatened against or relating to A Corp. or the transactions contemplated by this Agreement, which does, or would reasonably be expected to, affect materially and adversely the ability of A Corp. to enter into this Agreement, to fund the capital contributions of A Corp. required by this Agreement, or to carry out its obligations in this Agreement, except as has been fully disclosed by notice to, and approved by, B Corp. and as listed on Schedule ______ attached hereto.

(3) Neither the consummation of the transactions contemplated by this Agreement to be performed on the part of A Corp. nor the fulfillment of the terms, conditions, and provisions of this Agreement conflict with, or result in the breach of, any of the terms, conditions, provisions of, or constitute a default under, the articles or charter by which A Corp. was created or is regulated, or any agreement, indenture, instrument, or undertaking to which A Corp. is a party or by which A Corp. is bound.

B. In order to induce A Corp. to enter into this Agreement, B Corp. hereby makes the following representations and warranties and does hereby indemnify and hold A Corp. harmless from any and all loss, expense, or liability A Corp. may suffer as the result of any inaccuracy as of the date hereof in such representations and warranties:

(1) The execution of this Agreement has been duly authorized pursuant to the articles or charters by which B Corp. was created and is regulated, and this Agreement constitutes the legal, valid, and binding obligation of B Corp., which is, so far as B Corp. is aware, enforceable in accordance with the terms hereto.

(2) There is currently no claim, litigation, proceeding, or governmental investigation pending, or, so far as is known to B Corp., threatened against or relating to B Corp. or the transactions contemplated by this Agreement, which does, or would reasonably be expected to, affect materially and adversely the ability of B Corp. to enter into this Agreement, to fund the capital contributions of B Corp. required by this Agreement, or to carry out its obligations in this Agreement, except as has been fully disclosed by notice to, and approved by, A Corp. and as listed on Schedule ______ attached hereto.

(3) Neither the consummation of the transactions contemplated by this Agreement to be performed on the part of B Corp. nor the fulfillment of the terms, conditions, and provisions of this Agreement conflict with, or result in the breach of, any of the terms, conditions, provisions of, or constitute a default under, the

articles or charter by which B Corp. was created or is regulated, or any Agreement, indenture, instrument, or undertaking to which B Corp. is a party or by which B Corp. is bound.

24. *Indemnification.* Each venturer does hereby indemnify the other venturer against any loss or liability exceeding the proportions set forth in Paragraph 3 above stated by reason of the execution of any surety company bonds or indemnity agreements executed in connection therewith or by reason of any payments required to be made in connection with the performance of the Construction Contract. Each venturer does hereby indemnify the other venturer against all loss, cost, damage, expense, or liability, regardless of the proportions stated above, arising directly from such indemnifying venturer's negligent or wrongful act or omission, or negligent or wrongful performance or failure to perform its duties and obligations under Exhibit "A" attached hereto or under any other provision of this Agreement. In the event of a claim against the Joint Venture not due to either venturer's negligent act or omission, or negligent or wrongful performance or failure to perform its duties and obligations under Exhibit "A" attached hereto or under any other provision of this Agreement, each venturer agrees to indemnify the other venturer against any loss, cost, damage, expense, or liability suffered by such other venturer which exceeds its proportionate share set forth in Paragraph 3 above. Additionally, each venturer agrees to indemnify and save harmless the other venturer from any and all loss, cost, damage, expense, or liability arising from claims against such indemnifying venturer arising outside of the Joint Venture, and further agrees to pay all legal expenses incurred by the indemnified venturer in defending such claims. Should any sums be owed by one venturer to the other venturer under the provisions of this Paragraph, such sums, if not earlier paid, will be deducted from any distributions or returns to which the venturer obligated to pay such sums would otherwise be entitled under this Agreement and shall be paid instead to the other venturer; provided that such payment shall in no way limit any rights or remedies which the other venturer may have at law or in equity or by statute.

25. *Waiver.* No express or implied consent to, or waiver of, any breach or default by a venturer in such venturer's performance of its obligations under this Agreement shall be deemed or construed to be a consent to, or waiver of, any other breach or default in such venturer's performance of the same or any other obligations of such venturer under this Agreement. Failure on the part of either venturer to complain of any act or failure to act of the other venturer or to declare the other venturer in default, irrespective of how long such failure continues, shall not constitute a waiver of the rights of any venturer under this Agreement.

26. *Trust Funds.* All funds contributed by the venturers and all funds received by the Joint Venture shall be treated and regarded as, and are declared to be, trust funds for the performance of the Construction Contract and for no other purpose until the satisfactory completion of the Construction Contract and all other obligations and duties of the venturers shall have been paid or otherwise satisfied or discharged. No Joint Venture funds shall be commingled with any other funds of either of the venturers.

27. *Credit.* Neither venturer, nor its representative designated pursuant to Paragraph 2, nor the Joint Venture shall have the power to borrow monies, to pledge

the credit of either venturer, or to pledge the Joint Venture's joint credit without the express written consent of both venturers.

28. *Separability.* If any provision of this Agreement, or the application thereof, to any entity or circumstance shall be invalid or unenforceable to any extent, then the remainder of this Agreement and the application of such provisions shall not be affected thereby and shall be enforced to the greatest extent permitted by law.

29. *Time.* Venturers agree that time is of the essence in this Agreement.

30. *Counterparts.* This Agreement may be executed in any number of counterparts, each of which shall be deemed to be an original and all of which shall comprise but a single instrument.

31. *Arbitration.* Any dispute, claim, or controversy between the venturers arising out of, or relating to, this Agreement or any alleged breach hereof, shall be submitted to arbitration in accordance with the Construction Industry Arbitration Rules of the American Arbitration Association, which are in effect at the time a demand for arbitration is filed with such association. The Arbitration shall take place in ___________. The venturers shall select and agree on three arbitrators from a list of arbitrators provided by the American Arbitration Association. The decision of the arbitrators shall be by majority vote. The arbitrators shall have the power to issue injunctions, orders, and any other equitable relief that could be ordered by a court of competent jurisdiction. The arbitrators shall have authority to award damages, costs, interest, expenses, and attorney's fees in such amounts as the arbitrators shall deem appropriate. Judgment may be obtained on the arbitrators' decision or award and enforced in and through any court having appropriate jurisdiction.

Notwithstanding any demand for arbitration or any pending arbitration proceeding brought pursuant to this paragraph, the parties shall be obligated to continue to work on the Project diligently and to contribute or lease their proportionate share of funds, personnel, plant, and equipment regardless of whether the demand for arbitration or pending arbitration calls into dispute the obligation of either party to continue to work on the Project or to contribute or lease funds, personnel, plant, or equipment.

32. *Notices.* Any notices required to be given by the terms and provisions of this Agreement shall be in writing and shall be deemed to have been served and given on the day such notice was personally delivered, or five (5) calendar days after the date the note is deposited either by registered or certified mail, return receipt requested, postage prepaid, in the United States mail, addressed to the venturers at their respective address as follows:

For A Corp. ______________________	For B Corp. ______________________
______________________	______________________
______________________	______________________
with a copy to:	with a copy to:
(A Corp.'s attorneys) ______________________	(B Corp.'s attorneys) ______________________
______________________	______________________
______________________	______________________

33. *Merger.* This Agreement constitutes the entire agreement of the venturers with respect to the subject matter hereof. This Agreement and the provisions hereof may not be changed, waived, discharged, or terminated unless the change, waiver, discharge, or termination is in writing and duly executed by the venturer against which enforcement of the change, waiver, discharge, or termination is sought.

IN WITNESS WHEREOF, the venturers have set their hands and seals to this Agreement on the day and year first above written.

ATTEST:	A CORP.
______________________	BY: ______________________
SECRETARY	ITS: ______________________
[CORPORATE SEAL]	
ATTEST:	B CORP.
______________________	BY: ______________________
SECRETARY	ITS: ______________________
[CORPORATE SEAL]	

CHAPTER 4

INDUSTRIAL CONSTRUCTION PROJECTS

Walter G. Browning
A.H. Gaede, Jr.
John J. Park, Jr.

Walter G. Browning is Vice President/Legal and General Counsel of Rust International Corporation, a leading international and domestic engineering, construction, and project development company, where he is responsible for all legal aspects of Rust's activities. He received his B.A. from Birmingham Southern College in Birmingham, Alabama, and his J.D. from the University of Alabama School of Law.

A.H. Gaede, Jr., is a partner in the Birmingham, Alabama, law firm of Bradley, Arant, Rose & White, specializing in construction law on behalf of contractors, design professionals, and owners on a national basis. Mr. Gaede attended undergraduate school at Yale University in New Haven, Connecticut, and received his Bachelor of Laws degree from Duke University School of Law in Durham, North Carolina. He has written several articles and lectured extensively in national seminars to construction industry executives, design professionals, and other lawyers on all aspects of construction law, and has instructed on construction law for the University of Fribourg, Switzerland. He is a fellow in the American College of Construction Lawyers, and he is a member of the American Bar Association's Public Contracts Law Section and Forum Committee on the Construction Industry. He also serves as a construction arbitrator for the American Arbitration Association.

John J. Parks, Jr., is an associate in Bradley, Arant, Rose & White, where he concentrates his practice in the construction and procurement fields. He received his B.A. from the University of Virginia and his J.D. from Yale University in New Haven, Connecticut. He is a member of the American Bar Association's Public Contract Section and its Forum Committee on the Construction Industry.

---

§ 4.1 Overview

The flexibility of the joint venture structure lends itself equally to industrial construction projects as to other projects. Industrial projects involve facilities that turn raw materials into finished products and include paper mills, structural steel mills, and food processing plants. Joint venturers in the industrial construction arena can derive the same benefits and encounter the same risks as other joint venturers. They will also encounter specialized risks associated with the industrial arena. Joint venturers will need to take those common risks, and the unusual risks of industrial joint venturing, into account when drafting joint venture agreements for the industrial project.

This chapter discusses the merits of joint ventures, both generally and with respect to industrial projects, and assumes that a contractor is contemplating a joint venture with another contractor, an architect/engineer, or a specialty subcontractor. The joint venture may submit a hard bid or a competitive proposal to construct or improve an industrial facility that sells a product or products in the marketplace. Finally, a sample joint venture agreement, including bid or proposal teaming provisions, appears in **§ 4.21**.

§ 4.2 General Considerations

A *joint venture* may be defined as:

> an association of persons with intent, by way of contract, express or implied, to engage in and carry out a single business venture for joint profit, for which purpose they combine their efforts, property, money, skill, and knowledge, without creating a partnership or a corporation, pursuant to an agreement that there shall be a community of interest among them as to the purpose of the undertaking, and that each joint venturer shall stand in the relation of principal, as well as agent, as to each of the other coventurers, with equal right of control of the means employed to carry out the common purpose of the venture.[1]

A joint venture is not a partnership, but the law treats joint ventures like partnerships in nearly all respects.[2] If joint venturers prefer a different structure for their venture, such as a corporation, they should choose one expressly; otherwise, the partnership model will be the choice by default. The most significant effect of the partnership structure will be the application of joint and several liability, which means that each member of the joint venture will be fully liable for the obligations of the joint venture and for the acts of the other joint venturers undertaken in pursuit of the joint venture's goals. That liability scheme is completely unlike the scheme of corporate liability, in which the liability of a shareholder is normally limited to the equity interest in the corporation.[3]

Contractors form joint ventures for a variety of reasons. A joint venture partner may provide a geographical presence, bonding or insurance capacity, or skills not available to the contractor. For example, a joint venture with a strong local contractor may offer the opportunity to test a new market with a lesser degree of risk, or a joint venture with a designer or a supplier may permit a contractor to respond to a request for a design-build proposal or to utilize a

---

[1] 46 Am. Jur. 2d *Joint Ventures* § 1 (1969) (footnotes omitted); *compare* Browning v. Peyton, 918 F.2d 1516, 1520 (11th Cir. 1990) ("Under Florida law, a joint venture is defined as 'a special combination of two or more persons, who, in some specific venture, seek a profit jointly without the existence between them of any actual partnership, corporation, or other business entity'").

[2] *See, e.g.,* 48A C.J.S. *Joint Ventures* §§ 5a, 5b (1981) ("Although it has been held that a joint venture and a partnership are separate legal relationships, it has also been held that they are governed by the same rules of law. . . . [T]the principal difference is that [a joint venture] is usually, but not necessarily, limited to a single transaction, or a single series of transactions"); 46 Am. Jur. 2d *Joint Ventures* § 4 (1969); Meridian Homes Corp. v. Nicholas W. Prassas & Co., 687 F.2d 228 (7th Cir. 1982) (joint venture's rights and liabilities are just like those of partnership, except with respect to termination).

[3] *Cf.* Itel Containers Int'l Corp. v. Atlanttrafik Express Servs. Ltd., 909 F.2d 698, 702 (2d Cir. 1990) ("A joint venture and a corporation are mutually exclusive ways of doing business"), and cases cited therein (applying N.Y. law).

proprietary technology such as a patented process or unique piece of machinery, the ownership rights of which are vested in only one company. Also, if a contractor does not have an ongoing relationship with a particular owner, a joint venture with a firm that has such a relationship may give the contractor access to the owner or to the project in question. Of course, the contractor with the "inside track" will generally be reluctant to provide other contractors with access to "its owner." However, if the project is too large for one contractor or requires skills that contractor does not have, a joint venture may be mutually advantageous.

In the industrial context, these purposes remain equally valid. The joint venture, however, must anticipate the following risks that are present in the industrial arena but not always in others.

The Risks of Nonperformance

In the industrial context, construction projects often involve building new facilities or upgrading existing facilities so that the owner can produce more of a certain product. The owner contemplates selling the increased product quantity in the marketplace and views delays or nonperformance as lost sales. In addition, process quality, that is, the reliability of the established manufacturing process used to produce a quality product, is a crucial consideration. The failure to meet performance guarantees or to perform in timely fashion may result in substantial potential liability to the joint venture.

Licensing

When a contractor and an architect/engineer (A/E) form a joint venture, the A/E may be performing, furnishing, or rendering "architectural" services as they are defined in state licensing statutes. The same state licensing statutes may require those performing, furnishing, or rendering such services to be licensed, and although the A/E may be properly licensed, the joint venture itself may not be. Often, unlicensed persons who perform professional services are not entitled to enforce their contracts. Without minimizing the risk, it appears that the owner is most likely to invoke a licensing defense when it decides not to go forward with a project.[4]

Trade Secrets

Industrial projects often employ or develop new or proprietary technologies that the owner or developer is entitled to protect as intellectual property. The

---

[4] *See, e.g.*, Food Management, Inc. v. Blue Ribbon Beef, Inc., 413 F.2d 716 (8th Cir. 1969); Hospital Dev. Corp. v. Park Lane Land Co., 813 S.W.2d 904 (Mo. Ct. App. 1991).

parties to the project will want to protect their ownership rights in such technologies because each may contribute and define those rights in any intellectual property developed jointly or independently by the joint venturers. One author recommends:

> Generally, intellectual property previously owned by either party should continue to be exclusively owned by that party during the joint venture's performance of a . . . contract. Intellectual property jointly developed should be owned jointly unless either party elects not to participate in such ownership. This property should also be permitted to be used without consent of the other party or without payment of royalties or other compensation to the other reason of such use.[5]

The parties may also with to establish a procedure for protecting proprietary information, beginning with the identification of such information. Other considerations include defining the standard of care for protecting the information, identifying when protection is not applicable, and addressing the return of the information after use and forced disclosure.[6]

Fast-Track Considerations

Industrial projects are frequently fast-tracked which means that construction activities begin before the design is complete. On a fast-track project, it is not unusual for the construction work to be bid and awarded in several packages (for example, excavation and foundations, building superstructure, electrical, and mechanical) to separate contractors. This procedure requires increased communication and cooperation among the owner, A/E, and contractor. Otherwise, the prospects for both disruption related to incomplete design and gaps between the work of the various contractors are substantial.

§ 4.3 Selecting the Joint Venturer

Selection of a joint venturer may be the most significant risk in industrial projects. The proper joint venturer must, at a minimum, furnish something the contractor does not already have—market access, in the form of presence, assets, licenses, and so on. In addition, the joint venturer must represent a good corporate fit with respect to such considerations as centralization of control, willingness to assume risks, and image. The fit must also extend to a compatibility of goals and priorities; one venturer's goal of profit maximization in the short run may conflict with the other's long-run market development considerations, for example.

---

[5] Ingrao, *Joint Ventures: Their Use in Federal Government Contracting,* 20 Pub. Cont. L.J. 399, 413–14 (Spring 1991) [hereinafter Ingrao].

[6] *Id.* at 413.

The joint venturer must also be able to take care of its share of the joint venture's capital requirements, and potential liabilities. A/Es, for example, do not generally have the fixed asset base that is the prerequisite for bonding capacity; A/E firms' assets are concentrated in the ability of their employees, who can migrate, taking those assets with them. A/Es may, however, be able to compensate to a degree with their professional errors and omissions insurance coverage.

Finally, the joint venturer must be trustworthy. Joint venturers may owe each other a fiduciary duty and likely will be burdened with joint and several liability for the actions of fellow joint venturers. Each member of the joint venture must be able to rely on the judgment of its fellow joint venturers. In sum, each joint venturer must have confidence in the ability, stability, and integrity of its joint venturers.

§ 4.4 Joint Venture Agreement

In general, the joint venture is formed through an agreement between the parties. A joint venture may, however, result from something as informal as a letter to a third party[7] or, legally, by an implied contract. In the industrial construction context, the parties should always enter into a written agreement establishing the joint venture's purposes and the rights and obligations of the venturers.

The joint venture agreement should address all of the elements legally necessary for a joint venture. Some courts have identified four elements:

1. The intent or purpose to form a joint venture
2. The sharing of a common interest
3. The agreement to share profits and losses
4. The joint right to control the venture.[8]

Other courts identify the contribution of property, skill, financing, knowledge, or effort by each joint venturer as an additional prerequisite.[9] The joint venture agreement should also address all the elements of any other contract: purpose, time, money, termination, disputes, and so on. Following is an overview of the joint venture agreement's main provisions. See **§ 4.21**.

---

[7] *See, e.g.,* Trustees, Bricklayers Local No. 3 v. Reynolds Elec. & Eng'g Co., 747 F. Supp. 606 (D. Nev. 1990) (letter from one joint venturer to surety); Murphy v. Redland, 583 P.2d 1049 (Mont. 1978) (oral agreement, later partially confirmed in writing).

[8] *See, e.g.,* Karl's, Inc. v. Sunrise Computers, 901 F.2d 657 (9th Cir. 1990); Davidson v. Enstar Corp., 848 F.2d 574 (5th Cir.), *rev'd on rehearing on other grounds,* 860 F.2d 167 (5th Cir. 1988); *cf.* Nature's Share, Inc. v. Kutter Prods., Inc., 752 F. Supp. 371 (D. Kan. 1990) (three elements under Kansas law: joint ownership, joint operation, and express agreement to share profits and losses).

[9] Itel Containers Int'l Corp. v. Atlanttrafik Express Servs. Ltd., 909 F.2d 698, 701 (2d Cir. 1990).

Recitals. The recitals may address the general purposes of and basis for organizing the joint venture. The recitals should be consistent with the terms of the agreement.

Purpose. The purpose behind an industrial construction joint venture is ordinarily to submit a bid or proposal for a particular project and, if a contract is awarded, to perform the work in accordance with the construction contract and the joint venture contract. Joint venture agreements need not be limited to a single specific project, but become more complex when they are not so limited.

Parties, joint venture name, and respective interests. The agreement should identify the parties and their interests in the control, profits, and losses of the joint venture. In addition, the parties may wish to designate the name of the joint venture and its office location. The joint venturers could choose to combine their business names or might select another name, commonly called a *fictitious name* for the venture. Selection of a name may involve more than it would initially appear, especially on federal government contracts. If the contract is subject to the federal Cost Accounting Standards or if the joint venturers are subject to government approval of their initial purchasing, quality control, or other systems, a fictitious joint venture may require independent approval, but a nonfictitious joint venture would pass because of the prior approvals of its members.[10]

Management. The parties should establish a management structure empowered to direct the joint venture's activities. Most often, a committee structure is used, appointing representatives and alternates of each party. Alternately, one party may be delegated authority with respect to certain aspects of the joint venture, but the retention of the legal right to control the joint venture's activities by the other is a prerequisite to the existence of a joint venture.[11] When one joint venturer is designated to speak to the owner, has a majority ownership interest, or both, that joint venturer is commonly referred to as the *sponsor.*

Capital contributions. The parties should establish the method of funding the joint venture's activities. Although some of that funding will be derived from progress payments for the work performed, frequently those progress payments will neither cover mobilization expenses nor match the expenses of performance once retainage is taken into account. In addition, unrecognized

---

[10] *See* Ingrao at 407–11.

[11] *See, e.g.,* Hellenic Lines, Ltd. v. Commodities Bagging & Shipping, 611 F. Supp. 665, 679 (D.N.J. 1985) ("Although a joint venture is not present absent a *right* of mutual control, mutual control over every aspect of the venture need not be actual"); Shain Inv. Co. v. Cohen, 443 N.E.2d 126, 130 (Mass. App. Ct. 1982) ("Substantial authority underscores the importance of the . . . consideration that '[a] right of mutual control or management of the enterprise' is an essential element of joint venture").

changes or delays or bid errors may cause unreimbursed expenses. The management committee should be empowered to require the joint venturers to contribute capital whenever a call is made, and should establish the consequences of failing to meet a capital call.

Finances. The joint venture should have records and accounts separate from those of its members. It is frequently advisable to have the financial records and accounts audited by an independent auditor. The parties may wish to establish the mechanics of their banking arrangements, either expressly or by delegating the necessary powers to the management committee. The use of a bank as the depository and disbursement agent for progress and other payments owed to the joint venture will aid in speeding disbursement of funds to the joint ventures.

Distributions. Distributions may be made in two ways, either pay-as-you-go in response to invoices, or periodically as determined by the management committee. Once the project's progress payment mechanism is established and operating, the progress payments received from the owner can be matched to the joint venture's invoices. The joint venture's management committee may, in its discretion, be empowered to make periodic distributions, to return capital contributions, or to distribute profits, but, for that to occur, the project needs to be generating a profit, exclusive of contingencies (amounts reserved to cover unexpected costs). In addition, any distribution should not affect the ultimate responsibilities of the joint venturers. Obviously, the final distribution, to be made during the winding up of the joint venture's affairs, may be either positive or negative.

Provision of services, employees, and equipment. The parties may wish to agree in advance which assets they will contribute in terms of personnel and equipment. It is vital to consider the effect that changing employers may have on the pension and benefit rights of the employees in question. If a rental charge is to be paid to one or more of the joint venturers for equipment, the rental rate should be specified in the agreement. Alternately, the joint venture management committee may be empowered to use third-party rentals or to purchase equipment as joint venture property. The method of paying for such equipment should be dealt with in the joint venture agreement. Normally, purchased equipment will be disposed of in the winding up of the joint venture and the proceeds included in the final distribution. Joint venturers may want to have the option to purchase joint venture property; if so, the basis for determining a purchase price should be included in the joint venture agreement. If all parties are to contribute to the management of the venture in proportion to their share interests, there should probably be no reimbursement for such services.

Indemnity/liability. The joint venturers are subject to joint and several liability for claims against the joint venture even though one party may be factually blameless. If they wish to assess liabilities based on fault, the parties should establish an internal indemnity obligation so the consequences of joint and several liability may be allocated according to the agreement.

Default. The parties should address the consequences of a joint venturer's failure to perform its obligations. By doing so, the joint venturers may avoid gridlock and its consequences if a joint venturer refuses to meet a capital call, fails to perform its share of the work in a timely fashion, or declares bankruptcy.

Duration and termination. Ordinarily, the joint venture continues until the end of the project, at which time its affairs are concluded. The parties may wish to consider whether other conditions, such as a joint venturer's bankruptcy or failure to contribute capital, might cause them to dissolve the joint venture. They should also consider how the joint venture's affairs will be wrapped up through the making of distributions, disposal of equipment, assumption of warranty obligations, and so on.

Disputes and dispute resolution. Two dispute resolution mechanisms are needed, one to resolve disputes with the owner, which will not be part of the agreement, and the other to resolve disputes within the joint venture, which will be part of the agreement. As with all construction projects, the work of the joint venture should normally continue even though there is a dispute either with the owner or within the joint venture. The agreement should specify how to proceed, in a manner consistent with the ownership interest of the joint venturers. For example, a 50-50 joint venture agreement may provide a deadlock-breaking procedure. Without one, the parties would be required to compromise.

Special provisions. For foreign industrial projects or for the relatively rare federal government industrial projects, the agreement should address the special kinds of statutory liability that may arise. The Foreign Corrupt Practices Act[12] prohibits various activities of contractors working outside the United States. The False Claims Act[13] and other statutes prohibit certain activities on government projects. In appropriate cases, the parties may wish to anticipate the consequences of statutory violations.

Miscellaneous provisions. As with other contracts, some provisions have become so customary that they are regarded as *boilerplate.* Provisions such as those addressing third-party beneficiaries, notice, merger, governing law, and amendments, are wisely included even if viewed as *boilerplate.* See **Chapter 3**.

---

[12] 15 U.S.C. § 78M(b), 78dd-1, 78ff.

[13] 18 U.S.C. § 287; *see also id.* § 1001.

§ 4.5 —Funding

The parties to a joint venture must each contribute something to the common purpose. The something contributed may be property, skill, financing, knowledge, or effort. Each party's contribution need not be of the same value or the same character; indeed, joint ventures are often premised on the contribution of different kinds of things by each party. The parties should, however, agree on what each will contribute in order to meet its obligation to the joint venture and earn its share interest in the joint venture.

The parties may wish to address the issue of responsibility for the joint venture's losses. This can be particularly important when the parties' contributions are of different kinds. As one court has stated:

> [W]here a joint venture involves the contribution of capital by one party and services by the other, neither party is required to reimburse the other for losses sustained. In the event of loss, the party contributing capital loses his capital and the one contributing labor loses the value of his efforts.[14]

In this situation, the capital initially contributed was sufficient to cover the losses. Problems between the joint venturers more frequently occur when the losses, or need for operating capital, exceed the capital contributed by the parties. If only one of the parties contributed capital initially, there must be an understanding of, and mechanism for the payment of, each parties' obligation for such additional capital. One simple solution is to require that additional capital be contributed comparable to the venturers' respective interests in the joint venture.

When the agreement contemplates that the joint venture will submit a bid or proposal (see **Chapter 3**), the parties can reasonably expect the costs of bid preparation, which are usually almost completely internalized, to be roughly equal to the share interest of each party and that those costs will not be charged to the joint venture. If bid costs are to be joint venture expenses, a provision for determining each party's portion and the timing of reimbursement should be included in the agreement. Once the bid or proposal has been accepted, the parties will need to decide what they will contribute, how that contribution will be determined, and how they will be compensated.

On a construction project, the parties generally expect their receipt of progress payments to fund most of the work. However, the parties must provide for working capital to cover mobilization expenses, delays in payment, unrecognized changes or delays, and retainage. The agreement should provide a

---

[14] April Enters., Inc. v. KTTV, 147 Cal. App. 3d 805, 195 Cal. Rptr. 421, 428 (1983). *See* Snellbaker v. Herrman, 462 A.2d 713 (Pa. Super. Ct. 1983); Dugan v. Pettijohn, 285 P.2d 339, 342 (Cal. Ct. App. 1985).

mechanism for making capital calls and for the consequences of the failure to meet such a call.

§ 4.6 —Personnel

Contributions of personnel raise a potential loyalty issue. If key personnel remain on the joint venturer's payroll or remain part of the venturer's organization, those personnel may put loyalty to the venturer ahead of loyalty to the venture. If the joint venturers decide to contribute personnel to a separate venture, there is the possibility that the personnel contributed will be those the venturer finds easiest to spare. This difficulty may be minimized in the agreement by allocating control and separating the spheres of work and billings. Such a solution may be difficult to put into practice, however.

The joint venturers may wish to distinguish salaried supervisory personnel from hourly personnel. Salaried supervisory personnel who are dropped from the joint venturer's payroll and transferred to the joint venture may find their pensions and other benefit entitlements compromised, however. The hourly personnel generally do not have the same concern which simplifies their hiring by the joint venture. The joint venture may also provide the flexibility needed to enter into project agreements with labor unions, which might not be the case with the individual contractor if it is bound by existing labor contracts.

§ 4.7 —Reimbursement of Joint Venturers

The parties will want to address the manner in which they will recover the value of their contributions from the project revenues. While the project is underway, such recovery will have to take a back seat to completion of the work; the owner wants a completed project, not happy joint venturers. In addition, the premature return of capital or distribution of anticipated profits can lead to undercapitalization and additional capital calls. Moreover, with retainage being customary on the prime contract, it is unlikely the joint venturers will be made completely whole before the end of the project. Generally, the safest practice is to retain capital and anticipated earnings until the project is complete or nearly complete.

Even so, the joint venturers may choose to have their contributions reimbursed and anticipated profits distributed through periodic distributions. If so, the periodic distributions should be directed by the joint venture's management, leaving it the discretion to schedule distributions in response to the joint venture's overall cash position. Any such distributions should be provisional and should not affect the final accounting or interim needs for capital.

In the author's view, the joint venture should function as a separate entity and thereby reduce the reimbursable expenses incurred by the parties. Examples of the expenses that may be incurred by each joint venturer even in a stand-alone joint venture (when the joint venture functions as a separate entity) are:

1. Costs to attend management committee meetings
2. Special bookkeeping services
3. Scheduling services, including corporation time
4. Home office overhead, if one of the venturers is responsible for overall management of the venture.

Of course, in some instances the parties provide services to the joint venture and even function as if they were subcontractors. The detail necessary with respect to reimbursement schemes will depend in part on whether the basis of the underlying contract is hard-bid or cost-reimbursable. On a lump-sum contract, payments by the owner are usually based on the percentage of work completed without regard to expenses. To the extent the parties are providing services to the joint venture, the parties' invoices to the joint venture could either reflect the appropriate percentage of completion or be based on costs incurred. If the underlying contract is a cost-reimbursable contract, the parties should define which expenses will be reimbursable and at what rates. The parties' invoices to the joint venture or to the owner should then reflect an appropriate basis for reimbursement.

Absent an agreement, a joint venturer may not be entitled to charge the joint venture for overhead,[15] interest on advances,[16] or attorneys' fees incurred in defending the joint venture.[17] Indeed, absent an agreement, a joint venturer may not be entitled to be reimbursed for its services.[18]

§ 4.8 —Project Finance

One author notes that the term *project finance*

> is generally used to refer to the arrangement of debt, equity and credit enhancement for the construction or refinancing of a particular facility in a capital-intensive industry, in which lenders base credit appraisals on the projected revenues from the operation of the facility, rather than on the general assets or the corporate credit of the promoter of the facility, and in which they rely on the

---

[15] *See* Anderson v. Property Developers, Inc., 555 F.2d 648 (8th Cir. 1977).

[16] *Id.*

[17] *See* Interstate Properties v. Pyramid Co., 581 F. Supp. 982 (S.D.N.Y. 1984).

[18] *See* 48A C.J.S. *Joint Ventures* § 35 (1981); Interstate Properties v. Pyramid Co., 581 F. Supp. 982, 988; Murphy v. Dees, 307 So. 2d 1 (Ala. 1975).

assets of the facility, including the revenue-producing contracts and cash flow, as collateral for the debt.[19]

Project finance is most often encountered on cogeneration, solid waste/recovery, waste water treatment, and privatization projects.[20] See **Chapter 7**.

In general, the project finance scheme may introduce a more aggressive construction lender to the project equation. The lender, which has secured its loan with the expectation that a performing facility will produce a product which sells profitably in the marketplace, often becomes more aware of its interest in the timely completion and proper operation of the facility. Owners, too, have become more aware of their payment obligations on construction loans. Industrial and cogeneration projects sometimes tie liquidated damages for late completion or failure to fulfill performance guarantees to loan payment obligations, which results in massive figures. Contractors may wish to try to negotiate those figures downward to a more acceptable level, but may find that owners feel themselves hemmed in by their loan agreements.

Project finance and construction-loan-linked liquidated damages shift substantial risks to the members of joint ventures. Project finance not only introduces a lender to the equation, just like many other construction projects, but a nonrecourse loan limits the lender's security to the project itself. As a consequence, the lender will, in effect, tie up all the security (the project), leaving none for the contractor other than the project funds. The owner and lender can be counted on to tie up a substantial portion of the project because one goal of project finance is to substitute debt for equity. Indeed, in the "go-go" 1980s the leverage percentage, or the percentage of the project cost borrowed, was often between 80 and 98 percent.[21] As *ENR* puts it, "In the 1980s, lenders were loose and would even finance 100% of commercial buildings with no significant preleasing."[22] Today, lenders are more reluctant to lend to projects, both generally and on a nonrecourse basis, and, when loans are made, the leverage percentage is lower.[23] However, lenders still insist on having the full security of the project, frequently denying liens to the contractor.

Contractors should not lose sight of the fact that project finance represents a means of financing projects that might not otherwise be built; the lender shifts its focus from the general assets of the owner to the merits of the individual

---

[19] Hoffman, *A Practical Guide to Transactional Project Finance: Basic Concepts, Risk Identification, and Contractual Considerations,* 45 Bus. Law. 181, 181 n.1 (1989).

[20] Feldman & Hoffman, *Basic Concepts of Project Finance Documentation: Risk Allocation, Drafting, Contractual and Regulatory Considerations, in* Project Financing 1986; Power Generation, Waste Recovery, and Other Industrial Facilities 2 (Practising Law Institute 1986).

[21] *Id.* at 5.

[22] Krizan, *Money Is out There for Projects That Make Lots of Sense,* 228 ENR 24 (May 4, 1992).

[23] *Id.* at 25 ("Lenders also want more equity than in the past . . . . [T]he commonly acceptable range is 10% to 20%").

project. Contractors, too, have formed capital subsidiaries to put financing deals together and fund projects to be designed or built by their parents.[24] In sum, project finance represents both risk and reward to the joint venture.

§ 4.9 —Organization, Management, and Control

One of the prerequisites to a joint venture is mutuality of control. One commentator explains, "The better-reasoned view is that the *right* of control must exist as a matter of law, but the *exercise* of such control may be surrendered or entrusted to another by agreement."[25] Thus, the parties to a joint venture may divide responsibility and "defer . . . to each other's different areas of expertise."[26] For example, an A/E joint venturer may be delegated design responsibility and the contractor/joint venturer responsibility for constructing the project.

In the joint venture agreement, the parties need to establish a management structure and identify the joint venture's representative to the rest of the world. Often, the management structure is established when each party appoints one or more representatives or alternates to a management committee empowered to run the joint venture. The parties may also appoint one management committee member, for example, the representative of the sponsor, as the joint venture's representative. The agreement should also establish a voting mechanism for approving the joint venture's action and may set forth a procedure to break deadlocks. These issues are addressed in **§ 4.21**, the sample joint venture agreement at ¶ 10.

A second alternative would be to appoint a controlling or managing partner, often called the *sponsor*. That partner would have control over the ordinary, daily activities of the joint venture, although other joint venturers would have input on significant decisions. Those decisions might include the timing and amount of distributions and capital calls, or the addition of a new party. One author explains:

> In considering how a joint venture should operate, priority should be given to those few items in which one of the partners can say "no." These are more important than the issues for which positive agreement is needed. Casting a veto is often harder than declining to agree. And, therefore, the veto should be reserved only for key decisions.[27]

---

[24] *Id.* at 25–26.

[25] Ginsburg, Keup & Villet, *Joint Ventures: Basic Principles and Guidelines,* 84-7 Construction Briefings 3 (July 1987) (emphasis added).

[26] *See* Halloran v. Ohlmeyer Communications Co., 618 F. Supp. 1214, 1219 (S.D.N.Y. 1985).

[27] Ehrenhaft, *International Joint Ventures: Setting Them Up, Taking Them Apart, in* Going International: International Trade for the Nonspecialist 5 (American Law Institute, 1990).

The importance of preventing deadlocks cannot be overstated. The owner does not want happy joint venturers, but rather a completed project. Because a deadlock between the joint venturers threatens timely completion of the work, it also threatens each joint venturer with joint and several liability for any damages. The power to break deadlocks should follow the percentage of control. Thus, a joint venturer with a controlling interest could break a deadlock by dictate, but a 50-50 joint venture would remain deadlock. The prospect of joint and several liability, however, is likely to force a compromise. In addition, the parties might consider a provision requiring that the decision of one joint venturer be followed if a compromise cannot be reached.

§ 4.10 —Scope of Services

In general, one distinction between joint ventures and partnerships is that joint ventures are usually limited to specific projects.[28] The sample agreement (see **§ 4.21**) addresses this consideration in the preamble and in section 16 and expressly states what might otherwise be implied, that is, that the parties are free to contract as they wish with respect to matters outside the joint venture. This consideration is important because joint venturers have a fiduciary relationship with each other; fiduciaries cannot appropriate to themselves the business opportunities of the joint venture.[29] Ordinarily, this rule applies to business opportunities the joint venture might pursue while it is in existence, similar to the corporate opportunity doctrine. The absence of a limitation of the joint venture's purposes in the agreement, however, may create an ambiguity with respect to opportunities arising after a specific project has been performed. The parties should identify the project(s) with respect to which they are cooperating with specificity, and should also identify the scope of work for each member. Identification of the scope of work may also extend to defining responsibility for warranty matters.

Although joint ventures are often limited to a single project, they need not be so limited. Expanding their scope to more than one project, however, adds complexity to the joint venture and the agreement. One element of this complexity may be antitrust considerations. When competitors team up, the resulting combination may be construed as an attempt to monopolize a particular market. The longer such a pairing continues, the more competitors or the government may see a threat of monopolization, even if intent is lacking or the relevant market is impossible to monopolize.

---

[28] *See, e.g.,* 46 Am. Jur. 2d *Joint Ventures* § 10 (1969).

[29] *See, e.g.,* Leff v. Gunter, 33 Cal. 3d 508, 658 P.2d 740, 189 Cal. Rptr. 377 (1983); J. Leo Johnson, Inc. v. Carmer, 156 A.2d 499, 503 (Del. 1959) ("The fiduciary relationship between the parties was such as to preclude one of them from dealing with property relating to the enterprise, either for himself or another, in the absence of full disclosure to his associates").

For federal government contracts, the Federal Acquisition Regulation requires contracting agencies to report suspected antitrust violations to the attorney general.[30] The regulations offer examples of practices that may show a violation, including, "[t]he filing of a joint bid by two or more competitors when at least one of the competitors has sufficient technical capability and productive capacity for contract performance."[31] One author points out that there may be potential antitrust problems for both a *horizontal combination* (one between prime contractors), and a *vertical combination* (one between a prime contractor and a subcontractor).[32] A joint venture between a general contractor and an A/E for a design-build project would not appear likely to cause concern because neither joint venturer is likely to have both the technical capability and the productive capacity necessary to complete the project on its own. The same may hold true for a joint venture between a general contractor and a supplier of specialized equipment.[33]

Industrial joint ventures are often formed for design-build projects, so licensing considerations may also be important. First, some states may require the licensing of the joint venture, separate and apart from any professional licensing.[34] Other states have exempted design-build from their design professional licensing laws.[35] As for the remaining states, most prohibit the unlicensed practice of architecture and engineering, and define such practice in terms of "performing," "rendering," or "furnishing" certain services. If the joint venture is a separate entity from the contractor and A/E who compose it, must the joint venture be independently professionally licensed? Alternatively, if a contractor fronts a design-build entity, does the unlicensed contractor's furnishing of plans prepared by a licensed A/E to the owner constitute the rendering of professional A/E services? If the contractor serves only as a conduit for the plans, is the contractor "performing" design services? If the A/E fronts the joint venture and contracts with the owner, is the resulting construction the product of a licensed contractor? There is no uniform answer to these questions because the laws of each state are different. Both the joint venture and the

---

[30] 48 C.F.R. § 3.303(a) (1991).

[31] *Id.* § 3.303(c)(7).

[32] Sherrer, *Joint Venturers on Government Contracts: A Walk Through a Rose Garden Planted over Land Mines,* 19 Pub. Cont. L.J. 331, 342–47 (Winter 1990).

[33] *But cf. id.* at 346–47 (raising competitors' costs by using improper strategies and tactics may be antitrust violation; relying on Krattenmaker & Salop, *Anticompetitive Exclusion: Raising Rivals' Costs to Achieve Power over Price,* 96 Yale L.J. 209 (1986)).

[34] California requires joint ventures composed of two or more licensed contractors to obtain a joint venture license in order to be awarded a contract or to act as a contractor. Cal. Bus. & Prof. Code § 7029.1 (Supp. 1991).

[35] *See, e.g.,* Fla. Stat. Ann. § 481-229(3) (West); N.C. Gen. Stat. § 83A-13(b); R.I. Gen. Laws § 5-1-7(b); Wash. Rev. Code Ann. § 18.08.410 (West). *See also* Seaview Hosp., Inc. v. Medicenters of Am., Inc., 570 S.W.2d 35 (Tex. Civ. App. 1978); Charlebois v. J.M. Weller Assocs., Inc., 531 N.E.2d 1288 (N.Y. 1988).

design-build subcontractor relationships have potential licensing problems; in many states, the resulting validity of the arrangements is not certain.[36]

When the parties are providing separate parts of a single unified project, they may wish to address "handoff" issues. Such issues might include acceptance, the obligation to identify defective work, the obligation to remedy defective work, and the consequences of any defect and associated delay. These issues would not represent a defense to an owner's claim, but may be very important internally.

§ 4.11 —Taxes

The parties should consider the tax consequences of selecting a corporation as the form of a joint venture rather than a partnership. Under the Internal Revenue Code, partnerships are not taxed; instead, the participating joint venturers are taxed on their respective shares of the venture's profits and losses. In contrast, a corporation has a separate identity for tax purposes; it is taxed on its earnings and the shareholders are taxed on dividends, but not on returns of capital. When the joint venture expects to incur losses initially, the joint venturers will want to look at their ability to use those losses to offset other income.[37] If those losses can be used by the joint venturers, the partnership form may permit the losses to produce tax benefits more quickly. Such tax benefits will also depend on the accounting method employed; the completed contract method will generally be slower than the percentage of completion method in recognizing gains and losses. With the completed contract method, there may not be a substantial difference between corporations and partnerships with respect to how quickly they recognize gains and losses.

§ 4.12 —Risk Allocation

In non-joint venture contracts, just as in every agreement, a critical element is the identification of and response to risks. In the industrial context, the standard construction risks are present as well as those associated with design-build or fast-track projects. There is also typically a greater degree of self-performed work, and less subcontracting, on industrial projects. These additional elements introduce different risks that the parties should anticipate, allocate, and, if possible, diffuse.

---

[36] *See generally* Park, Rogers & Sears, *The Effect of Licensing Laws on Design-Build Projects, in* Design-Build Contracting Handbook (R. Cushman & K. Taub eds., John Wiley & Sons 1992).

[37] *See generally* Ginsburg, Keup & Villet, *Joint Ventures: Basic Principles and Guidelines,* 84-7 Construction Briefings 3, 6 (July 1987).

In general, there are two kinds of risks on an industrial construction project: construction risks (including the risks associated with design) and operating risks. Construction risks include the possibility of cost overruns, delays, changes to the work, and design issues. Where the joint venture is offering design and engineering services as part of the package, the adequacy of that work is heavily dependent on the parties' success in defining the program and in keeping the owner committed to that program. With respect to the owner, construction risks are generally allocated in the construction contract. Between the joint venturers, such risks may be allocated according to the scope of work defined in the agreement. See **§ 4.11**. With the exception of warranty and performance issues, operating risks should be borne by the owner. Operating risks include changes in regulations affecting plant operations, availability of raw materials, the market for the product, and consequential loss or damages.

§ 4.13 —Liability to Third Parties

The similarities between joint ventures and partnerships extend to the issue of liability to third parties. As with partnerships, the liability of joint venturers is joint and several, which may extend to some frightening situations, such as tax liability,[38] liability for punitive damages,[39] or withdrawal liability under the Multiemployer Pension Plan Amendments Act.[40] In one case, a joint venturer's failure to qualify to do business in a state made it ineligible to use that state's courts: because that ineligible venturer was an indispensable party to any suit against the owner, the joint venture was denied the opportunity to sue the owner.[41] The scope of this potential liability is another indication of the significance of the selection of the joint venture partner.

In addition, the joint venture's potential liability to third parties should spark attention to the standard forms of contractual protection—insurance and indemnity. With respect to insurance, the standard commercial general liability policy does not extend protection to joint ventures including the insured. Coverage for joint venture activities may be procured at additional cost through a rider. Alternatively, the joint venture might procure insurance coverage on its own.

One treatise favors the joint venture's procuring of separate insurance coverage, finding the benefits of the named insured approach outweighed by the detriments.[42] It notes that although naming the joint venture as an additional

---

[38] *See, e.g.*, Schaffer v. Commissioner, 779 F.2d 849 (2d Cir. 1985); Burde v. Commissioner, 352 F.2d 995 (2d Cir. 1965), *cert. denied*, 383 U.S. 966 (1966).

[39] *See* Blue v. Rose, 786 F.2d 349 (8th Cir. 1986).

[40] 29 U.S.C. §§ 1381–1453 (1990). *See* Teamsters Pension Trust Fund v. H.F. Johnson, 830 F.2d 1009 (9th Cir. 1987).

[41] *See* Scott Co. v. Enco Constr. Co., 264 So. 2d 409 (Miss. 1972).

[42] Woodward et al., I Construction Risk Management VI. N. 25–28 (International Risk Management Institute 1984).

insured avoids the effort of obtaining a new policy and may result in cost savings on premiums, a loss by the joint venture will travel with the insured's coverage, affecting future premiums and depleting liability limits. In addition, the failure of one joint venturer to procure insurance will skew the potential joint and several liability and would prevent insurability under the contractual liability coverage.[43] The treatise also recommends:

> Even when a separate CGL and umbrella policy are used to insure a joint venture, a contractor should attempt to endorse his own CGL and umbrella policy to provide a form of difference-in-conditions coverage and additional limits of liability over and above that provided by the policies purchased for the joint venture.[44]

For completed operations coverage, the venturers may want to purchase extended coverage for the joint venture's policy; an extension of coverage for three to five years may cover most of the injuries or property damage that occur in relation to the completed project. Each venturer should then arrange its own coverage for occurrences after the extension period.

The parties may also bargain for cross-indemnification, making each responsible for the work it performs for the joint venture or for that portion of the project that is commensurate with the profit-/loss-sharing ratio in the agreement. The security of a cross-indemnity promise depends on the assets and integrity of the promisor. It has proven difficult, if not impossible, to bond cross-indemnity obligations. On the other hand, if the commercial general liability policy for the individual joint venturers does not exclude coverage of joint venture activities, the policy may cover the contractually assumed indemnity obligation.[45] Letters of credit may also prove useful as security for cross-indemnity obligations.

§ 4.14 —Indemnification

As noted in **§ 4.13**, the parties to a joint venture may bargain for cross-indemnification as a possible means of protection from joint and several liability for a coventurer's actions. Those actions need not be limited to claims for injury by third parties because the basis for a claim against the joint venture may arise from the prime contract or from one joint venturer's subcontract.

---

[43] *See, e.g.*, Reliance Ins. Co. v. Giannini, 158 Ill. App. 3d 657, 511 N.E.2d 755 (1987) (failure to procure insurance not covered under incidental contract rider). *Cf.* Reliance Ins. Co. v. Gary C. Wyatt, Inc., 540 So. 2d 688 (Ala. 1989) (failure to name person as additional insured not an "occurrence").

[44] I Construction Risk Management, VI. N. 27 (International Risk Management Institute 1984).

[45] The standard Commercial General Liability Policy § II (Insurance Services Office 1988) states, "No person or organization is an insured with respect to the conduct of any current or past partnership or joint venture that is not shown as a Named Insured in the Declarations."

For example, a failure of performance, either in terms of delay or quality of workmanship, may result in a claim by the owner against the joint venture, and may be attributable to one of the parties. The parties should be aware that some states bar indemnity for the consequences of one's sole or partial negligence.[46] In addition, there may be no basis for common law indemnity for other obligations.[47]

If the joint venturers wish to make themselves responsible for the consequences of their errors, they should expressly provide for allocation of responsibility. Otherwise, they may not be able to recover for mere negligence on the part of their fellow joint venturers. The Texas Court of Appeals has asserted:

> [A]s a matter of law . . . negligence in the management of the affairs of a general partnership or joint venture does not create any right of action against that partner by other members of the partnership. It is only when there is a breach of trust, such as when one partner or joint venturer holds property or assets belonging to the partnership or venture, and converts such to his own use, would such action lie.[48]

In most instances, these cross-indemnity obligations cannot be bonded. Sureties are willing to bond the work of the joint venture, but often demand that each joint venturer guarantee 100 percent of the obligation. To accept a lesser percentage guarantee would deprive the surety of the benefit to it of the partnership model, that is, joint and several liability. Alternatively, the joint venturers and their respective sureties may be able to enter into a four-party agreement allocating the risk of nonperformance along percentage of control lines.

§ 4.15 —Warranty

The joint venture's warranty obligations will be derived from both the law and the construction contract. Although construction services are generally not considered to be subject to the Uniform Commercial Code, other non-Code warranties may be applicable by law. For example, a designer conveys an implied warranty of reasonable results to the owner in several jurisdictions.[49] The

---

[46] *See, e.g.*, Cal. Civ. Code § 2782 (West 1974 & Supp. 1992); Ga. Code Ann. § 13-8-2 (Michie 1982 & Supp. 1991); Ill. Rev. Stat. ch. 29, para. 61 (1969 & Supp. 1991); Mich. Comp. Laws § 691.991 (1987); Minn. Stat. §§ 337.01 *et seq.* (1966 & Supp. 1992); N.Y. Gen. Oblig. Law § 5-322.1 (McKinney 1989).

[47] *See* United States v. Nardone, 782 F. Supp. 996 (M.D. Pa. 1990) (defendant liable under False Claims Act not entitled to indemnification from third-party defendant, even if third party would be jointly and severally liable).

[48] Ferguson v. Williams, 670 S.W.2d 327, 331 (Tex. Ct. App. 1984). *See also* Shain Inv. Co. v. Cohen, 443 N.E.2d 126, 131 n.3 (Mass. App. Ct. 1982).

[49] *See* Acret, Architects & Engineers § 6.03 (2d ed. 1984) (such an implied warranty applies in Alabama, South Carolina, and Washington).

construction contract is likely to include express warranty provisions, for example, obligating the joint venture to replace defectively performed work for a year after completion. The parties will need to decide how performance and financial responsibilities for warranty complaints are to be handled. That allocation depends on the particular project at hand, but may also depend on the identity of the joint venturers. If a problem is a construction deficiency, the contractor is likely to be in the best position to provide a remedy. When the problem is a design problem, however, the contractor may have to perform the repair but the designer will have to be involved and, possibly, assume responsibility for the redesign and the repair costs. Alternatively, making the contractor and designer share the risk of the joint venture's deficient performance may keep the joint venture in a cooperative frame of mind and avoid fingerpointing during and after performance.

§ 4.16 —Guarantee

Depending on the project, the construction may obligate the joint venture's work to meet certain performance criteria. For example, clean rooms require a minimum established standard of cleanliness, and cogeneration plants often require achievement of specified heat output and fuel consumption standards. The penalty for failure to match any of those standards may be severe. In *Arkansas Rice Growers Cooperative v. Alchemy Industries, Inc.,*[50] for example, the failure to achieve performance criteria was held to be a material breach of contract. The court relieved the operator of a plant designed to burn rice hulls to generate power from its contract obligations, including the obligation to pay royalties and furnish fly ash which was a by-product of the process. The court reviewed the obligation to provide "the necessary engineering plant layout and equipment design and the on-site engineering supervision and start up engineering services" to produce a plant capable of meeting specified criteria, and deemed it a warranty.[51] The result in *Arkansas Rice Growers* illustrates the potentially dramatic effects of failing to meet performance criteria.

When performance criteria are specified, the joint venture should first attempt to determine their source. Sometimes, as with cogeneration plants, the performance criteria are directly related to the minimum standards of the pollution control permits. In such instances, the joint venture may have little or no input with respect to the criteria. When there are no such external constraints, the joint venture should seek to define the performance standards in its construction contract and to utilize its technical expertise to define standards it will

---

[50] 797 F.2d 565 (8th Cir. 1986).

[51] *Id.* at 569 (citing United States v. Spearin, 248 U.S. 132, 137, 39 S. Ct. 59 (1918) (party who furnishes plans and specifications warrants their sufficiency for the purpose in view)).

be comfortable with. Absent such definition, the owner may be able to impose its own performance tests.[52]

Arkansas Rice Growers illustrates other guarantee and warranty issues: responsibility for the work of subcontractors or vendors and allocation of responsibility between design and construction. The court affirmed a judgment that the engineer was not responsible for the failure of pollution control equipment supplied by another. This proved to be small relief to the engineer because the court found that the failure of the pollution control system did not cause the performance failure. If the owner or joint venture partner is the proponent of a process or equipment, it may be appropriate for the same person to assume responsibility for the adequacy of that process or equipment. Second, the engineer in *Arkansas Rice Growers* argued that the contractor's deviations from the plans relieved the engineer of responsibility for the performance deficiencies. The court rejected this argument, noting that the contractor's deviations were minor and the design was defective and insufficient. The court made that allocation in *Arkansas Rice Growers* because there was no joint venture; the parties to a design-build joint venture will face the same problem of allocating responsibility for deficiencies to design or to construction.

§ 4.17 —Default

Termination by completion represents the basis for an orderly distribution and winding up of the joint venture's affairs. Sometimes, however, one party to a joint venture ceases to perform because of a disagreement with the management or otherwise. A party's withdrawal may result in the dissolution of a joint venture, but termination may have to wait until after an accounting takes place.[53] Alternatively, the bankruptcy of one member may dissolve the joint venture but may not terminate it. In *Allan Constr. Co. v. United States,*[54] the court of claims held that the solvent member was entitled to administer the joint venture property and was obligated to complete the work.[55]

Although this result may be desirable, the Bankruptcy Code may invalidate the clauses in a joint venture agreement giving the performing joint venturer

---

[52] Richelo, *Legal Implications of Design-Build Method in High Technology Projects, in* Design/Build: Issues for the 90's and Beyond 31 (American Bar Association 1990).

[53] Design Cast Stone Sys., Inc. v. NAB Constr. Co., 760 F. Supp. 68, 69 (E.D. Pa. 1991) (N.Y. law). *See* Stram v. Miller, 663 S.W.2d 269 (Mo. Ct. App. 1983) (equitable action for accounting is prerequisite to action for contribution, but may be joined in a single suit for breach of joint venture agreement).

[54] 227 Ct. Cl. 193, 646 F.2d 487 (1981).

[55] 646 F.2d at 495. *Cf.* Keppner v. Gulf Shores, Inc., 462 So. 2d 719, 723 (Miss. 1985) ("Whether a joint venture terminates when one of the joint venturers becomes bankrupt turns upon proper construction of the joint venture agreement").

the right to act unilaterally. The Code invalidates so-called ipso facto clauses, which terminate executory contracts unilaterally when one party declares bankruptcy or on other similar events, with the exception of contracts to make a loan or extend financing to or issue financing for the debtor.[56] Thus, in one case, the surviving partners were not entitled to oust a general partner from its management role through the operation of an ipso facto clause.[57] It may be necessary for the nondebtor joint venturer to ask the bankruptcy court to require the debtor to accept or reject the executory contract more quickly than the debtor is otherwise entitled to do under the Bankruptcy Code. The presence of ipso facto language, even if legally ineffective without court action, will assist the nondebtor joint venturer in obtaining relief by showing the intent of the joint venturers.

§ 4.18 —Termination of Joint Venture

The joint venture agreement should establish a time and format for termination of the joint venture. Absent such provisions, the joint venture may become subject to state laws pertaining to the termination of partnerships, which may allow termination at will. One court explained that under Illinois law:

> (1) Joint venture agreements which lack a provision regarding termination may be terminated only when the joint venture purpose has been accomplished, or when accomplishment has become impracticable;
>
> (2) Where the agreement does not permit a determination whether or not a purpose has been accomplished, the joint venture will be terminable at will.[58]

The possibility that a disgruntled joint venturer could terminate the joint venture at will should be sufficient warning to those drafting the agreement to specify purposes for the joint venture and to include termination and default provisions.

The agreement should also establish a format for the division of the joint venture property. The agreement may provide for the distribution of monetary assets (bank accounts, profits, or losses) in other provisions. It might also provide for distribution of the joint venture's property, such as equipment and

---

[56] *See* 11 U.S.C. § 365(e) (1979).

[57] *See In re* Cardinal Indus., Inc., 116 B.R. 964, 982 (Bankr. S.D. Ohio 1990).

[58] Meridian Homes Corp. v. Nicholas W. Prassas & Co., 687 F.2d 228, 231 (7th Cir. 1982). *See* Deauville Corp. v. Federated Dep't Stores, Inc., 756 F.2d 1183 (5th Cir. 1985) (Texas statutory law gives absolute right to terminate at will absent agreement to contrary); Sheridan v. McBaine, 660 S.W.2d 189 (Mo. Ct. App. 1983) (when no termination date is fixed, agreement continues until purpose is accomplished).

other physical assets. Absent a prior agreement, capital contributions are to be refunded before profits are distributed.[59]

§ 4.19 —Dispute Resolution

Dispute resolution procedures merit consideration on two grounds. First, the procedure for resolving contractual disputes with third parties should be addressed in the joint venture's contract with those third parties. The joint venturers should be aware that, unless the agreement provides otherwise, all of the joint venturers will be indispensable parties in any action against a third party alleging an injury to the joint venture's property or interests.[60]

With respect to internal disputes, the joint venture agreement should provide a means for resolving disputes between the joint venturers, provided they wish to use a mechanism other than litigation. Absent a contractual selection of a dispute resolution procedure, the parties will likely resort to litigation, and the equitable remedy of an accounting may be a prerequisite to such a suit.[61] During any dispute, the agreement should permit, if not require, the joint venture's work to proceed, even on a unilateral basis by one joint venturer. Otherwise, the completion of the project may become leverage for one or another of the disputing joint venturers.

Finally, if the parties decide in advance to arbitrate or mediate their disputes, they should be aware that not all states are equally willing to support such provisions. When the joint venture agreement (possibly including the project contract) is a contract in interstate commerce and there is a basis for federal jurisdiction, a joint venturer can go into federal court to enforce the arbitration provision in accordance with the Federal Arbitration Act.[62] If there is no basis for federal jurisdiction, the state courts should supply the Federal Arbitration Act to contracts in interstate commerce.[63] State court factual findings, state

---

[59] *See* Zdroy v. Dickenson, 60 Or. App. 596, 654 P.2d 1127 (1982) (applying Oregon partnership law).

[60] *See, e.g.*, Pine Prods. Corp. v. United States, 15 Cl. Ct. 11 (1988); General Eng'g Corp. v. Virgin Islands Water & Power Auth., 636 F. Supp. 22 (D.V.I. 1985); Heinz v. Simon & Flynn, Inc., 444 F. Supp. 114 (S.D.N.Y. 1978).

[61] *See* Meridian Homes Corp. v. Nicholas W. Prassas & Co., 687 F.2d 228 (7th Cir. 1982); Deauville Corp. v. Federated Dep't Stores, Inc., 756 F.2d 1183 (5th Cir. 1985); Sheridan v. McBaine, 660 S.W.2d 189 (Mo. Ct. App. 1983). *See also* VMS/PCA Ltd. Partnership v. PCA Partners Ltd. Partnership, 727 F. Supp. 1167 (N.D. Ill. 1989) (Texas law, action for accounting not a condition precedent to joint venturer's action for damages).

[62] 9 U.S.C. §§ 1–16 (1970).

[63] *See* Moses H. Cone Memorial Hosp. v. Mercury Constr. Co., 460 U.S. 1, 103 S. Ct. 927 (1983); *see also* Southland Corp. v. Keating, 465 U.S. 1, 104 S. Ct. 852 (1984).

legal rules, or both may, however, frustrate an attempt to enforce an arbitration provision.[64]

§ 4.20 Sample Joint Venture Agreement

SAMPLE JOINT VENTURE AGREEMENT

TABLE OF CONTENTS

This Joint Venture Agreement is executed at ____________ as of the ______ day of ____________, 199____ between ____________, a [business entity] with principal offices at ____________ (hereinafter referred to as ____________), and ____________, a [business entity] with principal offices at ____________ (hereinafter referred to as ____________).

WITNESSETH:

WHEREAS, the parties heretofore have associated themselves with each other for the purpose of submitting a proposal to ____________ for the construction of a ____________ known as ____________; and

WHEREAS, said proposal was accepted by ____________ and a contract was awarded to the parties hereto as Joint Venturers, dated ____________, hereinafter called "the Construction Contract" (copy attached hereto); and

---

[64] *See, e.g,* Volt Info. Sciences, Inc. v. Board of Trustees, 489 U.S. 468, 109 S. Ct. 1248 (1989) (state court finding that parties intended to apply California law pertaining to arbitration through choice-of-law provision was binding on Supreme Court); *Ex parte* Warren, 548 So. 2d 157 (Ala.), *cert. denied sub nom.* Jim Skinner Ford, Inc. v. Warren, 493 U.S. 998 (1989).

WHEREAS, it is the desire of the parties hereto to perform the Construction Contract as Joint Venturers, and to set forth herein their mutual understanding relative to their respective duties and obligations under, and their respective rights and interests in, the Construction Contract and in any profits to be derived therefrom the liabilities incurred in connection therewith.

NOW, THEREFORE, in consideration of the premises and the mutual agreements herein contained, the parties hereto agree as follows:

1. *Purpose and Name.* The parties hereto associate themselves with each other for the sole purpose of carrying out and performing the work under the Construction Contract as Joint Venturers. The Construction Contract shall be performed in the name of ____________, so far as carrying out the obligations of the Construction Contract are concerned and so far as enforcing the rights under the Construction Contract are concerned.
2. *Contract Performance.* Each of the parties hereto is acquainted with the terms and conditions of the Construction Contract and the applicable regulations of ____________, and each of the parties hereto shall cooperate in obtaining applicable licenses, bonds, and other matters incidental to the performance of the Construction Contract.
3. *Interest of Parties.* It is agreed that the interests of each of the Joint Venturers in and to the performance of the Construction Contract and in and to any and all materials, supplies, tools, equipment, and other property real or personal to be acquired in connection with the performance of the Construction Contract, and in and to any and all profits and monies which may be derived from the performance thereof, and in and to any and all losses, liabilities, and obligations which may be incurred in connection therewith, shall be in accordance with the following percentages of the whole thereof:

NAME	*PERCENTAGE*
____________________________	____________________
____________________________	____________________

4. *Capital and Equipment.* All necessary working capital and all funds when and as and in the amounts required for the performance of the Construction Contract shall be furnished expeditiously by each and all of the Joint Venturers proportionately in accordance with their respective interests, as set forth in Paragraph 3 hereof. The Joint Venturers shall provide sufficient and suitable personnel and labor, materials, tools, equipment, supplies, and all other property, real and personal, requisite for the completion of the Construction Contract, and shall cooperate with each other to the end that the Construction Contract will be performed and carried to completion in the manner therein provided. If personnel, labor, materials, tools, equipment, supplies, and/or property, real or personal, is furnished by either of the Joint Venturers for actual use in performance of the work of the Construction Contract, with the express approval of ____________, the Sponsor of the Joint Venture, compensation, rental and/or costs relating to such personnel, labor, materials, tools, equipment, supplies, and/or other property, real or personal, shall

be paid to any such Joint Venturer out of Joint Venture funds and be deemed costs incurred by the Joint Venture in the performance of the Construction Contract.

5. *Financial Obligation.* Subject to the provisions of Paragraph 8 hereof, all financial obligations assumed by the parties hereto, or any of them, in connection with and for the benefit of the performance of the Construction Contract, all liabilities assumed by or charged to them, or any of them, as contractors, guarantors, or indemnitors in connection with any surety bond, indemnity agreement, or other bond or undertaking which may be given or executed in connection with the Construction Contract, and all other obligations and liabilities of any kind or character which are assumed or undertaken by the parties hereto, or any of them, in connection with and for the benefit of the performance of the Construction Contract shall be shared by each of the parties hereto proportionately and in accordance with their respective interests as set forth in Paragraph 3 hereof.

6. *Share of Profits.* Subject to the provisions of Paragraph 8 hereof, any and all profits realized or losses suffered or obligations or liabilities incurred in the performance of, or as the result of, the Construction Contract shall be participated in, shared, and borne by each of the Joint Venturers proportionately and in accordance with their respective interests as set forth in Paragraph 3 hereof; provided, however, that in the event of the inability or failure of a Joint Venturer to furnish its proportionate share of the required working capital, as provided in Paragraph 4 hereof and within one (1) calendar week after written notification by ___________ or if ___________ fails to furnish its proportionate share of working capital within one (1) calendar week after written notification by ___________, then, without prejudice to any other remedy or right of enforcement of the parties hereto, the profits shall be divided by the Joint Venturers proportionately in accordance with the amount of working capital actually furnished by each of the parties hereto, notwithstanding any provision in this Agreement to the contrary, and furthermore, the party failing to furnish its proportionate share of working capital required in accordance with Paragraph 4 hereof shall, in addition to its obligations and liabilities under this Agreement, pay interest at the rate of ___________ per annum upon the working capital in accordance with its respective interest under Paragraph 3 hereof; and, provided further, that nothing herein contained shall increase or decrease the proportionate liability of each of the Joint Venturers, as established in Paragraph 3 hereof, for any and all losses suffered or sustained and for any and all liabilities and obligations incurred in connection with the performance of the Construction Contract. It is agreed that the offer to make such contribution at a later date by any party hereto who has failed to contribute its proportionate share of the required working capital shall not cure the default of such party, except by the express written consent of the other party hereto not so in default.

7. *Sponsor and Representatives.* ___________ is hereby designated as Sponsor of the Joint Venture and of the work to be performed under the Construction Contract and as the managing director and agent of the Joint Venture shall

have full and complete authority to manage, supervise, and carry on all matters necessary to and connected with the performance of the Construction Contract. __________ is authorized by __________ to use its own business discretion and judgment in acting as Sponsor of the Joint Venture and of the work to be performed under the Construction Contract, and in so acting, __________ has, and shall have, no duties, responsibilities, or liabilities to __________ other than the duties, responsibilities, or liabilities which it shares with __________ as Joint Venturers.

Without limiting the authority hereby conferred upon by __________, __________ is granted the authority to employ personnel and labor, acquire and lease materials, equipment, tools, supplies, and facilities, enter into subcontracts, leases, and purchase orders, obtain bonds and insurance, receive and disburse funds and working capital and incur any and all obligations for and on behalf of the Joint Venture with respect to performance of the Construction Contract and the administration and management thereof.

The parties hereto agree that __________ and __________ of __________, and each of them, are the Authorized Representatives of the Joint Venture and are authorized to act jointly or separately with the same authority as that conferred upon __________ as Sponsor.

The parties hereto further agree that the Project Manager for the performance of the Construction Contract and his successors shall be designated by __________ and shall be and is granted full power and authority to take all action on behalf of the Joint Venture necessary to carry out and perform the construction work.

8. *Commitments and Obligations.* Subject to the provisions of Paragraph 7 hereof and to the authority hereby conferred upon __________ by __________, no party hereto is the representative of the other party hereto, and it is agreed that no party hereto shall make commitments of any kind whatsoever or incur obligations or liabilities binding upon the other party hereto without first obtaining from the other party hereto the written consent and approval of any such commitment, obligation, or liability, and no commitment made or obligation or liability incurred by any party hereto shall be binding upon the other party hereto who has not given written consent and approval to any such commitment, obligation, or liability. In the event __________ enters into any commitment, obligation, or liability without obtaining the written consent and approval of __________, __________ agrees to indemnify and hold harmless __________ from any and all such commitments, obligations, and liabilities.

9. *Bankruptcy, Insolvency, Dissolution.* In the event of the bankruptcy, insolvency, or involuntary dissolution of any party hereto, this Joint Venture shall continue with respect to the remaining party. Upon the occurrence of any such event, the successors, assigns, receivers, trustees, or legal representatives, hereinafter called "the Representatives," of the party involved in bankruptcy, insolvency, or involuntary dissolution proceedings, shall cease to have any interest in the performance of the Construction Contract and shall cease to have any interest in and to this Joint Venture or any assets held or acquired in connection therewith, except to share, for and on behalf of the party so

represented, in profits and losses as hereinafter provided. In any such case, the remaining party shall wind up the affairs of the Joint Venture, and in that connection carry out and complete the performance of the Construction Contract, and upon such completion, or sooner termination, and receipt of the payment of all amounts due thereunder, the remaining party shall account to the Representatives of the party whose bankruptcy, insolvency, or involuntary dissolution has occurred, and such Representatives shall then be entitled to receive from the remaining party an amount equal to the monies advanced by the party represented, plus such party's proportionate share of the profits resulting from the performance of the Construction Contract computed to the completion or termination of the entire Construction Contract; provided, however, that the profit computed as of the date of such bankruptcy, insolvency, or involuntary dissolution shall be that percentage of the whole profit resulting from the performance of the Construction Contract as the amount of work done thereunder as of the date of such bankruptcy, insolvency, or involuntary dissolution bears to all of the work done or to be done thereunder. In the event the share of the losses chargeable to the party so represented exceeds the sums advanced by such party, the Representatives shall promptly pay unto the remaining party hereto all of such excess and share of all losses in accordance with the respective interest of the party so represented pursuant to Paragraph 3 hereof.

In the event of the voluntary dissolution or reorganization of any party hereto, this Joint Venture shall continue and the performance of the Construction Contract shall be completed by the Joint Venture, and the dissolution or reorganization of any party hereto shall not in any manner whatsoever release such party from its obligations and liabilities under this agreement.

10. *Overhead Expenses.* No party hereto shall make any charges against the Joint Venture for any ordinary overhead expenses or for time which may be expended in connection with the performance of the Construction Contract by any party, its officers, or employees, except in actually carrying on the performance of the Construction Contract with the express approval of ____________, and except for travel expenses of officers or employees related to performance of the Construction Contract.

11. *Deposit and Disbursement of Funds.* All Capital Contributions paid or advanced by parties hereto, and all monies, if any, borrowed for the account of this Joint Venture, and all progress and final payments and other revenue received in connection with the Construction Contract shall be deposited in a bank or banks selected by ____________ in an account or accounts designated by ____________, and all such capital contributions, payments, monies, and revenue shall be received and disbursed by ____________, in accordance with the terms of this Agreement, provided, however, that when any return of capital contributions or payment of profits is made to any party hereto, the other party hereto shall then be paid proportionate returns of capital contributions or payment of profits subject to the terms of this Agreement; and provided further, that the unanimous consent of the parties hereto shall be obtained before any return of capital and/or payment of profits is made before final settlement of the affairs and accounts of this Joint Venture.

12. *Books and Records.* A complete set of books, records, and accounts correctly showing all payments on account of capital or otherwise made by each Joint Venturer, or costs incurred and monies received in connection with the performance of the Construction Contract, and correctly reflecting all transactions pertaining thereto shall be kept and maintained, and the parties hereto shall be furnished with periodic statements and reports reflecting the current financial condition of the construction project. Any Joint Venturer shall have access to and the right to inspect such books, records, and accounts at all reasonable times. The books of the Joint Venture shall, except in the case of demonstrable error, be conclusive in establishing whether a profit has been realized or a loss sustained, the amount thereof, and the proportionate amount of work done as of any given time or date.
13. *Assignment.* No party hereto shall sell, assign, or in any manner whatsoever transfer its interest in the Construction Contract, any assets acquired in connection therewith, or any part of its interest under this Joint Venture Agreement without first obtaining the written consent of the other party hereto.
14. *Ownership.* Each Joint Venturer shall be the owner of an undivided proportionate interest in and to any and all equipment, materials, machinery, supplies, and other property, real and personal, which may be acquired in connection with the construction project; such interest shall be in the same proportions as the parties hereto have actually contributed working capital in accordance with the provisions of Paragraphs 3, 4, and 6 hereof.
15. *Final Settlement.* Upon the completion of the performance of the Construction Contract, the parties hereto shall render a true and correct accounting, each to the other, of all authorized expenses incurred in connection with the performance of the Construction Contract, all monies received as the result thereof, and all assets acquired in connection therewith. The parties hereto agree, upon such completion or the termination thereof by ____________, to settle and adjust all accounts and obligations incurred in connection with said Construction Contract, to return all working capital and other cash funds to the party or parties having contributed such funds, and thereupon to make full and final settlement with each other in such manner as will cause each party to receive that percentage of all profits or bear that percentage of all losses arising from the performance of the Construction Contract, as is set forth opposite its respective name under Paragraph 3 hereof, subject, however, to the provisions of Paragraph 6 hereof. If, after final settlement of the accounts of the Joint Venture, claims, liabilities, or obligations shall arise for which the Joint Venture is liable, the parties shall advance the funds, when and as needed, to satisfy same.
16. *Scope of Agreement.* It is expressly understood and agreed by the parties hereto that this Joint Venture Agreement extends only to the performance of the aforesaid Construction Contract, together with any changes or additions thereto and/or extra work thereunder, and in no event shall this Agreement extend to or cover any other, or different work; and upon final accounting and settlement among the parties hereto, this Agreement shall terminate, subject to the provisions of Paragraph 15 hereof. The term Construction Contract as used in this Agreement is intended to and shall include the changes,

additions, and/or extra work hereinabove mentioned. This Joint Venture Agreement supersedes any and all prior agreements between the parties hereto with respect to the aforesaid Construction Contract.

17. *Binding Agreement.* Subject to the foregoing provisions herein contained, this Agreement shall inure to the benefit of, and be binding upon, the parties hereto, their successors, trustees, assigns, heirs, administrators, and legal representatives, but shall not inure to the benefit of any other person, firm, or corporation.

18. *Third-Party Claims.* Subject to the provisions of Paragraph 7 hereof and the authority thereby conferred upon ___________, no claims arising out of or related to the operation or conduct of this Joint Venture asserted against one or both of the Joint Venturers by a claimant other than a Joint Venturer shall be settled except with the unanimous consent of the Joint Venturers, provided that the consent of any insolvent Joint Venturer, or of any Joint Venturer who shall deny liability to the other Joint Venturer with respect to such claims, shall not be required.

IN WITNESS WHEREOF, the parties hereto have executed this Agreement as of the date first above written.

Attest:	By
______________________________	______________________________
Attest:	By
______________________________	______________________________

CHAPTER 5

INSURANCE AND BONDING FOR JOINT VENTURE CONSTRUCTION PROJECTS

Richard W. Miller

Richard W. Miller is the senior partner at Miller Law Firm, P.C., in Kansas City, Missouri, which specializes in representing contractors in legal matters throughout the country. Mr. Miller received an A.B. from Rockhurst College in Kansas City, Missouri, and his LLB and LLM from the University of Missouri at Kansas City. He is a member of the Kansas City and American Bar Associations and the Lawyers Association of Kansas City. He has addressed state and national construction, surety, accounting, and banking groups, as well as the Superconference of Construction, and has authored a number of books on construction and surety matters.

INSURANCE AND BONDING

§ 5.1 Introduction

A joint venture has been described in different ways with various elements. For the purpose of this discussion, a *joint venture* is a combination of two or more persons to carry out a single business enterprise or a series of business enterprises for profit, during which the parties combine property, money, skill, and knowledge to achieve such purpose. The amount of money and property normally is either contributed equally or in specific percentages, but there is no way to measure accurately the skill and knowledge each party brings to the joint venture.

Generally, the rules that apply to members of a partnership also apply to members of a joint venture. One venture member can bind its associates by a contract in furtherance of the enterprise or within the scope of activity of the enterprise. Each party to a true joint venture is liable for the performance of the entire contract and the payment of all labor, material, equipment, and other obligations. There is no limitation of liability as between the joint venture and the owner and, if any member of the joint venture defaults, the remaining financially responsible members of the joint venture are required to complete the job.

Despite the risk that one member of the joint venture may have to satisfy a greater percentage of the loss than originally contemplated, there are certain advantages to a joint venture in construction:

1. It spreads the risk among the members
2. It combines specialized abilities and pools specific talents
3. It aids in estimating and permits members to compare estimates
4. It permits using a contractor with local knowledge
5. It increases the ability to bid more projects and thereby spreads bonding capacity
6. It enables bids to be submitted on major projects
7. It enables a pooling of resources, equipment, manpower, and financing
8. It encourages future business with members
9. It keeps capital working
10. It allows venturers to increase their area of operation and expertise.

The following sections discuss some of the ways in which to joint venture, the risks inherent in certain methods, and possible ways to minimize such risks. Of course, one way to minimize loss is by way of insurance. Which parties are covered will depend on the type of joint venture arrangement they select. The extent of insurance should remain the same regardless of the joint venture arrangement. This chapter discusses the various joint venture arrangements and how the parties are covered and includes sample agreements for them.

§ 5.2 Role of Insurance Agents

In addition to deciding on insurance coverage, the venturers must also determine which agents will handle the bonds and insurance requirements. The following plan is one method for handling the insurance and bonding needs for a joint venture.

Identify sponsoring agent. The insurance agent of the sponsoring contractor becomes the *sponsoring agent,* with the immediate and total responsibility to the joint venture for all issues related to the insuring of the joint venture. Sponsoring agents can delegate this responsibility to others, but in no way does this lessen their total responsibility. The insurance agents for the other venturers, the *cooperating agents,* retain full responsibility for seeing that their principal's interest is properly covered.

Agreement of cooperating agents. It is the sponsoring agent's initial responsibility to gather all facts regarding the venture, analyze the risk, and submit the analysis and the facts related thereto to the cooperating agent(s) for approval. If agreement cannot be reached between the sponsoring and cooperating agent, then the sponsoring agent will submit the point of disagreement to the principals for their decision. The cooperating agent must advise the sponsoring agent of any special advantages the cooperating agent enjoys with respect to the analysis of the risk. This would include special forms, market entrees, and experience.

Market the program. The sponsoring agent prepares the joint venture insurance program, utilizing any special advantages enjoyed by the cooperating agent to find insurance coverage at the lowest premium from the highest-rated company.

Communication between agents. The sponsoring agent keeps the cooperating agent fully informed of developments related to the insurance program. This includes, at a minimum, furnishing each cooperating agent with a copy of the policies, endorsements, and agreement with the carrier, a copy of correspondence on material matters, and a memorandum of any important discussions with the insurance carrier. It normally does not include advice to the cooperating agent on such matters as mailing the certificates, small loss coverage, moving automobiles or other items on or off the policy, and so on. The cooperating agents should be kept fully informed on loss summaries, engineering reports, and similar information.

Remuneration of agents. Regardless of who issues the policy, all commissions are paid into a common pot, controlled by the sponsoring agent. At some convenient time, all agents submit to the sponsoring agent a list of their out-of-pocket expenses. This includes travel expenses, services purchased, and any other unusual expenses. It does not include internal expenses nor expenses for time invested by the agents. Covered expenses are reimbursed by the sponsoring agent out of the pot. Commissions remaining in the pot after paying expenses are distributed to each agent, in a proportion equal to the percentage interest of that agent's client in the profits of the joint venture. The commissions can also be divided equally if the agents prefer.

§ 5.3 Complexities of Joint Venture Coverage

Certain problems are unique to joint venture insurance. These include:

Minimum coverage. The agents and the venturers must agree on the minimum for any umbrella coverage of the venture.

Termination of liability. Because an accident occurring as a result of joint venture activities may not be reported until long after the joint venture is disbanded, care must be taken to stop any liability from flowing to the individual venturers after the venture is complete.

Completed operations. Completed operations is, of course, one hazard that continues after the joint venture is dissolved. It is suggested that this coverage be negotiated when the joint venture insurance is set, so as to extend the completed operations coverage for a period of at least five years after completion of the job. Even more preferable would be to continue coverage to the end of the statutory limitation for the liability. This may be done by paying a flat premium. An alternative is to negotiate with each of the venturers' insurance carriers to add the joint venture risk to each of their individual policies. The venturers would cover only their own risk arising out of the joint venture, extending coverage for the length of time deemed necessary.

Contractual liability. Any comment in the discussion of completed operations applies equally to contractual liability coverage.

Maintenance period. During the maintenance period following the completion of the joint venture project, the joint venture should consider subcontracting the maintenance responsibility to one of the venturers. This venturer would undertake the responsibility for insurance and file certificates with the other venturers.

Premium adjustments. Although it is quite improbable that a retrospective rating approach (increasing future premiums to cover losses incurred) will be used on a joint venture, the agents should consider the problems that will arise if retrospective premium adjustments are made two or three years after the venture is dissolved. It can be agreed that once the reserves for loss stabilize over time as losses are minimized, the insurance carrier will not adjust the premiums.

Employee benefits. On any joint venture of any length of time, special attention should be given to employee benefits such as group life and hospitalization for any employees loaned to the joint venture by the various venturers.

Equipment. If equipment is rented to the joint venture by one of the venturers, there should be an agreement regarding responsibility for damage to that equipment not insured under the owner's policy or subject to the deductible.

Fidelity coverage. The discovery period on fidelity coverage (to protect a company from embezzlement by an employee) should be extended beyond the one-year period because fidelity coverage will cease at the end of the joint venture.

Surety Coverage

Financial information. The agents handling the surety requirements for each venturer should be advised at the earliest possible date to contact the sponsoring agent to coordinate the necessary financial information.

Commissions. Commissions should be paid to the agents in proportion to each venturer's participation, unless unusual circumstances are encountered or the parties agree otherwise.

Participation. Each venturer's surety should have the opportunity to participate in the same proportion that their principals participate.

Pre-bid agreement. A pre-bid agreement establishing terms and conditions of the final joint venture agreement should be submitted to each surety by the sponsoring agent.

Terms and conditions. To avoid last-minute misunderstandings as to various sureties' requirements for such items as indemnity, the sponsor should advise all venturers well before the bid date of the final terms, conditions, and requirements of the sureties.

SILENT JOINT VENTURES

§ 5.4 Silent Joint Venture

In a *silent joint venture* one or more parties are named in the contract and bond but there also are one or more unidentified parties. This arrangement can be used when:

1. One of the parties to the venture does not want the relationship disclosed (for example, a supplier or subcontractor joint venturing with one general contractor, and at the same time bidding for projects with other general contractors)
2. One of the venturers is not licensed in the area of the job, which might cause the bid to be disallowed (note that this will not cure the licensing problem in certain states and on certain types of projects)
3. Because it is unable to obtain sufficient bonding, one of the venturers seeks coverage through association with another venturer.

Although the responsibilities and obligations of the silent joint venturers are limited to those defined in the joint venture agreement and application, certain common elements flow through all these arrangements. The silent joint venturer has no direct responsibility or obligation to the owner for completion of the work. Similarly, upon default or nonperformance by the joint venture, the silent joint venturer has no direct standing with the owner that would enable the silent venturer in its own right to step in and remedy the default. Consequently, the pitfalls of this arrangement include allocating to the silent venturer all the liability of a member of a regular joint venture without the necessary means to minimize liability.

Before issuing a bid bond to a silent joint venture, the surety should have a written commitment (pre-bid agreement) from all the parties, including the silent venturer, to execute the bond application and be bound by the bid and the obligations incumbent with a bid bond. Otherwise, the surety could find itself issuing a bid bond with the silent venturer unnamed and thus uncommitted. Similarly, if the party putting up the bonding capacity believes the bid is too low or for some other reason does not want to sign the take-out payment and performance bonds, then provision is made (see **§ 5.5**) to prevent the other venturer from going forward without the consent of all venturers.

Adequate protection of the silent inactive venturer whose capacity is little more than that of an indemnitor to obtain bonding is very difficult to achieve. A suggested form of joint venture agreement drafted for the protection of the silent inactive venturer appears in **§ 5.6**.

If the silent venturer is going to supply an equally proportionate amount of capital, equipment, personnel, and other items, then the standard form joint venture agreement (see § **5.10**) may be used, with the understanding that the contract will be taken and the bond issued in the name of only one member of the joint venture. It should be made clear that this in no way detracts from the fact that the arrangement is a joint venture and the parties are equal joint venturers.

Practice note. Under no circumstances should a silent joint venture be used on a government project that requires all the interested members of the joint venture to be named, or on any project in which such a disclosure is required. To do so could expose the parties to fraud and other charges, both civil and criminal.

§ 5.5 Sample Pre-Bid Silent Joint Venture Agreement

SAMPLE PRE-BID SILENT JOINT VENTURE AGREEMENT

TABLE OF CONTENTS

This Agreement made this _____ day of ___________, 199__, by and between ________________ (herein called "Contractor"), party of the first part, and ________________ (herein called "Silent Venturer"), party of the second part,

WITNESSETH:

WHEREAS, Contractor will bid on the Contract for ________________; and

WHEREAS, if the Contract is awarded to Contractor and an agreement is entered into for its performance by Contractor and the owner, Contractor and Silent Venturer intend to participate in a joint venture for the performance of Contract and as joint venturers to share in the profits or losses thereof, to be jointly and severally liable for its performance and to designate the respective obligations of the parties and authority to control the work or act as agent for each other;

NOW, THEREFORE, in consideration of the premises and the mutual agreements of the parties hereinafter set forth, and conditioned upon the issuance by ________________, as Surety, of a Bid or Proposal Bond in connection with said Contract, the parties hereto agree as follows:

1. Bonds. Contractor shall execute said Bond or Proposal Bond and any Performance and Payment Bonds required in connection with the Contract if the same is awarded to and accepted by said Contractor and if the Surety issues each such Bond.

2. Agreement to Proceed. Notwithstanding anything in the joint venture agreement to the contrary, the parties hereto agree to be joint venturers and as

such to be jointly and severally liable for the submission of said bid and the performance of the obligations of said Contract, Bid, or Proposal Bond and to execute all appropriate indemnification agreements indemnifying the Surety to the extent required by the Surety.

3. Share of Profits and Losses. If the Contract is awarded to and accepted by Contractor, and if the Surety issues the Payment Bond and the Performance Bond, the parties hereto shall be and become joint venturers for the performance of the Contract and as such the parties shall share in the profits or losses thereof equally, unless otherwise mutually agreed upon between them, shall be jointly and severally liable for its performance, shall designate both the respective obligations of the parties and the authority to control the work or act as agent for each other, and shall execute the Contract Bond Application of Surety and any other documents incident thereto.

4. Cancellation. Upon the execution by Surety of any Bid, Proposal, Performance, or Payment Bonds relating to the Contract given by Contractor as Principal to the owner as Obligee, this Agreement may be cancelled and the full Silent Joint Venture Agreement attached hereto shall be executed.

5. Surety. The parties recognize that Surety, although not a party hereto, is relying on this Agreement in the issuance of any bonds to Contractor and that Surety has a right to enforce the provisions of this Agreement to the same extent as though it were a party hereto. This Agreement shall in all its terms and obligations, in addition to being for the benefit of Surety, be also for the benefit of any other surety or sureties joining with Surety in executing said bond or bonds or executing at the request of Surety said bond or bonds, as well as any surety or sureties assuming reinsurance thereupon.

Signed and sealed the day and year first above written.

Witness or Attest:

____________________________ ____________________________

Contractor

____________________________ ____________________________

Silent Venturer

§ 5.6 Sample Silent Joint Venture Agreement

SAMPLE SILENT JOINT VENTURE AGREEMENT

TABLE OF CONTENTS

8. Default of Contractor.
9. Scope of Obligations.

THIS AGREEMENT, made and entered into this _____ day of ___________, 199____, by and between _________________, herein called "Contractor," First Party, and _________________, herein called "Silent Venturer," Second Party.

WITNESSETH:

WHEREAS, _________________, as Owner, has signified its decision and intention to award to the Contractor a Contract of general construction in accordance with drawings and specifications prepared by _________________, Architect; and

WHEREAS, Contractor needs to procure a Contract Bond, executed by itself as principal and by a corporate surety as surety, in the penal sum of $___________, conditioned in the manner approved by said Owner; and

WHEREAS, Contractor can obtain such a Contract Bond from ___________, herein called the "Surety," if and only if Silent Venturer will join it in the application therefor and in the agreements contained in said application; and

WHEREAS, Silent Venturer is willing to execute said application and make said agreements for the convenience of Contractor and pursuant to the request which Contractor heretofore made of it, only upon and subject to the terms and conditions set forth herein;

NOW, THEREFORE, in consideration of the premises and the covenants set forth herein, IT IS MUTUALLY AGREED:

1. Application for Bonds. Silent Venturer will join Contractor in the execution of an application to the Surety for a Contract Bond in the penal sum of $________, referenced in said Contract and conditioned in the manner approved by said Owner, and Silent Venturer will join Contractor in making the agreements contained in said application.

2. Payment to Silent Venturer. If the Surety shall execute such a bond after receiving an application joined in by Silent Venturer as aforesaid, then and in such event Contractor covenants and agrees to pay Silent Venturer the sum of $________, and to make and effect such payment in full upon completion of the work called for in said Contract, by whomsoever performed. Contractor acknowledges that its obligation to pay said sum to Silent Venturer is absolute and shall not be subject to abatement or diminution for any reason or under any circumstances. In addition, Silent Venturer shall receive ______ percent (____%) of the profits inuring from the performance of such Contract. Under no circumstances shall Silent Venturer be responsible for any losses incurred by Contractor as a result of, or in the performance of, this Contract.

3. Terms and Conditions. This instrument and Silent Venturer's joinder in said application and in the agreements provided for therein are conditioned upon each and all the following covenants, terms, and conditions, which Contractor agrees to perform, keep, and observe at its own sole cost and expense and without cost or expense to Silent Venturer, to wit:

(a) Contractor will pay the premium(s) on said bond as soon as the same shall become due;

(b) Contractor covenants and agrees faithfully to perform each and every obligation and punctually to make each and every payment incumbent on it under, by virtue of, or in relation to said Contract and the work provided for therein, and Contractor will not suffer or permit any default to arise under, or in relation to, said Contract or work;

(c) Contractor hereby covenants and agrees faithfully to perform each and every covenant and agreement set forth in the application for said Contract Bond and to observe all the other terms and conditions contained therein;

(d) Contractor hereby grants to Silent Venturer all and the same rights, privileges, and immunities under, in relation to, or in any manner concerning said Contract, the work provided for therein, or moneys payable thereunder as are granted to the Surety in and by said application and Indemnity Agreement given to the Surety;

(e) Without limiting the generality of the foregoing, Contractor hereby covenants and agrees:

  (1) To establish in such bank(s) as Silent Venturer may designate from time to time a separate and special bank account, herein called the "trust account," and to be identified as such on the records of the bank;

  (2) To receive all moneys due or to become due under or on account of said Contract in trust, to deposit such moneys as and when received in said trust account(s), and not to permit any moneys to be withdrawn from any such account except in the manner and for a purpose hereinafter provided; and

  (3) That in the establishment of each such trust account it shall be provided that until the arrangement shall be terminated upon the written consent of Silent Venturer delivered to the bank, no moneys may be withdrawn from the respective account except upon joint signature of an individual designated from time to time by Contractor and an individual designated from time to time by Silent Venturer or upon the sole signature of such person(s) as Silent Venturer alone may designate from time to time under and pursuant to paragraph 8 hereof.

(f) Contractor shall pay promptly, as the same become due, all obligations which it or any member or representative thereof did or may incur in connection with said Contract or prosecution of the work provided for therein, including the premium for said Contract Bond and all items of every character and description covered by or within the scope of said Contract Bond; and

(g) As soon as practicable after a progress payment received under said Contract has been deposited in a trust account so established, Contractor shall exhibit to Silent Venturer proof that it paid for all items covered by said Contract Bond in respect of the portion of the work covered by said progress payment, whereupon Contractor shall be entitled to reimbursement from said trust account, for the amounts which it expended to pay for such items, up to but not in excess of the lesser of (i) eighty-five percent (85%) of the estimate covered by said progress payment or (ii) the balance then on deposit in said trust account, such reimbursement to be by check on said trust account signed as herein provided.

4. Deficiency. If and to the extent that payments accruing to Contractor under the Contract or hereunder shall not suffice to pay all bills and expenses incurred in

the prosecution of said work, as the same accrue and become due, Contractor shall immediately supply any deficiency forthwith.

5. Limited Responsibility of Silent Venturer. Silent Venturer shall have no responsibility upon any promise or undertaking of Contractor, and Contractor shall have no right or authority to pledge or involve the credit or financial responsibility of Silent Venturer in any way or for any amount.

6. Nonwaiver. Silent Venturer shall have no duty or responsibility to enforce compliance with the provisions hereof and may waive any such provision, for as long as it shall elect, without waiving or otherwise affecting its right to insist upon complete and precise performance in accordance with the tenor hereof.

7. Validity. Silent Venturer's rights and privileges herein are intended to be exercisable from the date hereof and are not dependent on any default of Contractor under said Contract, application for Contract Bond, or other instrument.

8. Default of Contractor. If and at any time that Silent Venturer shall be of the opinion that Contractor shall have failed to perform or observe any covenant, agreement, condition, or restriction contained in said Contract or herein, or both, Silent Venturer shall have the right:

(a) to give notice of such opinion to the bank(s) in which any such trust account(s) shall be maintained at the time and on so doing, the authority of Contractor to sign, or to designate a representative to sign, checks for the withdrawal of funds therefrom, jointly with Silent Venturer, shall be terminated instantly at the election of Silent Venturer and said bank(s) thereafter shall honor checks for the withdrawal of funds from such trust account(s) when and only when signed solely by such person(s) as Silent Venturer alone may designate in writing from time to time; and

(b) in addition to other rights which Silent Venturer has, to have Contractor removed from the jobsite and perform the balance of the work itself or place a contractor of Silent Venturer's selection as completing contractor and Contractor shall forfeit all rights to any proceeds and shall immediately reimburse Silent Venturer for any losses then or thereafter incurred.

9. Scope of Obligations. Although this arrangement may be styled or considered for certain purposes a joint venture, it is specifically understood and agreed that Contractor shall perform all work under the Contract, provide all men, equipment, materials, and supplies necessary to complete such work and do everything else necessary to complete such work in strict accord with the Contract, and Silent Venturer will have no obligation to do anything in connection with the Contract except to join in the application for the Contract Bond and other documents incident thereto.

10. Binding Agreement. The provisions hereof shall bind the parties hereto and their respective successors and assigns.

IN WITNESS WHEREOF, the parties have executed this agreement in duplicate on the day and year first above mentioned.

____
Contractor

____
Silent Venturer

DISADVANTAGED PARTIES

§ 5.7 Joint Venture with a Disadvantaged Party

The last few years have seen the inauguration of governmental programs to enable contractors who have no independent bonding capacity to bid on (see **§ 5.9**) and perform work on (see **§ 5.10**) projects requiring bonds. These programs have caused joint ventures to be formed in order to provide bonding and financial capabilities. Under these programs, the minority or economically disadvantaged contractor must have at least 51 percent of the joint venture interest. The standard form of joint venture agreement is not applicable under such circumstances and should not be used.

In some degree, the protection accorded to the financially responsible member of such a joint venture is similar to the protection that exists in certain types of silent joint ventures. However, because this is not and should not be a silent joint venture arrangement, that form of agreement will not suffice.

In this arrangement, the financially responsible party must be in a position to take any tax losses. Because the parties designated as disadvantaged contractors do not have the financial capability to perform the contract, it is generally fruitless to require them to bear any percentage of the loss. Also, in order to have a joint venture approved, it sometimes is significant to the approving agency that the party lacking financial capability will not be required to bear any of the loss. If, as a practical matter, the responsible party will have to bear the loss anyway, the agreement might as well specify this.

Because the financially responsible party, whom the agreement designates as the contractor, is responsible for all the losses on the project, an administrative committee is appointed to run the project in order to achieve control for the contractor. If the administrative committee is unable to agree, then all decisions of the administrative committee under section 8 will be made "by the project manager, whose decision will be binding upon the parties." The agreement could also provide that, instead of the project manager, final decisions could be made by the contractor. See sample agreement in **§ 5.10**.

In order to permit the contractor, the financially responsible party, to control the project, the contractor must also control the project manager. Because the project manager has key responsibilities, section 6 of the agreement provides: "[I]f the employee designated to act as Project Manager shall fail, refuse or be unable for a period of 30 days to fully and completely perform the duties and obligations of the Project Manager, then Contractor . . . has the right to designate the Project Manager and any successors to said Project Manager."

The ability to control the operations is critical to the contractor's success in minimizing its potential losses. Therefore, a management agreement should be executed between the contractor and the disadvantaged contractor, recognizing the right and power of the contractor to control certain aspects of the joint venture as specified. A sample management agreement appears in **§ 5.8**.

§ 5.8 Sample Management Agreement with Disadvantaged Contractor

SAMPLE MANAGEMENT AGREEMENT WITH DISADVANTAGED CONTRACTOR

TABLE OF CONTENTS

THIS AGREEMENT, made and entered into this _____ day of __________, 199____, by and between ______________, a ___________ corporation, hereinafter referred to as "Contractor," First Party, and ______________, a __________ corporation, hereinafter referred to as "Disadvantaged Contractor," Second Party,

WITNESSETH:

WHEREAS, Disadvantaged Contractor is a minority contractor which neither has the staff nor expects at this time to be able to perform certain managerial functions, and Disadvantaged Contractor deems it advisable and in its best own interest to engage Contractor to perform certain managerial functions for it and for any joint venture entered into with Contractor, and Contractor is willing to perform such managerial functions;

WHEREAS, Contractor has been engaged in construction for a number of years and has developed a staff and expertise in managing and operating construction operations;

WHEREAS, Contractor has assisted other minority contractors and is interested in entering into a joint venture arrangement with Disadvantaged Contractor to assist Disadvantaged Contractor in expanding its business and improving its operation;

NOW, THEREFORE, in consideration of the premises and the mutual covenants expressed therein, IT IS AGREED:

1. Books and Accounting. Disadvantaged Contractor hereby engages and employs Contractor to keep complete books of account, including payment of all bills and payroll for all transactions and dealings of the parties in connection with any joint venture between them and for all services performed by Contractor for Disadvantaged Contractor; and any costs, expenses, and income of any joint venture in

which Disadvantaged Contractor and Contractor are involved shall be recorded therein. The records, books of account, and other papers of every character and description pertaining to this Agreement shall be kept at Contractor's office and shall not be removed therefrom, and shall be open to inspection and audit at all convenient times on reasonable notice by Disadvantaged Contractor and its respective authorized representatives.

2. Contractor's Scope of Work. Disadvantaged Contractor hereby further engages Contractor to perform for it such functions as supervision of the work on the projects undertaken by Disadvantaged Contractor in a joint venture with Contractor; administration and performance of all basic managerial functions normally performed in the management of a like contracting concern subject to direction from the directors of Disadvantaged Contractor; estimating the work bid by Disadvantaged Contractor in a joint venture with Contractor; arranging for insurance; and training employees of Disadvantaged Contractor to perform such services.

3. Remuneration. For and in consideration of such services, Disadvantaged Contractor and any joint venture for which services are performed by Contractor shall pay to Contractor $_________ per month per joint venture project for the records maintained and services performed by Contractor on each such separate project. Such payment shall not include payment for any employees of Contractor which shall become employees of, or be employed by, any joint venture between Disadvantaged Contractor and Contractor, and such employees shall be paid by the joint venture.

4. Termination. If either party shall fail to do anything incumbent on it hereunder as herein provided and shall fail to commence to rectify such default within five (5) days after the other party gives it written notice thereof, then and in such event said other party may terminate this contract forthwith by and upon giving the party in default notice of its intention so to do. Notwithstanding anything herein to the contrary, Disadvantaged Contractor cannot terminate Contractor and this Agreement until all the work on all the contracts taken in the name of a joint venture between Disadvantaged Contractor and Contractor are completed and accepted, and all liabilities and warranties in connection therewith are fully satisfied. Furthermore, Disadvantaged Contractor cannot terminate this Agreement and cannot terminate the rights of Contractor under this Agreement as long as there are outstanding a) any loans for Disadvantaged Contractor individually or loans for any joint venture between Contractor and Disadvantaged Contractor which Contractor has guaranteed, or b) any bonds on which Contractor acted as an indemnitor either for Disadvantaged Contractor or any joint venture between Contractor and Disadvantaged Contractor, or c) both the conditions set forth in a) and b).

5. Employees. Disadvantaged Contractor does not presently have anyone that performs the services hereby contracted to be performed by Contractor and Contractor shall perform such services with the primary intent of trying to train others connected with Disadvantaged Contractor to perform those services in connection with maintaining and establishing Disadvantaged Contractor as a minority contractor which ultimately can perform without such assistance by Contractor. Other than training as herein provided, Contractor shall have a) no authority to direct or

in any way control employees of Disadvantaged Contractor, b) no voice whatsoever in the hiring or firing of employees of Disadvantaged Contractor, and c) no responsibility for the compensation of employees of Disadvantaged Contractor. Contractor, except during the time it is training employees of Disadvantaged Contractor, shall have no control whatsoever over the time, manner, or wages of employees of Disadvantaged Contractor. At no time shall Contractor have any responsibility or obligation for, or in respect of, compensation due or payable to the working force, taxes measured by, or in relation to, the amount of such compensation, insurance premiums, other direct or indirect costs, or otherwise.

6. Contract Terms. This Agreement, unless terminated prior thereto as herein provided, shall continue in force until ___________, 199____, and it shall then and at the end of each succeeding contract year thereof renew itself automatically for another contract year, unless at least ninety (90) days prior thereto either party shall give the other party written notice that the same shall expire at the end of the contract year then in force. The term "contract year," as said term is used herein, shall be deemed to have commenced on ___________ 1 of each year during continuance of this agreement and end on the last day of the next succeeding ___________. Notwithstanding anything herein to the contrary, Disadvantaged Contractor cannot exercise its right not to renew the contract until (a) all the work on any joint venture between Disadvantaged Contractor and Contractor on all the contracts that such joint venture has are completed and accepted and all liabilities and warranties in connection therewith are fully satisfied, and b) any loans which Contractor has guaranteed for Disadvantaged Contractor individually or loans for any joint venture between Disadvantaged Contractor and Contractor which Contractor has guaranteed are satisfied and no longer remain unpaid, and c) any bonds or indemnification agreements as to which Contractor has acted as an indemnitor remain open and not cancelled either for Disadvantaged Contractor or any joint venture between Disadvantaged Contractor and Contractor.

7. Relationship of Parties. It is expressly understood that the parties are not associating themselves, hereunder or otherwise, for any other purposes, and are not associating themselves generally, permanently, or as partners, and nothing in this Agreement shall be construed as a limitation or restriction upon the right and power of either party to carry on its separate business for its sole benefit. Nothing herein contained shall be considered to constitute the parties hereto partners nor to constitute any party hereto as the general agent of any other party. The only arrangement between the parties separate from this Agreement would be any joint venture agreements between the parties which are or will be set forth in specific written agreements.

8. Choice of Law. Irrespective of the fact that any one of the parties now is or may become a resident of a different state, this Agreement and all questions relative to the execution, validity, interpretation, and performance of this Agreement shall be governed by and construed and enforced in accordance with the laws of the State of ___________ and, if there is any dispute between the parties, then the parties agree that suit can only be brought and maintained in the ___________ Court of ___________ County, ___________ and venue and jurisdiction shall rest solely in ___________ County, ___________ and nowhere else.

IN WITNESS WHEREOF, the parties hereto have caused this Agreement to be executed by their respective officers hereunto duly authorized on the day and year above written.

CONTRACTOR

Attest: By ______________________________

President

First Party

____

Secretary

DISADVANTAGED CONTRACTOR

Attest: By ______________________________

President

Second Party

____

Secretary

§ 5.9 Sample Pre-Bid Agreement with Disadvantaged Contractor

SAMPLE PRE-BID AGREEMENT WITH DISADVANTAGED CONTRACTOR

This Pre-Bid Agreement, made and entered into this _____ day of __________, 199____, by and between __________________, a ___________ corporation, with its principal office and place of business in _________________, ___________ (hereinafter called "Disadvantaged Contractor") and _______________________, a _____________ corporation, with its principal office and place of business in __________, ___________ (hereinafter called "Contractor"), both of whom collectively are sometimes referred to as the "Joint Venturers,"

WITNESSETH:

WHEREAS, the Joint Venturers are planning to submit a bid to ___________ (hereinafter referred to as the "Owner") for the construction of project no. ___________ (hereinafter referred to as the "Project"); and,

WHEREAS, Disadvantaged Contractor does not have the financial capacity to obtain the necessary payment and performance bonds and does not have sufficient financial capability and does not have the staff or supervisory experience nor the funds to handle the financial and supervisory commitments arising from this bid, and Contractor on certain terms is willing to provide the bonds, finances, staff, and supervisory assistance; and

WHEREAS, the parties hereto desire to enter into this Pre-Bid Agreement so as to define, if the joint venture is the low bidder and a contract is awarded to the joint venture, their interest and the services to be rendered by each and the work to be done under the contract and how the profits derived therefrom and how any liability for losses arising out of the performance thereof shall be divided.

NOW, THEREFORE, the parties hereto hereby constitute themselves as Joint Venturers for the purpose of submitting a bid to the Owner on the Project, and if the joint venture is the successful bidder and if a contract is awarded by the Owner to the joint venture, then the parties agree that the standard form joint venture agreement, a copy of which is attached, and the Management Agreement shall be utilized and executed by both parties in connection with performing the contract for the Owner and to set out the respective rights, obligations, and duties of both parties to the joint venture.

IN WITNESS WHEREOF, the parties have executed this Pre-Bid Agreement on the day and year above written.

CONTRACTOR

Attest: By ______________________________

President

First Party

____

Secretary

DISADVANTAGED CONTRACTOR

Attest: By ______________________________

President

Second Party

____

Secretary

§ 5.10 Sample Joint Venture Agreement with Disadvantaged Contractor

SAMPLE JOINT VENTURE AGREEMENT WITH DISADVANTAGED CONTRACTOR

TABLE OF CONTENTS

15. Accounting and Audits.
16. Final Distribution.
17. Other Compensation.
18. Plant and Equipment.
19. Sale of Equipment.
20. Insolvency.
21. Relationship of Venturers.
22. Assignment.
23. Claims.
24. Settlement of Claims.
25. Choice of Law.
26. Duration of Agreement.
27. Notices.
28. Binding Agreement.
29. Counterparts.

This Joint Venture Agreement made and entered into this __________ day of __________, 199____, by and between ________________, a ______________ corporation, with its principal office and place of business in __________, __________ (hereinafter called "Disadvantaged Contractor") and __________, a ____________ corporation, with its principal office and place of business in ________________, __________ (hereinafter called "Contractor"), both of whom collectively are sometimes referred to as the "Joint Venturers,"

WITNESSETH:

WHEREAS, the Joint Venturers submitted a bid to and a contract (hereinafter referred to as "Contract" as more fully defined in paragraph one hereof) has been awarded by ________________ (hereinafter referred to as the "Owner"), for the construction of Project No. __________ (hereinafter referred to as the "Project"); and

WHEREAS, Disadvantaged Contractor does not have the financial capability to obtain the necessary payment and performance bonds and does not have sufficient financial and managerial experience and funds to handle the financial and managerial commitments arising from this bid and Contract, and Contractor on certain terms is willing to provide the bonds, finances, and managerial assistance; and,

WHEREAS, the parties hereto desire that their interest and the service to be rendered by each and the work to be done under the Contract and any profits derived therefrom and any liability for losses arising out of the performance thereof be defined by an agreement in writing:

NOW, THEREFORE, said parties hereto hereby constitute themselves as Joint Venturers for the purpose of performing and completing the said Contract, but not for any other purposes, it being expressly understood that this agreement contemplates only the furnishing and performance of the work, labor, service, materials, plant, equipment, and supplies necessary for the completion of the said Contract and that the parties are not making any permanent partnership agreement or joint venture agreement to bid for or undertake any contracts other than the said Contract, and nothing in this agreement shall be construed as a limitation of the powers or rights of any party hereto to carry on its separate business for its sole benefit except, however, the parties hereto shall cooperate with each other according to the terms and spirit hereof in the performance of the said Contract.

To carry out the Joint Venture the parties hereto mutually agree as follows:

1. Contract. The work to be performed by the Joint Venture shall consist of the Contract and any change orders or supplemental agreements entered into with the Owner in connection with the aforedescribed project, all of which are hereinafter referred to as the "Contract" and shall be performed by the Joint Venture operating under the name of Disadvantaged Contractor Joint Venture.

2. Share of Profits and Losses. Each of the parties shall have an undivided interest in the Joint Venture, and shall participate in its net gains and profits and share in its losses and liabilities in the proportion set opposite its name in the next succeeding sentence. In addition, the interests of the parties hereto in and to the Contract, and in and to any and all moneys which may be derived from the performance thereof, and the obligations and liabilities of each of the parties hereto as between themselves in connection with the Contract, and with respect to any and all liabilities, costs, and expenses in connection therewith, shall be in the following proportions, viz.:

Name	Percentage of Profit	Percentage of Loss
Disadvantaged contractor	51%	0%
Contractor	49%	100%

3. Administrative Committee. In order to facilitate the handling of all matters and questions in connection with the performance of the Contract by the parties hereto, an Administrative Committee shall be formed and each of the parties shall appoint the following representatives (herein called the "designees" and "alternates") to act for it in all such matters with full and complete authority in its behalf in relation to any matters or things in connection with, arising out of, or relative to, this Joint Venture and to act for and bind the respective parties appointing such designees to any and all matters of things involving the performance of the Contract: Disadvantaged Contractor appoints ______________ as its designee and ____________ as its alternate. Contractor appoints ____________ as its designee and ____________ as its alternate. The aforesaid members of the Administrative Committee and their alternates have been designated by the Joint Venturers to act for them with full authority in any matter or thing in connection with or relating to the Contract, including, but not limited to, the negotiation of contracts, the determination of working funds, materials, plant, and equipment to be supplied, the manner of performance, assignment of work between the Joint Venturers, settlement of disputes with the Owner and with others, changes and modifications in the extent or scope of the work, organization, and personnel. Actions and decisions of the Administrative Committee shall be by unanimous vote and shall as to any and all matters having to do with the Joint Venture, the Project, the Contract, or the performance thereof under this agreement or otherwise, or as to the interpretation of the agreement, or as to any claim or dispute thereunder, be final,

conclusive, and binding on the Joint Venturers with the same force and effect as if each Venturer had specifically or affirmatively taken such action or decision. The Administrative Committee shall be given such specific powers in addition to the foregoing as the Joint Venturers may from time to time unanimously delegate and they shall also have the power to delegate to such person or persons as they may unanimously determine such of their powers as they deem necessary or convenient in the best interests of the parties hereto. If necessary or desirable, each of the parties hereto shall execute and deliver to their respective designees such powers of attorney as may be required to enable them to perform the duties entrusted to them properly. It is understood and agreed that none of the parties hereto nor any of the designees or alternates shall have the power to borrow moneys for, in the name of, or to pledge the credit of the other party to this agreement or on their joint credit.

4. Successor Member/Alternate. In the event that either member of the Administrative Committee shall be temporarily incapacitated or temporarily not available to act or if either member of the Administrative Committee shall die or become permanently incapacitated or unavailable to act, and if the Joint Venture does not want the alternate to fulfill the position of designee, then a successor for such member shall be named by the Joint Venturer who appointed such member. In the event of the temporary incapacity or nonavailability or death or permanent incapacity or nonavailability of any alternate, the Joint Venturer which appointed such alternate shall appoint a successor alternate either temporarily or permanently as may be necessary. Any successor member or alternate appointed as hereinabove provided shall have every power to act hereunder that was possessed by his predecessor under this agreement. Either party at any time and from time to time may change its designee or alternate by advising the other of such appointment, but until the appointment and notification of the appointment to the other party as aforesaid, each party shall be bound conclusively by the acts and decisions of the designee or alternate previously appointed by it hereunder in the same manner and with the same effect as if such action had been taken or decision made by authority of its proper officers thereunto duly authorized by its board of directors.

5. Administrative Committee Meetings. Meetings of the members of the Administrative Committee for the transaction of the business of the Joint Venture may be called at such time and such place, subject to reasonable notice, by either Joint Venturer or by any member of the Administrative Committee as may be considered necessary or desirable.

6. Project Manager. The Administrative Committee shall appoint a Project Manager whose duties and responsibilities shall include:

(a) the general direction and supervision of the Contract to be performed directly by the Joint Venturer;

(b) the employment and discharge of all supervisory, skilled, and unskilled employees, and representation of the Joint Venture in matters relating to labor;

(c) the supervision and coordination of the work in accordance with the terms and conditions of the Contract;

(d) the submission, certification, and appropriate documentation of all vouchers and payment requests to the Owner for payments due the Joint Venture;

(e) the establishment and operation of the administrative functions of the Joint Venture such as payroll;

(f) the power in the name of the parties to negotiate, execute, and deliver purchase orders, rental agreements, subcontracts, and other agreements, and to take such steps and otherwise obligate the parties as Contractor may deem necessary in connection with the carrying out of the Contract.

If the Administrative Committee is unable to agree on the Project Manager or if the employee designated to act as Project Manager shall fail, refuse, or be unable for a period of 30 days to fully and completely perform the duties and obligations of the Project Manager, then Contractor, until all the obligations of the Joint Venture are completed and satisfied or until any loans or other financial commitments of Contractor are concluded and satisfied in full, or until the obligations of the Joint Venture and Contractor on the Bonds and related Indemnity Agreements posted in connection with the Contract are released, whichever is later, has the right to designate the Project Manager and any successor to said Project Manager.

7. Books and Bank Accounts. A Joint Venture office shall be established at the office of Contractor, until its financial commitments are concluded, where all accounting payroll, general office procedures, and all other Joint Venture books and records will be located and handled. The working capital and general funds of the Joint Venture shall be deposited in one or more general checking accounts of the Joint Venture. Withdrawals from such general accounts shall be made upon the joint signatures of the Designees or by any two persons from time to time mutually agreed upon by the respective Designees. In addition there will be established by mutual agreement of the parties one or more payroll and tax or other accounts in the bank as designated or in such other bank or banks and subject to withdrawal upon the sole joint signatures of the Designees or by any two persons from time to time mutually agreed upon by the respective Designees.

8. Disputes Between the Parties. Notwithstanding anything in this agreement to the contrary, it is specifically understood and agreed that in the event of a disagreement between Disadvantaged Contractor and Contractor, that disagreement or dispute shall be resolved by the Project Manager, whose decision shall be binding upon the parties.

9. Contribution of the Parties. The Joint Venturers shall furnish such parts of their respective organizations and personnel for the performance of the Contract as may be requested by the Administrative Committee, and each Joint Venturer further expressly agrees that it shall contribute and make available for the Joint Venture as far as is reasonably practicable for the performance of the Contract the utmost skill, experience, and knowledge of their respective organizations.

10. Moneys Received. All moneys received from the Owner and from others in connection with the performance of the Contract shall be deposited in the Joint Venturers' bank account.

11. Reimbursement of Contractor. On completion of the Project, any working capital advanced by Contractor shall be repaid to Contractor prior to the distribution of any profits as hereinafter provided.

12. Business Done in Name of Venture. The business of the Joint Venture shall be conducted and its property and effects held solely and exclusively in the joint names of both parties or in the coined name of the Joint Venture.

13. Contract Costs. Cost of the Contract shall consist of the costs of all subcontracts, labor, material, services, supplies, plant and equipment purchased or rented, bonds, insurance, taxes on labor and material, property taxes on equipment, permits, customs, imports, duties, charges, legal fees, accounting fees, liabilities and losses not covered or compensated by insurance or otherwise, and all other expenses and obligations incurred or suffered in and about the performance of said Project of a nature under sound accounting practices properly chargeable as a cost of the performance of the Project. Said costs shall not include any charges against the Joint Venture for any overhead expenses or charges of the main or branch offices of the parties hereto or for the time which may be expended in connection with the work by any of the parties hereto or their officers or employees, unless assigned to this Project, and except as may be approved by the designees. Travel expenses and subsistence during travel reasonably incurred in the performance or interest of the work under the Contract shall be treated as a part of the cost of the Project and shall be paid with Joint Venture funds.

14. Insurance. The Joint Venture shall carry adequate public liability, property damage, and workers' compensation insurance, as well as any other insurance that may be required or advisable from time to time, so as to protect the parties hereto adequately and hold them harmless from any accident or claim which may arise in the course of the performance of the Contract, the cost of which insurance attributable to the Joint Venture shall be chargeable thereto. Fidelity bond coverage in amounts and form satisfactory to the designees shall be maintained on such persons directly connected with performance of the Contract as the designees may require and all such fidelity bond premiums shall be part of the Contract. All such insurance and bonds that may from time to time be carried shall be obtained through the insurance agency for Contractor and the designees on the Administrative Committee can determine how the brokerage commissions will be divided, if at all, between the insurance agency for the Disadvantaged Contractor and the insurance agency for the Contractor if those are not the same agency.

15. Accounting and Audits. The Administrative Committee shall prescribe the methods of accounting in all matters relating to the affairs of the Joint Venture and the performance of the Contract. The books of account of the Joint Venture may be audited from time to time by an independent auditor selected by the Administrative Committee, the cost of any such audit to be paid from the funds of the Joint Venture. Periodic audits upon the request of either party hereto, shall include comparison between the items of cost and the items set up in the estimate of the cost. Upon completion of the Contract, a complete and final audit and true and correct accounting shall be had of all expenses and all accounts, vouchers, records, and data relating to the Contract and Joint Venture. The cost of all such audits shall be a part of the Contract of the Project and to the extent that records must be kept subsequent to the completion of the Contract, pursuant to the provisions of law, the same shall be kept at such place or places as the designees may from time to time determine and the cost hereof shall be borne equally by the parties.

16. Final Distribution. Upon completion and satisfaction of all obligations of the Joint Venture, the completion of all work in connection with the Project, upon satisfaction in full of all loans and other financial commitments of Contractor in connection with the Project and Contract, upon release of all obligations of the Joint

Venture and Contractor on the bonds and related indemnity agreements posted in connection with the Contract, after payment of and provision for all costs and liability incurred in the performance of the Contract, including liability admitted or reasonably anticipated on or in relation to claims not secured by insurance, and after provision for such reserves in respect of guarantees and contingencies as the Project Manager shall deem necessary, and after repayment to any party of the amount(s) it advanced to the Joint Venture as working capital or otherwise, any funds of the Joint Venture then and thereafter remaining, inclusive of reserves and unexpected balances thereof when determined by the Project Manager to be no longer required, shall be distributed to and divided among the parties in the proportions set forth in Paragraph 2 hereof.

17. Other Compensation. Except as otherwise expressly agreed between the Joint Venturers, no Joint Venturer shall be entitled to any compensation other than by participation in the profits and earnings of the Joint Venture as hereinbefore provided for services rendered by it on behalf of the Joint Venture, nor for any part of its or their overhead expense, including salaries of their executives, officers, or employees, except the salaries, if any, allowed by the Owner as reimbursable under the Contract and the salaries of all personnel of the Joint Venturers assigned to, and performing services for, the Joint Venture, which shall be paid out of the funds of the Joint Venture. Nonreimbursable costs incurred for the benefit of the work or the undertaking shall, subject to the approval of the Administrative Committee, be paid out of the Joint Venture funds and be deemed costs of the Contract and Project.

18. Plant and Equipment. It is contemplated that in the performance of the work under the Contract, plant and equipment owned by the parties hereto may be used. Each party agrees to rent to the Joint Venture on terms, if any, established in the Contract or on terms approved by the Administrative Committee such of its plant and equipment as is available and suitable for the performance of said work and as requested by the Administrative Committee. The proceeds of such plant and equipment rentals shall belong to and be credited and paid to the Joint Venturer furnishing such plant and equipment, and the other Joint Venturer shall have no interest in such plant and equipment rentals and no responsibility in connection therewith.

19. Sale of Equipment. Upon completion of the Project, the parties, through their respective representatives designated herein, will secure a bona fide bid for each item or group of items of equipment or tools purchased by the Joint Venture from one or more reputable equipment dealers, and each of the parties shall have the right to purchase any item or group of items at the highest prices bid therefor by such dealers. If more than one party shall desire the same item or items of equipment or tools, at a price(s) so determined, and a mutually satisfactory adjustment is not effected by agreement between or among them, then such item or items or equipment or tools, in like manner as items therefor not desired by the parties, shall be disposed of by sale, for the best price obtainable, to outsiders.

20. Insolvency. In the event of the bankruptcy or insolvency of one of the parties hereto, or should one of the parties hereto commit any act of bankruptcy or take advantage of any bankruptcy, reorganization, composition, or arrangement statute, then notwithstanding anything in this agreement to the contract, such

party (hereinafter referred to as the insolvent party) from and after said date, and its designee and alternate, shall cease to have any say or voice in the management of the Project and the Contract, and whenever it is provided in this agreement that the act, consent, or decision of the parties hereto is required, it shall be deemed to mean the act, consent, or decision of the other party hereto, excluding the insolvent party. However, the insolvent party shall remain liable for its share of any of the losses as provided in this agreement, to be paid at the time and in the manner as in this agreement provided. Should such insolvency, bankruptcy, or other proceeding of the type above described caused damage or extra cost to the other party, such damage or extra cost shall be charged against the interest of the insolvent party.

21. Relationship of Venturers. The relationship between the Joint Venturers shall be limited to the performance of the Contract under the terms of this agreement, which shall be construed and be deemed to be a Joint Venture for the performance only of the Contract between the joint venturers and the Owner. Nothing herein contained shall be construed to designate either Joint Venturer as the general agent of the other Joint Venturer, or in any manner to limit either of the Joint Venturers in the conduct of their respective businesses or activities in the making of other contracts or the performance of other work, or impose any liability except that of performance of the terms, provisions, and conditions of this agreement.

22. Assignment. Neither this agreement nor any interest of the parties or either of them herein, including interest in any moneys belonging to or which may accrue to the Joint Venture in connection with the Contract or any interest in the joint accounts or in any property of any kind employed or used in connection with the Contract, may be assigned, pledged, transferred, or hypothecated, except that in the event one of the parties desires to obtain banking accommodations for the purpose of this agreement and the Contract, such party may, but only with the prior written consent of the other party first obtained, assign, pledge, or hypothecate its rights, title, and interest in and to such moneys as it may be entitled to receive hereunder to the lending institution as security for said banking accommodations.

23. Claims. The right of any person, firm, or corporation claiming by, through, or under any party hereto (including but not limiting the same to judgment administrators) to assert any claim against the right, title, and interest of any party hereto shall be limited solely to the right to claim or receive, after completion of the Project and the Contract, after the closing of the accounts of the Joint Venturers, and after the satisfaction and release of all obligations, bonds, and related indemnity agreements in accordance with Paragraph 16 hereof, the distributive share of such party in the net proceeds payable hereunder, whether consisting of the return of any contribution made to working funds hereunder, earnings, or other avails, and then only subject to the equities and prior rights of the other party as in this agreement set forth.

24. Settlement of Claims. No claims arising out of, or related to, the operation or conduct of the Joint Venture asserted against one or both of the Joint Venturers by a claimant other than a Joint Venturer shall be settled except with the unanimous consent of the members of the Administrative Committee, if then in existence, or of both of the Joint Venturers, provided that the consent of any insolvent Joint Venturer or of any Joint Venturer who shall deny liability to the other Joint

Venturer with respect to such claim shall not be required. Notwithstanding anything herein to the contrary, if the Joint Venturers or the members of the Administrative Committee cannot agree on the settlement or resolution of any claims, then such determination of the same will be made by the Project Manager.

25. Choice of Law. All questions relative to the execution, validity, interpretation, and performance of this agreement shall be governed by the laws of the State of ____________.

26. Duration of Agreement. This agreement shall remain in effect only for such length of time as may be necessary to carry out the undertaking and the terms, provisions, and conditions of this agreement.

27. Notices. All notices required to be given or which may be given under any of the provisions of this agreement by either party hereto to the other shall be given by sending such written notice to the Joint Venturer entitled thereto by mail addressed to the office of such Joint Venturer as first hereinabove set forth.

28. Binding Agreement. The foregoing provisions and stipulations of this agreement shall bind the Joint Venturers and their respective successors and assigns.

29. Counterparts. This agreement may be executed in any number of counterparts, each of which shall be deemed an original and together shall constitute a single instrument.

IN WITNESS WHEREOF, the parties have executed this Agreement on the day and year above noted.

CONTRACTOR

ATTEST: By: ______________________________

______________________________ Its ______________________________

DISADVANTAGED CONTRACTOR

ATTEST: By: ______________________________

______________________________ Its ______________________________

CHAPTER 6

CONSTRUCTION JOINT VENTURING INTERNATIONALLY

Robert H. Garb

Robert H. Garb is a senior counsel-special projects at Bechtel Corporation, an international engineering and construction firm. His practice has been principally in the international side of Bechtel's business. Mr. Garb received his undergraduate and law degrees from the University of Michigan. He has assisted in the establishment of Bechtel's operations in Brazil, Chile, China, Egypt, and Nigeria, and has held several overseas field assignments in Australia and Papua New Guinea. He authored a number of articles on various aspects of international joint ventures.

§ 6.1 Opportunities for International Joint Ventures

Joint ventures are often needed in the international construction industry because they allow diverse companies to bring together their special resources and to share and allocate risks among themselves. There are few firms in the world that could tackle a project worth $1 billion, but in South Korea, Taiwan, the United Arab Emirates, Hong Kong, Saudi Arabia, and the United Kingdom there are a number of individual projects valued at over $5 billion. This increasingly large scale of current international construction projects makes joint cooperation among construction contractors necessary. Construction firms considering whether to take on a large-scale project alone must evaluate the possible consequences if the project were suddenly suspended or terminated for reasons beyond their control or how the concentration of resources on one project would affect the company's ability to compete in other fields later.

Joint ventures are often needed in the international construction industry in order to satisfy a particular country's legal or political requirements for local participation. Many opportunities that would otherwise be closed to foreign contractors are open to a joint venture that includes a local partner. In addition, customs duties exemptions, tax concessions, and other incentives may be available to international construction joint ventures that involve a local partner. Because resident coventurers know the prospective client, the local business regulations, and the logistical considerations, joint ventures involving this type of coventurer will have a smoother entry into the proposed market.

In order to maximize the chances of success, coventurers should work out their business relationship in advance. The sample forms in **§§ 6.10** through **6.17** appear in a chronological order that allows the parties first to build a working relationship, then to finalize the exact legal vehicle for their arrangement. By reviewing the pre-bid agreements in **§§ 6.10** through **6.14**, the parties can consider how to provide for successful administration of their work and equitable allocation of risk and reward.

Combining technical skills and taking advantage of local experience were the major reasons that Groundwater Technology Inc. of Norwood, Massachusetts (Groundwater), teamed up with Kurita Water Industries Ltd. of Tokyo, Japan (Kurita), in a joint venture to assess opportunities in Japan's environmental cleanup market. Groundwater's skills as an environmental and cleanup contractor complemented Kurita's skills as a manufacturing firm specializing in wastewater treatment systems.[1] By working together, they anticipated tackling a

---

[1] *Firms Join to Ply Japanese Cleanup Market,* ENR, Jan. 13, 1992, at 13.

broader market with a combined business strength exceeding that of either coventurer.

Often, the initial need to form an international construction joint venture is perceived, and the opportunities follow. The sample protocol agreement appearing in § **6.10** facilitates this type of relationship. The agreement envisions the need for teaming a fictitious U.S. construction firm with a fictitious Chilean engineering firm to pursue projects in Chile in the field of mining and metallurgy. After identifying a specific opportunity and agreeing to pursue it, the parties then negotiate another more detailed agreement to collaborate jointly for qualifying, bidding, and, if successful, undertaking the specific project. A generic format of this type of agreement is set forth in the memorandum of understanding in §§ **6.11** and **6.12**.

§ 6.2 Advantages and Disadvantages

An international construction joint venture can provide the opportunity for one firm to obtain technology that it might not otherwise possess. This was the advantage gained by the South Korean construction firm, Dong Ah Company (Dong Ah), in joint venturing with the U.S. pipe machinery supplier, Price Brothers Company (Price), to construct the various pipelines associated with Libya's Great Man Made River (GMMR) project. The GMMR project involved constructing pipelines to carry water from wells dug deep in the Sahara Desert to Libya's Mediterranean cities, as well as to its fertile coastal plain. To carry this water required the expeditious assembly of approximately 250,000 prestressed concrete pipes measuring 13 feet in diameter and weighing about 70 tons each.[2] Price owned the pipe-making technology and manufactured the specialized equipment to make such pipes, skills that Dong Ah obviously needed to undertake the GMMR project.

One can argue that the advantages of securing the Price technology could have been as easily obtained if Price were a nominated subcontractor to Dong Ah or were to furnish a license of their pipe-making technology to Dong Ah in exchange for Dong Ah's purchase order to obtain the Price pipe-making machines. Perhaps these alternative contracting methods were considered by the parties and rejected for the following reasons:

1. Price may have wanted a direct relationship (as opposed to a prime/subcontractor relationship) with the Libyan governmental client to ensure a substantial share of the anticipated profit, prompt payment, and timely processing of visa requests for Price expatriate personnel travelling to Libya.
2. Price may have wanted to gain some meaningful exposure to working conditions in the Middle East and believed a direct relationship with the client through a joint venture arrangement would facilitate this objective.

---

[2] *Libya Readies Water Project,* ENR, Sept. 16, 1991, at 28.

3. Dong Ah may not have had time to train its employees to use the Price technology and machines needed to make the prestressed concrete pipes. The pipe manufacturing plants that were quickly built by Price at Brega and Sarir, Libya, were complex and incorporated production supply lines 1.5 miles long.[3]

Legal and political reasons are another market-driven advantage for firms to joint venture in order to undertake an international construction project. It rarely happens today that a foreign client will select another country's construction firm when the obvious political implications at home dictate otherwise. For example, when the Serbian government issued its invitation to tender in 1991 to upgrade 110 miles of an existing road from Belgrade to the Hungarian border, there was a special requirement for the successful firm to joint venture with GENEX, a Yugoslav state trading company.[4]

In many countries in the Middle East, such as Kuwait, the United Arab Emirates, Qatar, and Oman, there is a legal requirement to select a local national as an agent for the construction project. It is possible that the well-connected and well-respected candidates for local agent may not be satisfied with a passive role. Instead, they will insist on being active partners in the execution of the project. On the theory that half a loaf is better than none, sharing part of the construction project with a local agent/coventurer makes good business sense. Consequently, entering into joint venture relationships with these agents may be necessary.

Another advantage obtained by forming a construction joint venture internationally is to attract desirable financing to bid on a particular job. For example, the South Korean Ministry of Energy and Resources currently allows local firms to form joint ventures with international developers to build 12 or 13 power plants fired by coal or liquified natural gas. Several South Korean industrial companies have advised the Ministry that they are interested and will allow their subsidiaries involved in construction and engineering to be joint venture partners with such international developers. The ultimate goal of the program is to encourage the international developers as coventurers to supply 10 percent of the new generating capacity anticipated in South Korea's long-term power supply plan. In order to attain this objective, the utility involved, state-owned Korea Electric Power Company, is expected to purchase power at a price high enough to provide the international developers with a guaranteed return on investment of about 10 percent.[5]

Although these cases illustrate the advantages of a joint venture relationship, one needs to weigh the disadvantages as well. One disadvantage of an international construction joint venture is that the diversity of cultural backgrounds of

---

[3] *Id.*

[4] *War Halts Contract,* ENR, Sept. 9, 1991, at 31.

[5] *Korean Market Opens to Private Developers,* ENR, Mar. 2, 1992, at 23.

the coventurers frequently results in a tenuous working relationship. In order to overcome this cultural disparity, it is prudent to define carefully at an early stage the parties' precise intended relationships, including their rights and responsibilities.

One good technique for documenting each coventurer's responsibilities in an international joint venture is to design a table and attach it to the joint venture agreement. In one column, spell out all the major elements of the project. In the other column, use an X to identify which coventurer has the responsibility to complete the particular element. In addition, when both parties are to have responsibility in the completion of a particular task, use an asterisk to identify which party has the primary responsibility. Appendix A in **§ 6.16** provides an example of how to use this technique. In this way, the parties avoid misunderstandings as to exactly what was intended as each coventurer's responsibilities.

Another disadvantage of an international construction joint venture relationship is that, with respect to the client, each coventurer is liable for the acts or omissions of the other coventurers as they relate to the activities of the joint venture. To minimize this exposure, many coventurers (especially those with the deeper pockets, to whom the client would most likely look in the event of a deficiency) either designate a subsidiary corporation of lesser net worth as a party to the venture or incorporate the proposed joint venture.

For a construction joint venturer to gain protection from joint responsibility for the other coventurer's work, the client must make a declaration that only the particular joint venturer for a given portion of the work will be held responsible. When the client is unwilling to look only to the responsible coventurer for relief, the coventurer can still allocate specific task obligations and incorporate within the joint venture agreement an indemnity from the assigned coventurer for its sphere of work. The sample agreements in §§ **6.15** and **6.16** provide appropriate cross-indemnity clauses. However, this type of indemnity is meaningful only if the firms involved have substantial net worth and are thus able to fulfill their indemnity obligations.

A significant disadvantage to the international construction joint venture relationship is that in most countries there is no definitive body of law supporting and interpreting the joint venture relationship. Accordingly, unlike the task of creating a limited liability company, drafting joint venture agreements are often given no statutory guidance. Coupled with this legal problem is a practical problem: a joint venture is such a flexible arrangement that the coventurers often fail to specify in writing all the key commercial considerations of their agreement. Well-intentioned conceptualizers sometimes defer difficult decisions in a "we can work this out later" attitude. In order to address essential legal and commercial elements at a very early stage in the parties' relationship, the sample agreements in §§ **6.11** and **6.12** require the parties to address at the outset certain key principles to govern the establishment of the joint venture.

Other difficulties in forming an international construction joint venture include issues regarding protection of confidential information, increased management time and effort, and loss of control. Solving complicated construction problems is always more difficult in a joint venture scenario than in a sole undertaking. If the joint venture proves unworkable, it could result in foreign litigation, a default in performance under the contract, and a disgruntled client.

§ 6.3 Structuring International Joint Ventures

When a construction firm teams up with another firm to seek business opportunities overseas, the parties generally have the following options to consider in structuring their proposed relationship:

1. Partnership
2. Joint stock company
3. Joint venture
4. Prime/Subcontractor relationship.

The options of forming a partnership or a joint stock company have appeal because they create a defined legal relationship recognized in many countries. On a particularly risky project, a joint stock company may be especially appealing because it is a good way to limit liability to the assets of the joint company. The disadvantage of both of these options is that complying with the legal formalities necessary to establishing and maintaining these arrangements can prove quite costly and time-consuming. If the parties intend to undertake only a single project together of short duration, the expense of forming these legal entities may not be warranted. If the parties' cooperation is to be formalized for a longer period of time and for an indefinite number of contracts, organizing as a partnership or a joint stock company takes on greater appeal.

It needs to be recognized that operating as a joint stock company or a partnership may be unduly burdensome. One of the disadvantages of a joint stock company is the need for periodic board of directors and shareholders meetings. One of the undesirable characteristics of a partnership is that any of the partners can bind the other partners. Although a joint venture arrangement is generally treated internationally like a temporary partnership or an unincorporated association, the parties can be flexible in eliminating unwanted partnership attributes. In the sample agreements in **§§ 6.15** and **6.16**, the parties specifically agree that they are not creating a partnership or any other legal entity by entering into the joint venture agreement. Furthermore, neither party can serve as an agent or representative of the other parties except as designated in the joint venture agreement.

A construction firm undertaking an international project must determine whether to establish a joint venture or a subcontract relationship with a prospective team member. Hiring on as a subcontractor could be a good way to obtain experience in a particular overseas construction market and win a profitable slice of business while keeping risks to a minimum. As noted in the discussion of the Dong Ah/Price relationship on the Great Man Made River project in Libya (see § 6.2), there are also disadvantages to being a subcontractor internationally. Because the client looks to the prime contractor for performance, the subcontractor's direct exposure to business conditions in the overseas country may be minimal. Subcontractors enjoy a relatively safe, but quite limited, learning experience. Also, because prime contractors typically invest heavily in the bidding process to win the project—particularly when there has been fixed-price bidding—they will expect most of the anticipated profit.

Prime contractors dealing with a team of subcontractors enjoy the advantages of retaining total control of the international project and being in a position to reap most of the rewards. The major disadvantage is that these prime contractors also carry the total risk. No matter how careful the prime contractor might be in selecting the subcontractors and in transferring legal liabilities to them, the risk remains with the prime contractor vis-à-vis the client. The project size and associated risks may convince the contractor instead to form a multinational joint venture.

§ 6.4 Methods of Joint Venturing Internationally

The characteristics of international joint ventures among construction contractors generally include:

1. No separate entity distinct from the coventurers
2. Business activities that are limited to the performance of one or more specific projects
3. The right of each party to govern policy
4. Joint and several liability
5. Sharing of profits and losses
6. Taxability as a partnership.

The joint venture then takes either the format of either an integrated or nonintegrated relationship.

§ 6.5 —Integrated Relationship

This arrangement allows the construction coventurers to agree to perform their work as if it were performed by a single entity. All of the coventurers' personnel work together under the supervision of one or more of the coventurers to accomplish the project. The coventurers share profits and losses in accordance with an agreed ratio. For example, the integrated joint venture relationship proposed in

§ **6.11** indicates that Red Rock Construction Company of California, Inc. (Red Rock), and its coventurer White Crane Construction Company of Suritania, Ltd. (White Crane), shall each be liable only for a 50 percent proportionate interest for the joint ventures performance of its obligations. Such obligation matches the intent expressed that each coventurer must supply the necessary qualified manpower to the integrated joint venture to perform approximately 50 percent of the awarded work.

§ 6.6 —Non-Integrated Relationship

This arrangement permits construction coventurers, for the most part, to undertake their respective portions of the project separately. This arrangement is often entered into by coventurers with specialized areas of expertise, and each coventurer is responsible for only its portion of the work. For example, in the nonintegrated joint venture relationship proposed in § **6.12**, Red Rock has specialized expertise in desalination projects and its coventurer, White Crane, has specialized expertise in power projects. In order to capitalize on each other's respective strengths, note that the role of Red Rock on the proposed Egyptian desalination and power projects is to design, supply, install, and erect the equipment and machinery associated with the desalination plant and seawater intake portions of the project. The role of White Crane is to design, supply, install, and erect the equipment and machinery associated with the power plant portion of the project. Each party agrees to indemnify and hold harmless the other coventurer from claims arising in connection with the indemnifying party's scope of work.

The primary objective of forming a construction joint venture internationally is to obtain the edge to get to the negotiating table. Once at the negotiating table, one may find that the client's real needs require some modification of the planned joint venture agreement. For example, instead of designating the Japanese partner as the leader and sponsor of the joint venture, the client may indicate in the course of the negotiation that it really prefers that the American partner be the leader and sponsor. As another example, a joint venture's proposal may call for an integrated joint venture arrangement. After negotiating with the client, however, it may appear more advantageous to winning the job to do some of the work through an integrated joint venture and the balance through a non-integrated arrangement. One would then want to tailor the agreements in §§ **6.15** and **6.16** to create a hybrid joint venture.

Accordingly, joint venture arrangements should have some flexibility to allow the joint venture to modify its plan and revise certain provisions. One way of achieving this flexibility is to sign an agreement covering the bid stage of the negotiations (see §§ **6.11** and **6.12**) that will be superseded by the formal joint venture agreement upon award of the project (see §§ **6.15** and **6.16**).

§ 6.7 Foreign Corrupt Practices Act

After entering into a multinational construction joint venture, one may encounter explicit or implicit legal and cultural burdens imposed by the country of one or more of the coventurers. Because outright bribery is widely practiced in many nations around the world, any multinational joint venture involving a U.S. construction firm must withstand the scrutiny of the Foreign Corrupt Practices Act (FCPA).[6]

Aimed at reducing the incidence of bribery of foreign government officials by U.S. citizens and businesses, the FCPA delineates such criminal offenses. It prohibits certain conduct by U.S. firms in their dealings with foreign officials and politicians. In general, giving anything of value to foreign dignitaries, directly or indirectly, with the intention of influencing the outcome of a business decision is strictly prohibited. The penalties for violation of the FCPA can be a fine of up to $2 million for a corporation and up to $100,000 and five years of imprisonment for each individual involved.

To avoid falling within the ambit of the FCPA, it must be shown that one exercised the required level of due diligence, thus eliminating any notion that there was knowing participation in a corrupt activity. Document first that the local coventurer was carefully selected through reliable contacts attesting to the proposed coventurer's good reputation. Then show that a prudent agreement was negotiated with the proposed local coventurer, wherein the coventurer agreed to conduct its joint venture activities so as not to place the U.S. firm in violation of FCPA obligations.

The agreements in §§ **6.15** and **6.16** serve to obtain the local coventurer's agreement to refrain from the type of bribery of government officials that is the target of the FCPA provisions. The agreements specify that the managing joint venture and sponsor is a U.S. firm and that such firm appoints the project manager. The project manager is responsible for the day-to-day management of the joint venture's operations. In this way the opportunity for the local coventurer to violate the FCPA provisions is minimized.

However, one can easily imagine a scenario in which the local coventurer is the managing joint venture, and sponsor and/or the country involved is one where institutionalized bribery is known to prevail. In either of the above scenarios, it would be prudent to replace the "Officials Not to Benefit" clause in the joint venture agreement with a clause similar to the one in § **6.17**. This clause requires the non-U.S. coventurer(s) specifically to recognize the U.S. coventurer's obligations under the FCPA and to agree to conduct its respective joint venture assignments so as to not to place the U.S. firm in violation of its FCPA obligations. The clause has teeth because it entitles any of the nonbreaching parties to terminate the agreement immediately for default. However, the

---

[6] 15 U.S.C. § 78dd-1, 2 (1977).

best protection against potential FCPA violations is to select the coventurers carefully.

§ 6.8 Resolving Disputes

Resolution of disputes through litigation in foreign courts is generally not acceptable to foreign contractors. Although many international construction joint ventures reflect international arbitration as the alternative means of resolving disputes, the parties are often unhappy with the results and the expense of utilizing this particular forum. There are now promising signs in the international construction community of a willingness to identify new techniques for dispute resolution involving joint venture relationships. These new techniques, known as *alternative dispute resolution* (ADR), include those in which the dispute is decided by a third party and those that concentrate on merely encouraging the parties themselves to settle the dispute.[7]

The sample joint venture agreements in §§ **6.15** and **6.16** focus on encouraging the parties to settle the dispute so that not only is the immediate dispute resolved but the business conditions giving rise to the dispute are also rectified so as to prevent further problems from developing. The agreements require the parties first to enter into good faith negotiations to try to resolve the dispute. If this fails, the dispute is referred to the joint venture's board of control and then to a panel of senior executives with a broad business perspective and extensive experience.

If all three of these in-house methods fail to resolve the dispute, the matter is referred to arbitration. The parties can select the rules governing the arbitration from a number of highly capable arbitration administering agencies, including the London Court of International Arbitration, the International Chamber of Commerce, and UNCITRAL.

One cannot specify a generic locale for arbitration of disputes that may arise in an international construction joint venture arrangement. The identification of the locale depends on whether a particular site is convenient to the parties, the administering agency, and the arbitrators, and the availability of adequate facilities in which to conduct the hearings.[8]

The case for ADR is very strong when one considers its numerous advantages—the parties' retention of control, the potential savings in cost and time, and the avoidance of disruption in the coventurers' relationship. Unlike a judge or an arbitrator, the neutral facilitator does not impose a decision on the parties, but rather assists the parties in resolving the disputes themselves. The inherent

---

[7] For a complete discussion of ADR, see Alternative Dispute Resolution in the Construction Industry (R. Cushman, G. Hedemann & A. Tucker eds., John Wiley & Sons, 1991).

[8] Myers, *International Construction Dispute Resolution and New Alternatives,* Int'l Construction L. Rev., Apr. 1986, at 226.

flexibility of the ADR process allows the parties to control the proceeding directly and decide upon a commercial solution rather than one governed by unanticipated foreign legal principles.

§ 6.9 Explanation of Forms

Table 6–1 provides guidelines on using the various forms that appear in §§ **6.10** through **6.17**.

Table 6–1

Forms for Construction Joint Venturing Internationally

Title	When Used
Protocol Agreement to Collaborate (§ **6.10**)	This agreement, similar to a teaming or pre-bit agreement, is used when two or more construction coventurers wish to explore together jobs in a particular foreign country or countries that are mutually advantageous for joint participation. When a potential candidate for joint collaboration is subsequently identified, the parties then develop the terms of a second preliminary agreement (see §§ **6.11** or **6.12**) outlining the basic form of their planned joint participation for the particular project.
Memorandum of Understanding to Form an Integrated Joint Venture (§ **6.11**)	In general, the format of joint venture agreements in the international construction industry falls within two categories, namely, integrated or non-integrated. The *integrated* joint venture agreement allows the coventurers to agree to perform their construction work as if it were to be performed by a single corporation having several shareholders. The parties share profits and losses in accordance with each party's proportionate interest in the joint venture. The sample document in § **6.11** is a form of pre-bid agreement that serves to evidence the parties' intent to form an integrated joint venture agreement should they be successful in their bid for an international construction prospect.
Memorandum of Understanding to Form a Non-Integrated Joint Venture (§ **6.12**)	The *non-integrated* joint venture agreement allows the coventurers to agree, for the most part, to undertake their respective portions of the construction work separately. Generally, each party is responsible for the performance of only its discrete scope of work. The document evidences the parties' intent to create a non-integrated joint venture agreement should the coventurers be successful in their bid.

Table 6–1 *(continued)*

Title	When Used
Short Form International Integrated Joint Venture Agreement (§ **6.13**)	Frequently, on major international construction projects, the clients' requests for proposal indicate that, by submitting a bid as a joint venture, the parties must include a signed copy of their joint venture agreement as part of their qualification document or proposal. This request could present the following difficulties: (1) at the pre-bid stage, the parties may not have completed all of their negotiations as to the terms to be included in their joint venture agreement; (2) even if the parties have concluded their definitive joint venture agreement, they may regard the document as confidential and not to be shared with the client. To overcome these difficulties, § **6.13** provides an abbreviated version of an integrated joint venture agreement that the parties could use in qualification documents and proposals to evidence their formation of an integrated joint venture.
Short Form International Non-Integrated Joint Venture Agreement (§ **6.14**)	The sample agreement in § **6.14** is a short form joint venture agreement evidencing the formation of a non-integrated joint venture.
International Integrated Joint Venture Agreement (§ **6.15**)	The integrated joint venture agreement is drafted so that the parties' personnel work together to accomplish a single project under the general supervision of a board of control and the day-to-day supervision of a project manager.
International Non-Integrated Joint Venture Agreement (§ **6.16**)	The joint venture agreement in § **6.16** evidences the formation of a non-integrated joint venture. Each party is responsible for the performance of a discrete scope of work.
Foreign Corrupt Practices Act Covenant for International Joint Venture Agreements Involving an American Coventurer (§ **6.17**)	The clause in § **6.17** can be inserted into joint venture agreements when a U.S. firm wishes to make certain that its non-U.S. coventurer(s) recognize the U.S. firm's obligations under the Foreign Corrupt Practices Act of 1977. This clause would be particularly appropriate when a U.S. firm contemplates forming a joint venture with a foreign coventurer whose country practices institutionalized bribery.

§ 6.10 Sample Protocol Agreement to Collaborate

SAMPLE AGREEMENT TO COLLABORATE TO DEVELOP INTERNATIONAL PROSPECTS

Prelude to an International Construction Joint Venture Agreement

TABLE OF CONTENTS

PROTOCOL AGREEMENT

THIS AGREEMENT entered into this _____ day of __________, 199____, by and between AMERICAN HARD HAT CORPORATION (hereinafter called "AHHC") and BUENAVENTURA INGENIEROS S.A. (hereinafter called "BISA").

1. Purpose. This Agreement refers to activities to be developed by the parties in Chile for the engineering, procurement, and construction of projects in the field of mining and metallurgy.
2. Cooperation. Both parties will promote projects in Chile in the interest of both firms and will communicate to each other on business opportunities that come to their knowledge.
3. Job Prospects. Whenever one of the parties obtains or is offered a job assignment in Chile which requires the joint participation of Chilean and foreign engineering and construction expertise, it will disclose such a possible collaboration to the other party. In such case, it will be determined by discussion between the parties if such collaboration could be mutually advantageous. If, after the discussion, one of the parties wants to work with a third firm or desires not to further pursue such assignment, it will so advise the other party in writing, which advice will leave both parties free from any further obligations pursuant to this Agreement as it concerns such job assignment.
4. Future Agreements. When a prospect is deemed mutually advantageous for joint participation, the form of participation, whether by a joint venture arrangement, a joint stock company, or otherwise, the particular organization,

financing, work share, profit share, etc., will be the object of individual agreements to be entered into by the parties to this Agreement.

5. Expenses. Each party will bear its own business development expenses unless a different arrangement is agreed upon for special cases. Likewise, the expenses incurred in negotiating this Agreement shall be borne by the party incurring such expense.
6. Prohibitions. It is expressly understood that neither party to this Agreement shall have the right to represent the other party or to use in any way the name, characterization, or trademark of the other party. Neither party to this Agreement shall utilize or commit any of the money, property, or credit of the other party.
7. Evaluation. The parties will meet together whenever required but in no event less than six (6) months from the date hereof to evaluate the objectives and achievements of the parties' collaboration pursuant to this Agreement.
8. Notice. Any notice required to be given herein shall be deemed to have been sufficiently given to either party for all purposes hereof if mailed by registered airmail, postage prepaid, addressed as follows:

   To AHHC: American Hard Hat Corporation

   ____

   ____

   Attn: ____________________

   ____

   To BISA: Buenaventura Ingenieros S.A.

   ____

   ____

   Attn: ____________________

   ____

   or to such other address as either of the parties shall designate by notice given as herein required. Notice hereunder shall be effective when received.
9. Force Majeure. Neither party shall be in default of the terms of this Agreement if such default is directly or indirectly caused by an act of force majeure.
10. Term of Agreement. This Agreement will remain in force for two (2) years from the date of this Agreement or until one of the parties gives written notice of its desire to discontinue it with at least thirty (30) days' notice. If this notice is given while jobs already taken in collaboration between the parties are still outstanding, each of the parties will continue its performance until such work is properly accomplished. If none of the parties gives notice within the aforesaid two (2) years, this Agreement will automatically be renewed for another two (2) years, and so on.
11. Assignment. This Agreement shall not be assigned by either of the parties without the written consent of the other party.

IN WITNESS WHEREOF, the parties hereto have entered into the Protocol Agreement effective as of the day and year first hereinabove written.

AMERICAN HARD HAT CORPORATION

By: ______________________________

Title: ______________________________

BUENAVENTURA INGENIEROS S.A.

By: ______________________________

Title: ______________________________

§ 6.11 Sample Memorandum of Understanding to Form an Integrated Joint Venture

SAMPLE PRELIMINARY AGREEMENT TO FORM AN INTERNATIONAL *INTEGRATED* JOINT VENTURE AGREEMENT FOR UNDERTAKING SINGLE/MULTIPLE PROJECTS

Loss Sharing by Proportionate Interest

TABLE OF CONTENTS

MEMORANDUM OF UNDERSTANDING

THIS MEMORANDUM OF UNDERSTANDING is entered into this ______ day of ____________, 1992, by and between RED ROCK CONSTRUCTION COMPANY of California, Inc. ("Red Rock"), and WHITE CRANE CONSTRUCTION COMPANY OF SURITANIA, LTD. ("White Crane"), sometimes individually referred to as the "Party" and collectively referred to as the "Parties."

WHEREAS, Red Rock and its affiliated entities have extensive experience performing construction services for power projects in the Arab Republic of Egypt ("Egypt"), including the Shoubrah El Kheima Thermal Power Plant and the Damietta Combined Cycle Plant; and

WHEREAS, White Crane and its affiliated entities also have extensive experience performing construction services for power projects in Egypt, including the Abu Sultan Thermal Power Plant, the Helwan and the Talka Gas Turbine Plants; and

WHEREAS, the Parties wish to draw upon such experience by collaborating together in the preparation and submission of a pre-qualification document ("Qualification Document") and a proposal ("Proposal") for certain defined construction services in connection with the construction projects in implementation of Egypt's Emergency Plan for the addition of generation capacity at those Egyptian Electricity Authority ("EEA") facilities referenced in the *Commerce Business Daily* Notice dated ____________, at three (3) nominated Plant Sites (the "Nominated Plant Sites") and one (1) unidentified site (the "Unidentified Plant Site") hereinafter collectively referred to as the "Projects"; and

WHEREAS, the Parties wish to collaborate and effectively utilize the capabilities and experience of each to the best mutual advantage in the preparation of the Proposal and the promotional activities associated herewith; and

WHEREAS, the Parties further desire, as part of this Memorandum of Understanding ("MOU"), to develop the basis upon which they will establish a joint venture relationship in which to implement the Projects if they are successful in the Proposal efforts;

NOW, THEREFORE, the Parties have agreed as follows:

1.0 *DEFINITIONS*

Whenever the following terms are used in this Memorandum of Understanding, they have the following meanings:

1.1 "Joint Venture" or "Joint Venture Agreement" means the business relationship referred to in Sections 2.2 and 2.4 hereof, based upon the principles described in Sections 3.1 through 3.4, 4.6, and 4.7 hereof.

1.2 "MOU" means this instrument, as originally executed or as it may from time to time be supplemented or amended.

1.3 "Sponsor" means the party identified in this MOU to act as the leader in all activities undertaken by the Parties.

1.4 "Work" means all work, supplies, services, and matters necessary to fulfill the requirements of the Projects.

2.0 *PURPOSE OF THE MEMORANDUM OF UNDERSTANDING*

The purpose of this MOU is to establish the working arrangements, principles, and methods for the Parties to accomplish the following business objectives:

2.1 Jointly prepare the Qualification Document and the Proposal for submission to EEA based on the Scope of Work set forth in Attachment A hereto.

2.2 Participate jointly in the drafting, negotiation, and finalization of a Joint Venture Agreement which will become effective and operative only at such time as an agreed contract is to be executed by the Parties with EEA.

2.3 Jointly develop, negotiate, and conclude a contract or contracts with EEA for the Work.

2.4 Serve as the contractual arrangements between the Parties until such time as the Parties have entered into a Joint Venture Agreement which formally defines their joint cooperation. Such Joint Venture shall be established without judicial personality under the laws of the State of ________.

The participation by the Parties in this MOU shall be for the purposes set forth in this Section 2.0 and, except as expressly provided, nothing in this MOU shall be construed as a limitation upon the power or rights of any Party to carry on its separate business, not in conflict with the Projects, for its sole and exclusive benefit.

3.0 *PRINCIPLES TO GOVERN THE ESTABLISHMENT OF THE JOINT VENTURE*

The Parties agree to reflect the following principles in the development of the Joint Venture Agreement:

3.1 The personnel shall be seconded by each Party to the Joint Venture to work as an integrated team.

3.2 It shall be the intent to allocate the seconded Work associated with the Nominated Plant Sites and the Unidentified Plant Site such that each Party supplies the necessary qualified manpower to the integrated Joint Venture to perform approximately 50% of the awarded work.

3.3 Both Parties' prior written consent will be required in the determining the scope of Work to be subcontracted to third parties who are not affiliated entities of either Party hereto, as well as in approving the particular potential subcontractor(s).

3.4 The day-to-day management of the Work to be performed by the integrated Joint Venture shall be conducted by and under the direction of a Program Director appointed by Red Rock and approved by White Crane. The Deputy Program Director shall be appointed by White Crane and approved by Red Rock. A more detailed description of the duties and responsibilities of the Program Director and Deputy Program Director shall be set forth in the Joint Venture Agreement. Within five (5) business days from the date of this MOU, Red Rock shall designate the Program Director.

3.5 The principles set forth in Sections 3.1 through 3.4 above and those set forth in Sections 4.6 and 4.7 of this MOU shall be equally applicable to the performance of Work on any future combined cycle phases which may evolve from the Joint Venture's Work on the Projects relating to simple cycle plant(s), regardless of the timing when such additional work evolves, provided the Joint Venture Agreement has not been terminated.

4.0 *PREPARATION AND SUBMISSION OF THE QUALIFICATION DOCUMENT AND PROPOSAL*

The Parties shall jointly prepare the Qualification Document and the Proposal and submit such documents as a Joint Venture. The following principles shall apply in the preparation and submission of the Qualification Document and the Proposal:

4.1 The Parties shall jointly establish and determine the format and order of the sections for the Qualification Document and the Proposal.

4.2 Red Rock and White Crane will each be responsible for preparing its own portion of the Qualification Document and the Proposal, including the nomination of key personnel. In order to ensure complete and consistent documents, Red Rock, with the appropriate assistance and concurrence of White Crane, will carry out the final review and consolidation of such documents.

4.3 Each Party shall be solely liable for any and all costs related to the preparation of its input to the Qualification Document and the Proposal and in connection with any discussions and negotiations which may be conducted with EEA representatives.

4.4 The Parties shall equally share those common Qualification Document and Proposal costs which are of benefit to both Parties, including, for example, those associated with the joint acquisition of retained legal advice in Egypt regarding the conduct of the Work in Egypt by the Joint Venture; provided, however, that before any such costs are considered common costs, the Parties shall have first agreed that such costs are necessary and shall have agreed on a budget for such costs.

4.5 It is agreed by the Parties that a Party may, to the extent practicable, prepare its share of the Qualification Document and the Proposal at its premises and shall make members of its staff available to the other Party at the other Party's premises, as required, in order to enable the other Party to prepare its portion of such documents. The assembling of the respective parts of such documents shall take place at the offices of Red Rock in __________________. Each Party shall, to the extent required, make available to the other Party at its premises such offices and facilities as may be reasonably required in connection with the preparation and assembly of the Qualification Document and the Proposal.

4.6 Although the Proposal will indicate that all liabilities to EEA associated with the performance of the Work shall be the joint and several obligation of the Joint Venture, the Parties will reflect in their Joint Venture Agreement that each party shall be liable only for its 50% proportionate interest in the Joint Venture.

4.7 The Program Director shall be responsible for the following:

4.7.1 Coordination of the activities of the Parties in the preparation of the Qualification Document and the Proposal and in dealings with EEA.

4.7.2 Carrying out of all necessary correspondence with EEA and maintaining the appropriate correspondence files. However, in no event shall the Program Director make any commitment to EEA on behalf of the Parties without obtaining both Parties' prior consent.

4.8 The Parties shall use reasonable efforts to provide correct and accurate information concerning their respective portions of the Qualification Document and the Proposal. In this regard, each Party shall coordinate, control, and manage other specifically contributing to that Party's scope of the Qualification Documents and Proposal. However, no warranty is assumed by either Party as to the accuracy or completeness of the information provided, and the sole remedy required of each Party for any inaccurate information furnished is to use reasonable efforts to provide corrected information. Neither party shall be liable to the other if the Qualification Document or the Proposal as submitted and/or the negotiations which may take place do not result in the award to the Joint Venture of a contract or contracts for the Work. In no event shall either Party be liable to the other for any special, indirect, incidental, or consequential loss or damages whatsoever.

5.0 *DEVELOPMENT*

Upon the coming into force of this MOU, the Parties shall develop and agree upon:

5.1 The overall contract structure between the Parties and EEA as reflected and implied in the Proposal. Such structure will be arrived at by a judicious assessment of all factors such as, but not necessarily limited to, EEA's standard terms of contracting, the objectives, capabilities, and available expertise of the Parties, and the responsibilities assumed by the Parties.

5.2 The responsibilities and liabilities in the proposed EEA contract and modifications to reflect the contract with the Joint Venture as finally negotiated with EEA.

5.3 Each Party's respective obligations and liabilities associated with the sharing of common risks.

6.0 *CLIENT CONTRACT NEGOTIATIONS*

Following the submission of the Proposal and upon receipt of an invitation from EEA to negotiate a contract based upon the Proposal, the Parties shall so meet with EEA's representatives and jointly develop the contract based on the results of such negotiations. Each Party shall have the right to attend all meetings and to have access to all correspondence, minutes, and other documentation pertaining to and relevant to the negotiations where such is pertinent or affects its scope of Work.

7.0 *VALIDITY*

This MOU shall come into force upon the signature hereof by each of the Parties hereto and on the date first above mentioned and shall terminate upon the earliest to occur of the following:

7.1 Six (6) months shall have elapsed since the coming into force of this MOU, and the Parties shall not have otherwise agreed to supersede this MOU by a Joint Venture Agreement or agreed upon an extension of this MOU, and provided the validity of the Proposal or any extension thereof has expired.

7.2 By declaration of EEA in writing or other satisfactory evidence that the Qualification Document or the Proposal is not accepted by it.

7.3 If EEA postpones indefinitely, cancels, or disqualifies either Party from participation in the Project.

7.4 It becomes impracticable for either Party to participate in the Qualification Document and/or the Proposal for reasons beyond their respective control. Notwithstanding any termination or expiry of this MOU, the provisions of

Sections 4.3, 4.4, 8.0, and 11.0 shall survive any termination or expiry hereof and continue in full force and effect in accordance with their respective terms.

8.0 *CONFIDENTIALITY*

8.1 Each Party shall treat as confidential all proprietary and confidential information made available to it from the other Party which is clearly marked as being "CONFIDENTIAL" and limit access to such information to its personnel as may reasonably require the same in connection with undertaking the activities contemplated by this MOU. The receiving Party further agrees not to use any of such information otherwise than in connection with the activities contemplated herein. Nothing contained in this Section shall apply to information received by either Party which:

8.1.1 at such times is or becomes generally available to the public through publication or otherwise, except by the receiving Party's wrongful act;

8.1.2 was in the receiving Party's possession prior to disclosure to the receiving Party by the transmitting Party; or

8.1.3 is independently made available to either Party by any other third party who is legally authorized to do so.

8.2 It is agreed that no license under any patents of either Party is granted by any disclosure or proprietary information hereunder.

8.3 The confidentiality obligations as set forth in this Section 8.0 shall continue for five (5) years from the date of this MOU.

9.0 *NOTICES*

Any notice, which may or is required to be given pursuant to this MOU shall be in writing and shall be sufficiently given or made if served personally or sent by facsimile or registered mail to the following addresses:

9.1 Red Rock Construction Company of California, Inc.

____

____

Attn: ______________________________

9.2 White Crane Construction Company of Suritania, Ltd.

____

____

Attn: ______________________________

10.0 *EXCLUSIVITY*

During the continuance in force of this MOU, no Party shall, directly or indirectly, collaborate or make any other agreements or arrangements with other parties relating to its respective scope of Work, except for the sole and express purpose of carrying out the objectives of this MOU.

11.0 *PARTIES' RESPONSIBILITIES*

Neither Party shall enter into any commitments nor incur any liabilities or obligations on behalf of the other Party in connection with the purpose of this MOU without the prior written consent of the other Party.

12.0 *FORCE MAJEURE*

Neither Party shall be considered in default in the performance of its obligations hereunder, to the extent that the performance of any such obligation is prevented or delayed by any cause, existing or future, which is beyond the reasonable control of such Party.

13.0 *SEVERABILITY*

In the event that any of the provisions, or portions or applications thereof, of this MOU are held to be unenforceable or invalid by any court of competent jurisdiction, Red Rock and White Crane shall negotiate an equitable adjustment in the provisions of this MOU with a view toward effecting the purpose of this MOU; and the validity and enforceability of the remaining provisions, or portions or applications thereof, shall not be affected thereby.

14.0 *ASSIGNMENT*

Neither Party shall assign its rights or interest in this MOU, either totally or partially, without the prior written consent of the other Party.

15.0 *GOVERNING LAW AND DISPUTES*

This MOU shall be governed and construed in accordance with the laws of the State of ____________. The Parties agree to submit all disputes between them to the federal or state courts of ____________.

16.0 *PUBLICATION*

16.1 This MOU is a confidential document and shall not be released to any person except with the written consent of both Parties.

16.2 No news release in any way relating to either Party's activity concerning this MOU shall be made by either Party to any news media or the general public without prior approval of the other Party.

17.0 *OFFICIALS NOT TO BENEFIT*

No monies shall be knowingly used directly or indirectly to influence improperly or unlawfully any decision or judgment of any official of any government or of any subdivision, agency, or instrumentality thereof in connection with the subject matter of this MOU. Any proven breach of this obligation shall be a material breach of this MOU and entitle the nonbreaching Party to terminate this MOU immediately and, subject to the provision set forth in the last sentence of Section 4.8 hereof, to recover actual damages incurred from the breaching party.

18.0 *TITLE*

Neither Party to this MOU shall have the right to use in any way any name, characterization, trademark, or logo of the other Party.

19.0 *ENTIRE AGREEMENT*

19.1 This MOU constitutes the entire agreement between Red Rock and White Crane with regard to the subject matter of this MOU and supersedes all previous communications, understandings, and agreements between the Parties.

19.2 This MOU may be varied or amended by agreement between the Parties hereto. No such variation, amendment, or modification of this MOU shall be valid unless reduced to writing and signed by duly authorized representatives of both Parties.

IN WITNESS WHEREOF, the parties hereto have entered into this Memorandum of Understanding effective as of the day and year first hereinabove written.

RED ROCK CONSTRUCTION COMPANY OF CALIFORNIA, INC.

By: ______________________________

Title: ______________________________

WHITE CRANE CONSTRUCTION COMPANY OF SURITANIA, LTD.

By: ______________________________

Title: ______________________________

§ 6.12 Sample Memorandum of Understanding to Form a Non-Integrated Joint Venture

SAMPLE PRELIMINARY AGREEMENT TO FORM AN INTERNATIONAL *NON-INTEGRATED* JOINT VENTURE AGREEMENT FOR UNDERTAKING SINGLE/MULTIPLE PROJECTS

Loss Sharing by Who Has Responsibility for Particular Scope of Work

TABLE OF CONTENTS

MEMORANDUM OF UNDERSTANDING

THIS MEMORANDUM OF UNDERSTANDING is entered into this _____ day of __________, 1992, by and between RED ROCK CONSTRUCTION COMPANY of California, Inc. ("Red Rock"), and WHITE CRANE CONSTRUCTION COMPANY OF SURITANIA, LTD. ("White Crane"), sometimes individually referred to as the "Party" and collectively referred to as the "Parties."

WHEREAS, Red Rock and its affiliated entities have extensive experience performing construction services for desalination projects in the Arab Republic of Egypt ("Egypt"), including the Abu Sultan Desalination Plant and the Helwan Desalination Plant; and

WHEREAS, White Crane and its affiliated entities have extensive experience performing construction services for power projects in Egypt, including the Shoubrah El Kheima Thermal Power Plant and the Damietta Combined Cycle Plant; and

WHEREAS, the Parties wish to draw upon such experience by collaborating together in the preparation and submission of a prequalification document ("Qualification Document") and a proposal ("Proposal") for certain defined construction services in connection with the construction projects in implementation of Egypt's Emergency Plan for the addition of desalination and generation capacity at those Egyptian Electricity Authority ("EEA") facilities referenced in the *Commerce Business Daily* Notice dated __________, at three (3) nominated Plant Sites (the "Nominated Plant Sites") and one (1) unidentified site (the "Unidentified Plant Site") hereinafter individually referred to as the "Project," collectively referred to as the "Projects"; and

WHEREAS, the Parties wish to collaborate and effectively utilize the capabilities and experience of each to the best mutual advantage in the preparation of the Proposal and the promotional activities associated herewith; and

WHEREAS, the Parties further desire, as part of this Memorandum of Understanding ("MOU"), to develop the basis upon which they will establish a joint venture relationship in which to implement the Projects if they are successful in the Proposal efforts;

NOW, THEREFORE, the Parties have agreed as follows:

1.0 *DEFINITIONS*

Whenever the following terms are used in this Memorandum of Understanding, they have the following meanings:

1.1 "Red Rock Work" means the work to be performed by Red Rock for the Projects, as more specifically described in Section 1.0 of Appendix A.
1.2 "White Crane Work" means the work to be performed by White Crane for the Projects, as more specifically described in Section 2.0 of Appendix A.
1.3 "Joint Venture" or "Joint Venture Agreement" means the business relationship referred to in Sections 2.2 and 2.4 hereof, based upon the principles described in Sections 3.1 through 3.4, 4.7, and 4.8 hereof.
1.4 "MOU" means this instrument, as originally executed or as it may from time to time be supplemented or amended.
1.5 "Sponsor" means the party identified in this MOU to act as the leader in all activities undertaken by the Parties.
1.6 "Work" means all work, supplies, services, and matters necessary to fulfill the requirements of the Projects.

2.0 *PURPOSE OF THE MEMORANDUM OF UNDERSTANDING*

The purpose of this MOU is to establish the working arrangements, principles, and methods for the Parties to accomplish the following business objectives:

2.1 Jointly prepare the Qualification Document and the Proposal for submission to EEA based on the Scope of Work set forth in Appendix A hereto.
2.2 Participate jointly in the drafting, negotiation, and finalization of a Joint Venture Agreement which will become effective and operative only at such time as an agreed contract is to be executed by the Parties with EEA.
2.3 Jointly develop, negotiate, and conclude a contract or contracts with EEA for the Work.
2.4 Serve as the contractual arrangements between the Parties until such time as the Parties have entered into a Joint Venture Agreement which formally defines their joint cooperation. Such Joint Venture shall be established without judicial personality under the laws of the State of ___________.

The participation by the Parties in this MOU shall be for the purposes set forth in this Section 2.0 and, except as expressly provided, nothing in this MOU shall be construed as a limitation upon the power or rights of any Party to carry on its separate business, not in conflict with the Projects, for its sole and exclusive benefit.

3.0 *PRINCIPLES TO GOVERN THE ESTABLISHMENT OF THE JOINT VENTURE*

The Parties agree to reflect the following principles in the development of the Joint Venture Agreement:

3.1 The provisional Scope of Services to be undertaken by each of the Parties is set forth in Appendix A to this MOU.
3.2 It shall be the intent to allocate the Work associated with the Nominated Plant Sites and the Unidentified Plant Site such that Red Rock performs the Desalination Plant portion of the awarded Work and White Crane performs both the civil work and the Power Plant portion of the awarded Work.
3.3 Both Parties' prior written consent will be required in determining the scope of Work to be subcontracted to third parties who are not affiliated entities of either Party hereto, as well as in approving the particular potential subcontractor(s).

3.4 The day-to-day management of the Work to be performed by the Joint Venture shall be conducted by and under the direction of a Program Director appointed by Red Rock and approved by White Crane. The Deputy Program Director shall be appointed by White Crane and approved by Red Rock. A more detailed description of the duties and responsibilities of the Program Director and Deputy Program Director shall be set forth in the Joint Venture Agreement. Within five (5) business days from the date of this MOU, Red Rock shall designate the Program Director.

4.0 *PREPARATION AND SUBMISSION OF THE QUALIFICATION DOCUMENT AND PROPOSAL*

The Parties shall jointly prepare the Qualification Document and the Proposal and submit such documents as a Joint Venture. The following principles shall apply in the preparation and submission of the Qualification Document and the Proposal:

4.1 The Parties shall jointly establish and determine the format and order of the sections for the Qualification Document and the Proposal.

4.2 Red Rock and White Crane will each be responsible for preparing its own portion of the Qualification Document and the Proposal, including the nomination of key personnel. In order to ensure complete and consistent documents, Red Rock, with the appropriate assistance and concurrence of White Crane, will carry out the final review and consolidation of such documents.

4.3 The Parties shall jointly establish and agree upon the details pertaining to the interfaces between the Red Rock Work and the White Crane Work. Such interfaces shall be taken into account in the preparation of the respective portions of the Proposal by the Parties.

4.4 Each Party shall be solely liable for any and all costs related to the preparation of its input to the Qualification Document and the Proposal and in connection with any discussions and negotiations which may be conducted with EEA representatives.

4.5 The Parties shall equally share those common Qualification Document and Proposal costs which are of benefit to both Parties, including, for example, those associated with the joint acquisition of retained legal advice in Egypt regarding the conduct of the Work in Egypt by the Joint Venture; provided, however, that before any such costs are considered common costs, the Parties shall have first agreed that such costs are necessary and shall have agreed on a budget for such costs.

4.6 It is agreed by the Parties that a Party may, to the extent practicable, prepare its share of the Qualification Document and the Proposal at its premises and shall make members of its staff available to the other Party at the other Party's premises, as required, in order to enable the other Party to prepare its portion of such documents. The assembling of the respective parts of such documents shall take place at the offices of Red Rock in ________________. Each Party shall, to the extent required, make available to the other Party at its premises such offices and facilities as may be reasonably required in connection with the preparation and assembly of the Qualification Document and the Proposal.

4.7 Although the Proposal will indicate that all liabilities to EEA associated with the performance of the Work shall be the joint and several obligation of the Joint Venture, each Party ("Indemnifying Party") shall indemnify and hold harmless the other Party ("Indemnified Party") from any claim made against the Indemnified Party by EEA or third parties to the degree that such claim arises in connection with the Indemnifying Party's fault or negligence in the performance of its respective scope of work.

4.8 The Program Director shall be responsible for the following:

4.8.1 Coordination of the activities of the Parties in the preparation of the Qualification Document and the Proposal and in dealings with EEA.

4.8.2 Carrying out all necessary correspondence with EEA and maintaining the appropriate correspondence files. However, in no event shall the Program Director make any commitment to EEA on behalf of the Parties without obtaining both Parties' prior consent.

4.9 The Parties shall use reasonable efforts to provide correct and accurate information concerning their respective portions of the Qualification Document and the Proposal. In this regard, each Party shall coordinate, control, and manage others specifically contributing to that Party's scope of the Qualification Document and Proposal. However, no warranty is assumed by either Party as to the accuracy or completeness of the information provided, and the sole remedy required of each Party for any inaccurate information furnished is to use reasonable efforts to provide corrected information. Neither party shall be liable to the other if the Qualification Document or the Proposal as submitted and/or the negotiations which may take place do not result in the award to the Joint Venture of a contract or contracts for the Work. In no event shall either Party be liable to the other for any special, indirect, incidental, or consequential loss or damages whatsoever.

5.0 *DEVELOPMENT*

Upon the effectiveness of this MOU, the Parties shall develop and agree upon:

5.1 The overall contract structure between the Parties and EEA as reflected and implied in the Proposal. Such structure will be arrived at by a judicious assessment of all factors such as, but not necessarily limited to, EEA's standard terms of contracting, the objectives, capabilities, and available expertise of the Parties, and the responsibilities assumed by the Parties.

5.2 The responsibilities and liabilities in the proposed EEA contract and modifications to reflect the contract with the Joint Venture as finally negotiated with EEA.

5.3 Each Party's respective obligations and liabilities associated with the sharing of common risks.

6.0 *CLIENT CONTRACT NEGOTIATIONS*

Following the submission of the Proposal and upon receipt of an invitation from EEA to negotiate a contract based upon the Proposal, the Parties shall so meet with EEA's representatives and jointly develop the contract based on the results of such negotiations. Each Party shall have the right to attend all meetings and to have access to all correspondence, minutes, and other documentation pertaining to and relevant to the negotiations where such is pertinent or affects its scope of Work.

7.0 *VALIDITY*

This MOU shall come into force upon the signature hereof by each of the Parties hereto and on the date first above mentioned and shall terminate upon the earliest to occur of the following:

7.1 Six (6) months shall have elapsed since the coming into force of this MOU, and the Parties shall not have otherwise agreed to supersede this MOU by a Joint Venture Agreement or agreed upon an extension of this MOU, and provided the validity of the Proposal or any extension thereof has expired.

7.2 By declaration of EEA in writing or other satisfactory evidence that the Qualification Document or the Proposal is not accepted by it.

7.3 If EEA postpones indefinitely, cancels, or disqualifies either Party from participation in the Project.

7.4 It becomes impracticable for either Party to participate in the Qualification Document and/or the Proposal for reasons beyond their respective control. Notwithstanding any termination or expiry of this MOU, the provisions of Sections 4.4, 4.5, 8.0, and 11.0 shall survive any termination or expiry hereof and continue in full force and effect in accordance with their respective terms.

8.0 *CONFIDENTIALITY*

8.1 Each Party shall treat as confidential all proprietary and confidential information made available to it from the other Party which is clearly marked as being "CONFIDENTIAL" and limit access to such information to its personnel as may reasonably require the same in connection with undertaking the activities contemplated by this MOU. The receiving Party further agrees not to use any of such information otherwise than in connection with the activities contemplated herein. Nothing contained in this Section shall apply to information received by either Party which:

8.1.1 at such times is or becomes generally available to the public through publication or otherwise, except by the receiving Party's wrongful act;

8.1.2 was in the receiving Party's possession prior to disclosure to the receiving Party by the transmitting Party; or

8.1.3 is independently made available to either Party by any other third party who is legally authorized to do so.

8.2 It is agreed that no license under any patents of either Party is granted by any disclosure or proprietary information hereunder.

8.3 The confidentiality obligations as set forth in this Section 8.0 shall continue for five (5) years from the date of this MOU.

9.0 *NOTICES*

Any notice, which may or is required to be given pursuant to this MOU shall be in writing and shall be sufficiently given or made if served personally or sent by facsimile or registered mail to the following addresses:

9.1 Red Rock Construction Company of California, Inc.

____

____

Attn: ____

9.2 White Crane Construction Company of Suritania, Ltd.

____

____

Attn: ____

10.0 *EXCLUSIVITY*

During the continuance in force of this MOU, no Party shall, directly or indirectly, collaborate or make any other agreements or arrangements with other parties relating to its respective scope of Work, except for the sole and express purpose of carrying out the objectives of this MOU.

11.0 *PARTIES' RESPONSIBILITIES*

Neither Party shall enter into any commitments nor incur any liabilities or obligations on behalf of the other Party in connection with the purpose of this MOU without the prior written consent of the other Party.

12.0 *FORCE MAJEURE*

Neither Party shall be considered in default in the performance of its obligations hereunder, to the extent that the performance of any such obligation is prevented or delayed by any cause, existing or future, which is beyond the reasonable control of such Party.

13.0 *SEVERABILITY*

In the event that any of the provisions, or portions or applications thereof, of this MOU are held to be unenforceable or invalid by any court of competent jurisdiction, Red Rock and White Crane shall negotiate an equitable adjustment in the provisions of this MOU with a view toward effecting the purpose of this MOU; and the validity and enforceability of the remaining provisions, or portions or applications thereof, shall not be affected thereby.

14.0 *ASSIGNMENT*

Neither Party shall assign its rights or interest in this MOU, either totally or partially, without the prior written consent of the other Party.

15.0 *GOVERNING LAW AND DISPUTES*

This MOU shall be governed and construed in accordance with the laws of the State of __________. The Parties agree to submit all disputes between them to the federal or state courts of __________.

16.0 *PUBLICATION*

16.1 This MOU is a confidential document and shall not be released to any person except with the written consent of both Parties.

16.2 No news release in any way relating to either Party's activity concerning this MOU shall be made by either Party to any news media or the general public without prior approval of the other Party.

17.0 *OFFICIALS NOT TO BENEFIT*

No monies shall be knowingly used directly or indirectly to influence improperly or unlawfully any decision or judgment of any official of any government or of any subdivision, agency, or instrumentality thereof in connection with the subject matter of this MOU. Any proven breach of this obligation shall be a material breach of this MOU and entitle the non-breaching Party to terminate this MOU immediately and, subject to the provision set forth in the last sentence of Section 4.9 hereof, to recover actual damages incurred from the breaching party.

18.0 *TITLE*

Neither Party to this MOU shall have the right to use in any way any name, characterization, trademark, or logo of the other Party.

19.0 *ENTIRE AGREEMENT*

19.1 This MOU constitutes the entire agreement between Red Rock and White Crane with regard to the subject matter of this MOU and supersedes all previous communications, understandings, and agreements between the Parties.

19.2 This MOU may be varied or amended by agreement between the Parties hereto. No such variation, amendment, or modification of this MOU shall be valid unless reduced to writing and signed by duly authorized representatives of both Parties.

IN WITNESS WHEREOF, the parties hereto have entered into this Memorandum of Understanding effective as of the day and year first hereinabove written.

RED ROCK CONSTRUCTION COMPANY
OF CALIFORNIA, INC.

By: ______________________________

Title: ____________________________

WHITE CRANE CONSTRUCTION
COMPANY OF SURITANIA, LTD.

By: ______________________________

Title: ____________________________

APPENDIX A
SERVICES TO BE PERFORMED

1.0 The following is a preliminary listing of the services to be performed by Red Rock for a Project:

- To assume the role of the Joint Venture Leader as well as the role of the spokesperson of the Joint Venture when items related to Red Rock's Scope of Work are being addressed.
- To coordinate the activities of the Parties so that the timely preparation and submission of the Qualification Document and the Proposal can be realized.
- To conduct the commercial and technical negotiations with EEA's representatives in cooperation with White Crane.
- To negotiate in cooperation with White Crane the terms of the Contract or Contracts with EEA and to execute such Contract(s).
- To design, supply, install, and erect the equipment and machinery associated with the Desalination Plant Portion and Seawater Intake Portion of a Project.
- To perform commissioning, trial operation, maintenance, and training associated with the Desalination Plant Portion and Seawater Intake Portion of a Project.

2.0 The following is a preliminary listing of the services to be performed by White Crane for a Project:

- To assume the role of the spokesperson of the Joint Venture when items related to White Crane's Scope of Work are being addressed.
- To conduct the commercial and technical negotiations with EEA's representatives in cooperation with Red Rock and to execute any resulting Contract(s).
- To perform and maintain the civil works relating to the Site Preparation Portion of a Project.
- To design, supply, install, and erect the equipment and machinery associated with the Power Plant Portion of a Project.
- To perform commissioning, trial operation, maintenance, and training associated with the Power Plant Portion of a Project.

§ 6.13 Sample Short Form International Integrated Joint Venture Agreement

SAMPLE SHORT FORM INTERNATIONAL *INTEGRATED* JOINT VENTURE AGREEMENT TO BE USED IN QUALIFICATION DOCUMENTS AND PROPOSALS WHERE THE PARTIES' LONG FORM AGREEMENT IS TO REMAIN CONFIDENTIAL

TABLE OF CONTENTS

JOINT VENTURE AGREEMENT

THIS JOINT VENTURE AGREEMENT is entered into this _____ day of ___________, 1992, by and between RED ROCK CONSTRUCTION COMPANY OF CALIFORNIA, INC. ("Red Rock"), and WHITE CRANE CONSTRUCTION COMPANY OF SURITANIA, LTD. ("White Crane"), sometimes individually referred to as the "Party" and collectively referred to as the "Parties."

WHEREAS, Red Rock and its affiliated entities have extensive experience performing construction services for power projects in the Arab Republic of Egypt ("Egypt"), including the Shoubrah El Kheima Thermal Power Plant and the Damietta Combined Cycle Plant; and

WHEREAS, White Crane and its affiliated entities have extensive experience performing construction services for power projects in Egypt, including the Abu Sultan Thermal Power Plant and the Helwan Gas Turbine Plant; and

WHEREAS, the Parties wish to draw upon such experience by collaborating together in the preparation and submission of a prequalification document ("Qualification Document") and a proposal ("Proposal") for certain defined engineering, procurement, and construction services in connection with Egyptian Electricity Authority's ("EEA") Invitation to Tender EEA/EIC/006 dated __________ for the design, supply, erection, and commissioning of the Talka Gas Turbine Plant located at Talka, Egypt (the "Project"); and

WHEREAS, the Parties hereto desire to respond to the said tender and, if successful, to implement as a Joint Venture a contract with EEA for the work called for by the Tender.

1.0 *JOINT VENTURE*

The Parties hereby agree to form an integrated Joint Venture named the "Red Rock-White Crane Joint Venture" (hereinafter called the "Joint Venture") to participate jointly in the Proposal for the tender of the Project and to implement the contract to be made with EEA, if successfully awarded the Project (hereinafter called the "Prime Contract"). Each Party shall have a fifty percent (50%) proportionate interest ("Proportionate Interest") to any profits derived from the performance of the Prime Contract and to any losses incurred in the performance of the Prime Contract.

2.0 *COOPERATION*

The Parties shall maintain good communications between themselves and cooperate with each other so that their Proposal will be successful and the Prime Contract will be performed effectively.

In this regard, each Party shall:

- Provide the other Party with all data and information concerning their own share of supplies and services which will be necessary for preparing the Proposal and carrying out the Prime Contract.
- Provide the necessary qualified manpower to the integrated Joint Venture in numbers and salary grade to perform that portion of the awarded work which conforms to its Proportionate Interest.
- Take full responsibility for its 50% Proportionate Interest in the Joint Venture in the performance of the Prime Contract.

3.0 *LIABILITY OF THE JOINT VENTURE*

The Parties shall be jointly and severally liable to EEA for the Proposal referred to in Section 1.0 above and for all responsibilities of the Contractor under the Prime Contract.

4.0 *ALLOCATION OF RESPONSIBILITIES*

The provisional allocation of responsibilities to be undertaken by each of the Parties shall be as listed below. This initial allocation may be adjusted from time to time by mutual agreement of the Members.

Red Rock

- To assume the role of the Joint Venture Leader as well as the role of the spokesperson of the Joint Venture.
- To coordinate the activities of the Parties so that the timely preparation and submission of the Qualification Document and the Proposal can be realized.
- To conduct the commercial and technical negotiations with EEA's representatives in cooperation with White Crane.
- To negotiate in cooperation with White Crane the terms of the Prime Contract with EEA and to execute such Prime Contract.
- To provide the Joint Venture with personnel possessing the requisite qualifications and experience to carry out approximately 50% of the work required by the Prime Contract in accordance with the terms and conditions of the Prime Contract.

White Crane

- To conduct the commercial and technical negotiations with EEA's representatives in cooperation with Red Rock and to execute any resulting Contract.
- To provide the Joint Venture with personnel possessing the requisite qualifications and experience to carry out approximately 50% of the work required by the Prime Contract in accordance with the terms and conditions of the Prime Contract.

5.0 *EXPENSES*

5.1 Each Party shall be solely liable for any and all costs related to the preparation of its input to the Qualification Document and the Proposal and in connection with any discussions and negotiations which may be conducted with EEA representatives.

5.2 The Parties shall equally share those common Qualifications Document and Proposal costs which are of benefit to both Parties, including, for example, those associated with the joint acquisition of retained legal advice in Egypt regarding the conduct of the work in Egypt by the Joint Venture; provided, however, that before any such costs are considered common costs, the Parties shall have first agreed that such costs are necessary and shall have agreed on a budget for such costs.

6.0 *EXECUTION OF PRIME CONTRACT*

Red Rock hereby appoints its Senior Vice President and Regional Manager for the Middle East, ____________, or duly authorized substitute, as its authorized representative to execute the Prime Contract on its behalf as a member of the Joint Venture. White Crane hereby appoints its Managing Director, __________, or duly authorized substitute, as its authorized representative to execute the Prime Contract on its behalf as a member of the Joint Venture. Unless advised otherwise, the above-named personnel shall be directly responsible on behalf of the Joint Venture for the due performance of the Prime Contract. Such persons shall be responsible for receiving any notices or other correspondence directed to the Joint Venture and can give valid receipts of same on behalf of the Joint Venture.

7.0 *MEETING OF THE PARTIES' REPRESENTATIVES*

After the Prime Contract has been awarded to the Joint Venture, the Parties' authorized representatives shall meet on a regular basis as a Board of Control or from time to time at the request of either Party. All policy matters necessary for implementation of the Prime Contract shall be decided at such meetings.

Details of the conduct of such meetings will be separately decided promptly after the award of the Prime Contract to the Joint Venture.

8.0 *USE OF TECHNICAL DATA*

Any documents, drawings, or other information relating to this Agreement received by each Party from the other Party shall be used by it only for the purpose of this Agreement and not for any other purpose.

9.0 *RESPONSIBILITY TO THIRD PARTIES*

Each Party (Indemnifying Member) shall indemnify and hold harmless the other Party (Indemnified Member) from any claim made against the Indemnified Member by EEA or third parties in accordance with its Proportionate Interest.

10.0 *ASSIGNMENT OF AGREEMENT*

No Party has the right to assign or transfer any part of its rights and obligations created by this Agreement to any person outside the Joint Venture without the prior written agreement of the other Parties hereto.

11.0 *ARBITRATION*

All disputes arising out of or resulting from this Agreement or the Prime Contract shall be settled by arbitration under the Rules of Conciliation and Arbitration of the International Chamber of Commerce by three arbitrators appointed in accordance with the said rules.

Said arbitration shall be held in __________________, and conducted in the English language.

The arbitration award shall be final and binding, and there shall be no appeal therefrom to any Court.

No party concerned shall be entitled to suspend performance of its obligations hereunder by reason of the reference of such dispute of difference to arbitration.

12.0 *TERMINATION OF CONSORTIUM*

This Agreement shall cease and terminate in the event:

12.1 The Parties are unable to agree upon a mutually acceptable Proposal to the Employer.

12.2 The Proposal expires by its own terms as of a given date unless all Parties agree to extend the validity period of such Proposal.

12.3 The Prime Contract is not awarded to the Joint Venture or awarded to others.

12.4 The Project has been completed, all the payments due from EEA under the Prime Contract have been received by the Joint Venture, and all properties, claims, and liabilities of the Joint Venture have been completely disposed of between the Parties hereto.

IN WITNESS WHEREOF, this Joint Venture Agreement is signed in triplicate by the duly authorized representatives on the day first above written, and one copy thereof to be held by each Party and one copy to be submitted to EEA as a part of the Joint Venture's Proposal.

RED ROCK CONSTRUCTION
COMPANY OF CALIFORNIA, INC.

By: ______________________

Title: ______________________

WHITE CRANE CONSTRUCTION
COMPANY OF SURITANIA, LTD.

By: ______________________

Title: ______________________

§ 6.14 Sample Short Form International Non-Integrated Joint Venture Agreement

SAMPLE SHORT FORM INTERNATIONAL *NON-INTEGRATED* JOINT VENTURE AGREEMENT TO BE USED IN QUALIFICATION DOCUMENTS AND PROPOSALS WHERE THE PARTIES' LONG FORM AGREEMENT IS TO REMAIN CONFIDENTIAL

TABLE OF CONTENTS

10.0 Assignment of Agreement.
11.0 Arbitration.
12.0 Termination of Consortium.

JOINT VENTURE AGREEMENT

THIS JOINT VENTURE AGREEMENT is entered into this ______ day of ________, 1992, by and between RED ROCK CONSTRUCTION COMPANY OF CALIFORNIA, INC. ("Red Rock"), and WHITE CRANE CONSTRUCTION COMPANY OF SURITANIA, LTD. ("White Crane"), sometimes individually referred to as the "Party" and collectively referred to as the "Parties."

WHEREAS, Red Rock and its affiliated entities have extensive experience performing construction services for desalination projects in the Arab Republic of Egypt ("Egypt"), including the Abu Sultan Desalination Plant and the Helwan Desalination Plant; and

WHEREAS, White Crane and its affiliated entities have extensive experience performing construction services for power projects in Egypt, including the Shoubrah El Kheima Thermal Power Plant and the Damietta Combined Cycle Plant; and

WHEREAS, the Parties wish to draw upon such experience by collaborating together in the preparation and submission of a prequalification document ("Qualification Document") and a proposal ("Proposal") for certain defined engineering, procurement, and construction services in connection with Egyptian Electricity Authority's ("EEA") Invitation to Tender EEA/EIC/006 dated ________ for the design, supply, erection, and commissioning of the Talka Gas Turbine and Desalination Station "A" located at Talka, Egypt (the "Project"); and

WHEREAS, the Parties hereto desire to respond to the said tender and, if successful, to implement as a Joint Venture a contract with EEA for the work called for by the Tender.

1.0 *JOINT VENTURE*

The Parties hereby agree to form a Joint Venture named the "Red Rock-White Crane Joint Venture" (hereinafter called the "Joint Venture") to jointly participate in the Proposal for the tender of the Project and to implement the contract to be made with EEA, if successfully awarded the Project (hereinafter called the "Prime Contract").

2.0 *COOPERATION*

The Parties shall maintain good communications between themselves and cooperate with each other so that their Proposal will be successful and that the Prime Contract will be performed effectively.

In this regard, each Party shall:

- Provide the other Party with all data and information concerning their own share of supplies and services which will be necessary for preparing the Proposal and carrying out the Prime Contract.
- Observe such time schedule for delivery and erection of equipment belonging to their respective scope of work as will be established by agreement of the Parties in conformity with the requirements of the Prime Contract.
- Take full responsibility for his own Scope of Services in terms of proper execution, good workmanship, delivery time, and fulfillment of guaranteed perfor-

mances as set forth in the conditions of the Prime Contract and as these will be defined and agreed by the Parties prior to the submission of the Proposal.

3.0 *LIABILITY OF THE JOINT VENTURE*

The Parties shall be jointly and severally liable to EEA for the Proposal referred to in Section 1.0 above and for all responsibilities of the Contractor under the Prime Contract.

4.0 *DIVISION OF THE WORK*

The provisional scope of work to be undertaken by each of the Parties shall be as listed below. The scope will be adjusted from time to time by mutual agreement of the Members.

Red Rock

- To assume the role of the Joint Venture Leader as well as the role of the spokesperson of the Joint Venture when items related to Red Rock's Scope of Work are being addressed.
- To coordinate the activities of the Parties so that the timely preparation and submission of the Qualification Document and the Proposal can be realized.
- To conduct the commercial and technical negotiations with EEA's representatives in cooperation with White Crane.
- To negotiate in cooperation with White Crane the terms of the Prime Contract with EEA and to execute such Prime Contract.
- To design, supply, install, and erect the equipment and machinery associated with the Desalination Plant Portion and Seawater Intake Portion of the Project.
- To perform commissioning, trial operation, maintenance, and training associated with the Desalination Plant Portion and Seawater Intake Portion of the Project.

White Crane

- To assume the role of the spokesperson of the Joint Venture when items related to White Crane's Scope of Work are being addressed.
- To conduct the commercial and technical negotiations with EEA's representatives in cooperation with Red Rock and to execute any resulting Contract.
- To perform and maintain the civil works relating to the Site Preparation Portion of the Project.
- To design, supply, install, and erect the equipment and machinery associated with the Power Plant Portion of the Project.
- To perform commissioning, trial operation, maintenance, and training associated with the Power Plant Portion of the Project.

5.0 *EXPENSES*

5.1 Each Party shall be solely liable for any and all costs related to the preparation of its input to the Qualification Document and the Proposal and in connection with any discussions and negotiations which may be conducted with EEA representatives.

5.2 The Parties shall equally share those common Qualifications Document and Proposal costs which are of benefit to both Parties, including, for example, those associated with the joint acquisition of retained legal advice in Egypt regarding the conduct of the work in Egypt by the Joint Venture; provided, however, that before any such costs are considered common costs, the Parties shall have first agreed that such costs are necessary and shall have agreed on a budget for such costs.

6.0 *EXECUTION OF PRIME CONTRACT*

Red Rock hereby appoints its Senior Vice President and Regional Manager for the Middle East, ___________, or duly authorized substitute, as its authorized representative to execute the Prime Contract on its behalf as a member of the Joint Venture. White Crane hereby appoints its Managing Director, _________, or duly authorized substitute, as its authorized representative to execute the Prime Contract on its behalf as a member of the Joint Venture. Unless advised otherwise, the above-named personnel shall be directly responsible on behalf of the Joint Venture for the due performance of the Prime Contract. Such persons shall be responsible for receiving any notices or other correspondence directed to the Joint Venture and can give valid receipts of same on behalf of the Joint Venture.

7.0 *MEETING OF THE PARTIES' REPRESENTATIVES*

After the Prime Contract has been awarded to the Joint Venture, the Parties' authorized representatives shall meet on a regular basis as a Board of Control or from time to time at the request of either Party. All policy matters necessary for implementation of the Prime Contract shall be decided at such meetings.

Details of the conduct of such meetings will be separately decided promptly after the award of the Prime Contract to the Joint Venture.

8.0 *USE OF TECHNICAL DATA*

Any documents, drawings, or other information relating to this Agreement received by each Party from the other Party shall be used by it only for the purpose of this Agreement and not for any other purpose.

9.0 *RESPONSIBILITY TO THIRD PARTIES*

Each Party (Indemnifying Member) shall indemnify and hold harmless the other Party (Indemnified Member) from any claim made against the Indemnified Member by EEA or third parties to the degree that such claim arises in connection with the said Indemnifying Member's fault or negligence.

10.0 *ASSIGNMENT OF AGREEMENT*

No Party has the right to assign or transfer any part of its rights and obligations created by this Agreement to any person outside the Joint Venture without the prior written agreement of the other Parties hereto.

11.0 *ARBITRATION*

All disputes arising out of or resulting from this Agreement or the Prime Contract shall be settled by arbitration under the Rules of Conciliation and Arbitration of the International Chamber of Commerce by three arbitrators appointed in accordance with the said rules.

Said arbitration shall be held in ________________, and conducted in the English language.

The arbitration award shall be final and binding, and there shall be no appeal therefrom to any Court.

No party concerned shall be entitled to suspend performance of its obligations hereunder by reason of the reference of such dispute of difference to arbitration.

12.0 *TERMINATION OF CONSORTIUM*

This Agreement shall cease and terminate in the event:

12.1 The Parties are unable to agree upon a mutually acceptable Proposal to the Employer.

12.2 The Proposal expires by its own terms as of a given date unless all Parties agree to extend the validity period of such Proposal.

12.3 The Prime Contract is not awarded to the Joint Venture or awarded to others.

12.4 The Project has been completed, all the payments due from EEA under the Prime Contract have been received by the Joint Venture, and all properties, claims, and liabilities of the Joint Venture have been completely disposed of between the Parties hereto.

IN WITNESS WHEREOF, this Joint Venture Agreement is signed in triplicate by the duly authorized representatives on the day first above written, and one copy thereof to be held by each Party and one copy to be submitted to EEA as a part of the Joint Venture's Proposal.

RED ROCK CONSTRUCTION COMPANY OF CALIFORNIA, INC.	WHITE CRANE CONSTRUCTION COMPANY OF SURITANIA, LTD.
By: ________________________	By: ________________________
Title: ______________________	Title: ______________________

§ 6.15 Sample International Integrated Joint Venture Agreement

SAMPLE INTERNATIONAL *INTEGRATED* JOINT VENTURE AGREEMENT TO SUBMIT A PROPOSAL FOR AND TO UNDERTAKE A REIMBURSABLE COST PROJECT

Loss Sharing by Proportionate Interest

TABLE OF CONTENTS

JOINT VENTURE AGREEMENT

THIS AGREEMENT made the _____ day of __________, 1992, by and between American Hard Hat Corporation (hereinafter referred to as "AHHC"), Swiss Specialized Technology Company (hereinafter referred to as "SSTC"), and the Far East Company, Ltd. (hereinafter referred to as "FEC").

WITNESSETH

WHEREAS, the parties hereto have agreed to enter into a Joint Venture for the purpose of submitting a joint proposal(s) (the "Proposal") to the Rapid Transit Authority of Singapore, hereinafter referred to as "Client," to construct the Magnolia Flower Line of the Singapore Mass Rapid Transit Project (hereinafter referred to as the "Project"); and

WHEREAS, the parties desire to enter into this Joint Venture Agreement to prepare and submit the Proposal to the Client and to perform the contract(s) (the "Contract") which will result in the event that the Joint Venture's proposal is accepted and it is awarded a contract; and

WHEREAS, the parties hereto desire to agree upon their respective rights, interests, and obligations as between themselves with respect to the Contract and the performance thereof:

NOW, THEREFORE, the parties hereby agree as follows:

1.0 *JOINT VENTURE ENTITY*

1.1 The parties hereby associate themselves as a joint venture ("Joint Venture") for the purpose of performing the said Contract along with any amendment or supplement thereto or modification thereof.

1.2 Except as otherwise provided in this Agreement, the Joint Venture shall remain in existence for that period of time required to perform the work described in the Contract (including any warranty period), and to recover the compensation attributable thereto, plus any extension of time required to perform any additional work authorized for the Project.

1.3 In the event the Joint Venture's work is terminated prior to completion and it is determined that further contracts for the Project will not be forthcoming, the Joint Venture shall conclude its affairs at the earliest possible date. However, should the Joint Venture's work be suspended, the Joint Venture shall remain in effect during the period of such suspension in accordance with the terms of the Contract.

1.4 It is not the purpose or intent of the parties to create a partnership or any other legal entity between the parties nor to constitute either party as a partner, agent, or representative of the other party; and neither the Joint Venture Agreement nor operations or activities thereunder or pursuant thereto shall be construed or considered as creating such a relationship or constituting either party as a partner, agent, or representative of the other party; except that a party may be a representative of the other party to the extent that such party is designated as such in the Joint Venture Agreement or by action of the Board of Control (as described in Section 6.0 hereof) or by written consent of the other party.

2.0 *JOINT VENTURE BID TO THE CLIENT*

2.1 Without prejudice to the usual operation, aims, and purposes of their respective businesses, the parties agree that they will provide support for the preparation of a Bid to the Client.

2.2 Each of the parties shall bear its own expenses incurred prior to the effective date of the Contract. Such expenses shall not be attributable to the Joint Venture.

2.3 Following submission of the Bid, no variation thereto shall be accepted by any of the parties during negotiations with the Client unless such variation has first been reviewed and agreed to by the other parties.

2.4 The Bid to the Client shall be made in the name of the Joint Venture.

2.5 Neither party shall, without the written consent of the other, pursue or perform any separate work connected or related to the Project.

3.0 *NAME*

3.1 The name of this Joint Venture under which said Contract shall be entered into and performed shall be "ASF, a Joint Venture."

3.2 All work contemplated by the Contract shall be performed under the name of the Joint Venture, and all money, equipment, materials, supplies, and other property acquired by the Joint Venture shall be held jointly in its name.

4.0 *BUSINESS ADDRESS*

The principal office of the Joint Venture shall be located at such location as the Joint Venture Manager shall designate.

5.0 *SPONSOR AND MANAGING JOINT VENTURER*

5.1 AHHC shall be the sponsor of the Joint Venture and shall act as Joint Venture Manager in the performance of the Contract. The Joint Venture Manager shall have supervision, management, and control, subject to the direction and guidance of the Board of Control, of matters pertaining to the performance of the Contract, including the nomination and supervision of a Project Manager who shall maintain continuing liaison with the Joint Venturers through the Board of Control.

5.2 The Contract shall be negotiated jointly by the parties with the Client, under the leadership of the Managing Joint Venturer. Following execution of the Contract, any amendments, supplement, or modification to the Contract shall be made with the approval of the Board of Control, as provided in Section 6.0.

6.0 *BOARD OF CONTROL*

6.1 For the purpose of establishing Joint Venture policy and expediting decisions and approvals requiring the action of the Joint Venture, there is hereby established a Board of Control consisting of six members: two (2) appointed by AHHC, two (2) appointed by SSTC, and two (2) appointed by FEC. The senior member for the Joint Venture Manager shall act as Chairman of the Board of Control. Each member of the Board shall have one (1) vote, and the votes of each such member shall be of equal value. The member(s) of each Joint Venturer shall be authorized to act for and on behalf of and to bind that Joint Venturer, subject to the provisions of this Section 6.0. Immediately following execution of this Agreement, each of the parties shall notify the other, in writing, of their respective appointees to the Board of Control.

6.2 Each of the members of the Board of Control shall designate in writing an alternate to act in his place and stead. At any time, a Joint Venturer may replace any member or alternate member of the Board of Control designated by it, as herein provided, by notice in writing to the said Board and the other Joint Venturer.

6.3 Meetings will be held regularly on a schedule to be prepared by the Chairman of the Board of Control. Special meetings may also be called by any member of the Board of Control; and notice thereof shall be given to the other Board members in writing, by certified mail return receipt requested, no less than one (1) week in advance of said meetings. No meeting shall be convened unless a quorum of three (3), comprised of at least one (1) member from each Joint Venturer, is present.

6.4 There shall be quarterly reviews by the Board of Control of all financial matters, and a determination shall be made of working capital requirements or distributions of capital.

6.5 Each of the parties hereto authorizes its representative on the Board of Control to act on behalf of such party in the making of all decisions; provided that amendments, supplements, or modifications to the Contract or to this Joint Venture Agreement must be approved in writing or executed by the respective officers of the Joint Venture partners.

6.6 All decisions of the Board of Control shall be taken by unanimous vote; however, if the Board of Control is unable to reach a decision because of lack of quorum or lack of unanimity and such failure to reach a decision will in the Joint Venture Manager's opinion jeopardize the proper execution of the Work, then the Joint Venture Manager shall have the authority to direct the Project Manager and, through him, those reporting to him to proceed, within the terms of the Project Manager's authority, to take those steps necessary and appropriate to safeguard the best interests of the Project and the Joint Venture.

6.7 The Board of Control is hereby authorized to make all decisions that are necessary for the operation of the Joint Venture and (without limiting the generality of the foregoing) may:

6.7.1 approve the bank or banks for deposit of Joint Venture funds;

6.7.2 request from each party, on recommendation of the Project Manager, the provision of any necessary working capital for the performance of the work;

6.7.3 authorize the common Project costs;

6.7.4 recommend to the parties the commencing, settling, compromising, or abandoning of any arbitration or litigation on behalf of the Joint Venture;

6.7.5 determine the insurance program for the Joint Venture;

6.7.6 authorize or initiate audits of Joint Venture books of account and financial statements by any independent auditor; provided, however, that the foregoing shall not limit the rights of either party to initiate an independent audit of the Joint Venture, as provided in Section 12.9;

6.7.7 resolve problems, disputes, and differences that cannot be resolved by the Project Manager; and

6.7.8 provide overall direction of the Joint Venture.

7.0 *PROJECT DIRECTION*

7.1 The day-to-day management of the Contract work shall be conducted by and under the direction of the Project Manager who shall be responsible for coordinating execution of the work in accordance with the policies established by the Board of Control. The Board of Control shall delegate to the Project Manager (and, in his absence, his designated alternate) such authority to act for and on behalf of and to bind the Joint Venture as may be required by the Contract.

7.2 The Project Manager shall be available as an advisor to the Board of Control. In addition to other responsibilities delegated by the Board, the Project Manager shall be the primary contact with the Client, conduct the day-to-day operations of the Joint Venture, and serve the Board of Control as its recording secretary (but shall not be entitled to vote on any issue). Each of the parties shall be responsible for seconding sufficient competent personnel to the Joint Venture, as required by Section 9.1.

7.3 A Deputy Project Manager, selected from the Joint Venturer's staff, shall be responsible to the Project Manager and shall be responsible for liaison with the Client as directed by the Project Manager.

7.4 The Board of Control shall approve the final selection of management personnel, including replacements or successors.

8.0 *INTERESTS OF THE PARTIES*

8.1 The terms and conditions of the Contract to be entered into, including any amendment, supplement, or modification thereof, shall be subject to the approval of the Board of Control.

8.2 Thereafter, to the extent that each party is obligated hereunder, each of the parties hereto shall provide the Joint Venture with personnel possessing the requisite qualifications and experience to carry out the work required by the Contract in accordance with the terms and conditions of said Contract.

8.3 The interests of the Joint Venturers in and to any profits and equity derived from the performance of the Contract, and in and to any property acquired by this Joint Venture in connection with the work to be performed thereunder, and in and to all contributions required and losses incurred in the performance of the Contract shall be those percentages set opposite their respective names as follows:

AHHC	Forty percent	(40%)
SSTC	Thirty-five percent	(35%)
FEC	Twenty-five percent	(25%)

9.0 *COMPENSATION*

9.1 For the accomplishment of the Contract work, it is agreed that each of the Joint Venturers will second qualified personnel, as requested by the Joint Venture Manager, in numbers and salary grades that are generally proportionate to each Joint Venturer's proportionate interest, as described in Section 8.3 above. Seconded personnel will remain on the payroll of their originating employer. In addition to the direct salary of such seconded personnel, a surcharge shall be paid to each venturer for personnel seconded to the principal office in an amount to be determined of such personnel's direct salary, provided, however, that when overtime has been paid the surcharge shall not be applied to the premium portion of that overtime.

9.2 It is intended that each party shall invoice the Joint Venture for the compensation it is entitled to for the work performed, subject to the provisions of the Contract and supported by such documentation as the Contract or the Joint Venture (acting through the Board of Control) may require. Each party will bear its own costs arising out of the preparation and submission of the Proposal, with the exception of the following costs, which will be borne by the parties in accordance with the proportions detailed in Section 8.3 herein:

- Approved travel costs including accommodations and subsistence.
- Printing and binding of Proposal.
- Cost of bid bond.

Should costs arise out of the preparation of the Proposal over and above the normal scope of estimating work and the aforementioned costs, such costs which relate to the Joint Venture shall be assessed and submitted for approval by all the parties participating in the Joint Venture.

In connection with the foregoing approval, the parties incurring these costs will submit them to the Joint Venture Manager, who will process them and charge the parties with their respective proportions in accordance with Section 8.3 hereof. The total amount of proposal preparation costs incurred by the Joint Venture will be subject to the limitations agreed to in advance by the parties.

9.3 The Joint Venture shall invoice the Client. Upon receipt of payment therefrom, the Joint Venture shall pay each of the parties the same due to the extent reimbursed by the Client.

9.4 Upon completion or termination of the services hereunder, whichever occurs first, the Joint Venture shall promptly wind up its affairs.

9.5 Nothing contained herein shall obligate the Joint Venture to pay any party until or unless it has received payment from the Client on account of the amounts invoiced by the respective parties.

10.0 *BONDS*

Each of the parties agrees to execute all applications and indemnity agreements required by the sureties upon any bond or bonds required in connection with the Contract. All financial obligations assumed by the Joint Venture in connection with the performance of the Contract, all liabilities assumed by or charged to the Joint Venture as contractor, guarantor, or indemnitor in connection with any surety bond or other bonds which may be given or executed in connection with the Contract, and all other obligations and liabilities of any kind or character which are assumed or undertaken by the Joint Venture in connection with and for the benefit of the performance of the Contract shall be shared by the parties hereto proportionately and in accordance with their respective interests as set forth in Section 8.3 hereof.

11.0 *WORKING CAPITAL*

11.1 All necessary working capital, when and as required for the performance and prosecution of the Contract, shall be furnished by the parties hereto proportionately in accordance with their respective interests as set forth in Section 8.3 hereof. If any party borrows funds to meet its obligation hereunder, such borrowing and interest payable thereon shall be the sole and separate obligation of the party and shall not be the debt or obligation of the Joint Venture.

11.2 If any of the parties fails or is unable to provide an additional capital contribution within the time specified, the Joint Venture Manager shall send an additional notice to all parties setting forth such fact and the amount unpaid, and the party not having deposited its additional capital contribution as provided shall have a further period of ten (10) days to make such additional capital contribution. If at the end of such ten-day period such party shall still have failed to make such additional capital contribution, such party shall be a defaulting party within the meaning of Section 19.1, and the surviving parties may select an additional remedy from among the following options:

11.2.1 The surviving party or parties may advance for their own respective capital account the additional capital contribution required as well as the additional capital contribution of the defaulting party and cause the allocation percentages of the parties specified in Section 8.3 to be recalculated as of the date such additional capital contribution is made. In such reallocation, the income, gains, profits, expenses, losses, deductions, and credits (or basis therefor) which, absent this Section 11.2, would have otherwise been allocated to the defaulting party shall be allocated to the surviving parties making the additional capital contribution for the defaulting party until such time as the net income, gains, and profits so allocated to the surviving parties equal two hundred percent (200%) of the amount of the contribution which the defaulting party failed to pay. In addition, upon such failure, all distributions of available cash which, absent this Section 11.2, would otherwise have been distributed to the defaulting party shall be distributed to the surviving party making the contribution for the defaulting party until such time as the amount of such available cash so distributed to the surviving parties equals two hundred percent (200%) of the amount of the contribution which the defaulting party failed to pay. The allocation percentages of each party following such recalculation shall be equal to the amount of each party's capital account after such contribution, divided by the aggregate amount of the capital accounts of all parties.

11.2.2 The surviving party or parties may advance as a loan to the defaulting party the amount of additional capital contribution to be made by the defaulting party. Such loan shall bear interest at four (4) percentage points above the publicly announced "reference" rate charged at the time by __________ to short-term commercial borrowers of the highest credit rating, but not more than the highest rate permitted by law. The balance of such loan shall constitute a lien upon the defaulting party's interest in the Joint Venture. Such loan shall be repaid from the first proceeds to be distributed thereafter to the defaulting party, whether as cash flow or as profit from the sale of such interest or any assets of the Joint Venture as permitted herein. Such lien shall be subordinate to any other lien placed upon such Joint Venture interest, as approved by the parties or as permitted thereunder.

11.3 Nothing contained in Section 11.2 shall increase or decrease the proportionate liability of the parties for losses suffered or sustained by the Joint Venture.

12.0 *BUSINESS MANAGEMENT*

12.1 The Joint Venture Manager shall perform the Joint Venture banking and accounting services and maintain the books and accounting records in accordance with accepted accounting practices. The Joint Venture books and records shall be subject to inspection by the parties hereto or their designated representatives at any reasonable time during the term of this Joint Venture.

12.2 Reports of the financial condition of the Joint Venture and of expenses incurred by the Joint Venture shall be made monthly to each of the parties hereto.

12.3 The books of account shall be maintained on the accrual basis of accounting for management and cash basis for tax purposes.

12.4 At the end of each calendar year, or at such other times as the Board of Control may direct, an accurate accounting of all income, liabilities, and disbursements of the Joint Venture shall be made and furnished to each of the parties.

12.5 The Joint Venture Manager shall deposit all advances of the Joint Venturers and all sums received from the Client in a bank account established exclusively for the Joint Venture, and all income or instruments for the payment of money received on behalf of the Joint Venture shall be payable only to the Joint Venture and deposited only in such bank account and shall be subject to withdrawal by check only, signed by persons as may from time to time be designated by the Board of Control.

12.6 For its accounting services, the Joint Venture Manager shall be reimbursed by the Joint Venture as a Joint Venture expense its actual payroll and related personnel costs plus direct costs.

12.7 Operating accounts shall be maintained at levels sufficient for efficient operations, based upon estimated needs and cash flow projections.

12.8 Upon termination of the Joint Venture, any Joint Venture facilities and property shall be disposed of at the best price obtainable, and an accounting shall be made to the Joint Venture for the proceeds thereof. Records of the Joint Venture which are required by the Contract to be kept subsequent to completion of the Services shall be kept at such place or places as the Board of Control may determine.

12.9 Each party shall keep separate, complete, and detailed records and books of account relating to its contributions to and the work it performs for the Joint Venture. Such records shall be subject to inspection by the other party during regular business hours, except that neither party shall have the right to audit such costs of the other party as are expressed as a fixed rate, fixed amount, or percentage. Any such audit costs shall be borne by the party conducting such audit.

13.0 *ASSIGNMENT OF INTEREST*

Neither of the parties hereto shall sell, assign, transfer, mortgage, pledge, or in any manner encumber its interest in the Joint Venture, or in the Contract or in any other instrument or obligation of the Joint Venture, or in any of the proceeds from said Contract without the prior written consent of the other parties hereto.

14.0 *SUBCONTRACTING*

None of the work to be performed under the Contract shall be assigned or subcontracted to any person, firm, or corporation other than the parties hereto, or their related or affiliated entities, without the prior approval of the Board of Control.

15.0 *JOINT VENTURE INSURANCE AND BONDS*

15.1 Each party shall contract in its own name all necessary workers' compensation and employer's liability insurance for its own employees and all necessary insurance on such party's property. Such insurance, except when legally impossible, shall provide for a waiver of insurers' subrogation rights against the Joint Venture, the other party, and the Client. The cost of the premiums for such insurance policies shall be paid by the party taking out such insurance and shall not be payable by the Joint Venture or the other party.

15.2 The specifications for any Joint Venture insurance desired by the parties or required by the Contract and any Bid Bond or Performance Bonds required by the Contract will be mutually agreed prior to execution of the Contract and will be procured by and in the name of the Joint Venture. The cost of Joint Venture insurance and any Bid Bond and Performance Bonds required by the Contract will be divided between the parties on the basis of their respective interests in the Joint Venture in accordance with Section 8.3.

15.3 Any Joint Venture's property insurance shall include a clause waiving insurers' subrogation rights against the Joint Venture, the parties, and the Client. Any Joint Venture insurance for third-party liability shall include a cross-liability clause and a waiver of insurers' subrogation rights against the parties.

15.4 The details of all insurance to be issued pursuant to this Agreement shall be agreed upon by the parties prior to executing the Contract, and all such insurance shall be satisfactory in form and substance to each party.

15.5 Notwithstanding any provision in this Agreement to the contrary, in no circumstances shall a party be liable to the other party for damage in respect of which the other party has been compensated by insurance proceeds resulting from Joint Venture insurance coverage according to this Section 15.0 (but only to the extent of such compensation actually received). In the event any party has a claim under the aforesaid Joint Venture insurance coverage, each party covenants and agrees to execute and deliver any and all documents necessary to effectuate prompt and satisfactory settlement. The proceeds of any Joint Venture insurance claim shall be used to reimburse the party incurring such loss. Deductible amounts applicable under any of the Joint Venture insurance shall be the liability of the party receiving the proceeds of the applicable Joint Venture insurance policy.

16.0 *ALLOCATION OF LIABILITY*

16.1 Under the Contract, each joint venturer will be jointly and severally liable to the Client. Any such liability to Client shall be subject to allocation between the parties in proportion to the parties' interests in the Joint Venture specified in Section 8.3, and each party shall indemnify the others and hold them harmless from any liability to the Client in excess of such party's proportionate interest, except as set forth below:

16.1.1 Liability for reperformance of the work or termination by Client for default, which liability can be attributable to a failure to second sufficient competent personnel to the Joint Venture, shall be assumed by the party or parties who failed to second such personnel to the Joint Venture.

16.1.2 Liability for failure to comply with applicable laws (including taxation) and regulations shall be assumed by the party or parties failing to comply.

16.1.3 Liability arising out of or related to a subcontractor of a single party shall be assumed by the party which has contracted with such subcontractor.

16.2 In no event shall either party be liable to the other parties for any incidental, special, consequential, or punitive damages arising under or related to this Agreement, the Contract, or otherwise, except for such damages which are claimed by third parties and are subject to indemnification pursuant to Section 16.4 hereof.

16.3 If a dispute arises among the parties as to which shall assume liability for any claim, suit, damages, expense, or penalty, each party shall provisionally assume a share of such liability in proportion to its interest in the Joint Venture in accordance with Section 8.3 until the dispute is settled by agreement between the parties.

16.4 Subject to the application of Joint Venture insurance as provided in Section 15, each party agrees, at its expense, to defend, indemnify, and hold the Joint Venture and the other party harmless from any and all third-party claims, demands, damages, cases, expenses, suits, actions, liabilities, and losses arising out of the negligence of its employees, agents, or subcontractors, or the neglect or failure to perform in accordance with the terms and conditions of the Contract or in the manner herein specified.

16.5 The releases from liability and limitations on liability expressed in this Agreement shall apply even in the event of the fault, negligence in whole or in part, strict liability, breach of contract, or otherwise of the party released or whose liability is limited, and shall extend to its related entities and its and their directors, officers, and employees.

17.0 *CONFIDENTIALITY*

17.1 Each party shall treat as confidential all proprietary and confidential information made available to it from the other parties which is clearly marked as being "CONFIDENTIAL" and limit access to such information to its personnel as may reasonably require the same in connection with undertaking the activities contemplated by this Agreement. The receiving party further agrees not to use any of such information otherwise than in connection with the activities contemplated herein. Nothing contained in this Section shall apply to information received by any of the parties which:

17.1.1 at such times is or becomes generally available to the public through publication or otherwise except by the receiving party's wrongful act;

17.1.2 was in the receiving party's possession prior to disclosure to the receiving party by the transmitting party; or

17.1.3 is independently made available to either party by any other third party who is legally authorized to do so.

17.2 It is agreed that no license under any patents of either party is granted by any disclosure or proprietary information hereunder.

17.3 The confidentiality obligations as set forth in this Section 17.0 shall continue for three (3) years after the expiration of the term of this Joint Venture, as provided in Sections 1.2 and 1.3 hereof.

18.0 *FORCE MAJEURE*

Neither party shall be considered in default in the performance of its obligations hereunder to the extent that the performance of any such obligation is prevented or delayed by any cause, existing or future, which is beyond the reasonable control of such party.

19.0 *DEFAULT*

19.1 Should one of the parties, hereinafter referred to as the "defaulting party," (i) file or fail to discharge within thirty (30) days an involuntary petition in bankruptcy or reorganization, (ii) file a certificate of dissolution by election, by an order of a court of competent jurisdiction, or by operation of law, (iii) make a general assignment for the benefit of creditors or become insolvent, or (iv) default in its obligations hereunder, then and on the occurrence of any such default, the other parties hereinafter referred to as the "surviving parties" shall, upon notice or discovery thereof, do whatever is necessary for the continuance of the performance of the requirements of the Contract.

19.2 After the occurrence of any such default, the administrators, trustees, or representatives of the defaulting party shall have no right to participate in the administration of the Joint Venture or to any distribution of compensation from the Joint Venture. The defaulting party's share of any compensation at the time of such default shall be placed in a special account until the closing of the accounts of the Joint Venture, from which there shall be deducted all additional expenses incurred, if any, by the surviving parties as a result of such default. The defaulting party shall be liable for any losses sustained by the surviving parties or which are incurred by the Joint Venture. The surviving parties shall be solely entitled to all compensation arising from work done after the date of such default of the defaulting party. In the case of such default, the defaulting party shall continue to remain liable in every respect under this Agreement. The defaulting party shall immediately turn over to the surviving parties all plans, data, drawings, and all other documents and information relating to the Project which are in its possession or control. Any or all of the defaulting party's subcontracts relating to the Project shall be assigned to the surviving party.

20.0 *DISPUTE RESOLUTION PROCEDURE AND APPLICABLE LAW*

20.1 The parties agree that any dispute which arises under this Agreement shall be mutually resolved through good faith negotiations between each of the parties' authorized representatives. In conducting such negotiations, the parties recognize that in drafting this Agreement it is impracticable to make provisions for every contingency which may arise during its term. Accordingly, in trying to resolve any dispute, the parties concur in the principle that, to the extent that the subject matter of the dispute is not addressed by the terms and conditions of this Agreement, the parties' authorized representatives shall seek to resolve such dispute by the application of the principle of fairness.

20.2 If, despite good faith negotiations, the dispute is not resolved to the mutual satisfaction of the parties' authorized representatives within thirty (30) calendar days after the matter is referred to such representatives or such longer time as is mutually agreed, the parties agree to refer the dispute to the Board of Control. If the Board is unable to resolve such dispute within thirty (30) calendar days after the matter is referred to the Board, then each party shall each designate one of their Senior Executives ("Senior Executive") with appropriate authority to be its representative in negotiations relating to the dispute. Each party shall promptly designate said Senior Executives and provide written notice of its designation to the other parties.

20.3 After the Senior Executives have been selected, then each of the parties shall provide to such Senior Executives its written position statement regarding the matter in dispute. If the Senior Executives arrive at a consensus regarding the dispute, the Senior Executives shall so advise the parties, who shall be bound by such consensus.

20.4 Any controversy or claim arising out of or relative to this Agreement or the breach thereof not adjusted or disposed of by the procedure noted above shall be settled by arbitration before and under the Rules of ____________ by one or more arbitrators appointed in accordance with the said rules. Said arbitration shall be held in ____________, and conducted in the English language. No Member shall be entitled to suspend performance of its obligations hereunder by reason of the reference of such dispute or difference to arbitration.

20.5 Any decision or award of the arbitrators shall be based solely on the terms of this Agreement. The terms and provisions of this Agreement shall be interpreted and construed under the laws of the State of __________, U.S.A.

20.6 The arbitrators shall not be requested to nor shall they have the power to render any decision or award except in accordance with the two preceding sentences. Decision of the arbitrators in accordance with the provisions of this Article shall be final and binding on the parties. Judgment upon the award rendered may be entered into any court having competent jurisdiction thereof, or application may be made to such court for a judicial acceptance of the award and an order of enforcement, as the case may be.

21.0 *NOTICES*

All notices required to be given under any provision of this Agreement by either party hereto shall be given by air mail or facsimile, addressed to the office of the party named in this Agreement, as follows:

American Hard Hat Corporation

____

____

Attn: __________________________

Swiss Specialized Technology Company

____

____

Attn: ________________________

Far East Company, Ltd.

____

____

Attn: ________________________

22.0 *AMENDMENT*

This Agreement may be modified or amended from time to time in writing as required. Amendments shall be initiated by the parties or by the Board of Control and then ratified and executed by an officer of each Joint Venture party.

23.0 *OFFICIALS NOT TO BENEFIT*

No monies shall be knowingly used directly or indirectly to influence improperly or unlawfully any decision or judgment of any official of any government or of any subdivision, agency, or instrumentality thereof in connection with the subject matter of this Agreement and the Contract. Any proven breach of this obligation shall be a material breach of this Agreement and entitle the nonbreaching parties to terminate this Agreement immediately and, subject to the provision set forth in Section 16.2 hereof, to recover actual damages incurred from the breaching party.

24.0 *TITLE*

Neither party to this Agreement shall have the right to use in any way any name, characterization, trademark, or logo of the other Party.

25.0 *SUCCESSORS AND ASSIGNS*

25.1 None of the parties hereto may assign or otherwise transfer all or any portion of its rights or obligations under this Agreement without the prior written consent of the other parties. In addition, none of the parties may obtain some of the necessary seconded personnel by subcontract issued to third parties without the prior written consent of the other parties, provided, however, that any of the parties may obtain some of the necessary seconded personnel by subcontract to its related entities.

25.2 Subject to the foregoing provision, this Agreement shall inure to the benefit of, and be binding upon, the parties hereto, their successors, trustees, assigns, receivers, and legal representatives but shall not inure to the benefit of any other person, firm, or corporation.

26.0 *SEVERABILITY*

In the event that any of the provisions, or portions or applications thereof, of this Agreement are held to be unenforceable or invalid by any court of competent jurisdiction, the parties shall negotiate an equitable adjustment in the provisions of this Agreement with a view toward effecting the purpose of this Agreement; and the validity and enforceability of the remaining provisions, or portions or applications thereof, shall not be affected thereby.

27.0 *PUBLICATION*

27.1 This Agreement is a confidential document and shall not be released to any person except with the written consent of the other party.

27.2 No news release in any way relating to any of the parties' activity concerning this Agreement shall be made by any of the parties to any news media or the general public without prior approval of the other parties.

28.0 *LANGUAGE*

Communication between the parties and between the Joint Venture and the Client shall be in the English language.

29.0 *ENTIRE AGREEMENT*

This Agreement contains all of the agreements, representations, and understandings of the parties hereto and supersedes any previous understandings, commitments, or agreements whether oral or written.

IN WITNESS WHEREOF, the authorized representatives of the parties hereto have executed this Agreement the day and year first above written.

AMERICAN HARD HAT CORPORATION

By: ______________________________

Title: ______________________________

SWISS SPECIALIZED TECHNOLOGY COMPANY

By: ______________________________

Title: ______________________________

FAR EAST COMPANY, LTD.

By: ______________________________

Title: ______________________________

§ 6.16 Sample International Non-Integrated Joint Venture Agreement

SAMPLE INTERNATIONAL *NON-INTEGRATED* JOINT VENTURE AGREEMENT TO SUBMIT A PROPOSAL FOR AND TO UNDERTAKE A REIMBURSABLE COST PROJECT

Loss Sharing by Party Responsible for Particular Scope of Work

TABLE OF CONTENTS

JOINT VENTURE AGREEMENT

THIS AGREEMENT made the ______ day of __________, 1992, by and between American Hard Hat Corporation (hereinafter referred to as "AHHC"), Swiss Specialized Technology Company (hereinafter referred to as "SSTC"), and the Far East Company, Ltd. (hereinafter referred to as "FEC").

WITNESSETH

WHEREAS, the parties hereto have agreed to enter into a Joint Venture for the purpose of submitting a joint proposal(s) (the "Proposal") to the Egyptian Electricity Authority, hereinafter referred to as "Client," to construct the Abu Sultan Gas Turbine and MSF Desalination Station "A" located in Talka, Egypt (hereinafter referred to as the "Project"); and

WHEREAS, the parties desire to enter into this Joint Venture Agreement to prepare and submit the Proposal to the Client and to perform the contract(s) (the "Contract") which will result in the event that the Joint Venture's proposal is accepted and it is awarded a contract; and

WHEREAS, the parties hereto desire to agree upon their respective rights, interests, and obligations as between themselves with respect to the Contract and the performance thereof:

NOW, THEREFORE, the parties hereby agree as follows:

1.0 *JOINT VENTURE ENTITY*

1.1 The parties hereby associate themselves as a joint venture ("Joint Venture") for the purpose of performing the said Contract along with any amendment or supplement thereto or modification thereof.

1.2 Except as otherwise provided in this Agreement, the Joint Venture shall remain in existence for that period of time required to perform the work described in the Contract (including any warranty period), and to recover the compensation attributable thereto, plus any extension of time required to perform any additional work authorized for the Project.

1.3 In the event the Joint Venture's work is terminated prior to completion and it is determined that further contracts for the Project will not be forthcoming, the Joint Venture shall conclude its affairs at the earliest possible date. However, should the Joint Venture's work be suspended, the Joint Venture shall remain in effect during the period of such suspension in accordance with the terms of the Contract.

1.4 It is not the purpose or intent of the parties to create a partnership or any other legal entity between the parties nor to constitute either party as a partner, agent, or representative of the other party; and neither the Joint Venture Agreement nor operations or activities thereunder or pursuant thereto shall be construed or considered as creating such a relationship or constituting either party as a partner, agent, or representative of the other party; except that a party may be a representative of the other party to the extent that such party is designated as such in the Joint Venture Agreement or by action of the Board of Control (as described in Section 6.0 hereof) or by written consent of the other party.

2.0 *JOINT VENTURE BID TO THE CLIENT*

2.1 Without prejudice to the usual operation, aims, and purposes of their respective businesses, the parties agree that they will provide support for the preparation of a Bid to the Client.

2.2 Each of the parties shall bear its own expenses incurred prior to the effective date of the Contract. Such expenses shall not be attributable to the Joint Venture.

2.3 Following submission of the Bid, no variation thereto shall be accepted by any of the parties during negotiations with the Client unless such variation has first been reviewed and agreed to by the other parties.

2.4 The Bid to the Client shall be made in the name of the Joint Venture.

2.5 Neither party shall, without the written consent of the other, pursue or perform any separate work connected or related to the Project.

3.0 *NAME AND SCOPE*

3.1 The name of this Joint Venture under which said Contract shall be entered into and performed shall be "ASF, a Joint Venture."

3.2 All work contemplated by the Contract shall be performed under the name of the Joint Venture, and all money, equipment, materials, supplies, and other property acquired by the Joint Venture shall be held jointly in its name.

3.3 The Joint Venture will agree to perform the work to the Client as provided in the Contract. As between themselves, each party hereto shall perform the services and supply the elements of the Project allocated to such party in Appendix A ("Scope of Work and Division of Responsibility"), attached hereto and by this reference made a part hereof, together with such other services and responsibilities as may be allocated to such party by the Project Manager in accordance with Section 7.0.

3.4 It is the intent of the parties that the elements of the Scope of Work allocated to each such party, taken together, shall constitute all of the work to be performed by the Joint Venture for Client under the Contract.

If work arises in addition to that specified in the Scope of Work of the Contract (and reflected in Appendix A hereto), the Project Manager shall determine the reasonable allocation of responsibility for the performance of such work, and the party performing such additional work shall be compensated in accordance with the compensation provisions of this Agreement.

3.5 Neither party shall, without the written consent of the other, pursue or perform any separate work connected with or related to the Project.

3.6 Each party may subcontract any part of the work allocated to it.

4.0 *BUSINESS ADDRESS*

The principal office of the Joint Venture shall be located at such location as the Joint Venture Manager shall designate.

5.0 *SPONSOR AND MANAGING JOINT VENTURER*

5.1 AHHC shall be the sponsor of the Joint Venture and shall act as Joint Venture Manager in the performance of the Contract. The Joint Venture Manager shall have supervision, management, and control, subject to the direction and guidance of the Board of Control, of matters pertaining to the performance of the Contract, including the nomination and supervision of a Project Manager who shall maintain continuing liaison with the Joint Venturers through the Board of Control.

5.2 The Contract shall be negotiated jointly by the parties with the Client, under the leadership of the Managing Joint Venturer. Following execution of the Contract, any amendments, supplement, or modification to the Contract shall be made with the approval of the Board of Control, as provided in Section 6.0.

6.0 *BOARD OF CONTROL*

6.1 For the purpose of establishing Joint Venture policy and expediting decisions and approvals requiring the action of the Joint Venture, there is hereby established a Board of Control consisting of six members: two (2) appointed by AHHC, two (2) appointed by SSTC, and two (2) appointed by FEC. The senior member for the Joint Venture Manager shall act as Chairman of the Board of Control. Each member of the Board shall have one (1) vote, and the votes of each such member shall be of equal value. The member(s) of each Joint Venturer shall be authorized to act for and on behalf of and to bind that Joint Venturer, subject to the provisions of this Section 6.0. Immediately following execution of this Agreement, each of the parties shall notify the other, in writing, of their respective appointees to the Board of Control.

6.2 Each of the members of the Board of Control shall designate in writing an alternate to act in his place and stead. At any time, a Joint Venturer may replace any member or alternate member of the Board of Control designated by it, as herein provided, by notice in writing to the said Board and the other Joint Venturer.

6.3 Meetings will be held regularly on a schedule to be prepared by the Chairman of the Board of Control. Special meetings may also be called by any member of the Board of Control; and notice thereof shall be given to the other Board members in writing, by certified mail return receipt requested, no less than one (1) week in advance of said meetings. No meeting shall be convened unless a quorum of three (3), comprised of at least one (1) member from each Joint Venturer, is present.

6.4 There shall be quarterly reviews by the Board of Control of all financial matters, and a determination shall be made of working capital requirements or distributions of capital.

6.5 Each of the parties hereto authorizes its representative on the Board of Control to act on behalf of such party in the making of all decisions; provided that amendments, supplements, or modifications to the Contract, or this Joint Venture Agreement, must be approved in writing or executed by the respective officers of the Joint Venture partners.

6.6 All decisions of the Board of Control shall be taken by unanimous vote; however, if the Board of Control is unable to reach a decision because of lack of quorum or lack of unanimity and such failure to reach a decision will in the Joint Venture Manager's opinion jeopardize the proper execution of the Work, then the Joint Venture Manager shall have the authority to direct the Project Manager and, through him, those reporting to him to proceed, within the terms of the Project Manager's authority to take those steps necessary and appropriate to safeguard the best interests of the Project and the Joint Venture.

6.7 The Board of Control is hereby authorized to make all decisions that are necessary for the operation of the Joint Venture and (without limiting the generality of the foregoing) may:

6.7.1 approve the bank or banks for deposit of Joint Venture funds;

6.7.2 request from each party, on recommendation of the Project Manager, the provision of any necessary working capital for the performance of the work;

6.7.3 authorize the common Project costs;

6.7.4 recommend to the parties the commencing, settling, compromising, or abandoning of any arbitration or litigation on behalf of the Joint Venture;

6.7.5 determine the insurance program for the Joint Venture;

6.7.6 authorize or initiate audits of Joint Venture books of account and financial statements by any independent auditor; provided, however, that the foregoing shall not limit the rights of either party to initiate an independent audit of the Joint Venture, as provided in Section 12.9;

6.7.7 resolve problems, disputes, and differences that cannot be resolved by the Project Manager; and

6.7.8 provide overall direction of the Joint Venture.

7.0 *PROJECT DIRECTION*

7.1 The day-to-day management of the Contract work shall be conducted by and under the direction of the Project Manager, who shall be responsible for coordinating execution of the work in accordance with the policies established by the Board of Control. The Board of Control shall delegate to the Project Manager (and, in his absence, his designated alternate) such authority to act for and on behalf of and to bind the Joint Venture as may be required by the Contract.

7.2 The Project Manager shall be available as an advisor to the Board of Control. In addition to other responsibilities delegated by the Board, the Project Manager shall be the primary contact with the Client, conduct the day-to-day operations of the Joint Venture, and serve the Board of Control as its recording secretary (but shall not be entitled to vote on any issue).

7.3 A Deputy Project Manager, selected from the Joint Venturer's staff, shall be responsible to the Project Manager and shall be responsible for liaison with the Client as directed by the Project Manager.

7.4 The Board of Control shall approve the final selection of management personnel, including replacements or successors.

8.0 *INTERESTS OF THE PARTIES*

8.1 The terms and conditions of the Contract to be entered into, including any amendment, supplement, or modification thereof, shall be subject to the approval of the Board of Control.

8.2 Thereafter, to the extent that each party is obligated hereunder, each of the parties hereto shall provide the Joint Venture with personnel possessing the requisite qualifications and experience to carry out the work required by the Contract in accordance with the terms and conditions of said Contract.

8.3 The interests of the Joint Venturers in and to any profits and equity derived from the performance of the Contract, and in and to any property acquired by this Joint Venture in connection with the work to be performed thereunder, and in and to all contributions required and losses incurred in the performance of the Contract shall be those percentages set opposite their respective names as follows:

AHHC	Forty percent	(40%)
SSTC	Thirty-five percent	(35%)
FEC	Twenty-five percent	(25%)

8.4 Each party shall assign sufficient competent professional and/or technical personnel to perform the work allocated to it.

8.5 The Joint Venture shall not have employees of its own, but shall perform its work with the employees of each party and by utilizing special consultants to the Joint Venture, as determined by the Board of Control.

8.6 The Joint Venture shall perform any additional work which may be duly authorized by Client pursuant to the Contract. The Board of Control shall thereupon determine which party or parties shall perform such work and the compensation therefor.

9.0 *COMPENSATION*

9.1 Costs incurred by each party or its affiliated companies in the performance of the work under the Contract allocated to it in accordance with Appendix A hereto or assigned as otherwise provided herein shall be reimbursed to it by the Joint Venture based on the sum of the following:

9.1.1 The cost of wages, salaries, and payroll additives of personnel (including Board of Control members) while such personnel are engaged directly in the performance of the work under a specific work assignment made by the Joint Venture, subject to exceptions pertaining under the Contract.

9.1.2 An allowance for indirect costs to be agreed upon and in accord with each Joint Venturer's established policies and practices.

9.1.3 Actual expenses incurred incidental to the work of the Joint Venturer, including the costs of travel and subsistence, personnel relocation, reproductions, report printing, computer usage, long distance communications, special materials and supplies, and shipping, all in accordance with reimbursement provisions of the Contract.

9.1.4 The expenses of taxes, duties, and fees to the extent which the Joint Venture has been reimbursed by the Client.

9.1.5 Actual cost of authorized subcontracted services.

9.2 The Joint Venture Manager will establish budgets for any specific work item assigned to a party, and, upon acceptance by such party, such budgetary limits shall be considered controlling on reimbursement, except as may be provided for by the Board of Control. When an officer of a party performs work for the Joint Venture and is reimbursed by the Client, it is agreed that compensation may be paid by the Joint Venture to such party for time so spent.

9.3 It is intended that each party shall invoice the Joint Venture for the compensation it is entitled to for the work performed, subject to the provisions of the Contract and supported by such documentation as the Contract or the Joint Venture (acting through the Board of Control) may require. Each party will bear its own costs arising out of the preparation and submission of the Proposal, with the exception of the following costs, which will be borne by the parties in accordance with the proportions detailed in Section 8.3 herein:

- Approved travel costs including accommodations and subsistence.
- Printing and binding of Proposal.
- Cost of bid bond.

Should costs arise out of the preparation of the Proposal over and above the normal scope of estimating work and the aforementioned costs, such costs which relate to the Joint Venture shall be assessed and submitted for approval by all the parties participating in the Joint Venture.

In connection with the foregoing approval, the parties incurring these costs will submit them to the Joint Venture Manager who will process them and charge the parties with their respective proportions in accordance with Section 8.3 hereof. The total amount of proposal preparation costs incurred by the Joint Venture will be subject to the limitations agreed to in advance by the parties.

9.4 The Joint Venture shall invoice the Client. Upon receipt of payment therefrom, the Joint Venture shall pay each of the parties the same due to the extent reimbursed by the Client.

9.5 Upon completion or termination of the services hereunder, whichever occurs first, the Joint Venture shall promptly wind up its affairs.

9.6 Nothing contained herein shall obligate the Joint Venture to pay any party until or unless it has received payment from the Client on account of the amounts invoiced by the respective parties.

10.0 *BONDS*

Each of the parties agrees to execute all applications and indemnity agreements required by the sureties upon any bond or bonds required in connection with the Contract. All financial obligations assumed by the Joint Venture in connection with the performance of the Contract, all liabilities assumed by or charged to the Joint Venture as contractor, guarantor, or indemnitor in connection with any surety bond or other bonds which may be given or executed in connection with the Contract, and all other obligations and liabilities of any kind or character which are assumed or undertaken by the Joint Venture in connection with and for the benefit of the performance of the Contract shall be shared by the parties hereto proportionately and in accordance with their respective interests as set forth in Section 8.3 hereof.

11.0 *WORKING CAPITAL*

11.1 All necessary working capital, when and as required for the performance and prosecution of the Contract, shall be furnished by the parties hereto proportionately in accordance with their respective interests as set forth in Section 8.3 hereof. If any party borrows funds to meet its obligation hereunder, such borrowing and interest payable thereon shall be the sole and separate obligation of the party and shall not be the debt or obligation of the Joint Venture.

11.2 If any of the parties fails or is unable to provide an additional capital contribution within the time specified, the Joint Venture Manager shall send an additional notice to all parties setting forth such fact and the amount unpaid, and the party not having deposited its additional capital contribution as provided shall have a further period of ten (10) days to make such additional capital contribution. If at the end of such ten-day period such party shall still have failed to make such additional capital contribution, such party shall be a defaulting party within the meaning of Section 19.1, and the surviving parties may select an additional remedy from among the following options:

11.2.1 The surviving party or parties may advance for their own respective capital account the additional capital contribution required as well as the additional capital contribution of the defaulting party and cause the allocation percentages of the parties specified in Section 8.3 to be recalculated as of the date such additional capital contribution is made. In such reallocation, the income, gains, profits, expenses, losses, deductions, and credits (or basis therefor) which, absent this Section 11.2, would have otherwise been allocated to the defaulting party shall be allocated to the surviving parties making the additional capital contribution for the defaulting party until such time as the net income, gains, and profits so allocated to the surviving parties equal two hundred percent (200%) of the amount of the contribution which the defaulting party failed to pay. In addition, upon such failure, all distributions of available cash which, absent this Section 11.2, would otherwise have been distributed to the defaulting party shall be distributed to the surviving party making the contribution for the defaulting party until such time as the amount of such available cash so distributed to the surviving parties equals two hundred percent (200%) of the amount of the contribution which the defaulting party failed to pay. The allocation percentages of each party following such recalculation shall be equal to the amount of each party's capital account after such contribution, divided by the aggregate amount of the capital accounts of all parties.

11.2.2 The surviving party or parties may advance as a loan to the defaulting party the amount of additional capital contribution to be made by the defaulting party. Such loan shall bear interest at four (4) percentage points above the publicly announced "reference" rate charged at the time by ____________ to short-term commercial borrowers of the highest credit rating, but not more than the highest rate permitted by law. The balance of such loan shall constitute a lien upon the defaulting party's interest in the Joint Venture. Such loan shall be repaid from the first proceeds to be distributed thereafter to the defaulting party, whether as cash flow or as profit from the sale of such interest or any assets of the Joint Venture as permitted herein. Such lien shall be subordinate to any other lien placed upon such Joint Venture interest, as approved by the parties or as permitted thereunder.

11.3 Nothing contained in Section 11.2 shall increase or decrease the proportionate liability of the parties for losses suffered or sustained by the Joint Venture.

12.0 *BUSINESS MANAGEMENT*

12.1 The Joint Venture Manager shall perform the Joint Venture banking and accounting services and maintain the books and accounting records in accordance with accepted accounting practices. The Joint Venture books and records shall be subject to inspection by the parties hereto or their designated representatives at any reasonable time during the term of this Joint Venture.

12.2 Reports of the financial condition of the Joint Venture and of expenses incurred by the Joint Venture shall be made monthly to each of the parties hereto.

12.3 The books of account shall be maintained on the accrual basis of accounting for management and cash basis for tax purposes.

12.4 At the end of each calendar year, or at such other times as the Board of Control may direct, an accurate accounting of all income, liabilities, and disbursements of the Joint Venture shall be made and furnished to each of the parties.

12.5 The Joint Venture Manager shall deposit all advances of the Joint Venturers and all sums received from the Client in a bank account established exclusively for the Joint Venture, and all income or instruments for the payment of money received on behalf of the Joint Venture shall be payable only to the Joint Venture and deposited only in such bank account and shall be subject to withdrawal by check only, signed by persons as may from time to time be designated by the Board of Control.

12.6 For its accounting services, the Joint Venture Manager shall be reimbursed by the Joint Venture as a Joint Venture expense its actual payroll and related personnel costs plus direct costs.

12.7 Operating accounts shall be maintained at levels sufficient for efficient operations, based upon estimated needs and cash flow projections.

12.8 Upon termination of the Joint Venture, any Joint Venture facilities and property shall be disposed of at the best price obtainable, and an accounting shall be made to the Joint Venture for the proceeds thereof. Records of the Joint Venture which are required by the Contract to be kept subsequent to completion of the Services shall be kept at such place or places as the Board of Control may determine.

12.9 Each party shall keep separate, complete, and detailed records and books of account relating to its contributions to and the work it performs for the Joint Venture. Such records shall be subject to inspection by the other party during regular business hours, except that neither party shall have the right to audit such costs of the other party as are expressed as a fixed rate, fixed amount, or percentage. Any such audit costs shall be borne by the party conducting such audit.

13.0 *ASSIGNMENT OF INTEREST*

Neither of the parties hereto shall sell, assign, transfer, mortgage, pledge, or in any manner encumber its interest in the Joint Venture, or in the Contract or in any other instrument or obligation of the Joint Venture, or in any of the proceeds from said Contract without the prior written consent of the other parties hereto.

14.0 *SUBCONTRACTING*

None of the work to be performed under the Contract shall be assigned or subcontracted to any person, firm, or corporation other than the parties hereto, or their related or affiliated entities, without the prior approval of the Board of Control.

15.0 *JOINT VENTURE INSURANCE AND BONDS*

15.1 Each party shall contract in its own name all necessary workers' compensation and employer's liability insurance for its own employees and all necessary insurance on such party's property. Such insurance, except when legally impossible, shall provide for a waiver of insurers' subrogation rights against the Joint Venture, the other party, and the Client. The cost of the premiums for such insurance policies shall be paid by the party taking out such insurance and shall not be payable by the Joint Venture or the other party.

15.2 The specifications for any Joint Venture insurance desired by the parties or required by the Contract and any Bid Bond or Performance Bonds required by the Contract will be mutually agreed prior to execution of the Contract and will be procured by and in the name of the Joint Venture. The cost of Joint Venture insurance and any Bid Bond and Performance Bonds required by the Contract will be divided between the parties on the basis of their respective interests in the Joint Venture in accordance with Section 8.3.

15.3 Any Joint Venture's property insurance shall include a clause waiving insurers' subrogation rights against the Joint Venture, the parties, and the Client. Any Joint Venture insurance for third-party liability shall include a cross-liability clause and a waiver of insurer's subrogation rights against the parties.

15.4 The details of all insurance to be issued pursuant to this Agreement shall be agreed upon by the parties prior to executing the Contract, and all such insurance shall be satisfactory in form and substance to each party.

15.5 Notwithstanding any provision in this Agreement to the contrary, in no circumstances shall a party be liable to the other party for damage in respect of which the other party has been compensated by insurance proceeds resulting from Joint Venture insurance coverage according to this Section 15.0 (but only to the extent of such compensation actually received). In the event any party has a claim under the aforesaid Joint Venture insurance coverage, each party covenants and agrees to execute and deliver any and all documents necessary to effectuate prompt and satisfactory settlement. The proceeds of any Joint Venture insurance claim shall be used to reimburse the party incurring such loss. Deductible amounts applicable under any of the Joint Venture insurance shall be the liability of the party receiving the proceeds of the applicable Joint Venture insurance policy.

16.0 *ALLOCATION OF LIABILITY*

16.1 Under the Contract, each joint venturer will be jointly and severally liable to the Client. Any such liability to Client shall be subject to allocation between the parties in proportion to the parties' interests in the Joint Venture specified in Section 8.3, and each party shall indemnify the others and hold them harmless from any liability to the Client in excess of such party's proportionate interest, except as set forth below:

16.1.1 Liability for reperformance of the work or termination by Client for default, which liability can be attributable to the portion of the work assigned to a particular party hereto, shall be assumed by such party. If such liability is attributable to the portion of the work assigned to two or more parties, the liability shall be assumed by each such party in such share as is proportionate to its respective responsibility for the default.

16.1.2 Liability for failure to comply with applicable laws (including taxation) and regulations shall be assumed by the party or parties failing to comply.

16.1.3 Liability arising out of or related to vendor and subcontractor of a single party shall be assumed by the party which has contracted with such vendor or subcontractor.

16.1.4 Liability for failure to observe or fulfill obligations, including warranties or performance guarantees, if any, contained in the Contract shall be assumed by the party so failing to observe or fulfill such obligations or, in the case of failure by two or more parties, by each such party in such share as is proportionate to its respective responsibility for the failure.

16.1.5 Liability for claims, penalties and damages, including liquidated damages, if any, shall be assumed by the party whose act or omission has caused such liability or, in the case of liability caused by two or more parties, by each such party in such share as is proportionate to its respective responsibility for the default.

16.2 In no event shall either party be liable to the other parties for any incidental, special, consequential, or punitive damages arising under or related to this Agreement, the Contract, or otherwise, except for such damages which are claimed by third parties and are subject to indemnification pursuant to Section 16.4 hereof.

16.3 If a dispute arises among the parties as to which shall assume liability for any claim, suit, damages, expense, or penalty, each party shall provisionally assume a share of such liability in proportion to its interest in the Joint Venture in accordance with Section 8.3 until the dispute is settled by agreement between the parties.

16.4 Subject to the application of Joint Venture insurance as provided in Section 15, each party agrees, at its expense, to defend, indemnify, and hold the Joint Venture and the other party harmless from any and all third-party claims, demands, damages, cases, expenses, suits, actions, liabilities, and losses arising out of the negligence of its employees, agents, or subcontractors, or the neglect or failure to perform in accordance with the terms and conditions of the Contract or in the manner herein specified.

16.5 The releases from liability and limitations on liability expressed in this Agreement shall apply even in the event of the fault, negligence in whole or in part, strict liability, breach of contract, or otherwise of the party released or whose liability is limited, and shall extend to its related entities and its and their directors, officers, and employees.

17.0 *CONFIDENTIALITY*

17.1 Each party shall treat as confidential all proprietary and confidential information made available to it from the other parties which is clearly marked as being "CONFIDENTIAL" and limit access to such information to its personnel as may reasonably require the same in connection with undertaking the activities contemplated by this Agreement. The receiving party further agrees not to use any of such information otherwise than in connection with the activities contemplated herein. Nothing contained in this Section shall apply to information received by any of the parties which:

17.1.1 at such times is or becomes generally available to the public through publication or otherwise except by the receiving party's wrongful act;

17.1.2 was in the receiving party's possession prior to disclosure to the receiving party by the transmitting party; or

17.1.3 is independently made available to either party by any other third party who is legally authorized to do so.

17.2 It is agreed that no license under any patents of either party is granted by any disclosure or proprietary information hereunder.

17.3 The confidentiality obligations as set forth in this Section 17.0 shall continue for three (3) years after the expiration of the term of this Joint Venture, as provided in Sections 1.2 and 1.3 hereof.

18.0 *FORCE MAJEURE*

Neither party shall be considered in default in the performance of its obligations hereunder to the extent that the performance of any such obligation is prevented or delayed by any cause, existing or future, which is beyond the reasonable control of such party.

19.0 *DEFAULT*

19.1 Should one of the parties, hereinafter referred to as the "defaulting party," (i) file or fail to discharge within thirty (30) days an involuntary petition in bankruptcy or reorganization, (ii) file a certificate of dissolution by election, by an order of a court of competent jurisdiction, or by operation of law, (iii) make a general assignment for the benefit of creditors or become insolvent, or (iv) default in its obligations hereunder, then and on the occurrence of any such default, the other parties hereinafter referred to as the "surviving parties" shall, upon notice or discovery thereof, do whatever is necessary for the continuance of the performance of the requirements of the Contract.

19.2 After the occurrence of any such default, the administrators, trustees, or representatives of the defaulting party shall have no right to participate in the administration of the Joint Venture or to any distribution of compensation from the Joint Venture. The defaulting party's share of any compensation at the time of such default shall be placed in a special account until the closing of the accounts of the Joint Venture, from which there shall be deducted all additional expenses incurred, if any, by the surviving parties as a result of such default. The defaulting party shall be liable for any losses sustained by the surviving parties or which are incurred by the Joint Venture. The surviving parties shall be solely entitled to all compensation arising from work done after the date of such default of the defaulting party. In the case of such default, the defaulting party shall continue to remain liable in every respect under this Agreement. The defaulting party shall immediately turn over to the surviving parties all plans, data, drawings, and all other documents and information relating to the Project which are in its possession or control. Any or all of the defaulting party's subcontracts relating to the Project shall be assigned to the surviving party.

20.0 *DISPUTE RESOLUTION PROCEDURE AND APPLICABLE LAW*

20.1 The parties agree that any dispute which arises under this Agreement shall be mutually resolved through good faith negotiations between each of the parties' authorized representatives. In conducting such negotiations, the parties recognize that in drafting this Agreement it is impracticable to make provisions for every contingency which may arise during its term. Accordingly, in trying to resolve any dispute, the parties concur in the principle that, to the extent that the subject matter of the dispute is not addressed by the terms and conditions of this Agreement, the parties' authorized representatives shall seek to resolve such dispute by the application of the principle of fairness.

20.2 If, despite good faith negotiations, the dispute is not resolved to the mutual satisfaction of the parties' authorized representatives within thirty (30) calendar days after the matter is referred to such representatives or such longer time as is mutually agreed, the parties agree to refer the dispute to the Board of Control. If the Board is unable to resolve such dispute within thirty (30) calendar days after the matter is referred to the Board, then each party shall each designate one of their Senior Executives ("Senior Executive") with appropriate authority to be its representative in negotiations relating to the dispute. Each party shall promptly designate said Senior Executives and provide written notice of its designation to the other parties.

20.3 After the Senior Executives have been selected, then each of the parties shall provide to such Senior Executives its written position statement regarding the matter in dispute. If the Senior Executives arrive at a consensus regarding the dispute, the Senior Executives shall so advise the parties, who shall be bound by such consensus.

20.4 Any controversy or claim arising out of or relative to this Agreement or the breach thereof not adjusted or disposed of by the procedure noted above shall be settled by arbitration before and under the Rules of __________ by one or more arbitrators appointed in accordance with the said rules. Said arbitration shall be held in __________, and conducted in the English language. No Member shall be entitled to suspend performance of its obligations hereunder by reason of the reference of such dispute or difference to arbitration.

20.5 Any decision or award of the arbitrators shall be based solely on the terms of this Agreement. The terms and provisions of this Agreement shall be interpreted and construed under the laws of the State of __________, U.S.A.

20.6 The arbitrators shall not be requested to nor shall they have the power to render any decision or award except in accordance with the two preceding sentences. Decision of the arbitrators in accordance with the provisions of this Article shall be final and binding on the parties. Judgment upon the award rendered may be entered into any court having competent jurisdiction thereof, or application may be made to such court for a judicial acceptance of the award and an order of enforcement, as the case may be.

21.0 *NOTICES*

All notices required to be given under any provision of this Agreement by either party hereto shall be given by air mail or facsimile, addressed to the office of the party named in this Agreement, as follows:

American Hard Hat Corporation

____

____

Attn: __________________________

Swiss Specialized Technology Company

____

____

Attn: __________________________

Far East Company, Ltd.

____

____

Attn: __________________________

22.0 *AMENDMENT*

This Agreement may be modified or amended from time to time in writing as required. Amendments shall be initiated by the parties or by the Board of Control and then ratified and executed by an officer of each Joint Venture party.

23.0 *OFFICIALS NOT TO BENEFIT*

No monies shall be knowingly used directly or indirectly to influence improperly or unlawfully any decision or judgment of any official of any government or of any subdivision, agency, or instrumentality thereof in connection with the subject matter of this Agreement and the Contract. Any proven breach of this obligation shall be a material breach of this Agreement and entitle the non-breaching parties to terminate this Agreement immediately and, subject to the provision set forth in Section 16.2 hereof, to recover actual damages incurred from the breaching party.

24.0 *TITLE*

Neither party to this Agreement shall have the right to use in any way any name, characterization, trademark, or logo of the other Party.

25.0 *SUCCESSORS AND ASSIGNS*

25.1 None of the parties hereto may assign or otherwise transfer all or any portion of its rights or obligations under this Agreement without the prior written consent of the other parties. In addition, none of the parties may obtain some of the necessary seconded personnel by subcontract issued to third parties without the prior written consent of the other parties, provided, however, that any of the parties may obtain some of the necessary seconded personnel by subcontract to its related entities.

25.2 Subject to the foregoing provision, this Agreement shall inure to the benefit of, and be binding upon, the parties hereto, their successors, trustees, assigns, receivers, and legal representatives but shall not inure to the benefit of any other person, firm, or corporation.

26.0 *SEVERABILITY*

In the event that any of the provisions, or portions or applications thereof, of this Agreement are held to be unenforceable or invalid by any court of competent jurisdiction, the parties shall negotiate an equitable adjustment in the provisions of this Agreement with a view toward effecting the purpose of this Agreement; and the validity and enforceability of the remaining provisions, or portions or applications thereof, shall not be affected thereby.

27.0 *PUBLICATION*

27.1 This Agreement is a confidential document and shall not be released to any person except with the written consent of the other party.

27.2 No news release in any way relating to any of the parties' activity concerning this Agreement shall be made by any of the parties to any news media or the general public without prior approval of the other parties.

28.0 *LANGUAGE*

Communication between the parties and between the Joint Venture and the Client shall be in the English language.

29.0 *ENTIRE AGREEMENT*

This Agreement contains all of the agreements, representations, and understandings of the parties hereto and supersedes any previous understandings, commitments, or agreements whether oral or written.

IN WITNESS WHEREOF, the authorized representatives of the parties hereto have executed this Agreement the day and year first above written.

AMERICAN HARD HAT CORPORATION

By: ______________________________

Title: ____________________________

SWISS SPECIALIZED TECHNOLOGY COMPANY

By: ______________________________

Title: ____________________________

FAR EAST COMPANY, LTD.

By: ______________________________

Title: ____________________________

APPENDIX A
Scope of Work and Division of Responsibility

Legend

AHHC—American Hard Hat Corporation
SSTC —Swiss Specialized Technology Company
FEC —Far East Company, Ltd.
* —Party with Primary Responsibility

Scope of Work	*Engineering*	*Materials*	*Labor*
DESALINATION PLANT			
MSF Evaporator (8 × 6.25 MIGPD)	AHHC	AHHC	AHHC
Brine Heater	AHHC	AHHC	AHHC
SW Deaerator	AHHC	AHHC	AHHC
Vent Condensor & Ejector	AHHC	AHHC	AHHC
CO_2 Extraction Blower	AHHC	AHHC	AHHC
Water Vapor Separator	AHHC*/FEC	FEC	FEC
BR Pump (2 × 50%)	AHHC*/FEC	FEC	FEC
Blow Down Pump	AHHC*/FEC	FEC	FEC
Condensate Pump	AHHC*/FEC	FEC	FEC
Distillate Pump	AHHC*/FEC	FEC	FEC
CW Recycle Pump	AHHC*/FEC	FEC	FEC
Chemical Injection System (Anti-Foam, Anti-Scale)	AHHC*/FEC	FEC	FEC
Ball Cleaning System	AHHC*/FEC	FEC	FEC
Acid Cleaning System	AHHC*/FEC	FEC	FEC
DESALINATED WATER BLENDING PLANT			
Recarbonation Plant • CO_2 Compressor (1+1) • CO_2 Absorption Vessel • Limestone Filter	SSTC*/AHHC	AHHC	AHHC
SW Filtration	AHHC	AHHC	AHHC
Hypo. Generating Plant	SSTC*/AHHC	AHHC	AHHC
Fluoridation	AHHC	AHHC	AHHC
Limestone Storage	AHHC	AHHC	AHHC
WASTE HEAT AND AUX. BOILER			
AUXILIARY BOILER			
FDF (2 × 60%)	SSTC	SSTC	SSTC
Sealing Air Fan	SSTC		
Chemical Dosing System	SSTC	SSTC	SSTC
Sootblower	SSTC	SSTC	SSTC
Chimney	SSTC	SSTC	SSTC

APPENDIX A *(continued)*

Scope of Work	*Engineering*	*Materials*	*Labor*
AUXILIARY BOILER (cont.)			
Water Washing Facility	SSTC*/FEC	FEC	FEC
Blowdown System	SSTC*/FEC	FEC	FEC
WASTE HEAT REC. BOILER			
Supplementary Firing System	SSTC*/FEC	FEC	FEC
Sealing Air Fan	SSTC*/FEC	FEC	FEC
Steam Drum	FEC	FEC	FEC
Circulation Pump (if required)	FEC	FEC	FEC
Chimney	FEC	FEC	FEC
FUEL STORAGE & SUPPLY SYSTEM			
FUEL GAS TREATMENT PLANT			
Knockout Drum	FEC*/AHHC	AHHC	AHHC
Filter Separator	FEC*/AHHC	AHHC	AHHC
Pressure Reducing Valve	FEC	FEC	FEC
Heater	FEC	FEC	FEC
Control Equipment	FEC	FEC	FEC
S/D & Depressurizing Plant	FEC*/AHHC	AHHC	AHHC
Ground Flare	FEC	FEC	FEC
Blowdown Drum	FEC	FEC	FEC
Purge System	FEC	FEC	FEC
DISTILLATE FUEL OIL SYSTEM			
Fuel Oil Unloading Pump ($8 \times 47m^3/H$)	FEC*/AHHC	AHHC	AHHC
Station Transfer Pump (2+1) Spare	FEC*/AHHC	AHHC	AHHC
Fuel Oil Pump ($2 \times 100\%$/Block)	FEC	FEC	FEC
Duplex Strainer	FEC	FEC	FEC
Gas Turbine Forwarding Pump ($2 \times 100\%$)	FEC	FEC	FEC
Duplex Strainer	FEC	FEC	FEC
Distillate Oil Storage Tank ($4 \times 20{,}000m^3$)	FEC	FEC	FEC
Distillate Oil Day Tank ($2 \times 110\%$)	FEC	FEC	FEC
Filter Coaleser	FEC	FEC	FEC

§ 6.17 Sample Foreign Corrupt Practices Act Covenant

SAMPLE FOREIGN CORRUPT PRACTICES ACT COVENANT FOR INTERNATIONAL JOINT VENTURE AGREEMENTS INVOLVING AN AMERICAN COVENTURER

23.0 *COVENANT BY THE PARTIES*

The parties acknowledge that they are familiar with the United States Foreign Corrupt Practices Act of 1977 ("the Act"), which prohibits the payment or giving of anything of value either directly or indirectly by a U.S. company to an official of a foreign government for the purpose of corruptly influencing an act or decision in his official capacity, or corruptly inducing him to use his influence with the foreign government, to assist an entity as a company or a joint venture in obtaining or retaining business for or with, or directing business to, any person. The parties covenant that they are familiar with the Act and its purposes and represent that they will not take any action which would be in violation of the Act. Any proven breach of this obligation shall be a material breach of this Agreement and entitles the nonbreaching parties to terminate this Agreement immediately and, subject to the provisions set forth in Section 16.2 hereof, to recover actual damages from the breaching party.

PART II

JOINT VENTURE AGREEMENTS FOR SPECIFIC PROJECTS

CHAPTER 7

ENERGY/COGENERATION/ SEWAGE/WATER TREATMENT CONSTRUCTION PROJECTS

John A. Rudy
Robert G. Harvey
Dexter Ewel*

John A. Rudy is a partner in the law firm of Nixon, Hargrave, Devans & Doyle and chairman of the NHD&D Construction Group. He manages the firm's construction law practice, which includes drafting and negotiating contracts, counseling during project execution, and dispute resolution. He earned a B.S. from LeMoyne College in Syracuse, New York, an M.A. from the University of Pittsburgh, and his LL.B. from the New York University School of Law. Mr. Rudy's projects include the design and construction of manufacturing facilities, nuclear and fossil-fueled power plants, hydroelectric and cogeneration facilities, mass transit systems, research and development and demonstration projects, and transfer of technology arrangements in the United States and throughout the world. He is a member of the Construction Panel of the Center for Public Resources, serves as counsel to the Greater New York Construction User Council, and is a member of the New York bar.

Robert G. Harvey is a member of the law firm of Nixon, Hargrave, Devans & Doyle and is a member of its project finance and development, and environmental practice groups. His principal areas of expertise include drafting and negotiating agreements for the finance, development, and construction of waste management projects and small power production facilities. Mr. Harvey also has significant experience with environmental impact assessments, environmental law compliance audits, regulation of hazardous and nonhazardous waste, and

*The authors wish to acknowledge with appreciation the contribution of Philip F. Cronin, Jr., in the Washington, D.C., office of Nixon, Hargrave, Devans & Doyle.

Sample agreements appearing in **§§ 7.17** and **7.19** are used with permission of Nixon, Hargrave, Devans & Doyle © 1992.

siting of public utility facilities. He is a graduate of Hamilton College in Clinton, New York, and Boston University School of Law in Massachusetts.

Dexter Ewel is a member of the NHD&D Construction Group and the project finance group in the Washington, D.C., office of Nixon, Hargrave, Devans & Doyle. He specializes in the development and financing of large-scale construction projects in the fields of resource recovery, waste management, and environmental services. He serves as counsel to developers and municipalities in the structuring, negotiating, and drafting of project documentation such as service, operation, and maintenance agreements, construction contracts, and recycling and composting-related agreements. Mr. Ewel received his B.A. degree from the University of Maryland and his J.D. and LL.M. in taxation from the Georgetown University Law Center in Washington, D.C.

---

§ 7.1 Unique Joint Venturing Considerations

Joint venturing is a relatively new development in the areas of energy, cogeneration, sewage, and water treatment. As in other construction-related fields, the joint project structure may take several forms. The parties may:

1. Form general partnerships or limited partnerships
2. Remain individual parties in a prime contractor/subcontractor relationship
3. Become shareholders of a special-purpose corporate developer
4. Form an unincorporated association pursuant to a joint venture agreement.

The advantages and disadvantages of each form should be evaluated before selecting the structure for participating in a new project. Joint venturing in the energy/cogeneration/sewage/water treatment industries requires the parties to address a broad spectrum of economic, financial, technical, and legal issues. The issues likely to arise in any particular construction project will depend on the substantive purpose of the project, its size and location, the character of the facility and site, and the contractual and financial complexity of the structure contemplated by the project's sponsor (including the possibility of public/private partnership arrangements and the use of project financing techniques).

Many of these projects will be developed in response to a sponsor's request for proposals (RFP). Under the Public Utilities Regulatory Policies Act of 1978 (PURPA),[1] many state regulatory commissions have instituted public bidding procedures pursuant to which utilities allow independent power producers to bid for the capacity and energy needed to displace the future concentration of electric generation facilities. The sample *teaming (pre-bid) agreement* in **§ 7.17** contemplates the preparation of a joint venture's response to the RFP or, in the case of cogeneration facilities, the utility's invitation to bid. A teaming agreement should be structured so that it will terminate if the joint venture proposal is not accepted.

Under the joint venture structure, the parties join together for the purpose of developing a specific project for a specific customer. The teaming agreement and the joint venture agreement indicate that the parties wish to deal with each other as venturers in the project rather than as shareholders in a corporation or as individual parties in a prime contractor/subcontractor relationship.

Teaming agreements and joint venture agreements are typically drafted with the assumption that the facility will be designed to provide the project's sponsor with a specific service—the generation of electricity, the treatment of sewage effluent, or the disposal of refuse. Accordingly, the agreements contemplate acceptance testing and treatment specification requirements. It should also be noted that proposed cogeneration facilities are, under PURPA, subject to the design specifications required by the regulations of the Federal Energy Regulatory Commission, including the requirement for a second energy component of 5 percent or more of the energy output of the facility.

In general, when a response is made to a RFP or a bidding invitation for a facility, the joint venturers must realize that in many respects their arrangement in terms of risk allocation, liability, and indemnification, among other things,

---

[1] 16 U.S.C. § 2601 (19).

will be affected by the construction or service agreement contemplated by the project sponsor (the developer). For example, if the project sponsor expects certain guarantees of treatment capacity or energy production levels, the need to make such guarantees must be addressed by the joint venturers. Responsibility for the failure to achieve such guaranteed performance or energy production levels must be allocated among the parties, taking into account the relationships among the adequacy of design, construction, materials, and cooperation. A joint venture agreement, to a greater extent than a teaming agreement, must also contemplate how each joint venturer will provide security for its performance and whether that security will be in the form of a performance bond, letter of credit, insurance, or otherwise. The joint venturers must also determine who will be the beneficiary or beneficiaries of such security—the joint venture, its participants, and/or the project sponsor.

§ 7.2 Funding

In the context of a teaming agreement, the most straightforward funding arrangement is for each party to pay its own costs, based on a predetermined set of tasks and responsibilities to be undertaken by the parties in an attempt to secure selection under the RFP or otherwise to be awarded the project. After the joint venture has been awarded the project, a mechanism to provide working capital and, if appropriate, equity funds must be established, even if the proceeds of construction loans or municipal debt are then available. Typically, the joint venture will be allowed to draw on construction funds in accordance with an agreed-upon milestone payment schedule. The joint venturers must ensure the adequacy of their project's cash flow if they are to be paid only after the completion of project milestones. In addition, there is the possibility of late payments resulting from disagreements with the project sponsor, especially with respect to whether project milestones have been achieved. In many projects the funding arrangements may require that one joint venturer pay a disproportional amount of expenses during a particular stage of the project, especially as the project moves from the design phase to the construction phase. Of course, the ultimate cash flow problem, cost overruns, is a risk that must be allocated appropriately among the joint venturers. In project financing, a substantial portion of the cost overrun risk under a turnkey contract is allocated to the contractor (joint venture).

Another funding issue that should be addressed in the joint venture agreement is the mechanism for receiving and distributing project funds. The sample joint venture agreement in **§ 7.19** assumes that each joint venturer gets paid separately. The parties may find it easier from an administrative standpoint to direct all payments to one party, who then makes the appropriate distribution of available funds. The creditworthiness of this responsible joint venturer must be examined with respect to its ability to withstand potential cash flow problems during the course of the project. In a larger sense, the creditworthiness of individual joint venturers may have an effect on the allocation of responsibility for indemnification and warranty claims, as well as responsibility for the payment of project debt. It is possible that the financial relationship among the joint venturers may suggest a form of agreement other than the one set forth in the sample joint venture agreement. This issue is addressed in greater detail in **§ 7.4**.

§ 7.3 Privatization or Project Finance

Whenever public/private partnerships are involved, numerous municipal law questions are relevant to the preparation of the agreements. For example, the joint venturers must review the requirements of applicable public procurement processes, the types of debt financing and application restrictions that may apply to municipal projects, and other statutory or regulatory restrictions governing municipal involvement in a project.

For joint venturers, the viability of such projects will depend on factors such as: (1) the availability of a reliable public revenue stream, which will demonstrate to lenders that the debt can be repaid from project service activities; (2) whether the risks of project development are well defined, subject to reasonable controls, and allocated reasonably among the participating entities; and (3) whether there will be an adequate return on any infusion of equity.

If project financing is contemplated, it probably should be memorialized in the joint venture agreement. *Project financing* is essentially nonrecourse financing, supported only by the revenues and assets of the project itself (for example, revenue-producing project contracts) rather than by the credit of the project sponsors.

Of particular importance in the project finance context are energy or service contracts that represent a payment obligation into the project and facility. Revenues from these contracts depend on the predictability, efficiency, and production capability of the facility under construction. This, in turn, focuses the project sponsor's and lender's interests on both the construction and performance guarantees and the overall construction schedule, because the project will not generate any fees/revenues until the project has been successfully completed and tested. Therefore, when project financing a facility, the joint venturers should pay special attention to any output or service contract analysis that is dependent on facility performance. Also of concern is how the joint venturers' risk of nonperformance may be affected by certain events, such as a change in law. The joint venturers must ensure that there are appropriate construction reserves or opportunities to secure additional debt for the project if a force majeure or change in law results in delays or additional costs requiring more funds to complete the project. Successful project financing is predicated on the satisfactory allocation of project risks, minimization of interruptions to the cash flow, and development of mechanisms to guarantee the ability to service the debt of the project. It is also predicated on a stable regulatory environment.

It is important to note that the Clean Water Act, under its construction grant program and the new revolving fund loan program, requires that waste water treatment facilities be owned by the public sector. This will limit the opportunities for private sector investment in such facilities. However, there will be no limitation on private construction and/or operation of such facilities.

Conventional project financing will allow for these types of recognized changes in law, but little else.

§ 7.4 Organization, Management, and Control

The sample teaming and joint venture agreements (see §§ **7.16** and **7.17** give the principal management responsibility for the work of the joint venture to one of the joint venturers. This arrangement can be particularly important when municipalities or utilities request responses to RFPs or responses to bid requests. A substantial amount of resources will be expended by the joint venturers during the preparation of the proposal. Occasionally, the RFP will provide for negotiations among certain bidders which, in turn, requires one of the joint venturers to take the lead role in negotiating a final joint venture proposal.

The form of organization of the joint venture is an important consideration that the joint venturers must reconcile at the outset of the project. The sample agreements in this chapter are drafted for a project that involves a municipality and a joint venture that provides services rather than takes an ownership and equity position with respect to the project. If the parties contemplate a *merchant facility* (one built by themselves as project sponsors) or a project in which the joint venturers contribute equity, the adoption of another project structure may be advisable. Other project structures include a partnership, either general or limited, and a corporation, the stock of which would be owned by the joint venturers. If a new partnership or corporation is formed for purposes of the project, the new organization will often execute contracts with each of the joint venturers for the provision of their respective services.

The organizational documents must, in addition, include an evaluation of property that any of the joint venturers will contribute to the project. These documents must also contemplate a termination of the joint venture, whether voluntary or involuntary, and how property and funds will be distributed to the joint venturers upon such termination. They should also provide for the assignment of joint venture contracts upon termination, as well as a mechanism for the continued existence of the joint venture if one of the joint venturers withdraws, ceases to exist, or becomes insolvent. Potential joint venturers should also keep in mind any tax consequences relevant to the organizational structure contemplated by the joint venture.

Any potential joint venturer should also ensure that its counsel has determined that the joint venturer has the authority and legal power to execute the joint venture agreements, and that there are no restrictions in prior agreements that would adversely affect the joint venturer's entry into the joint venture (for example, restrictive covenants in loan agreements). Each joint venturer will be asked by the project lender to make certain representations and warranties, supported by an opinion from the joint venturer's counsel. The joint venture organizational documents should also address the extent to which any of the joint venturers has the authority to bind the joint venture. Although this determination will depend on the facts and circumstances, a joint venture will often appoint one party to act as its agent on behalf of the other joint venturers.

§ 7.5 Allocation of Responsibility

The allocation of responsibility among the joint venturers is one of the central tasks of the teaming and joint venture agreements. The primary division, of course, will be among the design, construction, and operations aspects of the project. However, a number of ancillary responsibilities must also be allocated. The joint venturers must consider who will be responsible for bookkeeping, recordkeeping, accounting, administering the project, permitting, distributing the construction funds and service fees, overseeing construction, selecting and ordering equipment, and testing the project. The appropriate allocation of these responsibilities will depend on the facts and circumstances existing at the outset of the project, as well as the key personnel involved. The project lender will require that responsibilities be allocated to the party best able to perform the relevant tasks.

§ 7.6 Capitalization

If a project is being financed through project financing, the issue of capitalization of the joint venture will rarely be of major importance. The primary capitalization will be derived from the proceeds of the construction loan, the contracts executed by the joint venture that represent a revenue stream to the project, and the facility itself. If the parties contemplate a more permanent existence for the joint venture—consolidated offices, recordkeeping, and administration—the joint venturers must provide for the capitalization necessary to pay the expenses incurred by the joint venture. The source of capitalization will typically be the joint venturers themselves, taking into account the value of any property or proprietary information contributed by the joint venturers.

§ 7.7 Tax Issues

Allocation of tax benefits among joint venturers will generally be an important part of the joint venture arrangements. It is essential that these factors be carefully considered and expert tax advice obtained. The nature and timing of tax benefits and consequences will have an important, often vital, impact on each joint venturer's expected return on a particular project.

§ 7.8 Risk Allocation

Risk allocation among the participants will depend on the type of facility being constructed, the nature of the contractual relationship between the joint venture and the project sponsor, and the relative abilities of the joint venturers to bear risk. Generally, risk allocation issues fall into the categories of:

1. Facility site issues
2. Facility capital cost issues
3. Debt issues
4. Construction responsibility issues
5. Facility performance issues (if the joint venture is to have a role beyond construction of the facility, for example, as an operator).

Facility and facility site issues include responsibility for zoning, title to the facility site, design questions, subsurface soil and other environmental conditions, the availability of specific technology needed for the service to be provided in the facility, and equipment supply questions.

Facility capital cost issues include an appropriate complete assessment of contributing costs for the project, including those related to technology license, credit enhancement, payment/performance bonds, utility requirements and interconnection costs, access roads, insurance, zoning approvals, permit applications, and cost escalation factors. Potential cancellation charges for large equipment items, if any, and project financing costs should also be considered.

Debt issuance issues include the amount and source of the funds that must be obtained, the risk of failure to obtain financing, and what guarantees related to the debt will be required—bonds, insurance, or a letter of credit.

Construction responsibility issues include initial funding of the project as capital costs, excess costs caused by a force majeure or a change in law, unexcused construction delays and late penalties, fixed or scheduled completion dates, early completion bonus, cash flow during construction, establishment of construction and payment milestones, retainage amounts, principle governing operation prior to acceptance or facility testing, performance or acceptance testing provisions, change order procedures, subcontractor bidding requirements, and federal/state labor laws.

§ 7.9 Liability for Trade Secrets

One of the important considerations in the joint venture, which should be reflected in the agreement, is the question of confidentiality and trade secrets. Proprietary information may be particularly pertinent in the case of a resource recovery facility or a wastewater treatment facility using special technology to fulfill contractual obligations to the project's sponsor. Typically, these technologies are obtained from licensors, which expect to be assured that the project agreements adequately protect technology secrets. The joint venture may have to negotiate with the project sponsor to determine how much access to technology will be given to the project sponsor or to its consultants, or whether they will be subject to written confidentiality agreements.

§ 7.10 Indemnification

A joint venture agreement should provide for cross-indemnification among the joint venture participants. Additionally, indemnification provisions specifying the indemnification requirements of the project sponsor may also be necessary. Project sponsors, for example, may seek indemnification with respect to losses arising out of a failure to complete construction on a specified schedule or for failure to meet appropriate acceptance testing requirements. This risk should be addressed in the joint venture agreement. In the event that the project involves site remediation or cleanup, indemnification provisions relating to environmental compliance should be included, addressing issues such as responsibility under laws regulating transportation and disposal of hazardous substances.

§ 7.11 Warranties

As in any construction project, the joint venture will be required to provide warranties with respect to labor and materials, and possibly a warranty with respect to defective design. The joint venturers must determine at the outset which participant will be responsible for paying any damages or performing any extra work if any of the warranties are violated. Any internal cap on expenditures for extra work must be reflected in the project documentation in order to avoid any inconsistency in obligations of the joint venturers with respect to the project contracts. Often, project sponsors will expect warranties on the performance of the facility being constructed. Energy, cogeneration, and sewage and water treatment facilities each will have its typical performance guarantees. The joint venturers must determine which of the participants will be responsible for curing any failure to achieve performance guarantees.

§ 7.12 Guarantees

When special-purpose, thinly capitalized corporate subsidies are formed to develop the project, project sponsors in the energy/cogeneration/sewage/water treatment area will often demand that the joint venture provide a performance guarantee from a creditworthy parent company. Such a *parent guarantee* secures the performance obligations of the joint venture under the project documents and possibly under the financing documents as well. This type of guarantee is typically considered to be a credit enhancement by the project lender. Depending on the creditworthiness of the joint venture, a parent guarantee can be given by one, some, or all the parents of the participants.

§ 7.13 Default

It is crucial that potential joint venturers contemplate the possibility that one of them may default in its obligations during the course of a project. Joint venturers typically find discussions of default distasteful, especially when all the participants are involved in planning for a series of future successes. However, the possibility of default must be addressed and the risk of default adequately allocated among the joint venturers. Often, potential participants will agree that each will be responsible for its own default. However, in the event of a default by the joint venture, the defaulting joint venturer may not have the resources or creditworthiness to assume responsibility for the joint venture's liabilities. Project sponsors will often require that other joint venturers assume some liability in such an event, even if the other joint venturers are not at fault. Joint venturers should address this issue during contract negotiations and protect themselves adequately in the joint venture agreement.

§ 7.14 Termination of the Joint Venture

The parties to a joint venture agreement must address the premature termination of the joint venture. A termination of the agreement can arise as a result of the insolvency, withdrawal, or death of an individual joint venturer. In any such event, the joint venture agreement may provide for the establishment of a new joint venture and the continued participation of the remaining joint venturers. This mechanism should contemplate the orderly distribution of funds, liabilities, and selected property to or from the withdrawing joint venturer.

§ 7.15 Dispute Resolution

The dispute resolution provisions in the sample agreements in **§§ 7.16** and **7.17** emphasize that it is important for each party to continue to proceed with its work pending final resolution of the dispute procedures. This approach may be critical in obtaining the financing for the project because project lenders do not want to lend into projects at risk for work stoppages every time there is a dispute between the parties. The teaming agreements address the potential need for performance bonds in these projects.

§ 7.16 Teaming/Pre-Bid Agreement Issues

The following issues, as addressed in the sample teaming agreement (see **§ 7.17**), carry special significance and should be carefully considered by the parties.

Allocation of responsibilities. The teaming agreement will designate the prospective roles and responsibilities of the joint venturers with respect to the submission of a joint proposal to design, construct, and operate a facility. Allocation of these responsibilities is particularly important in a construction project subject to competitive bidding or procurement award procedures. Therefore, the joint venturers should delineate their respective responsibilities clearly and in detail.

Environmental audits. The teaming agreement contemplates in Section 1.2(b) that pre-proposal and project environmental audits or site surveys may be required. Many resource recovery facility projects and energy facilities, for example, are sited at prior landfill locations. It is important to determine the need to undertake such audits as soon as possible in order to minimize costs and potential risks associated with projects proposed at environmentally sensitive sites. There may be other reasons for taking such audits, such as the need to comply with environmental permit requirements and compliance with the National Environment Policy Act and analogous state and local laws.

Performance guarantees. Section 1.2(e) recognizes that the project sponsor may require guarantees of the performance of the facility by the joint venture. *Performance guarantees* are typically required in public/private partnerships, along with a performance bond, letter of credit, or other surety, in order to cover the construction and performance of the facility (statutory requirements regarding bonding and operating levels may also apply). Performance guarantees are also important in a project finance context. *Project financing* requires the lender to look solely to the revenues generated by the project itself for collateral. The project assets become security for project loans, which are nonrecourse to the developing entities. Often a "deep pocket's" guarantee of performance is necessary to secure the appropriate debt for the project.

Permits and licenses. Section 1.2(h) contemplates that one of the joint venturers will be responsible for obtaining all permits, approvals, licenses, and consents necessary for the project. It should also be noted that in some states the project owner may be required to be named on the permits and other regulatory approvals.

Acceptance testing. The guarantee of performance is also likely to be necessary for the acceptance testing requirements contemplated for the project. These kinds of projects typically involve providing a service such as waste disposal, wastewater treatment, or energy production to a municipality or other public recipient. These services require a facility that will meet certain agreed-upon specifications. The guarantee of performance is intended to ensure that, if the facility as designed and constructed does not meet design/testing specifications, a deep pocket is available at the acceptance testing phase to remedy the deficiency or "buy down" the facility (provide liquidated damages for the performance shortfall).

Expenses. In Section 3.5 of the teaming agreement, each party agrees to bear all the losses and expenses incurred by it in connection with the preparation of the proposal and the teaming agreement. Once the project is secured for the joint venture, more detailed provisions on funding will be required. In the sample joint venture agreement, Section 3.2 addresses the need for working funds to allow the joint venture to pursue its responsibilities to the project sponsor.

Personnel. In the event that key personnel are necessary for the preparation of the proposal, a provision should be added designating those key personnel and committing them to undertake the work necessary to prepare and submit the proposal. Conditions specifying the nature, extent, and scope of their participation and conditions under which this commitment can be changed could also be added.

Confidential information. The sample joint venture agreement (see **§ 7.19**) contains additional terms and conditions related to the protection of confidential information and ownership of intellectual property rights.

§ 7.17 Sample Teaming or Pre-Bid Agreement

SAMPLE TEAMING AGREEMENT

____________ PROJECT

TABLE OF CONTENTS

10. Miscellaneous.
    10.1 Bid and Performance Bonds.
    10.2 Entire Agreement.
    10.3 Assignment.
    10.4 Governing Law.
    10.5 Severability.
    10.6 Counterparts.
    10.7 Further Assurances.

THIS AGREEMENT, dated as of ______________, 19___, is by and among __________, a __________ corporation (hereinafter referred to as "Managing Joint Venturer"), __________, a __________ corporation (hereinafter referred to as "__________") and __________, a __________ corporation (hereinafter referred to as "__________") (collectively referred to as the "Team"). The purpose of this Agreement is to define the parties' respective roles and responsibilities in connection with submission of a joint proposal to design, construct and operate a __________ facility and provide __________ services to __________ at a site located at __________ (the "Project").

In consideration of the mutual terms and conditions set forth herein, the parties agree as follows:

1. *THE PROPOSAL*

1.1 The Team, acting as a team, shall prepare a proposal (the "Proposal") for submission to ______________ for the design, construction and operation of a __________ facility to be located at __________, __________ (the "Facility"), in response to the Request For Proposal (the "Request") dated __________, 19___, issued by __________ (the "Sponsor").

1.2 The Proposal shall include the Team's proposals for the following tasks as set out in the Work Scope Allocation Matrix, Appendix 1.2:

a. For the Proposal and any contracts arising therefrom, the Managing Joint Venturer shall be the prime contractor responsible for overall Project management, including (i) integration of the design, engineering, equipment and systems developed and supplied by __________, (ii) contracting for erection of the Facility, installation of equipment and performance testing, (iii) contracting for operation and maintenance of the Facility, and (iv) compliance with __________ requirements and procedures in connection therewith;

b. __________ shall conduct any necessary pre-Proposal and Project environmental audits or surveys of the site and prepare any environmental impact analyses required in connection with the proposed construction and operation of the Facility;

c. __________ shall (i) design and construct the Facility, based on the criteria established by __________ and the site conditions, (ii) install the Facility equipment, and (iii) perform construction tests of the equipment and systems provided;

d. __________ shall be responsible for establishing the general Facility design criteria such as influent specifications and limitations, capacity, size and space requirements for the Facility, and supplying all the technical data, equipment specifications and drawings to support the Project in order to permit __________ to erect the Facility and __________ to operate the Facility in accordance with the specifications contained in the Request;

e. __________ shall provide the equipment specified by __________ and shall guarantee performance of the Facility equipment. Because the equipment is the integral part of the Facility, the overall performance of this equipment shall be the responsibility of __________ up to and including performing any acceptance tests and meeting the acceptance test criteria. Any penalties that accrue due to performance deficiencies resulting from the __________-supplied equipment or its failure to meet Facility design criteria shall be to __________'s account;

f. __________ shall provide to __________ a Facility capable of meeting all operating criteria and performance guarantees, all warranties and equipment performance guarantees obtained from all subcontractors and equipment vendors and a ______ year warranty on workmanship and materials;

g. __________ shall be solely responsible for the operation of the Facility, meeting Facility performance guarantees, repair and maintenance of the Facility; and

h. __________ shall be responsible for and use its best efforts to obtain all permits, approvals, licenses and consents necessary to construct and test the Facility in accordance with the terms of the Request and the Proposal and shall be responsible for ensuring that construction and the results of performance acceptance tests of the Facility comply with all of the terms and conditions of such permits, approvals, licenses and consents. ________ shall be responsible for and use its best efforts to obtain all permits, approvals, licenses and consents necessary to operate the Facility in accordance with the terms of the Request and the Proposal and shall be responsible for ensuring that operation of the Facility complies with all of the terms and conditions of such permits, approvals, licenses and consents.

2. *EXCLUSIVE PROPOSAL*

2.1 No member of the Team shall submit a proposal in response to the Request other than the Proposal to be submitted by the Team. No member of the Team shall associate in any way with any competitor of its own or of any Team member with respect to the Project.

3. *PARTIES' RESPONSIBILITIES*

3.1 Each member of the Team acknowledges that it has fully reviewed the Request, understands its requirements and has taken all steps it believes necessary or desirable to ascertain the nature and scope of work requested, the location of the Project site, any existing facilities related to the Project and local site conditions and to identify the general and specific conditions which would affect the performance of its obligations or the assumption of its responsibilities and costs under this Agreement, the Proposal and under any agreement with the Sponsor or other party entered into pursuant to the Proposal to be submitted.

3.2 Each member of the Team agrees to use its best efforts in preparing and submitting the portions of the Proposal which describe the services that it is to provide. No party hereto is bound to assist any other party in securing any contract except the contracts contemplated by the Request and the Proposal.

3.3 Preparation and submission of the Proposal shall be coordinated by and through the Managing Joint Venturer. Each member of the Team shall select and empower one person to act on its behalf with respect to all matters relating to its rights and obligations under this Agreement, the Proposal and under any contract with the Sponsor or Managing Joint Venturer arising out of the Proposal. A member may change its selection upon written notice thereof to each of the other Team members.

3.4 At least one complete copy of the Proposal shall be furnished to each member of the Team; provided, however, that the Managing Joint Venturer may delete therefrom such material as is identified to it as being proprietary information or a trade secret of a member of the Team except, subject to the provisions of Section 6.1, as necessary to another party's understanding or performance of its obligations set forth in the Proposal.

3.5 Each party hereto agrees to bear all charges, costs and expenses, including, but not limited to, counsel fees, incurred by it in connection with this Agreement, the preparation of the Proposal and selection and award of a contract for the Project.

3.6 In the event of the award to, and execution by, the Team of the contract(s) contemplated by the Request and the Proposal, it is agreed that the Managing Joint Venturer and each other party will, in good faith, negotiate a mutually satisfactory joint venture agreement for the work identified in Section 1.2 hereof, embodying, among other provisions, those terms and conditions required by each of the parties and the laws of the State of ____________.

3.7 The Managing Joint Venturer shall act as the Team's principal negotiator in connection with negotiations with the Sponsor. Each Team member shall, at its own cost, exert its best efforts toward the successful negotiation of the contracts contemplated by the Request and the Proposal and shall provide appropriate and high-quality personnel to perform and support such contracts. Each Team member shall, at its own cost and to the extent it deems necessary, participate in negotiations with the Sponsor to assure that the price, terms and conditions of the Project contracts are satisfactory to it and in agreement with the Team's objectives and this Agreement.

3.8 Each party shall maintain, as appropriate, adequate errors and omissions insurance coverage in an amount customarily carried by similar entities and with deductibles, self-insurance or coinsurance as is customary for entities engaged in the same or similar businesses similarly situated.

4. *TERM OF AGREEMENT*

4.1.1 This Agreement shall commence on the date hereof and, except as otherwise expressly provided in this Agreement or extended by mutual written agreement of all of the parties, shall automatically terminate upon the earliest of any one of the following events:

(i) execution of a contract or contracts between the Team and the Sponsor and a joint venture agreement among the parties to this Agreement to design, construct and operate a ____________ facility as contemplated by this Agreement, the Request and the Proposal;

(ii) any official announcement by the Sponsor to the effect that it will not award the contract(s) contemplated by the Request to the Team;

(iii) any official announcement by the Sponsor of the award of such contract(s) to a bidder other than a member of the Team;

(iv) any official announcement by the Sponsor of the cancellation of the Request;

(v) any official announcement by the Sponsor that no contract will be awarded for the Project described in the Request;

(vi) the elapse of ____________ (____) months from the date of this Agreement; or

(vii) the written agreement of all of the parties.

4.1.2 Any member of the Team which (1) makes any assignment for the benefit of its creditors; (2) suffers the entry of a decree or order for relief by a court having jurisdiction in an involuntary case under the federal bankruptcy laws, as now or hereafter constituted, or any other applicable federal or state bankruptcy, insolvency or similar law now or hereafter in effect; (3) commences a voluntary case under the federal or state bankruptcy laws, as now or hereafter in effect; (4) is the subject of the appointment of a liquidator, assignee, custodian, trustee or sequestrator (or similar official) for it or any substantial part of its general affairs or property and such appointment is not vacated within sixty (60) days; (5) has an attachment levied against any of its assets and such attachment is not vacated within thirty (30) days; (6) has an execution issued against its property which remains unbonded, unpaid, unsatisfied and unstayed for a period of thirty (30) days; (7) is dissolved or liquidated; or (8) is merged with another corporation and such party is not the surviving entity, shall immediately cease to be a member of the Team and shall not thereafter participate in or be a party to the Proposal.

4.2 Termination of this Agreement or of any party thereto for any cause shall not release any party hereto from any liability which, at the time of termination, has already accrued to any other party or which thereafter may accrue in respect of any act or omission prior to such termination.

5. *INDEPENDENT CONTRACTOR STATUS*

5.1 For the purposes set forth in this Agreement, each party hereto shall act as an independent contractor and not as an agent for, partner of or joint venturer with any other party for any purpose whatsoever. No party shall have any authority to bind any other party except to the extent expressly set forth herein.

6. *PROPRIETARY INFORMATION*

6.1 The parties anticipate that it may be necessary for one party to exchange information of a proprietary or confidential nature with another party. Each party agrees that it will enter into an appropriate confidentiality agreement with the owner of such proprietary or confidential information prior to becoming entitled to receive or use such information. Subject to the foregoing, each party agrees to disclose to the other parties all essential technology and information reasonably necessary to prepare a Proposal responding to the requirements of the Request. Without limiting the scope of the foregoing, the parties agree that the specific information and data identified on Appendix 6.1 shall be disclosed to the other parties by the party specified.

6.2 No party receiving confidential or proprietary information shall use such information for any purpose except as expressly set forth herein and in any agreement of the relevant parties made at the time of the disclosure thereof. Internal trade or pricing practices of any of the parties shall not be disclosed or in any way communicated to any other party or person without the prior approval of the party affected.

6.3 Upon expiration or termination of this Agreement and except as necessary to fulfill the terms and conditions of any contracts entered into pursuant to the Proposal, each party shall return to the owner thereof all proprietary and confidential information in its possession or control.

7. *INDEMNIFICATION*

7.1 Each Party agrees to defend, indemnify and hold harmless each of the other parties to this Agreement from and against all losses, liabilities, damages, claims, costs and expenses, including reasonable attorneys' fees and disbursements whether such fees and disbursements are incurred as a result of a third-party claim or a claim under this Agreement (collectively, "losses"), to the extent such losses arise out of such party's wrongful or negligent act or omission in connection with its performance under this Agreement or the Proposal.

7.2 Any party seeking indemnification shall notify the party from whom indemnification is sought as soon as possible after the occurrence of an event for which indemnification will be sought; shall not compromise or settle any such claims without the prior written consent of the party from which indemnification is sought; shall provide that party the opportunity to defend against third-party claims; and shall cooperate in all respects with such defense. These Sections 7.1 and 7.2 are intended solely for the protection of the parties to this Agreement and shall not establish any liability to or benefit for any third parties. Notwithstanding anything in this Agreement to the contrary, no party shall be liable to any other party, except to the extent of contributions to damages awarded to a person other than a party to this Agreement or an affiliate thereof, for indirect, special, incidental, consequential or punitive damages arising out of the performance of this Agreement or any contract with the Sponsor pursuant to the Proposal, whether such damages are based upon contract, tort, negligence, warranty or other legal theory.

8. *DISPUTE RESOLUTION*

8.1 In the event of any dispute between or among parties to this Agreement, each of the parties shall proceed diligently with performance of its obligations under this Agreement pending final resolution of any request for relief, claim, appeal or action arising under or relating to the Agreement.

8.2 Any controversy solely between or among parties to this Agreement and arising out of or relating to this Agreement or the breach hereof in which the claim for money damages of the initiating party is reasonably likely to be less than

$__________ shall be resolved by arbitration conducted in accordance with the Construction Industry Arbitration Rules of the American Arbitration Association (insofar as those rules do not conflict with the provisions hereof). Unless the parties otherwise agree, the arbitration will be held in ________________. The rules pertaining to discovery of information and appeals of judgments rendered in arbitration shall be those set forth in __________.

8.3 Any party may initiate arbitration proceedings by notifying the others in writing that it demands arbitration of such dispute pursuant to this Article 8. Once a demand for arbitration is made, the parties shall endeavor to appoint one mutually acceptable arbitrator, who shall be the sole arbitrator. If the parties are unable to designate one (1) mutually acceptable arbitrator within ten (10) days after the demand for arbitration, then the American Arbitration Association shall make the appointment. The parties will proceed with the arbitration expeditiously and a decision shall be rendered within ninety (90) days from the initial demand for arbitration (the "Return Date"). If, after exercising due diligence, the arbitrator is unable to render an award within ninety (90) days from the initial demand for arbitration, the parties may mutually agree on a later date when the award shall be rendered (the "Extension Date"). If no agreement on a later date can be reached, or if the arbitrator is unable to render an award by the date agreed upon pursuant to this Section 8.3, any rulings or awards issued subsequent to the applicable Return Date or Extension Date shall be void, and the parties may proceed with any action in a court of competent jurisdiction.

8.4 The award of the arbitrator shall be final and binding on all parties, and may be enforced in any court having jurisdiction over the party against which enforcement is sought. Each party shall bear its own expenses, including but not limited to counsel fees, except that all other fees and expenses of the arbitration shall be apportioned in the award of the arbitrator based on the respective merit of the positions of the parties.

9. *SURVIVAL OF OBLIGATIONS*

9.1 The provisions of Articles 6 and 7 shall apply for the duration of this Agreement and shall survive for a period of ______ years after the later of the termination or expiration of this Agreement.

10. *MISCELLANEOUS*

10.1 *Bid and Performance Bonds.* Each party shall be responsible for obtaining and maintaining, at its sole expense, all bid and performance bonds required for the Proposal and the Project to the extent applicable to the services and materials to be supplied by it pursuant to the Proposal and any contracts awarded pursuant thereto. Each party represents that, as of the date of this Agreement, it has the capacity to obtain such bonds as are reasonably anticipated to be required pursuant to the Request for Proposal and the Project and will have such capacity upon the dates of submission and acceptance by the Sponsor of the Proposal.

10.2 *Entire Agreement.* This Agreement constitutes the full and complete understanding and agreement among the parties with respect to the subjects hereof. This Agreement supersedes all prior oral or written agreements, communications and documents among the parties with respect to the subject matter hereof. The terms of any contract awarded pursuant to the Proposal or of any joint venture agreement entered into pursuant to Section 3.6 shall supersede this Agreement to the extent that they conflict with or alter this Agreement.

10.3 *Assignment.* This Agreement may not be assigned, in whole or in part, by any party without the prior written consent of each of the other parties, which consent shall not be unreasonably withheld or delayed. All of the terms and provisions of this Agreement shall be binding upon and inure to the benefit of the respective parties' successors and permitted assigns. Except as expressly provided herein, no party assumes any duty hereunder to any other person or entity which is not a party to this Agreement. This Agreement shall not be construed to provide any benefit to any other person or entity.

10.4 *Governing Law.* This Agreement shall be governed by the laws of the State of ___________ without reference to its principles of conflicts of law.

10.5 *Severability.* Any provision or provisions hereof, or any portion thereof, found to be unenforceable or prohibited by law will be ineffective only to the extent of such unenforceability or prohibition and no other provision of this Agreement will be invalidated thereby.

10.6 *Counterparts.* This Agreement may be executed in any number of counterparts, each of which shall be an original, but all of which together shall constitute one instrument.

10.7 *Further Assurances.* Each of the parties hereby covenants and agrees that it shall hereafter make, execute and deliver any and all such further and other instruments, documents and agreements, and do such other and further acts and things, as may be reasonably necessary or expedient to carry out and give full force to the intent and purposes of this Agreement and to the provisions hereof and to assure that each of the parties hereto enjoys the benefits contemplated by this Agreement.

IN WITNESS WHEREOF, the parties have executed this Agreement as of the date set forth above.

Attest:	______________________________
______________________________	By: ___________________________
	Date: _________________________
Attest:	______________________________
______________________________	By: ___________________________
	Date: _________________________
Attest:	______________________________
______________________________	By: ___________________________
	Date: _________________________

Appendices

Appendix 1.2—Work Scope Allocation Matrix

Appendix 6.1—Information and Data to Be Disclosed

§ 7.18 Joint Venture Agreement Issues

The sample joint venture agreement in **§ 7.19** specifically addresses the following issues, which are particularly important in drafting such an agreement.

Change in law. In section 1.11 of the joint venture agreement, force majeure includes "change in law." For some projects it may be important to establish a more definitive and elaborate definition of change in law. If the change in law risk is significant to the project or if the facility is to be project financed, thus requiring a stable regulatory environment, a change in law could interrupt the project's cash flow necessary to repay the debt. In general, it should be noted that in any project context involving a service agreement between the joint venture and the project sponsor, ultimately the joint venture agreement must be reviewed to ensure that any regulatory, environmental, and risk allocation responsibilities in the service agreement are properly addressed in the basic joint venture agreement. (Section 17.16.) In this way, each joint venture party knows exactly its responsibilities and the extent of those responsibilities, including the potential liabilities. Similarly, "strikes" are included in the definition of force majeure. It may be appropriate to limit the nature of strikes giving rise to relief under this clause.

Capital needs. The capital needs of a particular joint venture may vary according to circumstances. Generally, those needs fall into three categories: (1) construction; (2) operating capital (if the facility is going to be operated by the joint venture); and (3) working capital needs to meet ongoing expenses. The timing of the debt issue and drawdowns to the joint venture (payments under the contract) will be critical in determining how much working capital is required until payments are received from the lender or trustee. (A trustee's role is to ensure that all contractual conditions to payment are satisfied, thus protecting the bondholder.) A further capital need may arise if the joint venture is expected to contribute capital to the project. If the project is to be project financed, the lender(s) may require 15 to 20 percent equity in the project, albeit not from the joint venture engaged on a turnkey contract basis.

Risks. Complex projects require more specific identification of risks that have to be addressed in the agreement. For example, during the design and construction phase, risks include a delay in project completion or increased costs caused by the lack of experience of one of the joint venturers or a problem with a major supplier. Other risks involve the start-up and operating phases: technology failure, obsolescence, changes in law, force majeure or acts of God, changes in availability or price of raw materials, a shift in demand or price of output, and risks related to faulty operation and management. The likelihood of any risk increases or decreases depending on the nature of the project. The very structure of the joint venture approach serves to minimize some of these risks. A joint venture, for example, can be used to reduce equipment or material supply risks if one of the parties is an equipment manufacturer or fuel supplier. Three of the most difficult risks to mitigate, either by strategy or joint venture, are force majeure, changes in law, and shifts in demand. Insurance can cover certain kinds of force majeure risks; however, change in law and shift in demand represent risks requiring more careful analysis by the joint venturers and the project sponsor. Ultimately, the parties must assume responsibility for those risks. If the joint venture accepts any of these risks with respect to the project sponsor, the joint venture agreement should allocate those risks among the joint venturers.

Tax issues. When dividing the profits and losses of the venture (Section 3.1) in connection with the work to be performed thereunder, consider the various allocations of tax benefits to take into account, among other things, the variations in tax appetites and the tax basis of property, if any, contributed to the capital of the venture.

§ 7.19 Sample Joint Venture Agreement

Note. The following draft uses the development of a wastewater treatment facility as an example. Language that applies specifically to this type of facility is bracketed. When drafting agreements for other types of projects, similar provisions tailored to the specific type of facility should be substituted for the bracketed material. Brackets are also used to identify language that deserves special attention when preparing a specific argument.

SAMPLE JOINT VENTURE AGREEMENT
____________ PROJECT

TABLE OF CONTENTS

- 3.3 Failure to Contribute Working Funds.
- 3.4 Distribution of Assets.
- 3.5 Return of Advances.

4. Relationships with Third Parties
   - 4.1 Services and Materials.
   - 4.2 Use of Name.
5. Allocation of Project Responsibilities
   - 5.1 Responsibilities of Joint Venturers.
   - 5.2 Facility Site.
   - 5.3 Facility Design.
   - 5.4 Facility Operations.
6. Insurance
   - 6.1 Insurance.
   - 6.2 Certificates of Insurance.
7. Force Majeure
   - 7.1 Delay of Performance.
   - 7.2 Notice of Force Majeure.
   - 7.3 Mitigation of Effects.
8. Term of Agreement
   - 8.1 Term.
   - 8.2 Accrued Rights.
9. Independent Contractor Status
   - 9.1 Independent Contractor.
10. Proprietary and Confidential Information
    - 10.1 Exchange of Confidential Information.
    - 10.2 Restrictions on Disclosure.
    - 10.3 Ownership of Intellectual Property.
    - 10.4 Confidentiality Agreements.
    - 10.5 Internal Disclosure.
    - 10.6 Copies.
    - 10.7 Return of Confidential Information.
11. Indemnification
    - 11.1 Indemnification.
    - 11.2 Notice of Claim.
12. Dispute Resolution
    - 12.1 Continued Performances.
    - 12.2 Obligation to Arbitrate.
    - 12.3 Initiation of Arbitration.
    - 12.4 Award.
13. Bank Accounts
    - 13.1 Designation of Bank.
    - 13.2 Check Authority.
    - 13.3 Fidelity Bonds.
14. Books and Records
    - 14.1 Maintenance of Books and Records.
    - 14.2 Certification of Books and Records.
    - 14.3 Audit.

THIS AGREEMENT, dated as of ________________, 19____, is by and among, ______________, a ________________ corporation (hereinafter referred to as "____________"), ____________, a ____________ corporation (hereinafter referred to as "____________") and ____________, a ____________ corporation (hereinafter referred to as "____________"). In accordance with the terms and conditions of this Agreement, the parties hereto agree to enter into a joint venture to design, construct, test, operate and maintain a [wastewater treatment] facility and to provide [wastewater treatment] services to [host, municipality, etc.] at a site located at ____________.

In consideration of the mutual covenants and terms set forth herein, the parties agree as follows:

ARTICLE 1
DEFINITIONS

As used in this Agreement, the following terms have the meanings set out below:

1.1 *"Affiliate"* means any person controlling or controlled by or under the common control with any Joint Venturer.

1.2 *"Agreement"* means this Joint Venture Agreement entered into by the Joint Venturers, as amended from time to time.

1.3 *"Applicable Law"* means all legally enforceable local, state and federal laws, rules, regulations, ordinances, permits, licenses, authorizations and agreements applicable to the design, construction, operation, repair and maintenance of the Facility and [Residue disposal], including, or as modified by, legally enforceable judicial or administrative orders or rulings with respect thereto.

1.4 ["Average Daily Flow (or "ADF")" means the cumulative flow of Influent during a calendar month divided by the number of days in the given month expressed in gallons (or fraction thereof) per day.]

1.5 *"Confidential Information"* means all technical information, trade secrets, data, know-how, drawings, computer programs, plans, and all other information of any kind and in whatever form, disclosed or otherwise made available to the Venture by or on behalf of a Joint Venturer and which is designated by the disclosing Joint Venturer as being proprietary or confidential, preferably but not necessarily being marked with legend identifying it as "proprietary" or "confidential."

1.6 [*"Effluent"* means all liquids and other process-related materials, other than storm water runoff and Residue, discharged or otherwise removed from the Facility.]

1.7 *"Eligible Expenditures"* means all reasonable and necessary expenditures which are incurred in connection with the design, construction, testing, operation, repair and maintenance of the Facility, including: (a) __________; (b) __________; (c) ____________; (d) the costs to the Venture of all Venture management; and (e) all debt service of the Venture.

1.8 *"Executive Officer"* means the highest ranking executive officer of each Joint Venturer or one of its affiliated organizations, as agreed upon by the Joint Venturers.

1.9 *"Facility"* means the wastewater treatment facility constructed and operated pursuant to the terms of the Prime Contract.

1.10 *"Fiscal Year"* means the period from January 1 through December 31 of each calendar year or such portion thereof as the Venture shall be in existence.

1.11 *"Force Majeure"* means an act of God, lightning, landslide, earthquake, severe and unusual weather, epidemic, fire, explosion, flood, subsidence, act of a public enemy, strike, government action, war, sabotage, riot, civil disturbance, loss of or inability to obtain utility services, [Influent having a characteristic exceeding the Influent Design Parameters], or any other cause which is beyond the reasonable control of the party affected and the effects of which could not have been avoided by the exercise of reasonable foresight or preventative action by the party seeking relief from its obligations. Force Majeure shall include a change in Applicable Law subsequent to the date of this Agreement.

1.12 ["Gpd" means gallons per 24-hour day.]

1.13 ["Gph" means gallons per hour.]

1.14 ["Influent" means untreated or partially treated sewage and associated liquid waste provided by the Municipality to the Facility for treatment and which may include extra water resulting from inflow, storm water inflow and/or infiltration [but which shall not include ____________].]

1.15 *"Net Profits"* or *"Net Losses"* means the difference between (a) gross revenues and proceeds of indebtedness of the Venture and (b) Eligible Expenditures.

1.16 *"Managing Joint Venturer"* means the Person designated pursuant to Section 2.8.

1.17 ["Peak Daily Flow (or "PDF")" means the maximum cumulative flow of Influent during any calendar day expressed in gallons per day.]

1.18 ["Peak Hourly Flow (or "PHF")" means the highest moving 60-minute arithmetic average of the flow rate of Influent expressed in gallons per hour.]

1.19 "*Municipality*" means ____________.

1.20 "*Person*" means a corporation, partnership, trust, joint venture, company, firm, incorporated organization or association, individual, a government or agency thereof, or public benefit corporation.

1.21 "*Prime Contract*" means the contract [or contracts collectively] between the Venture and the Municipality dated ____________, 19____, for the design, construction, testing, operation, repair and maintenance of the Facility and for the providing of wastewater treatment services, as amended from time to time.

1.22 "*Project*" means the development, construction, operation and maintenance of the Facility and the providing of wastewater treatment services pursuant to the Prime Contract.

1.23 "*Joint Venturers*" means ____________, ____________, and ____________. "Joint Venturer" means any one of the Joint Venturers.

1.24 ["Residue" means screenings, grit, sludge and other process-related materials, other than Effluent and storm water run-off, which are removed from the Facility for disposal, recycling or reuse.]

1.25 "*Venture*" means the joint venture formed and governed by this Agreement.

ARTICLE 2
ORGANIZATION

2.1 *Formation.* The Joint Venturers hereby create a joint venture under the [partnership] laws of the State of ____________ for the limited purposes and scope set forth in this Agreement.

2.2 *Certificates and Approvals.* Prior to conducting any business as or under the name of the Venture, (a) a certificate of doing business shall be filed with the [Office of the Secretary of State] of the State of ____________ and with the [Office of the Clerk of ____________ County] in accordance with Section ______ of the ____________ law of the State of ____________ and (b) all other such licenses, permits, approvals and authorizations required by law to be obtained prior to or as a condition to conducting business as the Venture pursuant to this Agreement shall be obtained.

2.3 *Name.* The name of the Venture is ____________ and the business of the Venture shall be conducted solely under such name.

2.4 *Purpose.* The sole purposes of the Venture are to design, construct, test, operate, repair and maintain a wastewater treatment facility in and to provide wastewater treatment services to [the Municipality] pursuant to the Prime Contract. The Joint Venturers shall do all things necessary, appropriate or advisable in connection with the foregoing purposes. The Venture shall not engage in any other business or devote itself to any other activities unless reasonably incidental thereto.

2.5 *Principal Office.* The principal office of the Venture shall be located at ____________ or at such other place in the State of ____________ as may be selected from time to time by the Joint Venturers. The Venture may maintain such other offices as the Joint Venturers deem advisable.

2.6 *Policy Committee.*

2.6.1 To establish and implement the policies of the Venture and expedite decisions and approvals requiring the joint action of the Joint Venturers, there is hereby established a Policy Committee consisting of one (1) representative appointed by each Joint Venturer who shall be the Executive Officer thereof. The representative of ____________ shall act as chairman of the Policy Committee. By written notice to the other Joint Venturers, each Joint Venturer may from time to time appoint one alternate representative who shall be an employee of the Joint Venturer. The alternate representative shall, in the absence of the principal representative, act as and have the power of the principal representative of the Joint Venturer on the Policy Committee, subject to the terms and to the extent set forth in the notice of appointment.

2.6.2 Each primary member of the Policy Committee shall have one (1) vote [and the votes of each primary member shall be weighted in proportion to its percentage of the Venture set out in Section 3.2]. All actions shall be taken by [unanimous] vote, except in the case where a Joint Venturer or Joint Venturers are in default in performance of the Prime Contract or any subcontract, in which case the [unanimous] vote of the other Joint Venturers not in default shall be required. The principal representative of each Joint Venturer shall be authorized to act for and on behalf of and to bind the Joint Venturer.

2.6.3 The initial Policy Committee shall consist of the following members:

Joint Venturer	Principal Representative
____________________	____________________
____________________	____________________
____________________	____________________

2.6.4 Except as otherwise provided in this Agreement, the business, property and affairs of the Venture shall be managed under the direction of the Policy Committee. The Policy Committee shall establish procedures for conducting its affairs and shall schedule meetings which shall be held at least once quarterly or more frequently as any Joint Venturer deems necessary, at such times and places as set forth by notice to each Joint Venturer. Failure to give notice to any Joint Venturer shall render all actions taken at any non-noticed meeting void unless taken by the unanimous written consent of all Joint Venturers.

2.6.5 The Policy Committee shall have and is hereby granted the following powers and responsibilities on behalf of the Venture and each of the Joint Venturers:

(1) establishment of broad policies to attain the objectives of the Venture;
(2) general management of the business affairs and property of the Venture;
(3) allocation of work assignments, determination and assignment of budgets and determination of personnel requirements from each of the Joint Venturers;

(4) distribution of profits and losses as set forth in Section 3.4 and return of working funds, advances or other assets as set forth in Sections 3.2 and 3.5; and

(5) review and approval of:

   (a) the determination of which portions of the work under the Prime Contract shall be done by which of the Joint Venturers and which portions may be subcontracted to other Persons;

   (b) the selection [consistent with applicable law, including municipal bidding requirements] of subcontractors and subconsultants, including Joint Venturers' parents, affiliates or subsidiaries;

   (c) all financial affairs of the Venture, including the preparation of necessary financial statements and tax returns; and

   (d) settlement of claims by or against the Venture.

2.7 *Managing Joint Venturer.* ____________ shall act as Managing Joint Venturer in all the activities by or on behalf of the Joint Venture. The Managing Joint Venturer shall have responsibility for the day-to-day supervision and management of matters pertaining to the Venture's performance under the Prime Contract or any subcontractor's performance thereunder, subject to the direction of the Policy Committee.

2.8 *Other Business Activities.* Except as set out in Articles 2 and 4, each Joint Venturer shall be free to engage in any other business activity at its sole discretion and for its sole benefit. Except as each Joint Venturer shall otherwise agree, no other Joint Venturer shall have any interest in such other business activity.

ARTICLE 3
CONTRIBUTIONS

3.1 *Percentage Participation.* The interests of the Joint Venturers in, to and under any contracts and the performance thereof in connection with the Venture, and in and to all property acquired, if any, and any and all profits and losses of the Venture in connection with the work to be performed thereunder, shall be divided among the Joint Venturers in the following proportions.

____________________ ______%

____________________ ______%

____________________ ______%

The percentage figures listed above shall be hereinafter referred to as each Joint Venturer's percentage of participation.

The Joint Venturers intend that at all times all losses of the Venture, whether jointly or severally incurred by the Joint Venturers, shall be shared in the proportions above stated and the same shall continue after and survive the completion of any contract entered into by the Venture or any Joint Venturer with [the Municipality].

[Consider differing allocations of tax benefits to take into account, among other things, variations in tax appetites and tax bases of property, if any, contributed to capital of the Venture.]

3.2 *Working Funds.* All necessary working funds when and as required for the Project and affairs of the Venture, and in each such event, shall be furnished by the Joint Venturers in proportion to their percentages of participation set out in Section 3.1 [up to a maximum cumulative amount for any one Joint Venturer of $__________]. Within __________ (_____) days after any call for working funds by the Policy Committee, each of the Joint Venturers shall advance and pay into the Venture its portion of the requested working funds. The need for additional working funds shall be determined from time to time by the Policy Committee. All working funds advanced shall be repaid to the Joint Venturer advancing the same prior to the distribution of any profits as hereinafter provided. No Joint Venturer shall have the power or right to borrow monies on the credit of any other Joint Venturer or the Venture.

3.3 *Failure to Contribute Working Funds.*

3.3.1 Unless and until all Joint Venturers have contributed their proportionate shares of working funds in respect to any single call therefor, each Joint Venturer's contribution toward such call shall be held by the Managing Joint Venturer in escrow and shall be treated as a loan, repayable on demand upon the failure of any one of the Joint Venturers to make its contribution as and when required by such call.

3.3.2 Should any Joint Venturer be unable or fail or neglect to contribute and deposit such initial or additional funds in the Venture Account within __________ (_____) days after the Policy Committee's request for contribution(s) set forth in Section 3.2 above, the other Joint Venturers may, collectively or individually, at their option, pay the share of the defaulting Joint Venturer. In this event, the Joint Venturer(s) paying the defaulting Joint Venturer's share may, at its/their sole discretion:

(1) elect to treat the monies advanced on behalf of the defaulting Joint Venturer as a loan to the defaulting Joint Venturer, with interest accruing at the rate of _____ percent per annum. The principal amount of the loan and all accrued interest shall be due and payable upon completion of the Prime Contract; or

(2) elect to have the Joint Venturers share in any profits of the Venture in the proportions that their actual contributions to the joint working funds bear to the total contributions made to such fund by the Joint Venturers.

3.3.3 The Joint Venturer(s) advancing the share of the defaulting Joint Venturer may make the election set forth in Subsection 3.3.1 no later than the __________ (_____) day after [completion of the Prime Contract and a final determination is made with respect to undistributed profits as set forth in Section 3.4 hereof].

3.3.4 Nothing herein shall be construed to limit or reduce the obligation of the defaulting Joint Venturer to bear its proportionate share of losses suffered by the Venture to the full extent of its percentage of participation.

3.4 *Distribution of Assets.*

3.4.1 The Policy Committee may, from time to time, during the course of the Prime Contract, distribute some of the joint assets held and acquired by the Venture to the parties. Said distribution shall be in accordance with the parties' respective interests in said assets as provided in this Agreement.

For federal, state and local income tax purposes, however, gain or loss shall be reported under the [completed contract method] of accounting and no distribution of cash in excess of the Joint Venturer's tax basis in the Venture shall be made [during the life of the Prime Contract]. In the event one of the Joint Venturers desires funds in excess of its tax basis, it may request a loan from the Venture to be repaid no later than upon completion of the Prime Contract. The Policy Committee shall be empowered to make such loans as it deems proper and at interest rates as determined thereby.

3.4.2 Upon the consummation and completion of the Prime Contract, the remaining assets of the Venture and the profits or losses accrued in the performance thereof shall be divided in accordance with the respective interests of the Joint Venturers as herein provided.

3.4.3 In no event will any advance distribution of any funds pursuant to Section 3.4 reduce the obligation for future expenses of the Venture.

3.5 *Return of Advances.* Except as the Joint Venturers may otherwise agree, no part of any advances for working funds deposited in the Venture bank account or accounts shall be returned to any Joint Venturer and no distribution of profits shall be made [prior to the completion of the Prime Contract] except upon the agreement of the Policy Committee. Except as otherwise provided in Section 3.3, any return of advances for working funds shall be in the ratio of the actual contribution thereof by the Joint Venturers. Except as otherwise provided in Subdivision 3.3.2, any distribution of profits shall be on the basis of the percentage of participation set forth in Section 3.1.

ARTICLE 4
RELATIONSHIPS WITH THIRD PARTIES

4.1 *Services and Materials.* The Joint Venturers agree that all services and materials provided by the Joint Venturers to and from the Project shall be made in the name of the Venture, and that no Joint Venturer will provide services or materials to or for the Project outside the terms of this Agreement [or the Prime Contract] as long as it remains in force without the express prior written approval of all other Joint Venturers.

4.2 *Use of Name.* The names of the Joint Venturers, if used, will be shown with equal prominence on all letterheads, drawings, or printed materials used in any Venture activity. The business of the Venture and the performance of the Prime Contract shall be carried out by the Venture. All money, equipment, materials, supplies and other assets acquired by the Venture shall be jointly held in the name of the Venture.

ARTICLE 5
ALLOCATION OF PROJECT RESPONSIBILITIES

5.1 *Responsibilities of Joint Venturers.* Each of the Joint Venturers has certain of the special skills and experience necessary for the Venture to perform its obligations under the Prime Contract. Each of the Joint Venturers is relying upon the special skills and experience of the other Joint Venturers in the performance of its obligations under the Prime Contract. In order to fulfill the obligations of the Venture under the Prime Contract, each Joint Venturer shall be responsible for performing those portions of the Venture's obligations allocated to it as set forth in Appendix 5.1.

5.2 *Facility Site.* The Facility to be designed, constructed, operated, repaired and maintained by the Venture pursuant to the Prime Contract shall be located on the site described in Appendix 5.2. Each Joint Venturer acknowledges that it has adequately inspected the site, reviewed the data pertaining to the site supplied by [the Municipality] and ___________, and conducted such surveys, analyses and tests at the site [and of any existing facilities] as are necessary or desirable to perform all of its obligations under the Prime Contract as allocated pursuant to Section 5.1.

5.3 *Facility Design.* Each Joint Venturer shall perform the obligations allocated to it under this Agreement and the Prime Contract in a manner such that the Facility shall be capable of meeting at least the minimum design standards set forth in Appendix 5.3 [5.3(a)].

5.4 *Facility Operations.* Each Joint Venturer shall perform the obligations allocated to it under this Agreement and the Prime Contract in a manner such that the Facility is at all times capable of [treating Influent] having the characteristics set out in Appendix 5.4 so that the [Effluent] meets the requirements of Applicable Law [as of the effective date of the Prime Contract].

ARTICLE 6
INSURANCE

6.1 *Insurance.* Each party shall use its best efforts to obtain and maintain, as appropriate, adequate general comprehensive, errors and omissions and such other insurance coverages in amounts customarily carried by similar entities for similar projects and with deductibles, self-insurance or coinsurance as is customary for entities engaged in the same or similar businesses similarly situated, and of the types and in at least the minimum amounts set forth in Appendix 6.1. Each policy shall list the other Joint Venturers as additional named insureds as their respective interests may appear.

6.2 *Certificates of Insurance.* Each Joint Venturer shall furnish to each other Joint Venturer at the conclusion of each fiscal year, and upon any change in the insurance coverages with respect thereto, a certificate signed by its chief financial officer containing a detailed listing of the insurance policies and coverages then outstanding and in full force with respect to the Project and stating that such insurance fully complies with all requirements of this Agreement.

ARTICLE 7
FORCE MAJEURE

7.1 *Delay of Performance.* No Joint Venturer shall be liable to any other Joint Venturer for any failure or delay in its performance of any of its obligations under this Agreement to the extent caused by the occurrence of a Force Majeure subsequent to the date of this Agreement; provided, however, this Section 7.1 shall not excuse a Joint Venturer from any of its obligations to pay any sum of money which such Joint Venturer is otherwise required to pay pursuant to this Agreement (except to the extent making any such payment is expressly prohibited or delayed by Applicable Law).

7.2 *Notice of Force Majeure.* The Joint Venturer whose ability to perform is adversely affected by a Force Majeure shall promptly notify the other Joint Venturers informally, including, but without limitation, by telephone, on the date the Joint Venturer experiencing such event first knows of the commencement thereof. Thereafter within ten (10) days after the date upon which it first knows of such event, the Joint Venturer affected shall provide a written notice to each other Joint Venturer stating (i) the date such event occurred, (ii) its estimated effect and duration, (iii) the requirement for and amount of any additional capital and/or operating expenditures which may become necessary to alter the Facility or its operations as a result of such event, (iv) its impact, if any, on the Facility operations, and (v) its estimated impact on any other obligations of any Joint Venturer under this Agreement or the Prime Contract.

7.3 *Mitigation of Effects.* The Joint Venturer affected by the Force Majeure shall immediately take all reasonable actions to mitigate or eliminate the cause or effect thereof, reduce costs incurred as a result thereof and resume performance of its obligations under this Agreement as soon as practicable. The Joint Venturer affected shall give prompt written notice of cessation of the Force Majeure or the effects thereof to each other Joint Venturer.

ARTICLE 8
TERM OF AGREEMENT

8.1 *Term.* This Agreement shall be effective as of the date hereof and, except as otherwise expressly provided in this Agreement or extended by mutual written agreement of all of the Joint Venturers, shall terminate automatically upon the earliest of any one of the following events:

a. the elapse of one (1) year after expiration or termination of the Prime Contract;
b. the elapse of ____________ (______) months from the date of this Agreement if the Prime Contract has not been executed by all proposed parties thereto within such period;
c. the written agreement of all of the Joint Venturers; or
d. any Joint Venturer: (1) makes any assignment for the benefit of its creditors; (2) suffers the entry of a decree or order for relief by a court having jurisdiction over it in an involuntary case under the federal bankruptcy laws, as now or hereafter constituted or any other applicable federal or state bankruptcy, insolvency or similar law now or hereafter in effect; (3) commences a voluntary case under the federal or state bankruptcy laws, as now or hereafter in effect; (4) is the subject of the appointment of a liquidator, assignee, custodian, trustee or sequestrator (or similar official) for it or of any substantial part of its general affairs or property and such appointment is not vacated within sixty (60) days; (5) has an attachment levied against a substantial portion of its assets and such attachment is not vacated within thirty (30) days; (6) has an execution issued against its general property which remains unbonded, unpaid, unsatisfied or unstayed for a period of thirty (30) days; (7) is dissolved or liquidated; or (8) is merged with another corporation and such Joint Venturer is not the surviving entity.

8.2 *Accrued Rights.* Termination of this Agreement for any cause shall not release any Joint Venturer from any liability which, at the time of termination, has already accrued to any other Person or which thereafter may accrue in respect of any act or omission prior to such termination.

ARTICLE 9
INDEPENDENT CONTRACTOR STATUS

9.1 *Independent Contractor.* Except to the extent necessary for the specific purposes of the Venture, each Joint Venturer shall act as an independent contractor and not as agent for, partner of or joint venturer with any other Joint Venturer for any purpose whatsoever. No Joint Venturer shall have any authority to bind any other Joint Venturer except to the extent expressly set forth herein.

ARTICLE 10
PROPRIETARY AND CONFIDENTIAL INFORMATION

10.1 *Exchange of Confidential Information.* The Joint Venturers anticipate that it may be necessary for one Joint Venturer to exchange Confidential Information with another Joint Venturer. Each Joint Venturer agrees that it will enter into an appropriate confidentiality agreement with the owner of such confidential or proprietary information prior to becoming entitled to receive or use such information. Subject to the foregoing, each Joint Venturer agrees to disclose to the other Joint Venturers all essential Confidential Information reasonably necessary to perform the obligations of the Venture. Each Joint Venturer agrees that the use of such Confidential Information is limited solely to furtherance of the purposes of the Venture. No Joint Venturer receiving Confidential Information shall use such Information for any purpose except in conjunction with its own work and services relating to carrying out its obligations pursuant to this Agreement and the Prime Contract unless otherwise expressly set forth in a written agreement between or among the relevant parties. Internal trade or pricing practices of any of the Joint Venturers shall not be disclosed or in any way communicated to any other Person without the prior approval of the Joint Venturer affected.

10.2 *Restrictions on Disclosure.*

10.2.1 The Joint Venturers and their respective employees, officers, directors, agents, representatives and consultants shall maintain in confidence and shall not further disclose or cause to be disclosed, at any time or in any manner, any Confidential Information except as otherwise provided in this Agreement or except as specifically authorized in writing by the Joint Venturer owning, developing or properly possessing such Confidential Information. Disclosure of Confidential Information by a Joint Venturer shall be limited to those employees, officers, directors, agents, representatives and consultants having a need to know such Information in order to fulfill the Joint Venturer's obligations under this Agreement or the Prime Contract. The Joint Venturers agree to use their best efforts to prevent the unauthorized disclosure of Confidential Information to other Persons.

10.2.2 The non-disclosure provisions of Subsection 10.2.1 shall not apply to information which: (i) is generally available to the public other than as a result of a disclosure by the receiving party or its employees, officers, directors, agents, representatives or consultants; (ii) becomes available to the receiving party on a nonconfidential basis from a source other than the disclosing party which has been represented to the receiving party (and which the receiving party reasonably believes) is entitled to disclose it without restriction; (iii) is required to be disclosed by the receiving party to any governmental authority or agency or other public body pursuant to any law, regulation or judicial or administrative order (provided the receiving party exercises its best efforts and exercises all its rights and takes all such steps in opposing disclosure of Confidential Information as are available to it and to protect the continuing confidential nature of such Information); or (iv) the receiving party can show the Information was previously known to it on a non-confidential basis.

A disclosing party's making of its own Confidential Information available on a confidential basis to other Persons in connection with other business arrangements, or its filing of any documents, papers, tapes or other sources of Confidential Information on a confidential basis pursuant to any law, regulation or requirement of any authorized governmental body or court order, shall not, in and of itself, render such information "generally available to the public."

10.2.3 Neither the disclosing party nor any of its representatives shall have any liability to any receiving party or to any of its representatives as a result of their use of the Confidential Information, it being understood that the disclosing party shall use its best efforts to insure that the Information is accurate and sufficiently complete for the purpose of its intended use. If any information provided to the Venture by a Joint Venturer is determined to infringe upon the rights of any other Person, the disclosing Joint Venturer shall take such steps as are necessary to eliminate the infringing material or obtain appropriate authorization for its use by the Venture.

10.3 *Ownership of Intellectual Property.* Anything patentable or copyrightable, any trade secrets and any proprietary or confidential information produced solely by one Joint Venturer shall remain the property solely of the originating Joint Venturer. Nothing in this Agreement shall be construed as granting any other Person, expressly or by implication, any right or license to use such property as any existing invention, patent application or patent except as previously set forth herein. Anything patentable or copyrightable, or any trade secret or any other information developed jointly by the Joint Venturers during their performance hereunder or under the Prime Contract (except those that relate to __________ proprietary equipment and know-how), shall be owned jointly by all the Joint Venturers. All inventions that relate to __________ technology shall belong to __________. Each Joint Venturer shall, upon request, account to the other Joint Venturers regarding the use and proceeds of use of jointly owned property.

10.4 *Confidentiality Agreements.* Each Joint Venturer agrees that prior to disclosure it will advise all Persons to whom Confidential Information is disclosed or made available of its confidential nature and will obtain their agreement to restrict subsequent disclosure in accordance with the terms of this Agreement. The Joint Venturers further agree that should any Joint Venturer deem it necessary or useful, that Joint Venturer shall obtain nondisclosure agreements from those Persons to whom said Confidential Information is disclosed or made available.

10.5 *Internal Disclosure.* Notwithstanding any provision to the contrary herein contained, the Joint Venturers may disclose, or cause to be disclosed, Confidential Information to those officers and employees of their affiliates who have a need to know such Information in connection with rendering service to the Venture, whether as a member of the Policy Committee, a consultant, or an agent of one of the Joint Venturers whose services are being employed for the Venture; provided, however, that any affiliate, officer or employee to whom such disclosure is made shall first be advised of its confidential nature and agree to the restrictions on disclosure contained in this Agreement.

10.6 *Copies.* Any reproduction or transcription of the Confidential Information made, directly or indirectly, in whole or in part by any means, including, without limitation, photographic, photostatic, electromagnetic, computer tape, or any other device now known or hereafter discovered, and any digest, summary or extract from the Confidential Information shall be made only [upon the prior approval of the disclosing party, and then only] for the purposes set forth in this Agreement.

10.7 *Return of Confidential Information.* Upon expiration or termination of this Agreement, except as necessary to fulfill the terms and conditions of the Prime Contract, each Joint Venturer shall return to the owner thereof all tangible embodiments of Confidential Information in its possession or control. The Joint Venturers agree that each shall hold in trust and confidence for a period no less than ____________ (______) years following expiration or termination of this Agreement, and for so long as the confidential nature thereof shall remain, Confidential Information received from another Joint Venturer pursuant to this Agreement.

ARTICLE 11
INDEMNIFICATION

11.1 *Indemnification.* Each Joint Venturer agrees to defend, indemnify and hold harmless each of the other Joint Venturers to this Agreement from and against all losses, liabilities, damages, claims, costs and expenses, including reasonable attorneys' fees and disbursements, whether such fees and disbursements are incurred as a result of a third-party claim or a claim under this Agreement (collectively, "losses"), to the extent such losses arise out of such Joint Venturer's wrongful or negligent act or omission in connection with performance of its obligations under this Agreement or under the Prime Contract.

11.2 *Notice of Claim.* Any Joint Venturer seeking indemnification shall notify the Joint Venturer(s) from whom indemnification is sought as soon as possible after the occurrence of an event for which indemnification will be sought; shall not compromise or settle any such claims without the prior written consent of the Joint Venturer from which indemnification is sought; shall provide that Joint Venturer the opportunity to defend against third-party claims; and shall cooperate in all respects with such defense. This Article 11 is intended solely for the protection of the parties to this Agreement and shall not establish any liability to or benefit for any other Persons. Notwithstanding anything in this Agreement to the contrary, no Joint Venturer shall be liable to any other Joint Venturer, except to the extent of contribution to damages awarded to a Person other than a Joint Venturer or an Affiliate thereof, for indirect, special, incidental, consequential or punitive damages arising out of performance of this Agreement or the Prime Contract, whether such damages are based upon contract, tort, negligence, warranty or other legal theory.

ARTICLE 12
DISPUTE RESOLUTION

12.1 *Continued Performances.* In the event of any dispute between or among the Joint Venturers, each of the Joint Venturers shall proceed diligently with performance of its obligations under this Agreement and the Prime Contract pending final resolution of any request for relief, claim, appeal or action arising under or relating to the Agreement.

12.2 *Obligation to Arbitrate.* Any controversy arising out of or relating to this Agreement or the breach hereof in which (a) the claim is for money damages which the initiating party reasonably believes is likely to be equal to or less than $____________, and (b) all Persons necessary to accord complete relief as to the claim or who might be inequitably affected by an arbitration thereof are able to be joined as parties to the arbitration, shall be resolved by arbitration conducted in accordance with the Construction Industry Arbitration Rules of the American Arbitration Association (insofar as those rules do not conflict with the provisions hereof). Unless the parties otherwise agree, the arbitration will be held in ____________. The rules pertaining to discovery of information and appeals of judgments rendered in arbitration shall be those set forth in ____________.

12.3 *Initiation of Arbitration.* Any Joint Venturer may initiate arbitration proceedings by notifying the others in writing that it demands arbitration of such dispute pursuant to this Article 12. Once a demand for arbitration is made, the parties thereto shall endeavor to appoint one (1) mutually acceptable arbitrator, who shall be the sole arbitrator. If the parties thereto are unable to designate one (1) mutually acceptable arbitrator within ten (10) days after the demand for arbitration then the American Bar Association shall make the appointment. The parties shall proceed with the arbitration expeditiously, and a decision shall be rendered within ninety (90) days from the date of appointment of the arbitrator (the "Return Date"). If, after exercising due diligence, the arbitrator is unable to render an award on or before the Return Date, the parties may mutually agree on a later date when the award shall be rendered (the "Extension Date"). If no agreement on a later date can be reached, or if the arbitrator is unable to render an award by the Return or Extension Dates, any rulings or awards issued subsequent to the applicable Return Date or Extension Date shall be void, and the parties may proceed with any action in a court of competent jurisdiction.

12.4 *Award.* The award of the arbitrator shall be final (except to the extent otherwise provided in Section 12.2) and binding on all parties, and may be enforced in any court having jurisdiction over the party against which enforcement is sought. Each party shall bear its own expenses, including but not limited to attorneys' fees, except that all other fees and expenses of the arbitration shall be apportioned in the award of the arbitrator based on the respective merit of the positions of the parties.

ARTICLE 13
BANK ACCOUNTS

13.1 *Designation of Bank.* The Policy Committee shall designate the bank or banks for the deposit of Venture funds, and the accounts to be established with such bank or banks. All monies of the Venture shall be deposited with, and all invoices received by the Venture shall be paid by, such bank or banks in such account or accounts in the name of the Venture.

13.2 *Check Authority.* Checks may be drawn on said account or accounts only for the purpose of paying or reimbursing approved expenses related to Venture activities and disbursing the profits, if any. Such checks and all deposits and withdrawals shall be by signature of such person or persons as may be designated from time to time by the Policy Committee.

13.3 *Fidelity Bonds.* All persons authorized to draw against the funds of the Venture shall be bonded by such company or companies and in such amounts as the Policy Committee shall determine. The premiums on such bonds shall be paid by the Venture.

ARTICLE 14
BOOKS AND RECORDS

14.1 *Maintenance of Books and Records.* The Managing Joint Venturer shall maintain the books of account for the Venture, and such books of account may be examined by any of the Joint Venturers at all reasonable times. Reports of the financial condition of the Venture and the progress of work or the Prime Contract shall be made monthly to each member by the Managing Joint Venturer. The cost of maintaining such books shall be a cost of the Venture. The Managing Joint Venturer shall permit representatives of the other Joint Venturers, at all reasonable times, to have access to and inspect, examine and make copies of the Venture's books and records, and of all accounts which in any way relate to the business of the Venture. The books of account shall utilize generally accepted accounting practices (GAAP) applied on a consistent basis throughout the duration of the Venture.

14.2 *Certification of Books and Records.* The books of the Venture as certified by an independent public accounting firm shall be conclusive in establishing whether a profit has been realized or a loss sustained, the amount thereof and the proportionate amount of work performed by any Joint Venturer as of any given time or date.

14.3 *Audit.* A periodic audit of such books of account shall be made by an independent firm of certified public accountants selected by the Policy Committee, and a like audit shall be made upon completion of the Prime Contract. Complete copies of such audits shall be furnished to each of the Joint Venturers. With respect to the periodic audits, there shall be included, if requested by any of the Joint Venturers, a periodic comparison between the items of cost and the items set up in the estimate of cost. The cost of these audits shall be a part of the costs of the Venture. For purposes of the Agreement, the certified figures of the firm of accountants retained to perform the periodic and/or final audits shall be final, conclusive and binding upon the Joint Venturers.

14.4 *Income Accounting.* Income shall be recognized on all work performed within the scope of this Agreement according to the __________ method of accounting.

14.5 *Fiscal Year.* The Venture will have a fiscal year commencing on __________ and ending on __________.

14.6 *Preparation of Tax Returns.* The tax returns for the Venture shall be prepared by __________.

14.7 *Retention of Records.* Records of the Venture which are required to be kept subsequent to the completion of the Prime Contract pursuant to the provisions of law shall be kept at such place or places as determined by the Policy Committee, and the cost thereof shall be borne by the Joint Venturers in accordance with their respective interests as described herein.

ARTICLE 15
NOTICES

15.1 *Giving of Notice.* Any notice required herein shall be in writing and deemed to have been given when sent by registered or certified mail, return receipt requested, or by nationally recognized courier service, addressed as follows:

To: ________________ ____________________________________

____

____

To: ________________ ____________________________________

____

____

To: ________________ ____________________________________

____

____

15.2 *Changes of Address.* Any Joint Venturer may change the address to which notice shall be sent at any time by written notice of such change sent to each of the other Joint Venturers.

ARTICLE 16
SURVIVAL OF OBLIGATIONS

16.1 *Survival of Obligation.* The provisions of Articles 10, 11 and 12 shall apply for the duration of this Agreement and shall survive for a period of ____________ (______) years after the later of the termination or expiration of (a) this Agreement or (b) the Prime Contract.

ARTICLE 17
MISCELLANEOUS

17.1 *Key Personnel.* In performing its obligations under this Agreement, each Joint Venturer shall assign qualified personnel at such time and in such manner as necessary to perform its obligations in accordance with the terms and conditions of this Agreement and the Prime Contract. Without limiting the generality of the foregoing, each Joint Venturer has designated the key personnel identified in Appendix 17.1 to have primary responsibility for and devote the stated percentages of time to the overall conduct and performance of its services hereunder. Provided the relevant key person remains an employee of a Joint Venture, any substantial change to the designation of, nature or scope of responsibilities assigned to, or the extent of the time devoted to, the Venture by any of those key personnel identified on Appendix 17.3 shall be subject to the prior approval of the other Joint Venturers, which approval shall not be unreasonably withheld or delayed.

17.2 *Bid and Performance Bonds.* Each Joint Venturer shall be responsible for obtaining and maintaining, at its sole expense, all bid and performance bonds required for its participation in the Project to the extent applicable to the services and materials to be supplied by it pursuant to this Agreement and the Prime Contract. Each Joint Venturer represents and warrants that (a) as of the date of this Agreement it has the capacity to obtain such bonds as are anticipated to be required pursuant to the Prime Contract and (b) it will have such capacity upon the dates such bonds are required to be provided pursuant to the Prime Contract.

17.3 *Dissemination of Information.* All informational releases, advertising and other publicity concerning the activities of the Venture which are made by or on behalf of the Venture shall be approved in advance by the Policy Committee. This does not preclude any Joint Venturer from disclosing and reporting on its own membership in the Venture.

17.4 *Entire Agreement.* This Agreement constitutes the complete understanding and agreement among the Joint Venturers with respect to the matters set forth herein. This Agreement supersedes all prior oral or written agreements, communications and documents among the Joint Venturers with respect to the subject matter hereof.

17.5 *Assignment.* This Agreement may not be assigned, in whole or in part, by any Joint Venturer without the prior written consent of each of the other Joint Venturers. All of the terms and conditions of this Agreement shall be binding upon and inure to the benefit of the respective Joint Venturers' successors and permitted assigns. Except as expressly provided herein, no Joint Venturer assumes any duty hereunder to any other Person which is not a party to this Agreement. This Agreement shall not be construed to provide any benefit to any other Person.

17.6 *Amendments.* This Agreement may be amended or modified only upon the written agreement of all of the Joint Venturers.

17.7 *Absence of Waiver.* The failure of a Joint Venturer to insist upon strict performance of any provision hereof shall not constitute a waiver of, or estoppel against, asserting the right to require such performance in the future, nor shall a waiver or estoppel in any one instance constitute a waiver or estoppel with respect to a later breach of a similar nature or otherwise.

17.8 *No Termination.* Notwithstanding any provision to the contrary in this Agreement, no Joint Venturer shall transfer all or part of its interest in the Venture to any person, other than another Joint Venturer or its own subsidiary, whether or not such transfer would otherwise be permitted hereunder, if such transfer would result in the termination of the Venture under the United States Internal Revenue Code or analogous law of the State of __________ (collectively the "Code"). At the request of a Joint Venturer and as a condition to the consummation of any transfer of all or any part of a Joint Venturer's interest to any Person other than another Joint Venturer, the Joint Venturer proposing to transfer all or any part of its interests shall, at its cost, provide an unqualified opinion of qualified counsel, which opinion and counsel must be reasonably satisfactory to the other Joint Venturers, that such transfer would not result in such a termination of the Venture under the Code. The Joint Venturer proposing to transfer all or any part of its interest to any Person other than another Joint Venturer shall defend, indemnify and hold harmless the other Joint Venturers from and against any and all loss, cost, liability or expense (including but not limited to reasonable attorneys' fees and disbursements) which such other Joint Venturers may suffer if such transfer, either by itself or together with any other prior transfers of an interest in the Venture of which the transferring Joint Venturer has knowledge at the time of such transfer, causes or would cause such a termination under the Code.

17.9 *Restraining Order.* In the event that any Joint Venturer shall at any time transfer or attempt to transfer its interest in the Venture in violation of the provisions of this Agreement, and any rights hereby granted, then the other Joint Venturers shall, in addition to all other rights and remedies at law and in equity, be entitled to an injunction or order of specific performance enjoining such transfer, and the offending Joint Venturer shall not plead in defense thereto that there would be an adequate remedy at law; it is hereby expressly acknowledged and agreed that damages at law will be an inadequate remedy for a breach or a threatened breach or violation of the provisions concerning transfer as set forth in this Agreement.

17.10 *Rights and Remedies Are Cumulative.* The rights and remedies provided in this Agreement are cumulative, and the use of any one right or remedy by any Joint Venturer shall not preclude or waive its right to exercise or use any or all other rights and remedies. Such rights and remedies are given in addition to any other rights or remedies a Joint Venturer may have by law, statute or otherwise.

17.11 *Representations and Warranties.* Each Joint Venturer represents and warrants to the other Joint Venturers as follows:

17.11.1 It is a [partnership] [corporation] duly organized, validly existing and qualified to do business under the laws of the State of ____________, is in good standing under its [partnership agreement/certificate of incorporation] and the laws of the State of ____________, has the requisite power and authority to own its properties, to carry on its business as now being conducted, to enter into this Agreement, the Prime Contract and the transactions contemplated herein and to perform and carry out all covenants and obligations on its part under and pursuant to this Agreement, and is duly authorized to execute and deliver this Agreement and consummate the transactions contemplated herein.

17.11.2 It is not prohibited from entering into this Agreement or discharging and performing all covenants and obligations on its part to be performed under and pursuant to this Agreement. The execution and delivery of this Agreement, the consummation of the transactions contemplated herein and the fulfillment of and compliance with the provisions of this Agreement will not conflict with or constitute a breach of or a default under any of the terms, conditions or provisions of any law, rule or regulation, any order, judgment, writ, injunction, decree, determination, award or other instrument or legal requirement of any court or other agency of government, its [partnership agreement/certificate of incorporation and by-laws] or any contractual limitation, corporate restriction or outstanding trust indenture, deed of trust, mortgage, loan agreement, lease, other evidence of indebtedness or any other agreement or instrument to which it is a party or by which it or any of its property is bound and will not result in a breach of or a default under any of the foregoing.

17.11.3 It has taken all such [corporate/partnership] actions as may be necessary or advisable and proper to authorize the execution and delivery of this

Agreement, the performance of its obligations assumed under this Agreement and the consummation of transactions contemplated hereby.

17.11.4 This Agreement is a legal, valid and binding obligation of the Joint Venturer, enforceable in accordance with its terms, except as limited by laws of general applicability limiting the enforcement of creditors' rights generally or by the exercise of judicial discretion in accordance with general principles of equity.

17.11.5 No approval, authorization, order or consent of, or declaration, registration or filing with, any governmental authority is required for the valid execution and delivery by the Joint Venturer of this Agreement, except such as have been duly obtained or made.

17.11.6 There is no action, suit or other proceeding, at law or in equity, before or by any court or governmental authority, pending or, to the Joint Venturer's knowledge, threatened against the Joint Venturer wherein an unfavorable decision, ruling or finding would materially and adversely affect the validity or enforceability of this Agreement or any other agreement or instrument entered into by the Joint Venturer in connection with the transactions contemplated hereby, or which would materially and adversely affect the performance by the Joint Venturer of its obligations hereunder or under the Prime Contract.

17.12 *Governing Law.* This Agreement shall be governed by the laws of the State of ___________ without reference to its principles of conflict of laws.

17.13 *Severability.* The Joint Venturers intend each provision of this Agreement to be construed as may be possible and reasonable in a manner which will make it legal, valid and enforceable. Any provision or provisions hereof, or any portion thereof, found to be unenforceable or prohibited by law will be ineffective only to the extent of such unenforceability or prohibition and no other provision of this Agreement will be invalidated thereby.

17.14 *Counterparts.* This Agreement may be executed in any number of counterparts, each of which shall be deemed an original, but all of which together shall constitute one instrument.

17.15 *Further Assurances.* Each of the Joint Venturers hereby agrees that it shall hereafter make, execute and deliver any and all such further and other instruments, documents and agreements, and do such other and further acts and things, as may be necessary or expedient to carry out and give full force to the intents and purposes of this Agreement and to the provisions hereof and to assure that each of the parties hereto enjoys the benefits contemplated by this Agreement. Without limiting the generality of the foregoing, each of the Joint Venturers agrees to amend this Agreement as and to the extent necessary to be consistent with the Joint Venturers' rights and obligations contained in the Prime Contract.

IN WITNESS WHEREOF, the parties have executed this Agreement as of the date set forth above.

Attest: ______________________________

______________________________ By: ______________________________

Date: ______________________________

Attest:	______________________________
______________________________	By: ______________________________
	Date: ______________________________
Attest:	______________________________
______________________________	By: ______________________________
	Date: ______________________________

Appendices
- Appendix 5.1—Work Scope Allocation Matrix
- Appendix 5.2—Site Description
- Appendix 5.3—Minimum Design Parameters for Facility
- Appendix 5.3(a)—Minimum Design Parameters for Cogeneration Facility
- Appendix 5.4—Influent Parameters
- Appendix 6.1—Minimum Insurance Coverage
- Appendix 17.1—Key Personnel

APPENDIX 5.1
WORK SCOPE ALLOCATION MATRIX

Scope of Work	*Joint Venturer Responsible*
1. Facility Design	
2. Obtaining Facility Construction Permits	
3. Facility Construction	
4. Performing and Passing Facility Acceptance Tests	
5. Facility Operation, Repair and Maintenance	
6. Obtaining and Renewal of Facility Operating Permits	
7. Performing and Passing Periodic Facility Performance Tests	
8. Ongoing Facility Environmental Monitoring and Permit Compliance	
9. Residue Disposal	

APPENDIX 5.2
SITE DESCRIPTION

APPENDIX 5.3
MINIMUM DESIGN PARAMETERS FOR FACILITY

1. (a) Annual Wastewater
   Treatment Capacity______ gpd
   (b) Peak Daily Flow______ gpd
   (c) Peak Hourly Flow______ gph

[Add other parameters from Prime Contract]

APPENDIX 5.3(a)
MINIMUM DESIGN PARAMETERS FOR FACILITY
[Cogeneration Facility]

1. Fuel Requirements (assumed fuel characteristics for oil, natural gas, solid waste, waste coal, tires or other fuel source for the Facility; fuel characteristics form the basis for performance guarantees)
2. Net Electricity Output
3. Net Steam Output
4. Steam Conditions
5. Boiler Heat Rate
6. Air Pollution Control Performance

APPENDIX 5.4
INFLUENT PARAMETERS

1. The flow rate of Influent is no greater than: (i) an Average Daily Flow of ____________ (______) gallons; or (ii) a Peak Hourly Flow of ____________ (______) gallons during dry weather; or (iii) a Peak Daily Flow from any storm event of ____________ (______) gallons or (iv) a Peak Daily Flow during dry weather of ____________ (______) gallons; and

2. The Influent contains no chemical, industrial, hazardous, toxic or radioactive materials, as each is defined by Applicable Law, in amounts which could cause or be capable of causing, either alone or by interaction with other substances in the Influent, (i) a materially adverse effect on the Facility or Site or the operation or maintenance of the Facility or, (ii) a danger to human health or safety, or (iii) a violation of any Effluent limitations under Applicable Law pertaining to the Facility; and

3. The Influent contains no more than ____________ (______) pounds per day of five-day biochemical oxygen demand (BOD_5) on an average basis; and

4. The Influent contains no more than ____________ (______) pounds per day of total suspended solids (TSS) on an average basis; and

5. The Influent contains no more than ____________ (______) pounds per day of Ammonia Nitrogen on an average basis; and

6. The Influent contains no more than ____________ (______) pounds per day of Phosphorus on an average basis; and

7. The Influent contains no more than ____________ (______) pounds per day BOD_5 and no more than ____________ (______) pounds per day TSS and no more than ____________ (______) pounds per day of Ammonia Nitrogen and no more than ____________ (______) pounds per day of Phosphorus, each on a moving 30-day average.

APPENDIX 6.1
MINIMUM INSURANCE COVERAGE

APPENDIX 17.1
KEY PERSONNEL

Name	*Position*	*Employer*	*% Devoted to Venture*

CHAPTER 8

PUBLIC SECTOR CONSTRUCTION PROJECTS

F. Alan Cummings
W. Robert Vezina III

F. Alan Cummings is a partner in the law firm of Cummings, Lawrence & Vezina, P.A. He is a graduate of the Florida State University School of Law and has a B.S. from Auburn University, in Auburn, Alabama.

Mr. Cummings handles all aspects of construction disputes from preconstruction and post-award bid disputes to construction litigation on behalf of contractors, owners, subcontractors and design professionals. He has extensive experience in litigating delay claims on major bridge projects throughout the Southeast. Mr. Cummings has authored numerous articles and is a frequent lecturer on the subjects of risk avoidance and construction claims preparation.

W. Robert Vezina III, is a partner in Cummings, Lawrence & Vezina, P.A. He began his practice in construction litigation upon graduation from Duke University School of Law in Durham, North Carolina. He has tried numerous major claims for delay damages regarding highway and bridge projects, as well as a wide variety of both public and private vertical projects. Mr. Vezina's litigation experience provides him with particular insight in the preparation of construction contracts and joint venture agreements. He has authored several articles and is a frequent lecturer on the subjects of delay and disruption claims, trial techniques and contract risk-shifting provisions.

§ 8.1 Introduction

Joint ventures often are used by contractors doing business with federal, state, and local governments, primarily because of the size and complexity of many public works projects. The benefits of spreading risks, pooling resources, combining forces with a contractor with unique expertise or local knowledge, and spreading bonding capacity virtually compel the use of a joint venture for many public projects.

The distinguishing element of public sector contracting is that statutory and regulatory controls attach to public funds. A joint venture seeking a government contract is subject to all procurement statutes and regulations applicable to any other public works contractor. The very nature of a joint venture can give rise to liabilities the coventurers would not have assumed if working alone. For public works joint ventures, these include the debarment of an "innocent" coventurer because of the joint venture's failure to prosecute its contract work timely, or a previously undisclosed contract crime. This chapter addresses matters unique to public sector joint venture work as well as considerations applicable to joint venture projects generally.

The sample teaming (or pre-bid) agreement (see §§ **8.14**) and the sample joint venture form (see § **8.15**) are "field tested." However, any teaming or joint venture agreement must be specifically tailored to the project involved. They must consider the goals of each coventurer and the law of the state governing the joint venture. In a word, such agreements must be flexible to meet the desires of the participants and the demands of a particular project.

§ 8.2 Teaming or Pre-Bid Agreements

The teaming agreement gets one to the altar, the joint venture agreement controls the marriage. There are several reasons why general contractors, designers, or specialty contractors may want to enter into a teaming agreement solely for the purpose of preparing a bid or proposal, and subsequently enter into a joint venture agreement for performing the contract if the bid is successful. The *teaming agreement* is short and addresses only the basic understandings that must be finalized before bidding. The parties can act quickly—an essential given the short lead time for most public procurements—and not get waylaid with details of the full-scale joint venture agreement. In addition, the issues of risk allocation are always critical. The teaming agreement allows the would-be joint venturers to retain the flexibility to negotiate these items at a more considered pace and in light of the realities of the bid and available resources of the participants at the time of contracting.

The sample teaming agreement (see **§ 8.14**) is for contractors who wish to cooperate in the preparation of a bid to be submitted in the name of a joint venture for construction of a project. Another common use of a teaming agreement is in the contractor/designer or contractor/specialty subcontractor context. In such cases, a designer or specialty subcontractor teams with one or more prime contractors during the bidding or proposal stage, with the intent to subcontract with the prime contractor upon award.

Most designers are not prepared to assume risks of construction by entering into a design/control joint venture agreement. Design firms usually do not have the capacity to bond major projects or the capital to share in the funding of a joint venture. The use of a teaming agreement between a contractor and a design firm may be appropriate for bids requiring alternate proposals for major structures with design aspects. The ultimate configuration of such a venture may depend upon the alternative selected by the owner. For example, a contractor/designer collaboration on a steel alternative would not proceed to a subcontract or design/build joint venture if the concrete alternative for the structure were awarded.

Specialty contractors or suppliers often will team with a prime contractor or joint venture in a bid to overcome some of the risks inherent in the normal contractor/subcontractor relationship. Structural steel fabricators, precast yards, or suppliers of stronghold castings for prestressed items or cable stays often can quote lower prices if they have a better understanding of the general contractor's schedule and intended method of construction. In such a teaming relationship, the prime and the specialty contractor can share in the savings and the specialty contractor advances its self-interest to acquire the subcontract.

Often, would-be joint venturers finalize a single joint venture agreement at the pre-bid stage in contemplation of contract award. See **§ 8.14**, Sample Teaming Agreement § 2. Such agreements should provide for termination of the relationship if there is no award. Sample Teaming Agreement § 1.d. The sample joint venture agreement (see **§ 8.15**) was drafted to provide the user maximum flexibility. It addresses issues of organization and management of the joint venture, the division of duties among the parties, cash calls (see **§ 8.7**), liabilities, and indemnification. Alternative approaches are provided for joint venture management and control as discussed in **§ 8.6**. Experience with both the sample teaming agreement and the sample joint venture agreement has shown that these documents reflect the realities of bidding and project management.

§ 8.3 Unique Joint Venturing Considerations in Public Projects

The following three issues are especially important to examine when contemplating a public project joint venture: federal regulations, antitrust constraints, and debarment risks.

Federal Regulations

Most federal regulatory requirements pertaining to joint ventures are contained in the Federal Acquisition Regulation (FAR) and its supplements.[1] The federal government has few express requirements directed to contracting with joint ventures. Likewise, federal and state case law regarding joint venture formation is virtually nonexistent. However, as a matter of federal policy, the government recognizes "contractor team arrangements," which include joint ventures formed to act as a prime contractor.[2]

Though there is no current regulatory requirements that a joint venture agreement be executed by the coventurers prior to submitting a bid or proposal, the federal government usually insists on disclosure of the joint venture in the response to the solicitation.[3] If the joint venture agreement is not signed at the time of submitting a response to the government solicitation, each joint venture participant must sign the government contract. Specifically, FAR 4-102(d), entitled *Joint Venturers,* states:

> A contract with joint ventures may involve any combination of individuals, partnerships, or corporations. The contract shall be signed by each participant in the joint venture. . . . When a corporation is participating, the contracting officer shall obtain from the corporation secretary a certificate stating that the corporation is authorized to participate in the joint venture.

If the joint venture sponsor or managing agent receives a power of attorney to act as the joint venture's attorney-in-fact to sign all contractual documents of the joint venture, this requirement can be met by the single signature.[4]

---

[1] 41 U.S.C. § 405(a); 48 C.F.R. ch. 1, Subchapters A–H. The government-wide federal procurement regulations became effective April 1, 1984.

[2] FAR 9.601(a).

[3] Ingrao, *Joint Ventures: Their Use in Federal Government Contracting,* 20 Pub. Cont. L.J. 399, 401 (Spring 1991) [hereinafter Ingrao] (citing FAR 52.215–6 n.4).

[4] *Id.* at 402 (citing FAR 4-102(c) n.6).

Antitrust

Federal government procurement policy clearly prohibits any joint venture arrangement in violation of antitrust laws.[5] However, antitrust violations do not pose a substantial risk for the typical joint venture construction project.

First, the federal contracting officer usually obtains a copy of the joint venture agreement prior to award of the contract. Therefore, the government has had an opportunity to review the agreement for antitrust violations prior to award. Though contract award does not act as an approval for antitrust law compliance, the likelihood of a subsequent attack on antitrust grounds appears remote.

Second, as compared to a purely commercial joint venture, a construction contract joint venture is typically limited to a single contract. Even though follow-on projects may be included within the contract, the joint venture is dealing with a single owner governed by stringent federal regulations insuring the integrity of the competitive process. This situation is ill-suited to fostering restraints on trade.

Debarment and Suspension

Federal and state (and usually local) regulations authorize public owners to disqualify, debar, or suspend contractors from bidding for various causes. Generally, grounds for disqualification fall into two categories: the contractor either is found guilty of some type of contract crime or other fraudulent or illegal conduct, or fails to prosecute its contract work timely. When the guilty or derelict contractor is a member of a joint venture, the ramifications can be particularly harsh to its fellow innocent coventurers.

Often, one joint venture firm has insufficient bonding capacity for large public works. Consequently, it forms a joint venture with a company with ample bonding capacity. The firm providing the bonding may expend little or no out-of-pocket expenses and perform little or none of the work. Although it may exact a substantial percentage of the contract profits in return for "lending" its bonding capacity to the joint venture, it also assumes a substantial risk of debarment even though it is not actively engaged in the prosecution of the work. If the venturer charged with responsibility for performing the work fails to perform competently, the joint venture may be found delinquent in the progress of the work or, at worst, be defaulted. On federal contracts and in most states, each coventurer will suffer the consequences of the joint venture's failure to perform.

Federal government regulations provide that the government is entitled to hold the joint venture fully responsible for contract performance.[6] Similar regulations

---

[5] FAR 9.604.

[6] *Id.* 9.601(a).

in some states make it clear that each coventurer is fully liable to the state for the joint venture's bid and contract performance.[7] Under these regulations, the government may consider each venturer jointly responsible for a delinquency even though the company providing nothing more than capital or bonding capacity did not participate in the defective execution of the work. Thus, a financially secure and responsible company may find itself facing debarment solely because of the failure of its joint venture partner to fulfill its responsibilities.

Contract crimes also can impact an innocent coventurer. Under the federal regulations, fraudulent or criminal conduct of one venturer may be imputed to the other if the improper conduct occurs in furtherance of the project for which the joint venture was formed or if the nonculpable venturer receives the benefit of the improper conduct.[8] The consequences may include debarment.

State regulations may be even more onerous. Typically, state rules provide that the public owner shall revoke or deny the qualification to bid of any contractor and its affiliates for several months or years when it is determined that the contractor has been convicted of a contract crime within the jurisdiction of any state or federal court.[9] Neither the contractor nor its affiliates may act as a prime contractor, material supplier, subcontractor, or consultant on any department contract or project during the period of revocation or denial.[10] The term "affiliate" often is broadly defined to include coventurers. Thus, if one venturer is disqualified for delinquency, the other venturer may also be disqualified.

For these reasons a company contemplating a joint venture should exercise due diligence with respect to the responsibility and contract crimes history of its would-be coventurer.

§ 8.4 Privatization of Public Projects

Privatization simply means building public projects with private funds. Some states expressly recognize the privatization alternative to the traditional financing of public transportation projects with public sources of revenue. For example, California statutorily authorizes privately funded "build-operate-transfer" projects whereby private entities obtain exclusive development agreements to build, with private funds, all or a portion of public transportation projects.[11] Under this scheme, the private entity has the right to lease the facility from the state and charge tolls sufficient to retire the private investment in the project (including a reasonable profit), operate and police the facility, maintain the

---

[7] *See, e.g.,* Fla. Admin. Code Ann. r. 14-22.0101(4).

[8] Ingrao at 403.

[9] *See, e.g.,* Fla. Admin. Code Ann. r. 14-22.012.

[10] *Id.*

[11] Cal. Sts. & High. Code § 143 (West 1992).

facility, retire any outstanding bonds issued in support of the facility, and make lease payments to the state.[12]

Teaming agreements and joint venture agreements are uniquely designed to take advantage of private sector efficiencies in design and construction and to allow for rapid formation of capital necessary for funding transportation projects. However, a proposal for a transportation project may take some time to develop and its character may change during the negotiation and approval process. Therefore, the teaming agreement must have the capability of releasing venturers and adding venturers, or terminating and reconstructing itself in a new form. This enables the surviving interested parties to go forward and protect themselves from former venturers who have dropped out but might prepare a competing bid or form a separate joint venture.

In a typical privatization project, the initial proposal likely will be governed by a teaming agreement in which the designer, contractor, and developer agree to share the costs of conceptual designs and estimates. When and if an award for a proposal is given, the contractor will form a joint venture with other general contractors, and that joint venture will subcontract a final design to the initial designer. This joint venture also could participate in a separate joint venture to bring the infrastructure portion of the project to a stage where the developer will operate and maintain the completed facility and develop any other assets provided as part of the privatization arrangements, for example commercial facilities servicing the highway users.

The California Department of Transportation broke new ground in privatization by developing several demonstration projects to test the feasibility of building privately funded transportation facilities. The developers were granted 35-year leases to recoup their investment through toll and land development revenues. In this way, the financial viability of the demonstration projects would be assured by the certainty of toll revenues. Other privatization schemes require funding guarantees from the public owner. For example, a cogeneration scheme depending on methane from a large county's landfill would probably require a guarantee of a minimum volume of waste and a minimum price for energy generated.

A privatization scheme in Pennsylvania involves 20-year leases with title transferring to the state at the end of that period. The prisons were built by joint ventures of contractors that first teamed with designers and made proposals to the state. The state prison authorities engaged bond counsel and financial advisors, selected proposals based on a guaranteed maximum price from the joint venturers, and sold bonds to fund the contracts.

The combinations of teaming and joint venture agreements for privatization works are limited only by the imagination and resources of the participants.

---

[12] *Id.*

§ 8.5 Organization, Management, and Control

Managerial and organizational provisions of teaming agreements are generally less complex than those employed in joint venture agreements because of the short-term nature of the relationship. All parties to a teaming agreement should participate in the final check of a bid or proposal to insure that the documents are in order and all requirements have been met. This procedure may avert mistakes and, if there is a mistake, the parties will share the error, thus reducing likelihood of recrimination.

The simplest teaming agreement organization involves two contractors; one takes the lead and the second contractor simply provides a check bid. That is, after each contractor prepares an independent bid, the lead contractor consolidates the bid documents and checks its bid against the second contractor's bid. Generally, the principals of the potential joint venturers will meet to review the estimates and make appropriate revisions. In this scenario, the parties have joint responsibility for every aspect of the bid price and, absent a further understanding, one party does not accept responsibility for a particular aspect of the work.

When a general contractor teams with a specialty contractor, a logical division of labor exists. The specialty contractor provides an estimate for the portion of the work relating to its expertise and, in most instances, agrees to subcontract that work at the price bid.

Ultimate authority for management of a joint venture is typically shared by a committee composed of one or more representatives of each venturer. The *management committee* usually delegates responsibility for day-to-day operations to one of the parties or to a project manager, but reserves certain key decisions for itself. The management committee should retain the authority to take over or reassign management of day-to-day operations as necessary throughout the course of the project.

The management committee can be organized to act either unanimously or by majority vote in proportion to the ownership interests of the venturers. Requiring decisions to be made unanimously provides each party with a veto of any possible overreaching by its coventurers and forces the parties to develop a consensus approach to management decisions. However, the requirement of consensus may cause the management committee to be too sluggish to be effective and presents the risk of a management deadlock.

If the management committee operates by majority vote based on participation interests, the parties with the most at stake in the joint venture's operations have the strongest voice in management. To protect the concerns of minority venturers, unanimity can be required for actions concerning particular key issues. Examples of such issues include:

1. Purchases, loans, or other transactions above a specified dollar amount
2. Bringing or settling lawsuits

3. Modification or termination of the contract with the project owner
4. Decisions to make a cash call (see § **8.7**).

Depending upon the specific concerns of the parties, particular items can be added to or deleted from this list.

The sample joint venture agreement (§ **8.15**) includes in §§ 2.3 and 2.4 alternative management committee approaches. Under the first alternative, all actions taken by the committee must be unanimous vote. Deadlocks are resolved by the chief executive officers of the coventurers. Under the second alternative, each coventurer has a voice in the management committee equal to its participation interest in the profits of the joint venture. The management committee acts upon consent of the party or parties having participation interests in profits totaling more than 50 percent.

§ 8.6 Scope of Services

In the simplest joint venture agreement, two general contractors jointly bid a project and one goes forward as the lead venturer and manages the project. The incentive for the arrangement is to share bonding capacity, with the added benefit of a check bid.

The incentive for a design/construct combination involving a specialty contractor and a general contractor is business opportunity. The designer and the specialty contractor provide technical expertise that gives the general contractor a marked advantage, and both venturers have an enhanced opportunity for business. The division of responsibility between a general contractor, designer, or specialty contractor is relatively simple because the technical abilities of the parties are readily discernible.

When assets such as equipment, supervision, or management capabilities are shared, the scope of services provided by the parties becomes a more difficult issue. Capital such as equipment must be fairly valued by the joint venturers and remuneration for management and services must also be determined. It is best to resolve equipment rental rates, labor charges, and service charges before signing a joint venture agreement because the potential for dispute over these issues is high. The joint venture agreement should incorporate a listing and schedule of values for equipment, labor, and service charges.

When a joint venturer also supplies a manufactured product to the project, a predetermined product price should be established. These products might include precast concrete products such as piles or girders, and specialty mechanical items that are produced when the specialty contractor both designs and manufactures a portion of the project. Normally, these manufactured products should be valued at the bid price.

§ 8.7 Capitalization and Funding

The common funding technique for most joint venturers is the *cash call*. A determination is made regarding the capital requirements of the joint venture and each venturer is called upon to contribute its proportionate share of the necessary capital. Thus, the venturers can delay capital contribution in the joint venture until the funds are actually needed, then they call upon their own resources to provide the necessary capital.

In many instances, capital contributions may include services, equipment, materials, or other property. The joint venture agreement should make clear that all capital contributions must be made in cash unless the parties specifically agree otherwise so that the joint venture is not placed in the position of liquidating or disposing of unwanted in-kind contributions. See **§ 8.15**, Sample Joint Venture Agreement § 4.3.

One of the most difficult problems a joint venture can face is a shortfall in capital contributions. Normally, a party that fails to meet a cash call will have its interest in profits of the joint venture reduced in proportion to its capital shortfall. In many instances, a venturer's failure to meet a cash call is merely symptomatic of more serious problems within the organization and the financially responsible party probably will be forced to perform virtually all of the obligations of the joint venture. A stringent agreement might exclude a venturer failing to meet a cash call from management of the joint venture, and cause a proportionate reduction in profit although its proportionate share of liability for losses remains unchanged. A less severe approach is to reduce that party's share of profits proportionately to its ultimate investment. This is the most common practice and the one employed in §§ 3.2 and 3.4 of the sample agreement (see **§ 8.15**).

§ 8.8 Tax Issues

Joint ventures are generally treated as partnerships for federal income tax purposes. A tax professional should be consulted regarding the federal and state tax consequences of contributions of property and services to the joint venture and of distributions made by the joint venture.

The joint venture agreement typically designates one of the parties as the "tax matters partner" for the joint venture. The tax matters partner is authorized by statute to act on behalf of the other venturers in certain dealings with the Internal Revenue Service.[13] The joint venture agreement also should specify the taxable year for the joint venture or provide a mechanism for its designation. The joint venture agreement should use the percentage of completion method for tax reporting purposes because of the danger of the tax attribution rules and the

---

[13] *See* I.R.C. §§ 6221–6231 (1992).

limited exceptions to the percentage of completion method for tax purposes.[14] See sample agreement § 7.5.

If the joint venture makes a taxable profit in any tax year, the taxable income will be attributable to the coventurers. The failure of joint venture management to distribute the profit will not excuse the payment of tax. Coordinating the timing and amount of partnership income with each joint venturer's tax advisor can prevent the unplanned receipt of taxable income or worse, the payment of income tax on money not received from the joint venture.

§ 8.9 Risk, Liability, and Indemnification

Generally, members of a joint venture are jointly and severally liable for the acts or omissions of coventurers except in certain limited circumstances. This means that any coventurer may be held responsible for the entire amount of a claim brought by a third party against the joint venture. The recourse for the coventurer who has paid the claim or satisfied the judgment is to seek reimbursement from the other venturers, ideally pursuant to the joint venture agreement's indemnification clause.

In addition to general law, public construction contracts with joint ventures usually contain express provisions establishing the joint and several liability of joint venturers for full performance of the requirements of the contract.[15] The federal government normally insists on such an express provision in its contracts even though no procurement regulations or federal law mandate its inclusion.[16]

In a construction context various claims may arise based on a single venturer's conduct that binds the other members. As between the owner and the joint venturer directly, a common claim is for liquidated damages. If one venturer is responsible for delaying the prosecution of the work so that the contract is not completed on time, the other members and the joint venture are each exposed to the liquidated damages assessment. Likewise, the joint and several liability of the joint venture and its members applies to subcontractors' claims arising out of the project.

Construction contracts usually contain provisions requiring the contractor to indemnify the project owner for claims brought by third parties. For example, when the public owner is sued because a car accident allegedly resulted from a dangerous condition caused by the construction, the contractor is required to defend and indemnify the owner. When the contractor is a joint venturer, the basic principles of joint and several liability would apply and each venturer may be independently liable.

---

[14] I.R.C. § 460 (1992).

[15] FAR § 9.604.

[16] Ingrao at 402.

Of course, if a venturer incurs liability as a result of conduct wholly unrelated to the joint venture, the other venturers are not responsible. For example, A and B might form AB joint venture for the purpose of building an interstate highway project. At the same time, A is independently constructing an entirely separate project on a state highway. B cannot be held liable for claims arising out of the state highway project, but will be liable for claims arising out of the interstate project even if A's conduct is the sole cause of the claim. If A's resources are overburdened because it is working on the state highway so that the interstate project falls behind, B will be liable for the consequences of the interstate delay. However, if the car accident scenario occurs on the state highway project, B would incur no liability.

Standard risk-shifting and risk-avoiding mechanisms such as insurance, indemnity agreements, payment and performance bonds, and limitations of liability should be employed. In most instances, each of the parties will have to accept the risk of the other venturer's financial failure. In some instances, it is possible to bond either the performance or the contributions of the other joint venturer, although practical difficulties and costs associated with these protections generally prohibit their use.

Given the application of joint and several liability, the indemnification clause of the joint venture agreement is critically important. In § 6.1 of the sample joint venture agreement (see **§ 8.15**), a coventurer accepts financial responsibility for its own negligence or breach of contract. Although joint and several liability exists to the outside world, a just reckoning among joint venture participants is assured through a well-drafted indemnification clause, assuming, of course, the parties' financial stability.

§ 8.10 Warranties and Guarantees

To the extent possible, the responsibility for guarantees should be attributed to the coventurer that performed the work or supplied the guaranteed equipment or material. If subcontract agreements and purchase agreements are carefully drafted, the liability for most guarantees will be assumed by manufacturers and subcontractors. A common problem is matching the guarantee period in the project contract with the guarantee period provided by the subcontractor or supplier.

Warranties are related to the performance of the work and the quality of that performance. Common provisions require the contractor to warrant to the owner that:

1. The materials and equipment furnished will be new unless otherwise permitted
2. The work will be free from defects and of the specified quality
3. The work will conform to the requirements of the contract documents.

Implied warranties that the work was performed in a workmanlike manner and that the labor and materials are of a merchantable quality also attach unless they are specifically disclaimed in the project contract.

Joint venturers typically agree to be held liable for any actions on warranties to the extent of a venturer's own work. This form of risk allocation applies only to joint ventures in which each party performs a definable portion of the work and there is no aspect of the work where a shared responsibility is required. For example, the specialty coventurer for a proprietary process will warrant only its portion of the work.

Another reason designers may want to avoid a joint venture design-build relationship[17] is that warranty liability for construction often approaches a standard of strict liability. A contractor does not have to be found negligent to breach its warranty obligations. Conversely, a designer must be negligent before it will be liable for providing a defective design. The increased risk to a designer involved in a design/build joint venture is significant and a designer may find that the increased cost of insurance may preclude such a relationship.

§ 8.11 Default Provisions

The possibility of the insolvency or bankruptcy of a joint venture participant must be considered in the joint venture agreement. The provisions reducing a venturer's share in the joint venture if it fails to make cash calls generally address the issue unless the other venturers are relying upon the financial resources of the insolvent venturer. If the joint venture is ongoing and successful, a loan might be sufficient to insure the performance of the venture and to prevent default.

Because of the uncertainties of ownership and management and the intercession of creditors, bankruptcy of a joint venture participant requires a more aggressive stance. One possible clause would provide that a bankrupt venturer loses all rights to have any voice in the joint venture from the effective date of any bankruptcy filing. See §§ **8.15**, sample Joint Venture § 10. The language should clearly state that the party will continue to have liability and responsibilities under the joint venture agreement, although such a clause may not be enforced fully in a bankruptcy proceeding.

§ 8.12 Termination of the Joint Venture

Every joint venture agreement should provide for an orderly termination after the purpose of the joint venture is fulfilled. The FAR and some state laws require designation of one of the venturers as the custodian of records and that

---

[17] See § **8.2**.

the records of the joint venture must be kept as required by contract, statute, or regulation. State contracts typically require that such records be maintained for periods of three to seven years.

It is not uncommon for a construction project never to receive a final completion certificate. Therefore, including a provision that the management committee can terminate the joint venture upon cause is recommended. Bonding and insurance companies may require evidence of the termination of a joint venture before expanding coverage.

§ 8.13 Dispute Resolution

Joint venture participants should realize that the purposes and responsibilities of the joint venture will continue despite an internal dispute. Because public sector contractors inevitably have a duty to proceed under the contract, any interruption of the work can lead to a default.

Addressing likely disputes when the parties enter into the joint venture is the best method of preventing disputes during the operation of the joint venture. The committee form of joint venture is more likely to lead to a deadlock than the sponsoring partner form of agreement. The sponsoring partner form provides wider latitude in day-to-day operations to the sponsoring partner, and the vast majority of possible disputes can be resolved by a vote of 51 percent of the joint venture. Remaining issues must be resolved through negotiation or other forms of dispute resolution.

Including several levels of review and resolution in the agreement is a process that has been found to be successful. Once an issue is raised, it should go to the management committee for resolution. If the committee reaches a deadlock, the dispute should be referred to the chief executive officers of the venture partners for resolution on an expedited basis. Construction industry experience indicates that most disputes can be resolved at this level.

The next level of resolution is either arbitration or a judicial proceeding. Arbitration is generally speedier and less costly than litigation. It is advisable that the joint venture agreement contain an arbitration clause specifying which rules will govern (for example, the Construction Industry Arbitration Rules of the American Arbitration Association). See sample § 11. Choice of law and venue are considerations that should also be addressed in the agreement. Arbitration is not available in some states if that state's law controls. The Federal Arbitration Act is available if a nexus to interstate commerce can be found.

With respect to claims between the joint venture and the owner, joint venture agreements often specify the parties' respective responsibility for attorneys' fees and other claim expenses. If a federal contract is involved, the Contract Disputes Act of 1978 will apply.[18] Under the Act, certification by each

---

[18] 41 U.S.C. §§ 601–613.

coventurer of joint venture claims over $50,000 may be required.[19] It is a relatively simple matter to provide in the joint venture agreement that each member will sign any owner-directed claim urged by one party if it appears to be in conformance with all applicable regulations. Any liabilities incurred by a coventurer based on submission of a fraudulent claim by one of the parties should be subject to indemnification under the joint venture agreement.

§ 8.14 Sample Teaming Agreement

SAMPLE TEAMING AGREEMENT

TABLE OF CONTENTS

This Teaming Agreement (the "Agreement") is entered into as of this ______ day of ____________ , 199____ , by and between Adam Construction Company, Inc. ("Adam"), a corporation organized and existing under the laws of the State of ____________ , Baker Construction Company, Inc. ("Baker"), a corporation organized and existing under the laws of the State of ____________ , and Charlie Construction Company, Inc., ("Charlie") a corporation organized and existing under the laws of the State of ____________ .

WITNESSETH

WHEREAS, ____________ ("Owner") is seeking competitive bids for construction of ____________ located in ____________ (the "Project"); and

---

[19] Boeing Co., ASBCA No. 36,612, 89-1 B.C.A. (CCH) ¶ 21,421 (1988).

WHEREAS, Adam is an experienced general contractor with expertise in project management and heavy construction; and

WHEREAS, Baker is a contractor with expertise in the area of __________ construction which is an important aspect of the Project; and

WHEREAS, Charlie is a general contractor with construction experience in the locale of __________; and

WHEREAS, Adam, Baker and Charlie (the "parties") wish to cooperate in the preparation of a bid for construction of the Project to be submitted to the Owner in the name of a joint venture to be formed by the parties; and

WHEREAS, In the event that the bid is successful, the parties, as joint venturers, wish to enter into and perform a contract with Owner for construction of the Project;

NOW THEREFORE, in consideration of the foregoing premises and the mutual covenants and agreements set forth below, and for other good and valuable consideration, the receipt and adequacy of which is hereby acknowledged, the parties agree as follows:

1. *Bidding.*

a. *Cooperation.* Each party shall cooperate fully in the preparation and submission of a bid for construction of the Project by a joint venture to be formed by the parties (the "joint venture"). The parties shall use all reasonable commercial efforts to ensure that the joint venture is awarded a contract to construct the Project.

b. *Noncompetition.* During the term of this Agreement, no party shall submit or collaborate on any competing bid for work on the Project or perform any work on the Project other than pursuant to the terms of this Agreement or for or on behalf of the joint venture.

c. *Preparation.* The bid shall be submitted in the name of the joint venture. Baker shall be primarily responsible for preparing the bid relating to the __________ phase of the work. Adam shall be primarily responsible for preparation of the remaining portions of the bid. Charlie shall solicit prices form local subcontractors as required by Adam and Baker. Wherever possible, the parties shall cooperate in all facets of bid preparation.

d. *Termination.* It is the intent of the parties hereto that the joint bid contemplated and provided for herein shall be satisfactory and acceptable to all parties. If the parties are unable to agree upon a joint bid, this Joint Venture shall terminate upon written notice by the dissenting party to the other parties, which written notice shall be delivered to the other party or parties prior to the time of the bid, and in such event no party shall have any liability to any other party or parties.

2. *Joint Venture Agreement.*

Prior to submission of a bid for construction of the Project, the parties shall enter into a joint venture agreement substantially in the form of Exhibit A.

3. *Costs and Liability.*

Each party shall be solely responsible for the costs and liabilities it incurs in connection with the preparation of the bid. No party shall assume any such liability or obligations of the others, nor shall a party reimburse any costs or expenses incurred by the others in connection with bid preparation.

4. *Confidential Information.*

Each party agrees to maintain in confidence any proprietary, confidential information owned or licensed by the other parties, provided that the confidential information is prominently identified as such by affixing a legend to any tangible embodiment of the information or, in the event the information is not in tangible form, by verbal identification of the information at or before the time of its disclosure, followed by prompt written confirmation of the confidential nature of the information. Except as expressly provided in this article 4, nothing in this Agreement shall prohibit a party from future use or disclosure of information learned or created in the performance of the work contemplated by the Contract.

Confidential information shall not include information which: (i) is known to the receiving party prior to its disclosure; (ii) is or becomes generally available to the public through no act or failure to act by the receiving party; (iii) has been or is disclosed to the receiving party by a third party who did not acquire such information under an obligation of confidentiality; or (iv) is independently developed by the receiving party who, at the time of such independent development, did not have access to confidential information provided pursuant to this Agreement.

5. *Miscellaneous.*

a. *Entire Agreement.* This Agreement, including exhibits, shall constitute the entire agreement and understanding between the parties pertaining to the subject matter hereof and shall supersede all prior or contemporaneous agreements, representations, negotiations, drafts and understandings of the parties.

b. *Attorneys' Fees.* In the event that any dispute between the parties should result in litigation, the prevailing party shall be reimbursed for all reasonable costs incurred in connection with such litigation, including, without limitation, expert witness fees and attorneys' fees for trial and appeal.

c. *Amendment and Waiver.* No supplement, modification, or amendment of this Agreement shall be binding unless executed in writing by all parties. No waiver of any provision of this Agreement shall be deemed, or shall constitute, a waiver of any other provision, whether or not similar, nor shall any waiver constitute a continuing waiver, unless expressly and unambiguously so specified. No waiver shall be binding unless executed by the party making the waiver.

d. *Assignment.* This Agreement is not assignable by either party, but shall be binding upon and inure to the benefit of each party and its successors (by operation of law or otherwise).

e. *Governing Law and Venue.* This Agreement shall be governed by and construed under the laws of the State of ____________ without regard to its choice of law rules. The venue for any proceeding relating to this Agreement shall be ____________ County, ____________.

f. *Counterparts.* This Agreement may be executed in one or more counterparts, each of which shall be deemed an original, but all of which together shall constitute one and the same Agreement.

g. *Titles and Subtitles.* The titles and subtitles for articles and paragraphs used in this Agreement are used for convenience only and are not to be considered in construing or in interpreting this Agreement.

h. *No Third-Party Beneficiaries.* No person or entity other than the parties hereto shall have any right hereunder or be entitled to the benefit of any provision hereof.

i. *Notices.* All notices, requests, demands or other communications required or permitted under this Agreement shall be given in writing and shall be deemed effectively given (i) on the date of service if served personally or transmitted by electronic facsimile on the party to whom notice is to be given, (ii) one day after prepaid dispatch by overnight courier to the party to whom notice is to be given, or (iii) five days after mailing to the party to whom notice is to be given by first class mail, registered or certified, postage prepaid. All such notices shall be addressed as follows:

To Adam at: Adam Construction Company, Inc.

____

____

Facsimile Number: ____________________

Attention: ________________________

To Baker at: Baker Construction Company, Inc.

____

____

Facsimile Number: ____________________

Attention: ________________________

To Charlie at: Charlie Construction Company, Inc.

____

____

Facsimile Number: ____________________

Attention: ________________________

Any party may change its address for purposes of notice by giving notice of the new address to the other parties in the manner set forth above.

j. *Further Assurances.* At any time or from time to time after the date of this Agreement, each party agrees that it shall, at the request of another party and at the expense of such requesting party, execute and deliver any further instruments or documents and take all such further actions as such requesting party may reasonably require in order to effect the provisions of this Agreement.

IN WITNESS WHEREOF, the parties hereto have executed this Agreement as of the date first written above.

ADAM CONSTRUCTION COMPANY, INC.,
a __________ corporation

By: ________________________

Title: ________________________

BAKER CONSTRUCTION COMPANY, INC.,
a __________ corporation

By: ______________________________

Title: ______________________________

CHARLIE CONSTRUCTION COMPANY, INC.,
a __________ corporation

By: ______________________________

Title: ______________________________

§ 8.15 Sample Joint Venture Agreement

SAMPLE JOINT VENTURE AGREEMENT

TABLE OF CONTENTS

SAMPLE

This Joint Venture Agreement (the "Agreement") is entered into as of this ______ day of ____________, 199____, by and between Adam Construction Company, Inc. ("Adam"), a corporation organized and existing under the laws of the State of ____________, Baker Construction Company, Inc. ("Baker"), a corporation organized and existing under the laws of the State of ____________, and Charlie Construction Company, Inc. ("Charlie"), a corporation organized and existing under the laws of the State of ____________.

WITNESSETH:

WHEREAS, __________ ("Owner") is seeking competitive bids for construction of __________ located in __________ (the "Project"); and

WHEREAS, Adam, Baker and Charlie (the "parties") wish to form a joint venture for the purpose of submitting a bid for construction of the Project; and

WHEREAS, in the event that the joint venture is the successful bidder for the project, the parties, as joint venturers, wish to enter into and perform a contract (the "Contract") with Owner for construction of the Project; and

WHEREAS, the parties wish to enter into this Agreement in order to define and express their mutual rights and obligations as joint venturers;

NOW THEREFORE, in consideration of the foregoing premises and the mutual covenants and agreements set forth below, and for other good and valuable consideration, the receipt and adequacy of which is hereby acknowledged, the parties agree as follows:

1. *Formation and Scope.*

1.1 *Formation.* The parties hereby associate themselves as joint venturers, solely for the purposes of preparing and submitting a bid on the Project and, if the joint venture is the successful bidder, entering into and performing the Contract.

1.2 *Name.* The name of the joint venture shall be "Adam Construction Company, Inc., and Charlie Construction Company, Inc., a Joint Venture."

1.3 *No Partnership.* This Agreement does not create a partnership or any agency beyond that expressly provided for in this Agreement.

1.4 *Noncompetition.* During the term of this Agreement, neither party shall submit or collaborate on any competing bid for work on the Project or perform any work on the Project other than for or on behalf of the joint venture. Nothing in this Agreement shall be construed to otherwise limit or impair the rights of any party to engage in any business activity not directly relating to the Project.

2. *Management.*

2.1 *Representatives.* Each party shall appoint a single representative with full authority to act on all matters related to the joint venture. Any party may designate a new representative by delivering written notice as provided in this Agreement. In the event a party's representative shall resign or otherwise be unable to perform his duties, a replacement representative shall be named within twenty-four (24) hours. The initial representatives shall be as follows:

For Adam: ______________________________

____

____

For Baker: ______________________________

____

____

For Charlie:____

____

____

2.2 *Project Manager.* Upon receipt of notification that the joint venture is the successful bidder on the Project, the management committee shall appoint a project manager to oversee the day-to-day management of the work of the joint venture on the Project. The project manager shall perform such duties as may be specified by the management committee and shall be under the control and direction of the management committee.

[Alternative 1—Unanimous Vote.

2.3 *Management Committee.* The representatives appointed by the parties shall constitute the management committee which shall have full authority to direct the affairs of the joint venture. All actions taken by the management committee shall be by unanimous vote.

2.4 *Deadlock.* In the event that the management committee is unable to agree upon the proper management of the affairs of the joint venture, any member of the management committee may so notify the chief executive officer of each of the parties. The notice shall briefly describe the subject and reasons for the deadlock. Within three (3) days after receipt of such notice, the chief executive officers or their designees shall meet to attempt to resolve the deadlock. In the event the deadlock unresolved, a party may institute a demand for arbitration as provided in this Agreement.]

[OR]

[Alternative 2—Voting by Participation Interest.

2.3 *Management Committee.* The representatives appointed by the parties shall constitute the management committee which shall have full authority to direct the affairs of the joint venture. Each party shall have a voice in the management committee equal to its participation interest in the profits of the joint venture. The management committee may act upon consent of the party or parties having participation interests in profits totaling more than fifty percent (50%).

2.4 *Unanimous Voting.* Decisions regarding the following matters shall be made only upon the unanimous vote of the management committee:

a. Commencement, presentation or settlement of any lawsuit or claim relating to the Project;

b. transactions between any party and the joint venture; and

c. any purchase, sale, loans, borrowings, guarantees or other financial transactions or commitments reasonably expected to exceed __________ dollars ($______).]

3. *Participation in Profits and Losses.*

3.1 *Percentage Interests.* Subject to adjustment as provided in this Agreement, the participation interests of the parties in the profits and losses of the joint venture shall be as follows:

Adam	____%
Baker	____%
Charlie	____%

3.2 *Default.* If a party shall default on its obligations to provide working capital as required by this Agreement, that party's participation interest in losses shall be unaffected, but its participation interest in profits shall be reduced, and the other parties' participation interests in profits shall be increased proportionately, so that the respective participation interests of the parties in the profits of the Joint Venture shall be in the same proportion as the total amounts of working capital contributed. A party whose participation interest in profits has been reduced under the terms of this paragraph shall not be permitted to cure its default or restore its participation interest in profits by a subsequent payment of its required capital contribution or otherwise. Each default of an obligation to provide required working capital shall result in a separate reduction of the defaulting party's participation interest in profits.

4. *Working Capital.*

4.1 *Capital Contributions.* The management committee shall determine from time to time the amount of working capital reasonably required for the orderly and efficient conduct of the joint venture's operations. Within ten (10) days after receipt of notice of any such determination, each party shall contribute a portion of the total capital required equal to that party's participation interest percentage in the profits of the joint venture.

4.2 *Failure to Make Contributions.* In the event a party shall fail to promptly make its required capital contribution, that party's interest in joint venture profits shall be reduced as provided in paragraph 3.2 above and the shortfall in such party's contribution shall be immediately contributed by the other parties.

4.3 *Contributions in Kind.* At the sole discretion of the management committee, all or a portion of a party's capital contribution may be made in the form of labor, equipment, materials or other services or property. In such event, the management committee and the contributing party shall mutually agree on the value of the services or property contributed. In the event that an agreed valuation cannot be determined, the contributing party shall make the required capital contribution in cash. Notwithstanding the foregoing, it is specifically agreed that Adam shall be permitted to contribute the property listed on Exhibit A, Baker shall be permitted to contribute the property listed on Exhibit B and Charlie shall be permitted to contribute the property listed on Exhibit C. Such property shall be valued as set forth in the exhibits.

4.4 *Borrowing.* The joint venture shall have authority to borrow or lend funds on such terms and for such purposes as it shall determine to be reasonably necessary to carry out the purposes of this Agreement.

4.5 *Bank Accounts.* The joint venture shall establish and maintain one or more bank accounts for the orderly administration of its working capital. The number and kind of such accounts and the persons entitled to draw thereon shall be determined from time to time by the management committee.

4.6 *Reimbursement.* Each party shall be reimbursed by the joint venture for actual expenses incurred in performing work required under the Contract and performed at the direction or request of the management committee; *provided, however,* that no reimbursement shall be made with respect to any expense which is incurred as a capital contribution under paragraph 4.3 above. No reimbursement shall be made for ordinary overhead or home office expenses, for interest on funds contributed as working capital or for services or other expenses incurred in connection with the formation or general management of the joint venture.

5. *Employees.*

5.1 *Employees of the Joint Venture.* The joint venture may employ personnel on a full- or part-time basis as necessary or appropriate to carry out its operations. In the event that any such personnel are employees of a party, the compensation of such personnel (including actual wages or salary, payroll taxes and a labor burden of ______% as an allowance for insurance, fringe benefits and other expenses) shall be paid by such party and shall be reimbursed as provided in paragraph 4.6 above.

5.2 *Employees of the Parties.* Each party shall be solely responsible for the employment, compensation and performance of its own employees. The employees of one party shall not be deemed to be employees of the other party.

6. *Indemnification and Insurance.*

6.1 *Indemnification.* Each party shall, to the fullest extent permitted by law, indemnify, defend and hold harmless the other parties to this Agreement, the joint venture, and the directors, officers, employees, agents and consultants of each party (each an "Indemnitee") from and against any loss, expense or liability, including attorneys' fees, incurred by reason of or in connection with any of the following acts by such indemnifying party or its directors, officers, employees, agents or consultants (collectively the "Indemnitor"):

(i) the sole negligence, recklessness or willful acts of any Indemnitor(s);

(ii) the partial or mixed negligence of any Indemnitor(s); provided that the liability of such Indemnitor(s) shall be reduced by the percentage of fault attributable to persons other than the Indemnitor(s);

(iii) any breach of the Contract, including any modifications, supplements or amendments thereof;

(iv) any breach of this Agreement, including any modifications, supplements or amendments hereof; or

(v) any Proceeding (as defined below) resulting from or concerning any event of the kinds described in subparts (i) through (iv) of this paragraph 6.1.

As used in this paragraph 6.1, "Proceeding" means any threatened, pending or completed action, suit or other type of proceeding, whether civil, criminal, administrative or investigative and whether formal or informal.

6.2 *Insurance.* The joint venture shall at all times maintain all insurance required by the Contract. The joint venture shall also maintain insurance providing the types and amounts of coverage set forth on Exhibit D. In addition, the joint venture may maintain additional insurance covering such risks and in such amounts as the management committee may deem appropriate from time to time.

7. *Accounting.*

7.1 *Books and Records.* The joint venture shall maintain its own books and records and shall make them available for inspection by the parties and their consultants at all reasonable times.

7.2 *Tax Matters Partner.* Adam shall be the "tax matters partner" for federal, state and local income tax purposes.

7.3 *Fiscal Year.* The management committee shall designate the fiscal year of the joint venture.

7.4 *Financial Statements.* The joint venture shall prepare unaudited financial statements within thirty (30) days after the end of each fiscal quarter and shall cause its accountants to prepare audited financial statements no later than ninety (90) days after the end of each fiscal year.

7.5 *Basis of Accounting.* The joint venture shall use the percentage of completion method to account for the Contract for both income tax and accounting purposes.

8. *Confidentiality.*

8.1 *Confidential Information.* In the course of performing this Agreement or the work encompassed by the Contract, the parties may disclose to each other certain proprietary information either (i) in writing and marked "confidential," "secret," or any other marking identifying such information as information which shall not be disclosed to unauthorized persons, or (ii) orally and identified orally as confidential at the time of disclosure and confirmed promptly thereafter by written notification to the other party, which notification shall be effective when delivered (the "Confidential Information"). Confidential Information shall not include information which: (i) is known to the receiving party prior to its disclosure; (ii) is or becomes generally available to the public through no act or failure to act by the receiving party; (iii) has been or is disclosed to the receiving party by a third party who did not acquire such information under an obligation of confidentiality; or (iv) is independently developed by the receiving party who, at the time of such independent development, did not have access to Confidential Information provided pursuant to this Agreement.

8.2 *Nondisclosure.* The parties agree that all Confidential Information regarding the Project has been or will be provided in good faith and confidence and constitutes valuable property to the disclosing party, the unauthorized disclosure of which would result in economic damage to the disclosing party. The parties agree that each will use due diligence to insure that Confidential Information originated by the other party is not disseminated or disclosed by it to any unauthorized person or persons. Upon the expiration or termination of this Agreement and the contract, a party may request the others to deliver it to all Confidential Information previously provided which is then in the receiving party's possession or control.

8.3 *Unauthorized Persons.* For purposes of this article 8, the term "unauthorized person" shall mean anyone other than (i) an employee of the joint venture or of a party who reasonably requires access to Confidential Information in order to perform work required under the Contract or this Agreement, or (ii) any other person to whom the disclosing party has authorized in writing disclosure of such Confidential Information.

9. *Dissolution and Winding Up.*

9.1 *Term of Agreement.* This Agreement and the joint venture created hereby shall commence as of the date first written above, and unless extended by agreement of the parties, shall terminate upon the first to occur of the following:

(i) the Owner's announcement that the Project has been canceled or that award of the Contract has been postponed indefinitely;

(ii) uncontested award of the Contract to another bidder;

(iii) termination of the Contract, whether upon full performance, default or otherwise; or

(iv) the agreement of all of the parties to terminate this Agreement.

9.2 *Provision for Payment of Debts.* Upon termination of this Agreement, the management committee shall make appropriate arrangements, including the establishment of adequate reserves, for the payment of all debts and the performance of all obligations of the joint venture.

9.3 *Distribution.* At the conclusion of the joint venture, the assets of the joint venture shall be allocated first to pay all debts and obligations of the joint venture and to fund all reserves established for such payments. All remaining assets shall be distributed to the parties in accordance with their respective participation interests in profits, as those interests may have been adjusted by the terms of paragraph 3.2 above.

10. *Bankruptcy.*

In the event that a party to this Agreement shall become bankrupt or insolvent, shall commit any act of bankruptcy or shall take advantage of any bankruptcy, reorganization, moratorium or similar protection from creditors, then such party shall immediately lose all rights to participate in the management or control of the joint venture or the performance of work under the Contract. The participation interest of such party in the profits and losses of the joint venture shall be determined in accordance with article 3 above.

11. *Disputes.*

In the event that any dispute shall arise between the parties relating to this Agreement, the management or operations of the joint venture, performance of the Contract or construction of the Project, the parties shall use their best efforts to promptly resolve such dispute by mutual agreement. In the event that a party deems such efforts to be unsuccessful, that party may request arbitration of any dispute under the Construction Industry Arbitration Rules of the American Arbitration Association. If any dispute between the parties affects or threatens the orderly or timely progress of the work, the joint venture shall proceed with the work as directed by the project manager. In no event shall any dispute be permitted to delay the progress of the work required by the Contract.

12. *Miscellaneous.*

12.1 *Entire Agreement.* This Agreement, including exhibits, shall constitute the entire agreement and understanding between the parties pertaining to the subject matter hereof and shall supersede all prior or contemporaneous agreements, representations, negotiations, drafts and understandings of the parties.

12.2 *Attorneys' Fees.* In the event that any dispute between the parties should result in litigation, the prevailing party shall be reimbursed for all reasonable costs incurred in connection with such litigation, including, without limitation, expert witness fees and attorneys' fees for trial and appeal.

12.3 *Amendment and Waiver.* No supplement, modification, or amendment of this Agreement shall be binding unless executed in writing by all parties. No waiver of any provision of this Agreement shall be deemed, or shall constitute, a waiver of any other provision, whether or not similar, nor shall any waiver constitute a continuing waiver, unless expressly and unambiguously so specified. No waiver shall be binding unless executed by the party making the waiver.

12.4 *Assignment.* This Agreement is not assignable by either party, but shall be binding upon and inure to the benefit of each party and its successors (by operation of law or otherwise).

12.5 *Governing Law and Venue.* This Agreement shall be governed by and construed under the laws of the State of __________ without regard to its choice of law rules. The venue for any proceeding relating to this Agreement shall be in __________ County, __________ .

12.6 *Counterparts.* This Agreement may be executed in one or more counterparts, each of which shall be deemed an original, but all of which together shall constitute one and the same Agreement.

12.7 *Titles and Subtitles.* The titles and subtitles for articles and paragraphs used in this Agreement are used for convenience only and are not to be considered in construing or in interpreting this Agreement.

12.8 *No Third-Party Beneficiaries.* No person or entity other than the parties hereto shall have any right hereunder or be entitled to the benefit of any provision hereof.

12.9 *Notices.* All notices, requests, demands or other communications required or permitted under this Agreement shall be given in writing and shall be deemed effectively given (i) on the date of service if served personally or transmitted by electronic facsimile on the party to whom notice is to be given, (ii) one day after prepaid dispatch by overnight courier to the party to whom notice is to be given, or (iii) five days after mailing to the party to whom notice is to be given by first class mail, registered or certified, postage prepaid. All such notices shall be addressed as follows:

To Adam at: Adam Construction Company, Inc.

____

____

Facsimile Number: ______________________________

Attention: ______________________________

To Baker at: Baker Construction Company, Inc.

____

____

Facsimile Number: ______________________________

Attention: ______________________________

To Charlie at: Charlie Construction Company, Inc.

____

____

Facsimile Number: ____________________________

Attention: ________________________________

A party may change its address for purposes of notice by giving notice of the new address to the other parties in the manner set forth above.

12.10 *Further Assurances.* At any time or from time to time after the date of this Agreement, each party agrees that it shall, at the request of any other party and at the expense of such requesting party, execute and deliver any further instruments or documents and take all such further actions as such requesting party may reasonably require in order to effect the provisions of this Agreement.

IN WITNESS WHEREOF, the parties hereto have executed this Agreement as of the date first written above.

ADAM CONSTRUCTION COMPANY, INC.,
a ____________ corporation

By: ____________________________

Title: ____________________________

BAKER CONSTRUCTION COMPANY, INC.,
a ____________ corporation

By: ____________________________

Title: ____________________________

CHARLIE CONSTRUCTION COMPANY, INC.,
a ____________ corporation

By: ____________________________

Title: ____________________________

CHAPTER 9

JOINT VENTURES FOR TELECOMMUNICATIONS PROJECTS

Andrew D. Lipman

Andrew D. Lipman is a partner with the Washington, D.C., law firm of Swidler & Berlin, where he heads the firm's telecommunications practice. The firm specializes in representing providers of competitive telecommunications services and emerging communications and computer technologies. Mr. Lipman is a graduate of the University of Rochester and Stanford Law School. A frequent author and speaker on telecommunications-related topics, he has published over 150 articles, and is the author of four books.

---

§ 9.1 Introduction

The judicially imposed breakup of AT&T[1] vastly expanded the construction opportunities in the telecommunications industry. The dissolution of monopolistic

---

[1] *See* United States v. American Tel. & Tel. Co., 552 F. Supp. 131 (D.D.C. 1982), *aff'd sub nom.* Maryland v. United States, 460 U.S. 1001 (1983) (Modified Final Judgment).

control over the United States telecommunications infrastructure, combined with the advent of pro-competitive and deregulatory policies at the Federal Communications Commission (FCC) and, to a lesser extent, state regulatory agencies, have made the construction of new and improved telecommunications systems a growth area. In addition, because telecommunications services are technology-driven, advances in technology provide a continual source of demand for construction of new and improved telecommunications networks.[2]

§ 9.2 Unique Considerations in Telecommunications Contracts

As with all construction projects, and particularly with telecommunications construction projects, each joint venture is unique. The precise terms and conditions of a joint venture agreement will depend on the undertaking of the joint venture, the nature of the telecommunications system to be constructed, and the distribution of responsibilities between the venturers. This chapter explores generally three major issues that are unique and apply to most joint ventures for construction of telecommunications networks. These issues are:

1. Regulatory approvals
2. Technical specifications and acceptance testing
3. Liability for network outages.

§ 9.3 Regulatory Approvals and Regulation

In the telecommunications industry, joint ventures often combine the construction experience and financial resources of two venturers. In some telecommunications ventures, one party may be responsible for contributing its substantial telecommunications industry experience and the other party is expected to bring its construction and financial resources to the table. As with other joint venture arrangements, it is imperative that the purpose of the joint venture, as

---

[2] Increasingly, opportunities for construction of telecommunications systems are found at the metropolitan and local level. For example, the emergence of competitive access providers offering services that compete with those of local telephone companies has led to a vast expansion of the number of fiber optic networks in major metropolitan areas. In addition, a potential high-growth area likely to open substantial new system construction opportunities in the near future upon authorization by the FCC is personal communications services (PCS). PCS, in some ways similar to cellular telephone systems, is anticipated to include the offering of radio-based stations strategically located throughout a metropolitan area that access a backbone network, which may consist of a newly constructed network or existing networks.

well as the specific responsibilities and rights of each venturer, be clearly defined in the joint venture agreement.

A thorough review and understanding of the federal, state, and local regulatory requirements applicable to a telecommunications network's construction and operation is essential to the success of this type of joint venture. Although the FCC and some state regulatory agencies have reduced (and continue to streamline) the regulation of many telecommunications carriers and their services, regulation remains a central consideration in telecommunications construction and its application should be fully considered. Indeed, in telecommunications joint ventures, the scope of the undertaking of the joint venture will determine the regulatory approvals required to construct and operate the network. From a regulatory perspective, a joint venture formed to construct a telecommunications network for a third party who will operate the network differs significantly from a joint venture formed both to construct and operate a telecommunications network. Accordingly, the undertaking of the joint venture will dictate, in large part, the regulatory issues that will arise and need to be addressed in a joint venture agreement.

For many telecommunications services and networks, the regulation is multilayered, emanating not only from the FCC but also from state public utility commissions and local governments. One factor that contributes to the multilayered regulatory environment is the unique expansive nature of telecommunications networks in general. Construction projects such as an office building or hospital may be confined to the borders of a defined tract of private property, but telecommunications networks are often designed to provide comprehensive coverage to end-users throughout a metropolitan area. As a result, they transverse public rights-of-way, private property, and government-owned property. Thus, one of the primary issues in telecommunications construction is where and how the network will be constructed and installed. For certain projects, regulatory authorizations will be required before construction. In other cases, although not required, it may be advantageous to obtain regulatory authorizations early on to gain access to public rights-of-way and facilitate access to private property. The regulatory authorizations necessary to construct a telecommunications network may include construction permits, permits to use public right-of-ways, FCC authorizations, certificates of public convenience and necessity from state public utility commissions and local franchises. The three levels of regulation that are involved in most telecommunication construction projects are explained briefly in §§ **9.4** through **9.6**.

§ 9.4 —Federal Regulation

As a general matter, the FCC exercises jurisdiction over communications that are both interstate and interexchange (that is, intrastate long-distance toll services).[3] The FCC rules and regulations that apply to a particular construction project and joint venture depend heavily on the communications services and the transmission media used to provide those services. For example, different FCC regulations apply to services that use the radio frequency spectrum than to fiber optic networks constructed in metropolitan areas that provide interstate services. Specifically, construction of networks to provide certain radio-based services, such as cellular services, often requires FCC authorization in the form of a radio station license prior to the commencement of construction.[4] The radio station authorization issued by the FCC typically specifies an effective date and an expiration date for the construction authority. The joint venture agreement to construct a telecommunications system must therefore take into account the FCC construction authority requirements in establishing a completion of work schedule based on specific time frames and milestones for project completion.

By contrast, the FCC currently does not require competitive access providers seeking to construct fiber optic networks in metropolitan areas to obtain a construction permit or other FCC authorization prior to the commencement of construction even if the network will carry interstate communications.[5] Accordingly, in creating a joint venture it is important to identify the services that will be provided and determine to what extent, if any, FCC regulations apply.

§ 9.5 —State Regulation

State law and the regulations of state public utility commissions may also apply to networks constructed to provide telecommunications services if all or a portion of the services are *intrastate* services. Statutes and regulations governing telecommunications carriers vary substantially from state to state. Generally, however, the legal status of jurisdictionally intrastate services depends, in the first instance, on whether they are classified as utility services under applicable state law. To the extent that a service is regarded as a public utility offering, it will likely be subject to various regulatory obligations arising under state law and ensuing public utility commission regulations.

Most states require that, prior to the offering of telecommunications services, the telecommunications company obtain a certificate of public convenience and

---

[3] The allocation of jurisdiction between federal and state regulatory agencies over a communications facility is not, however, based solely on whether the facility crosses state lines. The allocation of jurisdiction depends, rather, on the nature of the communications carried by the facility.

[4] *See, e.g.*, 47 C.F.R. § 22.43(a) (1991). *Cf. id.* § 22.43(d).

[5] Such a carrier could be classified as a private carrier by the FCC or as a nondominant common carrier exempt from entry and rate regulation by the FCC.

necessity, or similar authority, to provide intrastate telecommunications services. For strategic reasons and to facilitate the construction process, it is often advisable to obtain certification prior to commencing construction. For example, certificates of public convenience and necessity may be helpful (or essential) in obtaining access to public rights-of-way. In some states, certification by the state public utility commission will endow the company with the authority to condemn property by eminent domain proceedings. At a minimum, a certificate can be used as a persuasive negotiating tool for obtaining access to private property necessary for construction of the network.

State regulation can also hamper the prospects for construction of a telecommunications network. For example, although some states have followed the FCC's generally competitive and deregulatory policies, others continue to prohibit competitive service offerings.[6] Therefore, a threshold issue that must be resolved at the outset is whether the intrastate services to be provided over the network are permitted by state law and regulation. If the service is permitted, the scope and application of the state regulations should also be analyzed. For example, some states either require a regulated entity providing telecommunications services to obtain regulatory approvals prior to the issuance of forms of indebtedness or impose other, sometimes burdensome, obligations on the telecommunications carrier.[7]

§ 9.6 —Municipal Regulation

Municipal and local law may also apply to the construction and operation of a telecommunications project by a joint venture. With the growth of competitive entrants seeking to construct telecommunications networks in metropolitan areas, local governments increasingly have begun to assert jurisdiction over these telecommunications networks and their construction. For example, many local governments in metropolitan areas have begun to require competitive access providers to obtain permits or franchises in order to construct and operate fiber optic networks in their cities. As a condition of the franchise, local governments are beginning, with increasing regularity, to seek to impose a significant franchise fee on competitive access providers. In some metropolitan areas, a

---

[6] Some states do not permit the competitive offering of certain intrastate services. For example, Nevada does not permit companies other than the local exchange carrier to provide service that is within a local area transport area (LATA). LATAs are distinct geographical areas that were created and adopted for use in the *Modified Final Judgment* to define the permissible service territories of the local Bell companies such as Ohio Bell and interexchange carriers such as AT&T and MCI.

[7] *See, e.g.,* N.Y. Pub. Serv. Law § 101 (McKinney Supp. 1992).

franchise is required to obtain access to public right-of-ways and to obtain construction permits. Other cities have imposed limitations on access to public rights-of-way to prevent continual and disruptive construction. Restrictions on new construction and property access are likely to increase, especially in major metropolitan areas, as the number of entrants seeking to construct networks also increases. For example, some jurisdictions have imposed temporary moratoriums on construction in their central business districts; other jurisdictions have begun imposing annual franchise fees based on a percentage of gross revenues.

§ 9.7 —Checklist of Regulatory Issues

The different regulatory issues that apply to a specific joint venture for construction of a telecommunications construction project are as diverse and varied as the possible combinations of regulatory authorities who could assert jurisdiction over the project and the proposed network's services. It is beyond the scope of this article to provide a comprehensive listing of regulatory issues that could arise in joint venture agreements for telecommunications construction projects. As a starting point, however, the following checklist can be used as a guideline for spotting potential regulatory issues:

____ 1. Are the services to be provided over the constructed network permitted by federal, state, and local law?

____ 2. What regulatory authorizations are required to provide service over the completed system from the:

   a. FCC?

   b. State Public Utility Commission?

   c. Municipality?

____ 3. Is regulatory authorization required *prior* to construction of the project from the:

   a. FCC?

   b. State Public Utility Commission?

   c. Municipality?

____ 4. Would prior regulatory authorization be helpful to obtain access to property for construction of the system?

   a. Does state or local law grant telecommunications companies or public utilities that have received regulatory authorization a right to use public rights-of-way or invoke the right of eminent domain?

   b. Are private property owners, such as landlords, or government entities more likely to give permit construction on their property to entities that have received regulatory authorization?

____ 5. Where and how will the network be constructed and installed?
   a. How will access to property be obtained?
      i. Can existing right-of-ways be used?
      ii. Is joint use of existing facilities such as subway tunnels and utility conduit possible?
      iii. Can agreements be negotiated to construct on private property?
   b. Are there any restrictions on construction activities in the proposed network areas?
   c. Are there any environmental regulations or land use restrictions that would prohibit construction (for example, wetlands, zoning restrictions)?

____ 6. Who will bear responsibility for obtaining the regulatory authorizations? The joint venture? One venturer? A third party?

____ 7. If regulatory authorizations cannot be obtained, will the joint venture be dissolved?

§ 9.8 Technical Specifications and Acceptance Testing

Telecommunications construction is technology-intensive. As technology changes and evolves, so do the requirements and specifications for construction of telecommunications projects. Because technical specifications are a vital component of any telecommunications construction contract, they should delineate, at a minimum, the:

1. Capacity of the network
2. Transmission specifications (including the speed of transmission and acceptable error rate)
3. Service requirements
4. Performance standards (voice grade transmissions)
5. Equipment specifications.

The technical specifications will vary with the project and should be carefully reviewed and agreed to by the joint venturers. Detailed technical specifications should be included as a part of the agreement or contract for construction. Generally, the project's technical specifications are set forth in detail in an exhibit to the agreement or contract and should be specifically incorporated as part of the terms and conditions of the contract. Parties to the joint venture may establish their own technical standards or agree to accept specified industry standards. In addition, several industry associations such as the Telecommunications

Industry Association (TIA) and the Electronics Industry Association (EIA) formulate technical standards that serve as a reference for accepted industry technical standards. Although the FCC is generally reluctant to define technical standards, it has adopted specific technical standards for certain services and equipment, including networks, such as the cellular networks, that provide radio-based services.[8]

As validation of the importance of technical specifications to telecommunications construction contracts, most telecommunications construction contracts provide that acceptance of the network or facilities is conditioned upon the successful performance of acceptance testing. *Acceptance testing* requires the party constructing the system to test the system for conformance to the technical operation and performance specifications agreed to by the parties as set forth in the agreement. The testing procedure should be carefully described in the agreement and agreed to by the parties. Generally, the testing is performed by the constructing party and the accepting party is provided an opportunity to observe the testing. If a project is to be completed in stages, acceptance testing can be completed independently at each stage of the project pursuant to an agreed-upon work schedule. In a phased project, the venturer may agree to a systemwide test at the completion of all phases.

§ 9.9 Limitation on Damages

Changes in technology and increased reliance on telecommunications networks have increased the demand for assurances of network reliability, network security, transmission speed, quality of communications, and redundancy. Significantly, although network reliability has been a subject of intense interest recently, it is generally common practice in construction contracts for telecommunications ventures for the parties to disclaim any liability for damages (other than direct damages) resulting from a network failure or system outage. Specifically, lost profits and incidental and consequential damages for network outages generally are excluded as recoverable damages under a telecommunications construction contract. Without such a limitation, the potential liability of the joint venture for a systems outage could be immeasurable. If the joint venture maintains or operates the completed network, the relief provided for a system outage is usually prompt dispatch of a repair team and completion of repair work.

---

[8] *See, e.g.*, 47 C.F.R. pt. 22 (1990).

§ 9.10 Sample Joint Venture Agreement

The dynamic nature of the telecommunications industry, technology, and regulation inhibits the creation of a standard agreement for joint ventures constructing telecommunications networks. Each joint venture agreement must be tailored to address the particular requirements of the project involved and incorporate changing technological and regulatory parameters. The principles outlined in this chapter and the accompanying sample agreement are intended to provide a general example of an individual joint venture and should not be used as a substitute for consulting legal counsel or relied upon in lieu of an agreement drafted for the particular project.

The following joint venture agreement form is based on the following hypothetical scenario: Company A and Company B desire to enter into a joint venture to construct a state-of-the-art personal communications services (PCS) network in Anytown, USA. Service will be provided through microcell base stations operating on radio frequencies specified by the FCC and installed throughout the metropolitan area of Anytown, USA. As contemplated under PCS services, individual subscribers will carry lightweight portable phones that will communicate with compatible base stations, enable end users to initiate and receive calls, and interconnect with the public switched telephone network. The network will be operated by the joint venture. Because the FCC has *not* yet granted the joint venture a license to provide PCS or to construct its network, the joint venture will be dissolved if the requisite approval is not obtained. In addition, Company A has undertaken the responsibility to construct the network.

SAMPLE JOINT VENTURE AGREEMENT

TABLE OF CONTENTS

EXHIBIT C Network Design and Technical Specifications

EXHIBIT D Acceptance Testing Procedures

SAMPLE

THIS JOINT VENTURE AGREEMENT ("Agreement") is made this ______ day of ________________, 19____, between COMPANY A, a ________________ organized and existing under the laws of the State of ______________ and COMPANY B, a ____________, organized and existing under the laws of the State of ________.

W I T N E S S E T H:

WHEREAS, COMPANY A has experience in the construction and operation of fiber optic telecommunications networks;

WHEREAS, COMPANY B has experience in the operation and management of microwave telecommunications networks; and

WHEREAS, COMPANY A and COMPANY B desire to combine their expertise and have entered into this joint venture, a general partnership pursuant to the Uniform Partnership Act of the State of ____________, for the limited purpose of constructing and operating a personal communications services network in Anytown, USA.

NOW, THEREFORE, in consideration of the covenants and agreements contained herein and of other good and valuable consideration, the receipt and sufficiency of which is hereby acknowledged, the parties hereto, intending to be legally bound, agree as follows:

ARTICLE I

Definitions.

Section 1.1 *Definitions.*

(a) "*Affiliate*" means, any person, firm, corporation, trust or other person controlled directly or indirectly or under common control of a Venturer.

(b) "*Agreement*" means this Agreement and all exhibits and schedules hereto.

(c) "*Authority*" means any authorization, approval, or permit by whatever title required from a governmental agency to construct or operate the Network, including, but not limited to, the Federal Communications Commission, the Public Utility Commission of the State of ____________, and the City of Anytown, USA.

(d) "*FCC*" means the Federal Communications Commission.

(e) "*Joint Venture*" means the joint venture formed pursuant to the terms of this Agreement.

(f) "*License*" means a License issued by the Federal Communications Commission authorizing the Joint Venture to provide personal communications services in Anytown, USA, and to construct and operate the Network.

(g) "*Management Committee*" means the committee appointed by the Venturers pursuant to Article VI of the Agreement.

(h) "*Network*" means all property, facilities and equipment used and owned by the Joint Venture to provide personal communications services in Anytown,

USA, as set forth in the Network Design and Technical Specifications attached hereto.

(i) *"Venturer"* means either COMPANY A or COMPANY B.

Section 1.2 *Exhibits.*

Attached hereto and forming an integral part of this Agreement are the Statement of Work, Proposed Schedule of Major Events, Network Design and Technical Specifications, and Acceptance Testing Procedures, all of which are incorporated into this Agreement as fully as if the contents thereof were set out in full herein at each point of reference thereto.

ARTICLE II

Formation and Purpose of the Joint Venture.

Section 2.1 *Formation of Joint Venture.*

The Venturers hereby form and establish the Joint Venture under the terms and conditions of this Agreement and pursuant to the provisions of the Uniform Partnership Act of the State of ____________ for the limited purposes and business set forth in Section 2.4 hereof and in accordance with the terms and conditions set forth herein.

Section 2.2 *Name of Joint Venture and Principal Place of Business.*

The name of the Joint Venture shall be "____________________." The Joint Venture shall maintain its principal place of business at ____________. Upon approval of the Venturers, the Joint Venture may change the location of its principal place of business. Additional offices may be established to the extent deemed necessary by the Management Committee.

Section 2.3 *Filing of Certificates.*

The Management Committee shall, on behalf of the Joint Venture, file and publish all certificates, notices, statements or other instruments required by law for the formation and operation of a joint venture in all jurisdictions where the Joint Venture may elect to do business, including such partnership or assumed or fictitious name certificate or certificates as may be required by law.

Section 2.4 *Purposes and Business.*

The limited purposes and business of the Joint Venture are to do all things necessary, convenient and incidental to the design, construction and operation of the Network to provide personal communications services in Anytown, USA. In no event shall the business of the Joint Venture be extended beyond the matters described herein without the approval of each Venturer.

Section 2.5 *Certain Representations, Warranties and Covenants.*

2.5.1 *Authority to Enter Joint Venture.* Each Venturer hereby represents, warrants and covenants to the Joint Venture and to the other Venturer that:

(a) In the case of COMPANY A, it is a corporation duly organized, validly existing and in good standing under the laws of the State of ____________ and has all requisite corporate power and authority to enter into this Agreement and to carry out the transactions contemplated by this Agreement.

(b) In the case of COMPANY B, it is a corporation duly organized and validly existing under the laws of the State of __________ and has all requisite corporate power and authority to enter into this Agreement and to carry out the transactions contemplated by this Agreement.

(c) All proceedings required to be taken by the Venturers to authorize the execution, delivery and performance of this Agreement have been properly taken by each Venturer, and this Agreement constitutes a valid and binding obligation, enforceable against each Venturer in accordance with its terms.

(d) Neither the execution, delivery or performance of this Agreement by the Venturers will, with or without the giving of notice or the passage of time, or both, conflict with, result in a breach of or default or loss of rights under, or result in the creation of any lien, charge or encumbrance pursuant to, any provision of either Venturer's certificate of incorporation or bylaws or any franchise, mortgage, deed of trust, lease, permit, license, agreement, understanding, law, order, judgment, decree or other restriction to which either Venturer or any of their Affiliates are a party or by which any of them may be bound or affected.

(e) Each Venturer has complied, and will comply in all material respects, with all laws and all rules and regulations of all governmental bodies applicable to it and its business including, without limitation, the FCC; each Venturer hereby represents and warrants that it is, and will continue to be, qualified for a License from the FCC to provide personal communications services in Anytown, USA, under applicable FCC rules and regulations; neither Venturer has any knowledge of any fact or circumstances that would disqualify it or the Joint Venture from holding the License; and neither Venturer nor any of its Affiliates has engaged or will engage in any improper act or practice, or has failed or will fail to take any action required, which would result, absent timely corrective action, either in the License being rescinded, revoked or not renewed.

2.5.2 Each of the representations, warranties and covenants in this Section 2.5 is subject, where relevant, to obtaining all of the necessary regulatory approvals, including, without limitation, that of the FCC, which each Venturer hereby covenants to use its best efforts to obtain.

Section 2.6 *Title to Joint Venture Property.*

All property and interests in property owned by the Joint Venture, whether real or personal, tangible or intangible, shall be deemed owned by the Joint Venture as an entity and no Venturer, individually, shall have any ownership interest in such property.

Section 2.7 *Limits of the Joint Venture.*

The relationship between the Venturers shall be limited to the carrying on of business of the Joint Venture in accordance with the terms of this Agreement. Such relationship shall be construed and deemed to be a partnership for the limited purpose of carrying on such business. Except as otherwise expressly and specifically provided in this Agreement, neither Venturer shall have any authority to bind or act for, or assume any obligations or responsibility on behalf of, the other Venturer or the Joint Venture.

Section 2.8 *Covenant Not to Compete.*

Each of the Venturers agrees that during the Term of the Joint Venture it will not, without the prior consent of the other Venturer, engage, directly or indirectly, individually, as an advisor partner, coventurer, stockholder or other proprietor in any enterprise which is engaged in, or which represents or promotes others who are engaged in, the business of providing personal communications services in Anytown, USA, or sell or resell personal communications services in Anytown, USA. Except as otherwise set forth herein, each Venturer and any of its Affiliate(s) may engage in or possess an interest in another business venture or ventures of any nature and description (including, without limitation, the business of providing personal communications services in any place other than Anytown, USA) independently or with others, and neither the Joint Venture nor any Venturer or any of its Affiliates shall have any rights by virtue of this Agreement in or to such other ventures or to the income or profits derived therefrom.

Section 2.9 *Term.*

The Joint Venture shall continue until its termination and distribution of its assets as provided in Article VIII.

ARTICLE III
Percentage Interests and Capital Contributions.

Section 3.1 *Percentage Interests.*

The respective percentage interests of the Venturers shall be as follows:

COMPANY A	____%
COMPANY B	____%

Section 3.2 *Capital Contributions and Accounts.*

(a) *Capital Contribution of COMPANY A.*

COMPANY A hereby contributes to the Joint Venture its agreement to design and construct the Network, amounting to a capital contribution of $______.

(b) *Capital Contribution of COMPANY B.*

COMPANY B hereby contributes capital to the Joint Venture in the amount of $______.

Section 3.3 *Working Capital.*

In the event that, at any time or from time to time, the Management Committee determines that it is necessary or appropriate to provide funds or additional funds to the Joint Venture for the purpose of supplying or augmenting the working capital of the Joint Venture, the Management Committee shall notify the Venturers of the amount of such funds or additional funds that the Management Committee has so determined to be necessary or appropriate. After any such notification, the Venturers shall pay the amount specified in such notification to the Joint Venture either as an additional capital contribution or as a non-interest-bearing loan.

Section 3.4 *Rights in Respect of Capital Contributions.*

Neither Venturer shall have any right to demand or receive the return of any capital contribution to the Joint Venture. Neither Venturer shall be entitled to interest on any capital contribution or on the balance of such Venturer's capital account.

Section 3.5 *Accounts.*

The Joint Venture shall maintain for each Venturer an account designated its "Capital Account," to which will be credited the Venturer's initial capital contribution, any additional capital contributions and its distributive share of the profits of the Joint Venture, and from which shall be deducted the Venture's distributive share of the losses of the Joint Venture and all distributions made to the Venturer.

ARTICLE IV
Allocation of Profits and Losses.

Section 4.1 *Profits and Losses.*

(a) Profits and Losses of the Joint Venture shall be allocated to COMPANY A and to COMPANY B in accordance with the percentage of interests set forth in Section 3.1.

(b) The respective interests of the Venturers in Profits and Losses shall be changed only by amendment to this Agreement.

ARTICLE V
Responsibilities of the Venturers.

Section 5.1 *Construction.*

COMPANY A shall construct and maintain the Network described in this Agreement and set forth in the exhibits hereto, or if not expressly specified herein, in a manner that equals industry accepted performance standards for network quality, operation, planning, and testing which may be used from time to time during the effective period of this Agreement. COMPANY A shall complete construction of the network in conformance with the Statement of Work and Proposed Schedule of Major Events attached hereto and in accordance with terms of the License and any other Authority issued to the Joint Venture.

Section 5.2 *Compensation.*

COMPANY A shall be compensated by the Joint Venture for any and all reasonable costs incurred by COMPANY A in the design and construction of the Network. The terms and conditions of such compensation shall be agreed to by the Venturers upon award of a License to the Joint Venture by the FCC.

Section 5.3 *Acceptance and Testing.*

COMPANY A shall complete all construction and conduct acceptance testing in accordance with the Acceptance Testing Procedures attached as an exhibit hereto by the dates specified in the Proposed Schedule of Major Events, provided that upon agreement of the Venturers, the date for acceptance testing may be modified. COMPANY A shall notify the Management Committee and the other Venturer of the date of commencement of acceptance testing at least seven (7) days in advance of the commencement of testing. The Management Committee and each Venturer shall have the right to observe the acceptance testing. Within twenty-one (21) days of conclusion of the acceptance testing, COMPANY A shall provide the Management Committee and each Venturer with the test results. The Management Committee shall promptly review and approve the test results if the results satisfy the terms and conditions hereof. If the test results are unsatisfactory and do not meet the specifications contained in this Agreement, COMPANY A shall take all actions necessary, at no costs to the Joint Venture, or COMPANY B, until satisfactory acceptance testing is performed or waived, in writing, by each Venturer.

Section 5.4 *Limitation on Liability.*

COMPANY A, except when acting in its capacity as a Venturer as provided for under the terms of this Agreement, shall not be liable to the Joint Venturer or either Venturer for any damages, including incidental or consequential damages, regulatory fees or penalties that the Joint Venturer or either Venturer may incur as a result of any Network failure, malfunction, or outage of the Network unless such failure, malfunction or outage is caused by the willful and neglectful action or inaction of COMPANY A or its employees.

ARTICLE VI
Management of Joint Venture.

Section 6.1 *Management Committee.*

(a) The general management and control of the business of the Joint Venture shall be vested in the Management Committee.

(b) The Management Committee shall consist of four (4) individuals, two (2) of whom shall be designated by COMPANY A and two (2) of whom shall be designated by COMPANY B. Either Venturer shall have the right, at any time and from time to time, upon notice to the other Venturer, (i) to remove any member of the Management Committee designated by such Venturer and to designate a different individual as a member of the Management Committee and (ii) in the event of the death, retirement, resignation or other withdrawal of any member of the Management Committee appointed by such Venturer, to appoint a new member of the Management Committee to replace such deceased, retiring, resigning, or withdrawing member. Meetings of the Management Committee shall be held on a regular basis, and in any event not less frequently than once during each fiscal quarter of the Joint Venture. Meetings may be called at any reasonable time and place by any member of the Management Committee upon not less than two (2) weeks' notice to each other member of the Management Committee; provided that attendance, by person or by telephone conference, by any member of the Management Committee at a meeting of the Management Committee shall constitute a waiver of notice of such meeting by such member. The Management Committee shall not take any action or make any determination without the unanimous consent of all members of the Management Committee.

Section 6.2 *Authority of the Management Committee.*

(a) Except as provided in subsection (b) of this Section 6.2, or as otherwise expressly provided in this Agreement, all decisions respecting any matter set forth herein or otherwise affecting or arising out of the conduct of the business of the Joint Venture shall be made by the Management Committee, and the Management Committee shall have the exclusive right and full authority to manage, conduct and operate the Joint Venture's business. Except as otherwise expressly provided in this Agreement, the Management Committee is hereby granted the right, power and authority to do on behalf of the Joint Venture all things that it determines to be necessary or desirable to carry out the aforementioned duties and responsibilities, including, but not limited to, the right, power and authority from time to time to do the following:

(i) to borrow money in the name and on behalf of the Joint Venture, and to secure the same by liens on all or any part of the Joint Venture's assets;

(ii) to acquire, own, hold a leasehold interest in, maintain, use, lease, sublease, develop, improve, manage, operate, sell, exchange, transfer, or otherwise deal in assets and property as may be necessary or convenient for the purposes and business of the Joint Venture;

(iii) to secure and maintain insurance against liability or other loss with respect to the activities and assets of the Joint Venture;

(iv) to cause to be paid all amounts due and payable by the Joint Venture to any Person or entity;

(v) to employ such agents, employees, managers, accountants, attorneys, consultants and other Persons, including either Venturer, necessary or appropriate to carry out the business and affairs of the Joint Venture, whether or not any such Persons so employed are affiliated with or related to either Venturer, and to pay to such Persons such fees, expenses, salaries, wages and other compensation as it shall in its sole discretion determine;

(vi) to pay, extend, renew, modify, adjust, submit to arbitration, prosecute, defend or compromise, upon such terms as it may determine and upon such evidence as it may deem sufficient, any obligation, suit, liability, cause of action or claim, including taxes, either in favor of or against the Joint Venture;

(vii) to pay any and all fees and to make any and all expenditures which it deems necessary or appropriate in connection with the organization of the Joint Venture, the management of the affairs of the Joint Venture and the carrying out of its obligations and responsibilities under this Agreement;

(viii) to acquire, prosecute, maintain, protect and defend or cause to be protected and defended all claims or demands of or against the Joint Venture;

(ix) to enter into, execute, acknowledge and deliver any and all contracts, agreements or other instruments necessary or appropriate to carry on the business of the Joint Venture as set forth herein;

(x) to cause to be paid any and all taxes, charges and assessments that may be levied, assessed or imposed upon any of the assets of the Joint Venture, unless the same are contested by the Management Committee on behalf of the Joint Venture;

(xi) to engage in any kind of activity to and enter into and perform obligations of any kind necessary to or in connection with, or incidental to, the accomplishment of the purposes and business of the Joint Venture, so long as said activities and obligations may be lawfully engaged in or performed by the Joint Venture under governing law.

(b) Notwithstanding any other provision of this Agreement, neither the Management Committee nor either Venturer, acting alone, shall have the power, without the written consent of both Venturers or of the other Venturer, as the case may be, to cause the Joint Venture to enter into or otherwise become liable for or with respect to any arrangement which would result in liquidation of the Joint Venture otherwise than in accordance with this Agreement.

Section 6.3 *Regulatory Authorizations.*

The Management Committee, on behalf of the Joint Venture and each Venturer shall take all reasonable actions necessary to obtain and comply with all Authority, consents, licenses, notices, approvals, authorizations, filings, orders, registrations, building permits, rights-of-way, certificates, ordinances, franchises, assignments, and permits required by any governmental authority, including the FCC, necessary for the construction and operations of the network. Each Venturer shall cooperate fully with the Management Committee to obtain any and all Authority necessary to construct the system.

Section 6.4 *Books and Records.*

(a) The Management Committee shall keep, or cause to be kept, books and records for the Joint Venture which are usually maintained by Persons engaged in similar businesses, setting forth a true, current, accurate and complete account of the Joint Venture's business and affairs, including a fair presentation of all income, expenditures, assets and liabilities thereof. Such books and records shall be maintained on a cash basis. Each Venturer and its authorized representatives shall have the right at all reasonable times to have access to, inspect, audit and copy the Joint Venture's original books and records, which at all times shall be kept at the principal office of the Joint Venture.

Section 6.5 *Bank Accounts.*

All funds of the Joint Venture shall be deposited in its name in an account or accounts maintained with such federally insured banking or other financial institutions as may be designated by the Management Committee with the Approval of the Venturers. Funds of the Joint Venture shall not be commingled with funds of any other Person. Checks shall be drawn upon the Joint Venturer's account or accounts only for the purposes of the Joint Venture and shall be signed at least two (2) members of the Management Committee or by such other Person(s) as may be approved by the Venturers. Working capital or other funds of the Joint Venture not currently needed to fund the Joint Venture's operations shall be Invested by the Management Committee to the extent required in securities or instruments approved by the Venturers and otherwise to provide the greatest return to the Joint Venture consistent with prudent cash management principles.

(b) The Management Committee shall, at the Joint Venture's expense, cause the Joint Venture's independent certified public accountants to prepare the federal, state and local income tax returns of the Joint Venture and shall cause such accountants to review and sign such tax returns as soon as reasonably practicable and in any event not later than ninety (90) calendar days after the end of each fiscal year. The Management Committee shall cause such tax returns to be filed on a timely basis with the appropriate governmental authorities after being approved by the Venturers. Copies of each such return shall be furnished for review and approval by each Venturer at least thirty (30) calendar days prior to the statutory date for filing, including any extensions thereof. Tax decisions and elections for the Joint Venture as well as all material accounting decisions not provided for expressly herein must be approved by the Venturers.

(c) In the event that the Internal Revenue Service ("IRS"), or any other governmental agency with jurisdiction, shall conduct, commence or give notification of intent to conduct or commence any audit or other investigation of the books, records, tax returns or other affairs of the Joint Venturer, the Management Committee shall respond to such audit or other investigation for and on behalf of the Joint Venture and shall keep the Venturers fully advised with respect thereto. The

Management Committee shall have the right to engage counsel to represent the Joint Venture in connection with such audit or other investigation, and the fees and expenses of such counsel and of any litigation thereof shall be borne by the Joint Venture.

(d) The Management Committee shall prepare and file all reports required by governmental or administrative agencies, (including the FCC) to be filed by the Joint Venture.

Section 6.6 *Other Businesses of Venturers.*

(a) The Venturers shall devote to the Venture such time as may be necessary for the proper performance of their duties hereunder.

(b) Neither the Joint Venture nor either Venturer shall have any rights or obligations, by virtue of this Agreement, in or to any independent ventures of any nature or description, or the income or profits derived therefrom, in which a Venturer may engage.

Section 6.7 *Indemnification.*

Each Venturer shall be indemnified jointly and severally by the other Venturer and the Joint Venture against any claims, losses, judgments, liabilities, amounts and expenses (including reasonable attorneys' fees and legal costs and disbursements) arising out of any act or omission by such Venturer which was committed, or omitted, by the Venturer in good faith and in the reasonable belief that such act or omission was in the best interests of the Joint Venture, and such act or omission was within the scope of the authority conferred on the Venturer by this Agreement and did not constitute or involve a breach of any warranty, representation or contractual obligation or duty by the Venturer, or constitute or involve any gross negligence or willful misconduct of or by the Venturer; provided, however, that any indemnity under this Section 6.7 shall be paid only out of and to the extent of assets of the Joint Venture.

ARTICLE VII

Assignment of a Venturer's Interest.

Section 7.1 *In General.*

Except for transfers to an Affiliate of a Venturer, no Venturer shall have the right to sell, assign, transfer or otherwise pledge all or any part of its interest in the Joint Venture without the approval of the other Venturer, which approval shall not unreasonably be withheld and without first obtaining any Authority required by the FCC or other governmental agency.

ARTICLE VIII

Dissolution, Liquidation and Termination of the Joint Venture.

Section 8.1 *Events Causing Dissolution.*

The Joint Venture shall dissolve upon the earliest to happen of any of the following events:

(a) A final decision by the FCC or other applicable governmental agency *not* to issue a License or other Authority necessary for the Joint Venture to provide personal communications services in Anytown, USA;

(b) Revocation of the Joint Venture's License or other Authority necessary to provide personal communications services in Anytown, USA;

(c) A decision, approved by the Venturers, to dissolve the Joint Venture; or

(d) The happening of any other event causing the dissolution of a limited partnership under the laws of the State of __________;

Dissolution of the Joint Venture shall be effective on the day on which the event occurs giving rise to the dissolution. Any necessary certificate of dissolution shall be filed under the Uniform Partnership Act of the State of __________ upon the dissolution and the commencement of winding up of the Joint Venture; provided, however, that the Joint Venture shall not terminate until the assets of the Joint Venture have been distributed as provided in Section 8.2.

Section 8.2 *Liquidation.*

(a) As soon as practical after the dissolution of the Joint Venture, the last appointed members of the Management Committee shall prepare a plan as to whether and in what manner the assets of the Joint Venture shall be liquidated. With the approval of the Venturers, the property of the Joint Venture shall be transferred outright to a successor Person, upon such terms and conditions agreed to by the Venturers.

(b) If the Venturers fail to approve an outright transfer of the property of the Joint Venture to a successor person pursuant to Section 8.2(a), upon dissolution of the Joint Venture, the last appointed members of the Management Committee shall take full account of the Joint Venture's liabilities and assets, and the Joint Venture shall be liquidated as promptly as is consistent with obtaining the fair market value thereof. Except as otherwise provided herein, the proceeds shall be applied and distributed in the following order and priority:

(i) First, to secured creditors (including Venturers and their Affiliates) in accordance with the priority of their security interests;

(ii) Next, to the payment of debts and liabilities of the Joint Venture to general unsecured creditors (excluding Venturers and their Affiliates who are general creditors of the Joint Venture);

(iii) Next, to the payment of debts and liabilities of the Joint Venture to Venturers and affiliates of venturers who are general unsecured creditors;

(iv) Next, to the establishment of any reserves which are reasonably necessary for contingent, unmatured, unliquidated, disputed, or unforeseen liabilities and obligations of the Joint Venture; and,

(v) Last, to the Venturers in proportion to their respective interests in the Joint Venture.

ARTICLE IX

General Provisions.

Section 9.1 *Word Meanings.*

In this Agreement, the singular shall include the plural and the masculine gender shall include the feminine and vice versa, unless the context otherwise requires.

Section 9.2 *Binding Provisions.*

The covenants and agreements contained herein shall be binding upon, and inure to the benefit of, the legal representatives, successors and permitted assigns of the respective parties hereto.

Section 9.3 *Applicable Law.*

This Agreement shall be construed and enforced in accordance with the laws of the State of ____________ without regard to principles of conflict of laws, and the rights, duties and obligations of the Venturers shall be as stated in the Uniform Partnership Act of the State of ____________ except as provided herein.

Section 9.4 *Counterparts.*

This Agreement may be executed in any number of counterparts, each of which shall be deemed to be an original as against any party whose signature appears thereon, and all of which shall together constitute one and the same instrument. This Agreement shall become binding when one or more counterparts hereof, individually or taken together, shall bear the signatures of all the Venturers.

Section 9.5 *Separability of Provisions.*

Each provision of this Agreement shall be considered separable and if for any reason any provision or provisions hereof are determined to be invalid and contrary to any existing or future law, such invalidity shall not impair the operation of or affect those portions of this Agreement which are valid.

Section 9.6 *Section Titles.*

Section titles are for descriptive purposes only and shall not control or alter the meaning of this Agreement as set forth in the text.

Section 9.7 *Entire Agreement.*

This Agreement, including the Exhibits and Schedules attached hereto, constitutes the entire understanding and agreement between the Venturers with respect to the subject matter hereof, and supersedes all prior and contemporaneous agreements and understandings, inducements or conditions, express or implied, oral or written, except as herein contained. This Agreement may not be modified, amended, discharged or waived other than by an instrument in writing and signed by the Venturers sought to be charged with such modification, amendment, discharge or waiver.

Section 9.8 *No Third-Party Beneficiary.*

This Agreement is made solely and specifically between and for the benefit of the Venturers and their respective legal representatives and successors, and no other Person whatsoever shall have any rights, interests, or claims hereunder or be entitled to any benefits under or on account of this Agreement as a third-party beneficiary or otherwise.

Section 9.9 *Arbitration.*

Any controversy or dispute arising out of or relating to this Agreement or the breach hereof (exclusive of matters which are expressly within the discretion of either Venturer) shall be settled by arbitration. Such arbitration shall be effected by arbitrators selected as hereinafter provided and shall be conducted in the State of ____________ in accordance with the Rules of the American Arbitration Association existing at the date thereof. The dispute shall be submitted to three arbitrators who are listed on the construction panel of the American Arbitration Association, one arbitrator being selected by COMPANY A, one arbitrator being selected by COMPANY B and the third being selected by the two arbitrators so selected. In the event that either Venturer, within fifteen (15) days after any notification of any demand for arbitrator hereunder, shall not have selected its arbitrator and given notice thereof to the other, such arbitrator shall be selected by the American Arbitration Association. Judgment may be entered on any decision rendered by the arbitrators in any federal or state court having jurisdiction. Each Venturer shall bear the costs of the fees and expenses of the arbitrator selected by or for it, and the fees and expenses of the third arbitrator shall be borne by the Venturers equally.

IN WITNESS WHEREOF, COMPANY A and COMPANY B have executed this Agreement under seal as of the day and year first above written.

WITNESS:	COMPANY A
______________________	By: ______________________
ATTEST:	COMPANY B
______________________	By: ______________________

EXHIBIT A
STATEMENT OF WORK

EXHIBIT B
PROPOSED SCHEDULE OF MAJOR EVENTS

EXHIBIT C
NETWORK DESIGN AND TECHNICAL SPECIFICATIONS

EXHIBIT D
ACCEPTANCE TESTING PROCEDURES

CHAPTER 10

HEALTH CARE CONSTRUCTION PROJECTS

Steven R. Olson
Peter Petrakis*

Steven R. Olson is a partner in the law firm of Katten Muchin & Zavis in Chicago, Illinois. He devotes a substantial portion of his practice to the development, construction, acquisition, and financing of health care facilities. He has represented numerous health care providers nationally in development and transactional matters. Mr. Olson received a B.S. from Andrews University in Berrien Springs, Michigan and his J.D. from the John Marshall Law School in Chicago, Illinois.

Peter Petrakis is a partner in the law firm of Katten Muchin & Zavis in Chicago, Illinois. He represents owners, developers, contractors, and construction managers in all types of commercial, residential, and mixed-use construction projects. His practice encompasses both counseling and dispute resolution. Mr. Petrakis received his B.A. and J.D. at Loyola University, in Chicago, Illinois.

*The authors acknowledge the contribution made to this chapter by Thomas J. McFadden of Katten Muchin & Zavis.

§ 10.1 Introduction

The participants in health care joint venture construction projects traditionally have included two or more health care providers that pool their resources to construct, own, and operate health care facilities or other health care projects. In recent years the category of participants has expanded to include nonproviders such as developers, contractors, and management organizations. In an increasingly competitive health care environment, providers have recognized the importance of combining their expertise and resources with nonproviders to accomplish their objective. These joint venture projects have included hospitals, nursing homes, medical office buildings, outpatient facilities, and retirement communities.

A health care joint venture contains many of the same legal, structural, financial, and operational issues associated with non-health care joint venture projects. However, several distinguishing characteristics that are particular to health care joint ventures are discussed in this chapter. Although there are numerous potential transactions for which a developer, contractor, management company, and health care provider may come together, this chapter focuses on the particular joint venture arrangement described in the sample agreement in **§ 10.18**.

The sample agreement, based on a general partnership arrangement, was drafted for a transaction in which a taxable subsidiary of a tax-exempt hospital combines forces with a development company. The developer, through its subsidiaries, is to provide architectural, construction, leasing, marketing, and management services for retirement housing projects. The proposed retirement housing project will be located adjacent to the hospital's campus and consists of congregate care units, residential care units, and skilled nursing beds.

The hospital, which had no prior experience in retirement housing, sought out developers who could provide the development, marketing, construction, leasing, and management expertise. The hospital considers the project to be an essential element in maintaining its role as the premier health care provider in the community. The project will enable the hospital to provide the entire continuum of health care services.

After the developer successfully bid for the project in accordance with the sample teaming agreement in **§ 10.17**, the parties then entered into the joint venture agreement. Although the developer heretofore had not participated in the ownership of a health care facility, it considers the project a long-term investment. The developer also expects greater potential for success in the community by associating the project with the hospital. The reputation of the hospital lends credibility to the project and thereby enhances marketing to prospective residents.

The sample agreement is designed to take into account the particular statutory and regulatory considerations imposed on health care joint ventures. These aspects are discussed specifically in §§ **10.4–10.6**, and generally throughout, to indicate to the reader where the agreement reflects these unique considerations.

§ 10.2 Teaming Agreement

In our sample transaction (see **§ 10.17**), the developer has put together a "team" of professionals to pursue a project presumably advertised by the hospital, which was seeking the right developer to join it in the health care venture. Once this developer and "team" successfully bids on the project, it is anticipated that the continuing relationship between the developer and its subcontractors and suppliers will be governed by any construction subcontracts.

An additional issue with regard to joint venture termination actually pertains to the teaming agreement: When does the parties' relationship end if the team does not successfully pursue the project? The teaming agreement pulls together entities from various disciplines to pursue the construction project and it is important that the teaming agreement preclude members of the team from leaving or joining the competition. The team must be constrained to stay together until a formal, binding announcement by the owner of the project that the contract has been let. Anything short of a formal award might allow members of the team to leave the group to make overtures to a more likely recipient of the project.

§ 10.3 Tax Concerns

Tax considerations are important in health care joint ventures because tax-exempt and taxable organizations are often participants. As discussed in the following sections, federal tax law restricts both the types of activities in which a tax-exempt organization may engage and the manner in which the organization may operate, and imposes restrictions on ventures with taxable entities.

§ 10.4 —Tax-Exempt Participants

A transaction between a taxable subsidiary of an exempt organization and a nonexempt entity raises a number of tax concerns for the exempt sponsoring organization. If not properly structured, the IRS may look "behind" the subsidiary and scrutinize the transaction as if the hospital were a direct participant.

Because many hospitals are exempt from federal income taxation pursuant to § 501(c)(3) of the Internal Revenue Code as organizations "organized and operated exclusively for . . . charitable, scientific, . . . or educational purposes," they are subject to operational restrictions not encountered by taxable entities. To maintain tax-exempt status, no part of the hospital's assets or net earnings may inure to nonexempt persons or entities. Nor may the hospital be operated in a manner to benefit private—as opposed to public—interests. These restrictions on exempt hospitals are commonly referred to as the prohibitions against private inurement and private benefit. When an exempt hospital, either directly or indirectly, participates in a transaction with taxable entities, the transaction must be examined to ensure that it does not violate these prohibitions.

By way of example, if in our hypothetical transaction the hospital's taxable subsidiary were the only general partner to provide a guaranty or other form of credit enhancement for project financing, this might be evidence of impermissible private inurement and private benefit unless the taxable subsidiary was compensated by receiving a guaranty fee or by obtaining a greater ownership percentage in the project. Another example arises when, during construction, the hospital's taxable subsidiary makes below-market interest rate loans to the project with inadequate or no security. If in fact the loans bear below-market interest rates or the security is inadequate, the IRS might conclude that the exempt hospital was violating the prohibitions against private inurement and private benefit, resulting in jeopardy to the hospital's exempt status.

The economic consequences of an exempt hospital's losing its exempt status are severe. For example, any tax-exempt bonds issued on behalf of the hospital would become taxable, an event which could likely result in an acceleration of the outstanding indebtedness. That is why Section 4.05 of the sample agreement, which contemplates loans to the project by the parties, specifically provides that such loans be at "commercially reasonable rates," in an effort to avoid this potential problem for the hospital.

A recent General Counsel Memorandum, published on December 4, 1991,[1] underscores the IRS's heightened scrutiny of transactions involving exempt hospitals and taxable participants. For the exempt hospital to justify participating, either directly or indirectly, in a transaction such as our sample transaction, it must demonstrate benefit to the community as distinguished from benefit to the

[1] Gen. Couns. Mem. 39,862 (Dec. 4, 1991). Note that general counsel memoranda do not have force of law as statutes or case law do, but are utilized in predicting the Internal Revenue Service's response to legal developments in tax law.

hospital itself and its financial viability. In order to demonstrate community benefit and thereby justify participation in a project with a taxable party, an exempt hospital must show that it is:

1. Providing a new service to the community
2. Bringing a new provider to the community
3. Sharing the risk inherent in a new activity
4. Pooling diverse and distinct areas of expertise
5. Improving patient convenience
6. Increasing physician accessibility to patients.

The IRS considers the following justifications inadequate to demonstrate the requisite community benefit:

1. Obtaining patient referrals
2. Avoiding new competition
3. Improving the hospital's financial health
4. Improving efficiency through increased utilization of the hospital's facilities.

§ 10.5 —Unrelated Business Income

Exempt hospitals are required to pay federal income taxes on income derived from activities unrelated to the hospital's exempt purposes. Income that is unrelated to an exempt hospital's purposes, referred to as *unrelated business income* (UBI), does not jeopardize a hospital's exempt status provided the amount of UBI is an "insubstantial portion" of the hospital's total revenues. By using a taxable subsidiary, the hospital's risk of UBI income is eliminated because dividend income is currently excluded from UBI treatment in the Internal Revenue Code.[2]

When the joint venture project is located on a hospital's campus, the joint venture may sometimes acquire use of the land by means of a ground lease from the hospital. UBI limitations should be considered when land is ground leased from an exempt organization, such as a hospital. Ordinarily, rental income received by an exempt organization is excluded from UBI treatment.[3] However, if the project is financed, then the rental income may be characterized as UBI to the extent of the financing. As indicated, if an exempt organization has more than an insubstantial amount of UBI, this may threaten its tax-exempt status. The risk of UBI to the hospital did not occur in our sample transaction because

---

[2] I.R.C. § 512(b)(1) (1986).

[3] *Id.* § 512(b)(3)(A)(i).

no rental income was received by the hospital; instead, the land was acquired by deed.[4]

§ 10.6 —Management Contracts

Projects that are financed with tax-exempt bonds and managed by taxable entities require particular attention and structuring to ensure compliance with Revenue Procedure 82-14.[5] In our sample transaction, tax-exempt bond financing is unavailable because the joint venture is not an exempt organization. However, many joint ventures are owned by tax-exempt organizations that finance project costs through the issuance of tax-exempt bonds. If a project financed with the proceeds of tax-exempt bonds is managed by a taxable manager, the management contract must be in compliance with the provisions of Revenue Procedure 82-14. Failure to comply causes the interest paid to investors purchasing the bonds to become taxable, thereby causing a default and probable acceleration of the underlying indebtedness.

A management contract generally can comply by being structured in the following ways:

1. The manager's compensation must be based on a periodic flat fee (which may be subject to automatic percentage increases if based on a particular external standard)
2. The term of the contract (including renewal options) may not exceed five years and must be cancellable at the option of the tax-exempt owner at the end of any two-year period and
3. The total compensation must be reasonable.

or

1. In the case of new operations without operating history, compensation may be based on a percentage of gross revenues for a period generally not exceeding one year
2. The compensation must be reasonable
3. The owner of the project and the manager may not be subject to common control and
4. The owner and the manager must represent that if any new contract is negotiated, the new contract will comply with Revenue Procedure 82-14.

---

[4] *Id.* §§ 512(b)(4), 514(a)(1).

[5] Rev. Proc. 82-14, 1982-1 C.B. 459 (1982).

§ 10.7 Certificate of Need and Licensure

Certificate of Need (CON) programs were established by Congress in 1975[6] as a system of national health planning and development designed to foster controls in the distribution, efficiency, and cost of health care services. A CON (or an exemption) is required before a provider can add new institutional services, make expenditures for the acquisition of health care equipment or facilities, or discontinue health care services. Although the federal law that created the CON program was repealed effective January 1, 1987,[7] CON programs remain active in many states. In the initial development stages of a health care project, a thorough review of the CON law of the particular state must be undertaken. If a CON is required, sufficient time must be allotted to obtain a permit. In the initial development process, the particular state licensure requirements should also be reviewed. Design and architectural compliance with licensure requirements is an essential component of the project. In most states the CON and licensure requirements are tandem regulations requiring advance planning to insure compliance and avoid project delays.

Proceeding without obtaining a CON when one is required could result in sanctions on the participants, including civil or criminal penalties. If a CON is required for the proposed project, it is advisable to notify and make application with the state agency as early as possible. This may also serve to preclude a competitor from preempting the project by submitting an application to fill the same need.

The significance of obtaining a CON is reflected in Section 9.02 of the sample agreement (**§ 10.18**), which provides that failure to obtain a CON (hopefully early on in the planning and development process) will result in dissolution of the joint venture.

§ 10.8 Medicare/Medicaid Issues

The system by which hospitals are paid by the federal government for treating Medicare patients was altered significantly in the mid-1980s when the payment system converted from a cost-based reimbursement method, whereby the hospital was paid its actual costs for services rendered to Medicare patients (subject to certain limitations), to a prospective payment system in which the hospital is paid a predetermined rate regardless of its actual costs in treating a Medicare

---

6 42 U.S.C. § 300k-1 to 300k-3, 300*l* to 300*l*-5, 300m to 300m-6, 300n to 300n-6, *repealed by* Act of November 14, 1986, Pub. L. No. 99-660, 1986 U.S.C.C.A.N. (100 Stat.) 3799.

7 Act of November 14, 1986, Pub. L. No. 99-660, 1986 U.S.C.C.A.N. (100 Stat.) 3799.

patient.[8] This new payment system creates financial incentives for a hospital to discharge a patient as early as possible to avoid the risk of financial loss.

This change has actually served to benefit projects similar to the sample transaction because it can provide a steady flow of patients to the project's nursing home, thereby increasing revenues for the project while simultaneously protecting the hospital from having to maintain a patient at a financial loss.

Joint venture participants need to be aware of the Medicare and Medicaid Anti-Fraud and Abuse statute.[9] The solicitation, offering, or receipt of remuneration in exchange for referring a person for the furnishing of goods or services reimbursed by Medicare or Medicaid, or for participating in or recommending a sale, lease, or order of any item reimbursed by Medicare or Medicaid, is a federal felony. Hospitals may consider the prospective payment reimbursement system adequate incentive to discharge patients to a lesser level of care sooner than if cost reimbursement were available for a patient's hospital stay. The hospital may decide to contract with the project's nursing home to hold beds open for transfers from the hospital.

The hospital may pay a fee to the project nursing home for each day a bed is held open, or agree to provide personnel or services to the nursing home, so long as the payment of consideration for holding beds open—whether monetary or the provision of additional staff—is not dependent on admissions of or services to Medicare patients. Exclusive transfer agreements or bonus payment arrangements generally should be avoided.

§ 10.9 Religious Organizations as Joint Venture Participants

Many health care organizations are sponsored by religious orders or denominations. A joint venture that provides health care services and includes a religious organization may preclude the performing of certain medical or surgical procedures within the project's health care facilities. These restrictions should be incorporated into the joint venture documentation. In addition, if real estate is to be transferred by a religious organization to the project, restrictions regarding that conveyance may also need to be documented in the instruments of conveyance. The transfer of the property itself may also require pre-approval by church authorities. For example, pursuant to its canon law, the Roman Catholic church requires that transfers of certain property of a specified value

---

[8] Pub. L. No. 98-21, 97 Stat. 65 (1983) (codified in scattered sections of 26 U.S.C., 42 U.S.C., and other titles).

[9] 42 U.S.C. § 1320a-7b (1990).

be approved by the Vatican. This requirement is designed to provide the church with a review process to ensure that church property is not transferred in a manner adverse to the interests of the church.

§ 10.10 Financing Covenants

Many hospitals are subject to financing documents that contain restrictions on participation in joint ventures. Typical covenants include restrictions on the transfer of assets, prohibitions on participating in an entity that it does not wholly own, and transfer of assets that will cause the hospital to fail to meet certain financial tests such as debt service ratios.

If the hospital's financing documents prohibit it from participating directly in a legal entity it does not wholly own, the hospital might be able to utilize a subsidiary to participate in the joint venture. If the subsidiary arrangement is used, the asset transfer provisions of the financing documents must be reviewed carefully because the subsidiary may have to rely on transfer of funds from the hospital as a source of its capital contribution to the joint venture. Existing debt covenants may preclude a hospital or a subsidiary of the hospital from participating in a joint venture. For this reason, Section 9.02(d) has been incorporated into the joint venture agreement (**§ 10.18**) to allow for dissolution of the joint venture if subsequent review of the relevant financing documents discloses that the hospital, either directly or through its subsidiary, is precluded from participating in the joint venture for any reason.

§ 10.11 Capitalization Issues

The development of a health care construction project generally requires a significant amount of capital to fund initial development. Section 4.01 of the joint venture agreement delineates the items typically required in the development phase of a health care project, including market feasibility studies; architectural and engineering fees; legal fees for zoning, certificate of need, and licensure applications; and marketing the project to prospective residents. As with most joint ventures, estimated capital need requirements can never be predicted with certainty. Therefore, the joint venture agreement (**§ 10.18**) provides in Section 4.02 that the management committee can require the parties to make additional capital contributions. If a party does not make the additional capital contribution, the agreement provides that such party's ownership interest in the project will be diluted. As an additional source of capitalization, Section 4.05 provides that participants, without increasing their capital contribution, may make loans to the project at commercially reasonable interest rates determined by the management committee.

§ 10.12 Organizational, Management, and Control Issues

There are certain advantages and disadvantages to the forms of organization commonly used in joint ventures.

General partnership. A general partnership has certain advantages, such as ease of formation, no minimum capitalization requirements, and federal income tax benefits flowing directly to the individual partners. It also has disadvantages: partners are jointly and severally liable for partnership obligations, and a partnership interest is generally not transferable.

Limited partnership. A limited partnership structure is widely utilized in health care joint venture projects, particularly those involving members of a hospital medical staff. The primary reason for its popularity is that limited partners incur no liability beyond the amount of their initial investment. Limited partners may transfer their interest in the venture without causing a dissolution of the joint venture, subject to certain restrictions on transfer. Although a limited partner may not actively participate in the business of the joint venture, some joint venture arrangements grant the limited partners approval rights with respect to certain major transactions. The limited partnership form is common when the venture's business is to construct a medical office building, the hospital serves as general partner, and the physician/investors are the limited partners. Like the general partnership, the federal income tax benefits flow directly to the individual investors.

Corporation. A joint venture utilizing a corporation may either be a for-profit or not-for-profit corporation. The principal difference between the two is that not-for-profit corporations are dedicated to public interests and may not distribute their net earnings to private individuals or entities. By contrast, for-profit corporations serve private interests and typically distribute their earnings by paying dividends to shareholders. The advantages are: the corporation's shareholders ordinarily have no personal obligation to pay the corporation's liabilities; the stock is generally transferable subject to certain restrictions; and the corporation has continuity of existence. However, corporations are subject to statutory and minimum capitalization requirements, their powers and authority may be limited by statute, and, if profitable, their shareholders are subject to double taxation.

In our sample transaction, the parties chose the general partnership form because both parties wanted to exercise an active role in decision making. To simplify management and control issues, while enabling full participation by the parties, a management committee was established. Described in Article V of the joint venture agreement, the management committee consists of two members—one representative for each party—who report to their respective organizations on all major decisions. Because the construction aspects predominate, the transaction contemplates that the developer act as the managing partner for the project and exercise the day-to-day responsibility for operations, subject to oversight by the management committee.

In light of the considerable investment of time, effort, expense, and the sharing of confidential information among the parties, there was incorporated into the joint venture agreement (**§ 10.18**) a noncompete clause, set forth in Section 6.03, which prohibits either party from competing with the project within the project's primary market area. Exceptions to this prohibition are that either may do so provided the other party consents, or if a competing project is already more than 90 percent occupied.

§ 10.13 Funding Issues

One of the primary benefits of participating in a joint venture is the pooling of financial resources to obtain the best possible financial arrangements for a project. Financing options for health care joint ventures include:

1. Equity
2. Tax-exempt bonds
3. Taxable bonds
4. Conventional mortgage financing
5. HUD programs consisting of either direct loans or mortgage insurance.

The financing option chosen depends upon a number of considerations, including the legal structure of the joint venture, the financial strength of the parties, the type of amenities the project provides to its residents, the percentage of project equity required by the lender, timing of construction, and other variables. Article 5 of the joint venture agreement (**§ 10.18**) is drafted to allow the parties the greatest flexibility in choosing financing options. Because in our sample transaction the project is not owned by an exempt organization, tax-exempt bonds are not available as a financing option. Prevailing conditions in the financial markets make HUD programs once again a viable option. However, if timing is an issue, HUD programs may prove unworkable, because it can frequently take six to nine months to close on this type of financing. Taxable bonds are another reasonable option for projects of this kind. However, the parties must factor in the costs of issuance, which can be considerable.

§ 10.14 Risk Allocation, Liability, and Indemnification Issues

By selecting the general partnership form of ownership for the joint venture entity, the general partners become exposed to the general liabilities of the project. Exposure to general liability would not ordinarily deter entities like the parties to our sample transaction because the nature of their respective businesses routinely exposes them to considerable liabilities. However, to minimize their exposure, the parties chose to designate subsidiary corporate organizations as general partners for this project.

Also, because of the financial strength of the parties, both have access to extensive general liability and professional insurance coverage. Accordingly, Section 6.04 of the joint venture agreement (**§ 10.18**) regarding indemnification is relatively standard and requires each participant to indemnify the other for payments made and liabilities reasonably incurred in the ordinary and proper course of the project's business. Section 6.05 provides that if a party to the agreement institutes or is made a party to any litigation to enforce or defend the agreement against the joint venture or the other party, the prevailing party shall be entitled to recover from the other party all of its costs and reasonable attorneys' fees.

§ 10.15 Dispute Resolution

Section 6.07 of the joint venture agreement (**§ 10.18**) designates a dispute resolution mechanism that culminates in litigation unless the parties mutually agree to arbitration at the time a dispute arises. Alternative dispute resolution mechanisms, such as mediation and/or binding arbitration, are increasingly in vogue as a way of avoiding the delay and expense of judicial resolution. However, the possible inaccessibility in arbitration of documents, witnesses, and statements and the perceived propensity of arbitration tribunals to "split the baby" raise significant questions about whether this more timely, and presumably less expensive, alternative is really preferable to litigation. Because the dispute resolution section of the sample agreement leaves much latitude for tailoring by the parties, they should consult with legal counsel before deciding which mechanism is preferable.

§ 10.16 Default and Termination of Joint Ventures

In health care projects subject to state licensure, the parties cannot automatically dissolve and terminate the relationship, even in the event of a default, without exposing themselves to civil or criminal penalties. In our sample transaction, because the project's nursing home required both a CON and a state license, Section 9.03(e) of the joint venture agreement (**§ 10.18**) requires that the parties apply for governmental approval for discontinuation and/or the transfer of licenses and permits as a precondition to dissolving the joint venture.

§ 10.17 Sample Teaming Agreement

SAMPLE TEAMING AGREEMENT

This Teaming Agreement (the "Agreement") is made and entered into this _____ day of ____________, 199____, by and between __________________, having an office at ____________, hereinafter referred to as "Developer," and ____________, having an office at ____________, hereinafter referred to as "Contractor"; collectively, Developer and Contractor are hereinafter referred to as "the parties."

W I T N E S S E T H:

WHEREAS, the parties hereto desire to jointly pursue and perform, as a team, Program Management/Construction Management, Design/Build, General Contracting or Consulting Contracts for a project currently proposed, or anticipated by the parties to be proposed, by Hospital, Inc., a ____________ not-for-profit corporation (the "Hospital"). The project presently being contemplated by Hospital includes, but is not necessarily limited to:

> The development, design, construction, and management of a retirement community located adjacent to the Hospital's campus at ____________ Street, City of ____________, ____________, consisting of a _____ unit congregate care facility, a _____ unit residential care facility and a _____ bed skilled nursing facility (the "Project").

NOW THEREFORE, in consideration of the mutual promises herein given, the parties hereby agree as follows:

1. That the parties hereby constitute themselves a single-purpose entity for the purpose of preparing and submitting a proposal for the Project to the Hospital.

2. That the parties shall each bear their own costs and expenses in the preparation and submittal of all proposals and will share, on a confidential basis, all necessary information required for the submission of proposals.

3. That the parties shall work exclusively with each other in any efforts to pursue and perform Program Management/Construction Management, Design/Build, General Contracting or Consulting Contracts for the Project, or any other agency or entity awarding such contract for the Project.

This Agreement shall remain in effect only for such length of time as may be necessary to carry out the undertaking and the terms, provisions and conditions of this Agreement. In no event will this Agreement terminate prior to a formal award of the Project to the parties or to some other entity or group of entities, unless earlier terminated by mutual agreement of the parties. In the event either party to this Agreement breaches the terms hereof, the other party shall have all rights and remedies available at law or in equity.

Contractor and Developer acknowledge that __________ may assist in obtaining any bonds necessary for the submission of proposals and/or the performance of the contemplated Project and the parties agree to incorporate and comply with any terms reasonably required by __________ for the production of such bonds.

IN WITNESS WHEREOF, the parties hereto have duly set their hands and seals this _____ day of __________, 199____.

DEVELOPER

By: ______________________________

____

Name & Title

CONTRACTOR

By: ______________________________

____

Name & Title

§ 10.18 Sample Joint Venture Agreement for Health Care Projects

SAMPLE JOINT VENTURE AGREEMENT FOR HEALTH CARE PROJECT

TABLE OF CONTENTS

THIS JOINT VENTURE AGREEMENT (the "Agreement") is entered into as of __________, 199____, by and between Development Company, Inc., a Delaware corporation ("Developer") and Healthcare Corporation Enterprises, Inc., a __________ business corporation, and an affiliate of Hospital, Inc. ("Hospital"), a __________ not-for-profit corporation (the affiliate is hereinafter referred to as "HCE"). Hereinafter, Developer and HCE are sometimes referred to as "Participant" or collectively as "Participants."

RECITALS

WHEREAS, the participants hereto desire to form an entity, the principal business of which shall be to develop, construct, own, and operate a retirement community, consisting of a _____ unit congregate care facility, a _____ unit residential care facility and a _____ bed skilled nursing facility (the "Project") located on that certain real property in __________ County, State of __________, owned by Hospital and adjacent to Hospital's campus located at __________ Street, City of __________, __________, more particularly described on Exhibit A, which is attached hereto and incorporated herein by reference (the "Property");

WHEREAS, Developer is an experienced developer and manager of retirement housing;

WHEREAS, Developer, through its various Affiliates, is experienced in marketing and managing health care projects; and

WHEREAS, HCE is an affiliate of Hospital which operates a 500-bed acute care hospital in the City of __________, __________.

NOW, THEREFORE, in consideration of the mutual promises herein contained, the parties hereby agree as follows:

ARTICLE 1
FORMATION

1.01 *FORMATION.* The Participants have agreed to form, and do hereby form, the Joint Venture under the __________ Uniform Partnership Act (the "Act").

1.02 *NAME.* The business of the Joint Venture shall be conducted under the name "HEALTHCARE VENTURE."

1.03 *OFFICE.* The address of the Joint Venture's place of business shall be __________, __________, or such other place as the Participants may determine from time to time.

1.04 *TERM.* The Joint Venture shall commence on the date hereof, and shall end on __________, unless sooner dissolved as provided below.

ARTICLE 2
DEFINED TERMS

DEFINED TERMS. Certain terms are defined elsewhere in the text of this Agreement. However, the following defined terms used in this Agreement shall have the meanings specified below:

2.01 *"Act"* means the _______ Uniform Partnership Act, Chapter _____, supplemented or superseded from time to time.

2.02 *"Affiliate"* means (a) any partner or officer of a Participant; (b) any trust, corporation, partnership, association or any other organization or entity controlling, controlled by or under common control with a Participant or any such partner or officer of a Participant; and (c) any officer, director, trustee, general partner or holder of 10% or more of the outstanding voting securities of any corporation, partnership, trust or other entity controlling, controlled by or under common control with the Participant, or any such partner or officer of a Participant.

2.03 *"Agreement"* means this Joint Venture Agreement as originally executed and as amended, modified or restated from time to time, as the context may require.

2.04 *"Capital Account"*: A Capital Account shall be maintained for each Participant. The Capital Account of each Participant shall consist of the original Capital Contribution made by each Participant and increased by (a) all additional contributions, if any, by a Participant to the capital of the Joint Venture; (b) any amounts credited to the Capital Account as a result of any profit allocated to a Participant and decreased; (c) by any amounts debited to the Capital Account as a result of any losses allocated to a Participant and any reductions to the Capital Account of a withdrawing Participant and (d) by the amount of all distributions made to a Participant.

2.05 *"Capital Contribution"* means the total amount of money or other property contributed or agreed to be contributed, as the context requires, to the Joint Venture by each Participant pursuant to the terms of this Agreement.

2.06 *"Code"* means the United States Internal Revenue Code of 1986, as amended.

2.07 *"Developer"* means Development Company, Inc., a Delaware corporation.

2.08 *"Distributions"* means cash or other property, from any source, distributed to the Participants by the Joint Venture, but shall not include any payments to any Participant for services or repayment of loans.

2.09 (a) "HCE" means Healthcare Enterprises, Inc., a ____________ business corporation and an affiliate of Hospital, Inc., a ____________ not-for-profit corporation.

(b) "Hospital" means Hospital, Inc., a ____________ not-for-profit corporation, owner of 100% of the stock of Healthcare Enterprises, Inc., a ____________ business corporation.

2.10 *"Joint Venture"* means the ____________ general partnership formed and governed by this Agreement.

2.11 *"Managing Participant"*: Developer shall be the Managing Participant for the Joint Venture.

2.12 *"Participants"* means Developer and HCE, plus any other person or persons who may become a substitute or additional Participant and who are elected or admitted hereto as a Participant pursuant to the terms hereof. The term "Participant" or "Participants," as the case may be, as used in this Agreement, shall include the singular and plural as the context of the provision requires and shall include each and every Participant hereof unless otherwise specified.

2.13 *"Percentage Interest"* means the respective interests of the Participants in and to all assets, proceeds, gain, income and profits of the Joint Venture and the respective shares of all losses, expenses, liabilities and obligations of the Joint

Venture. The initial Percentage Interest of each Joint Venture Participant is as set forth in Section 4.06 hereof.

2.14 *"Person"* means any natural individual or entity, and the heirs, executors, administrators, legal representatives, successors and assigns of such individual or entity.

2.15 *"Project"* means the Property and the buildings and improvements that comprise the _____ unit congregate care facility, the _____ unit residential care facility and the _____ bed skilled nursing facility, which are to be constructed on the Property.

2.16 *"Property"* means the real property identified and described in Exhibit A attached hereto.

2.17 *"Purpose"* means the reason and intent for forming the Joint Venture as set forth in Section 3.01 hereof.

ARTICLE 3
PURPOSE AND BUSINESS OF THE JOINT VENTURE

3.01 *PURPOSE.*

(a) The purpose of the Joint Venture is to own, develop, construct, and operate the Project and related facilities thereon.

(b) In furtherance of the above purpose, the Joint Venture shall have the power:

(i) To finance the construction and operation of the Project.

(ii) To enter into, perform and carry out contracts of any kind, including contracts with Affiliates of the Participants, necessary to, in connection with, or incidental to, the accomplishment of the purposes of the Joint Venture, specifically including, but not limited to, the execution and delivery of all agreements, certificates, instruments or documents required by a financial institution or other governmental entities in connection with the construction, development, financing, improvement, maintenance and operation of the Project or the Property.

(iii) To acquire any property, real or personal, in fee or under lease, or any rights therein or appurtenant thereto, necessary or convenient for the construction and operation of the Project, and to grant easements for the purposes of acquiring services for the Project or for the other purposes consistent with the purposes of the Joint Venture.

(iv) Subject to any applicable regulations, to borrow money and to issue evidences of indebtedness and to secure the same by mortgage, pledge or other lien on the Property, or any other assets of the Joint Venture, in furtherance of any and all of the purposes of the Joint Venture.

(v) To prepay in whole or in part, refinance, recast, increase, modify or extend the mortgage or any other mortgages affecting the Property and in connection therewith to execute any extensions, renewals or modifications of the mortgage or any such other mortgages on the Property.

(vi) To employ a licensed general contractor (which may be an Affiliate of a Participant) to construct the Project.

(vii) To contract with a mortgage company, to obtain the appropriate construction and permanent financing for the Project.

(viii) To employ a management company (which may be an Affiliate of a Participant) to manage the Project.

(ix) To sell the Project to third parties, the Participants or Affiliates of the Participants, or to joint ventures, general partnerships, limited partnerships, or corporations that this Joint Venture is a party to.

(x) To engage in any joint venture, general partnership, limited partnership or corporation that is formed for the purpose of developing or owning the Project.

(xi) To carry on any other activities necessary to or in connection with, or incidental to, the accomplishment of the purposes of the Joint Venture, so long as such activities may be lawfully carried on or performed by a joint venture under the laws of the State of ____________ and under the provisions hereof.

(c) The Joint Venture shall not engage in any business not included with Section 3.01(a) and Section 3.01(b) hereof without the prior consent of all the Participants.

3.02 *TITLE TO JOINT VENTURE PROPERTY.* All property owned by the Joint Venture, whether real or personal, tangible or intangible, shall be deemed to be owned by the Joint Venture as an entity, and no Participant shall have any ownership of such property.

ARTICLE 4
PARTICIPANTS' CAPITAL CONTRIBUTIONS AND PERCENTAGE INTERESTS

4.01 *INITIAL CAPITAL CONTRIBUTION.*

(a) *Cash Contribution.* Upon execution and delivery of this Agreement, each of the Participants shall have contributed to the capital of the Joint Venture the cash necessary to fund the initial development costs of the Project, including a market feasibility study, architectural and engineering fees, legal fees for zoning, Certificate of Need ("CON") and licensure applications, and marketing the Project to prospective Project residents. The sum of cash contributed by each Participant is set forth opposite each Participant's name, as follows:

Name of Participant	*Capital Contribution*
Developer	$______________
HCE	$______________
TOTAL	$______________

(b) *Real Property Contribution.* HCE shall cause Hospital to transfer title to the Property as part of HCE's Capital Contribution to the Joint Venture on or before closing on the construction financing for the Project. The Capital Contribution made pursuant to this Subsection is equal to $____________, representing the fair market value of the Property.

(c) *Work Product Contribution.* Each of the Participants possesses unique expertise which when coordinated and combined shall enable the Joint Venture to develop and construct the Project. As further initial Capital Contributions, each of the Participants shall contribute the following work product:

(i) ____

____

____

(ii) ______________________________

____

____

(iii) ______________________________

____

____

4.02 *ADDITIONAL CAPITAL CONTRIBUTIONS.*

(a) The Participants agree to make additional Capital Contributions as described in this Section 4.02.

(b) At any time after the execution of this Agreement, as and when the Joint Venture shall require additional funds as determined by the Joint Venture acting through its Management Committee, the Participants shall each contribute their respective share of such amounts as may be necessary as additional Capital Contributions pro rata in accordance with their Percentage Interest as of the date the notice is received which requests the additional Capital Contributions. If any additional Capital Contribution shall be required to be made pursuant to this Section 4.02(b), the Management Committee shall send a notice thereof to each Participant, stating the amounts required and the specific purpose for which such additional Capital Contributions are required. Each Participant shall, within five (5) days of the receipt of such notice, contribute the amount required by such notice to the Joint Venture.

(c) In the event that a Participant fails to make any additional Capital Contribution within the time specified, the Percentage Interests shall be recalculated as of the date the additional Capital Contribution was due. No creditor of the Joint Venture shall be a third-party beneficiary of the provision of this Section 4.02(c).

4.03 *NO INTEREST ON CONTRIBUTIONS.* No interest shall be paid upon any Capital Contributions.

4.04 *WITHDRAWAL AND RETURN OF CAPITAL.* Except as expressly set forth herein, no Participant may withdraw any portion of its Capital Contribution and no Participant shall be entitled to the return of its Capital Contribution except upon consent of the other Participants or on dissolution of the Joint Venture.

4.05 *LOANS FROM PARTICIPANTS.*

(a) Subject to the consent of the other Participant, a Participant may lend money to and transact other business with the Joint Venture and, subject to applicable law, shall have the rights and obligations with respect thereto as a person who is not a Participant. Any loans from a Participant to the Joint Venture shall bear interest at commercially reasonable rates as determined by the Management Committee. If any Participant makes any loan or loans to the Joint Venture, the amount of such loan shall not be an increase in the Capital Contribution of the lending Participant or entitle such lending Participant to any increase in Participant's share of the distributions of the Joint Venture or subject the Participant to any greater proportion of the losses the Joint Venture may sustain. No Participant shall be under any obligation to make any loan to the Joint Venture nor shall the Joint Venture be under any obligation to borrow money from any Participant.

4.06 *PERCENTAGE INTEREST.* Subject to an adjustment provided in Section 4.02(c) hereof, the Percentage Interest of each Participant shall be as follows:

Name of Participant	*Percentage Interest*
Developer	________
HCE	________
TOTAL	100%

ARTICLE 5
MANAGEMENT OF THE JOINT VENTURE

5.01 *MANAGEMENT OF THE JOINT VENTURE.* Except as otherwise expressly provided in Section 5.02, the Participants shall have all of the rights, powers, and authority conferred upon them by law. The Participants may delegate certain of their rights and responsibilities to the Management Committee as delineated in Section 5.02.

5.02 *MANAGEMENT COMMITTEE.* A Management Committee shall be established for the Joint Venture. The Management Committee shall consist of two (2) members, one representative for each Participant being the Participant's chief executive officer, or designee.

The Participants shall act through their respective representatives on the Management Committee. Both members of the Management Committee shall constitute a quorum for the transaction of business at any meeting of the Management Committee. All actions of the Management Committee shall require mutual agreement of the Participant's respective members of the Management Committee.

The power and authority of the Management Committee shall include the following:

(a) To acquire any land or interest therein.

(b) To finance or refinance the Joint Venture, including but not limited to, the financing of the acquisition of any of the Project, construction and permanent financing or refinancing of the improvements (including any public financing of onsite or offsite improvements) and financing operations of the Joint Venture.

(c) To sell or otherwise transfer, mortgage or place or suffer any other encumbrance on the Property or the improvements or any part or parts thereof.

(d) To construct the improvements for the Project or make any capital improvements, repairs, alterations or changes or cause the Joint Venture to enter into any other general partnership, limited partnership or any other venture involving the Project or otherwise.

(e) To select or vary depreciation and accounting methods and make other decisions with respect to the treatment of various transactions for state or federal income tax purposes, consistent with the other provisions of this Agreement.

(f) To approve all consultants' contracts pertaining to improvements, construction and architectural contracts and all architectural plans, specifications and drawings prior to the construction and/or alteration of the improvements contemplated thereby, and any modifications of such contracts, plans, specifications and drawings.

(g) To place and acquire all casualty and liability insurance to protect the Joint Venture's properties and business and to protect the Participants.

(h) To develop and approve a Project budget and to make any expenditure or incur any obligation with respect to any line item on such budgets.

(i) To file any formal applications pertaining to the Project with any public, quasi-public or private organizations.

(j) To make any expenditure or incur any obligation for any litigation concerning the Joint Venture or the Project.

5.03 *MANAGING PARTICIPANT.* Developer shall be the Managing Participant for the Joint Venture. In such capacity, Developer shall be responsible for the day-to-day operations of the Joint Venture, subject to the power and authority of the Management Committee and the terms and conditions of this Agreement.

5.04 *OPERATING RESTRICTIONS.*

(a) Each Participant agrees that unless it has the prior, written consent of the other Participant, it will not do any of the following:

(i) Use any money, property or effects belonging to the Joint Venture or contract any debt on behalf of the Joint Venture, except at the direction of the Management Committee; or

(ii) Settle or discharge any debt due the Joint Venture without receiving the full amount owing.

(b) Each Participant agrees that unless it has the prior written consent of the other Participant, it will not, for purposes other than the benefit of the Joint Venture, directly or indirectly:

(i) Use the Joint Venture's name for the benefit of any other entity; or

(ii) Make or endorse any financial instrument that purports to obligate the Joint Venture in any way.

ARTICLE 6
RIGHTS, OBLIGATIONS AND POWERS OF PARTICIPANTS

6.01 *NEGATION OF FIDUCIARY DUTY.* The Participants agree that, notwithstanding the fact that Developer and HCE are Participants herein, either Participant, individually, or in concert with others, may act as a subcontractor of the Joint Venture. In such event, such Participant agrees that the Joint Venture may act (including, without limitation, to declare defaults, assert rights and remedies which it may possess by subrogation or otherwise on account of satisfying its obligations under guaranties, or insist upon strict performance) without regard to any fiduciary or other duty the Joint Venture may have or the Participant may have to the other Participant because of such relationship. In the instance of such sub-contractual relationship, each Participant hereby agrees that the other Participant or the Joint Venture may act in such instance as if such Participant owed no fiduciary duty to the other Participant or this Joint Venture and may act as though such Participant had no interest in this Joint Venture.

6.02 *PERMISSIBLE ACTIVITIES.* Subject to the Noncompete Clause in Section 6.03 herein, any Participant and any Affiliate of a Participant may engage in or possess interests in other business ventures of every kind and description for their own account. Neither the Joint Venture nor any of the Participants shall have any rights by virtue of this Agreement in or to such other business ventures or to the income or profits derived therefrom.

6.03 *NONCOMPETE CLAUSE.* All of the Participants and their Affiliates, subsidiaries, joint ventures, or related organizations agree that they will not compete in any way with the Project or the existing programs of the Project. Except as otherwise provided in this Section 6.03, none of the Participants shall advise, build, construct, joint venture, market or manage licensed or unlicensed senior housing serving older adults which competes with the Project. A project will be competitive if it is located in the Project's primary market area. For purposes of this clause, the primary market area for the Project shall be defined as the geographic area described in Exhibit B attached hereto and incorporated herein by reference. Any unlicensed senior housing project serving older adults which is similar in pricing, residential, social and medical options to those offered by the Joint Venture on the site of the Project will be considered to be in competition with the Project. If any Participant believes that a project they wish to advise, build, construct, joint venture, market or manage does not compete with the Project, then that Participant may provide information to the Joint Venture explaining why the proposed project does not compete with the Project. The Joint Venture by the unanimous consent of the Participants may determine that a project located in the primary market area, or a project with a primary market overlapping the primary market area of the Project, does not compete and therefore waive the provisions of this clause with respect to that particular project. Any such waiver of this clause with respect to one project shall not be deemed to be a waiver of the clause with respect to any other project. As a further exception to the coverage of this restriction, all of the Participants shall be permitted to manage any competing project in the Joint Venture's primary market area or which competing project's primary market area overlaps the primary market area of the Project so long as such competing project is more than ninety percent (90%) occupied.

6.04 *INDEMNIFICATION.* The Joint Venture shall indemnify each Participant in respect of payments made and personal liabilities reasonably incurred by such Participant in the ordinary and proper conduct of the Joint Venture's business or for the preservation of Joint Venture business or property.

6.05 *COST OF ENFORCEMENT.* In the event a Participant institutes or is made a party to any litigation to enforce or defend any term, provision or covenant of this Agreement against the Joint Venture or the other Participant, the prevailing party in such litigation shall be entitled to recover from the other party hereto, comprised of either the Joint Venture or the other Participant or both of them, such costs and reasonable attorney's fees as the prevailing party shall have incurred therein. Further, if as a result of such litigation the result thereof is that the prevailing party thereto is entitled to, among other things, a money award, such prevailing party shall be entitled to have added to such award any interest thereon from the date the court determines such money award should have been paid, until it is in fact paid at the rate compounded per annum of twelve (12) percent.

6.06 *PROPRIETARY INTERESTS.* Each of the Participants hereby acknowledges that the employees of each Participant, the technical experience developed by each Participant and trademarks, servicemarks, trade names and logos of each Participant is individually and are collectively unique and that each such Participant has a proprietary interest in the continued employment of each such employee, in the technical experience so developed and in the trademarks, servicemarks, trade names and logos of each such Participant, whether or not registered. As a result, during the period commencing on the date hereof and on the first to occur of five (5) years following either the dissolution of this Joint Venture or of substantial completion of the obligations of the Joint Venture, each Participant agrees:

(a) Not to make any offers, proposals or advances (whether initiated by or solicited from a Participant) to any employee of the other Participant, the result of which would reasonably be intended to induce such employee to terminate his then-engaged employment with such Participant; and

(b) Not to use for its own benefit or the benefit of any of its Affiliates any of the surveys, data, reports, studies, or other information that was developed by a Participant through its technical experience or to use the other Participant's trademarks, servicemarks, trade names or logos without, in each instance, first obtaining such Participant's prior written consent, which consent may be arbitrarily withheld.

6.07 *DISPUTES.* If any dispute arises between the Participants or between a Participant and the Joint Venture, such disputing parties shall meet as promptly as possible and negotiate in good faith in an effort to resolve such dispute extrajudicially. In the event that such dispute cannot be resolved by mutual agreement after good faith negotiations, the Participants hereby agree that all such unresolved disputes must be, if resolution is desired, litigated in the ____________ Judicial Circuit in and for ____________ County, ____________, as the only forum in which a Participant or the Joint Venture may litigate such unresolved disputes. Notwithstanding the foregoing, if, in writing, the Participants subsequently agree (but they are under no duty to do so) to submit any unresolved dispute to binding arbitration, the resolution of such dispute shall be in accordance with the terms, provisions and conditions of such mutual agreement.

ARTICLE 7

COMPENSATION TO PARTICIPANTS OR THEIR AFFILIATES

7.01 *COMPENSATION.* The Participants or their Affiliates shall be entitled to receive each and all of the amounts as fees and compensation as set forth in this Section.

7.02 *DEVELOPMENT FEE.* The Joint Venture shall pay to Developer a development fee in an amount equal to five percent (5%) of the development cost for the development of the Project. The term "development cost" shall mean the total Project costs minus the fair market value of the Property, as established herein, costs of carrying the Property and costs for offsite improvements. The development fee shall be paid by the Joint Venture as follows: one-half (1/2) of said fee shall be paid on the date construction for the Project commences and the remaining one-half (1/2) shall be paid when certificates of occupancy are issued by the appropriate governmental authority.

7.03 *FINANCING FEE.* The Joint Venture shall pay to Developer a financing fee in an amount equal to one percent (1%) of the total construction financing placed on the Project. The financing fee shall be paid by the Joint Venture on the date the construction financing for the Project is funded by the lender providing such financing for the Project.

7.04 *MARKETING FEE.* The Joint Venture shall pay to Developer or an Affiliate of Developer a marketing fee in the amount of ____________ ($______). The marketing fee shall be paid to Developer in ____________ (______) equal monthly installments. The first monthly installment paid shall be paid on ____________, and continuing on the same day of each month thereafter until the ____________ (______) installments are fully paid.

7.05 *ARCHITECT'S FEE.* The Joint Venture shall pay to Developer an architect's fee in the amount of ____________ ($______), payable as set forth in Section 7.05(a) below. The fee schedule includes all consultants that would be utilized, the costs of which shall be paid for by Developer, except for interior design and all offsite engineering costs, which shall be additional costs incurred by the Joint Venture.

(a) The payment schedule for the above-referenced architect's fee shall be as follows:

(i) Upon commencement of the initial design for the Project, the Joint Venture shall pay to Developer an amount equal to fifteen percent (15%) of the total fee.

(ii) Upon completion of all the required detail work with respect to the working drawings for the Project, the Joint Venture shall pay to Developer an amount equal to fifteen percent (15%) of the total fee.

(iii) Upon completion of the working drawings and up to the bidding process for the Project, the Joint Venture shall pay to Developer in monthly progress payments from the completion of the working drawings and up to the bidding process an amount equal to fifty percent (50%) of the total fee.

(iv) Throughout the construction of the Project, the Joint Venture shall pay to Developer an amount equal to twenty percent (20%) of the total fee. Said twenty percent (20%) of the total fee shall be paid in quarterly installments based upon the percentage amount of construction completion.

(b) The Joint Venture and Developer shall enter into an architectural fee agreement for the payment of the above-referenced fee which shall denote in detail the above-referenced terms.

7.06 *MARKET STUDY FEE.* The Joint Venture shall pay to Developer, or an Affiliate of Developer, a market study fee in the amount of ____________ ($______) for providing the Joint Venture a market study for the Project. The market study fee shall be paid by the Joint Venture to Developer when the construction financing for the Project is closed and funded.

7.07 *PROPERTY MANAGEMENT FEE.* The Joint Venture shall pay to the Developer, or an Affiliate of Developer, a property management fee equal to five percent (5%) of the monthly gross receipts collected from the Project. The Joint Venture shall enter into a separate management agreement for the Project with the Developer, or an Affiliate of Developer, which shall delineate all of the pertinent terms and conditions of the day-to-day management of the Project.

7.08 *JOINT VENTURE ADMINISTRATION FEE.* The Joint Venture shall pay to Developer a Joint Venture administration fee in the amount of ____________ ($______) for monitoring the construction aspects of the Project. Said fee shall be paid when the construction financing for the Project is closed and funded. The Joint Venture shall also pay to Developer an ongoing Joint Venture administration fee during the rental operation of the Project. The ongoing Joint Venture administration fee paid to Developer shall equal the sum of one percent (1%) of monthly gross receipts collected on the Project. Said ongoing one percent (1%) Joint Venture administration fee shall be paid on a monthly basis promptly after collection of receipts for a given month.

ARTICLE 8
TRANSFERS OF PARTICIPANTS' INTERESTS

8.01 *TRANSFER RESTRICTIONS.* Except as otherwise provided in Section 8.02, neither Participant shall sell, assign, give or otherwise transfer its Joint Venture interest, or any part thereof, to any person or entity without the prior written consent of the non-transferring Participant. In the event the non-transferring Participant consents to such transfer, the person or entity to which the Participant's interest is being transferred shall be substituted as a Participant, subject to all the rights and obligations of a Participant under this Agreement.

8.02 *PERMITTED TRANSFERS.* Section 8.01 shall not apply to a transfer by either Participant of its entire Joint Venture interest to any entity that directly or indirectly controls the transferring Participant, is controlled by the transferring Participant or is under common control with the transferring Participant (for this purpose, control shall mean ownership of over 50% of the effective voting rights), provided that in each case all of the following conditions are met:

(a) The transferee assumes in writing in a form satisfactory to the non-transferring Participant all of the transferor's obligations under this Agreement; and

(b) Unless waived by the non-transferring Participant, an opinion is obtained from the transferee's counsel (which opinion and counsel shall both be satisfactory to the non-transferring Participant) stating that such assignment will not jeopardize the status of the Joint Venture as a partnership for Federal income tax purposes, will not materially affect the taxable income of the Joint Venture, will not cause a termination of the Joint Venture for purposes of the then applicable provisions of the Code, will not violate, or cause the Joint Venture to violate, any applicable law or governmental rule or regulation, including, without limitation, any applicable Federal or State securities law, and that registration under State and Federal securities law is not required in connection with such assignment.

8.03 *PARTICIPANT WITHDRAWAL.* Neither Participant shall withdraw from the Joint Venture unless a substitute Participant has been found by the withdrawing Participant, the non-withdrawing Participant has given prior written consent to the withdrawal and substitution, and the substitute Participant assumes in writing in a form satisfactory to the non-withdrawing Participant all of the withdrawing Participant's obligations under the Agreement.

ARTICLE 9
DISSOLUTION

9.01 *DISSOLUTION.* The Joint Venture shall be dissolved before expiration of its ____________ (______)-year term on the happening of any of the following events:

(a) Upon one hundred and twenty (120) days' prior written notice by either Participant to the other Participant.

(b) At any time during the term of the Agreement upon mutual consent of the Participants.

(c) The occurrence of a Dissolving Event as specified in Section 9.02.

9.02 *DISSOLVING EVENTS.* A Dissolving Event occurs:

(a) When either Participant is adjudicated a bankrupt or insolvent.

(b) When a trustee, receiver, or liquidator is appointed for either Participant's property or when an assignee for the benefit of either Participant's creditors has been appointed.

(c) Upon the filing of a voluntary petition in bankruptcy by either Participant.

(d) Upon the filing of a petition by either Participant seeking any reorganization, arrangement, composition, readjustment, liquidation, dissolution or similar relief with respect to either Participant.

(e) If, upon review of either Participant's existing debt instruments, either Participant is precluded by the terms thereof from participating in the transactions contemplated by the Joint Venture.

(f) If the market feasibility study referenced in Section 4.01(a) indicates the Project is not financially feasible within the Project's primary market area.

(g) If the Joint Venture fails to obtain a CON or any other required licenses or permits for the Project by ___________.

(h) If the Joint Venture fails to secure zoning, variances or other approvals necessary for the construction and operation of the Project by ___________.

(i) If the Joint Venture fails to obtain suitable commitments for construction financing for the Project by ___________.

(j) If the Joint Venture fails to negotiate and execute a property management agreement to manage the day-to-day operations of the Project with Developer or Developer's Affiliate, by ___________.

9.03 *LIQUIDATION OF THE JOINT VENTURE.*

(a) *Liquidation.* HCE and Developer, by mutual agreement, shall select a third party to act as liquidator (the "Liquidator") to wind up the Joint Venture. The Liquidator shall have full power and authority to sell, assign and encumber any or all of the Joint Venture's assets and to wind up and liquidate the affairs of the Joint Venture in an orderly and businesslike manner. All proceeds from liquidation shall be distributed in the following order of priority: (i) to pay the debts and liabilities of the Joint Venture and the expenses of liquidation, (ii) to set up such reserves as the Liquidator reasonably deems necessary for any contingent liabilities of the Joint Venture, and (iii) the balance, if any, to the Participants in the same manner as other distributions from the Joint Venture are made to the Participants.

(b) *Distribution in Kind.* If the Liquidator shall determine that a portion of the Joint Venture's assets should be distributed in kind to the Participants, it shall obtain an independent appraisal of the fair market value of each such asset as of a date reasonably close to the date of liquidation. Any unrealized appreciation or depreciation with respect to such assets shall be allocated among the Participants (in accordance with the provisions of Section 10.01 hereof regarding the allocation of Participants' profits and losses), assuming that the assets were sold for the appraised value and taken into consideration in determining the balance in the Participants' capital accounts as of the date of liquidation. Distribution of any such assets in kind to a Participant shall be considered a distribution of an amount equal to such asset's fair market value for purposes of Section 9.03 hereof. Except as otherwise determined by the Liquidator pursuant to this Section 9.03, no Participant shall have any right to receive distributions of property, other than cash, from the Joint Venture.

(c) *No Negative Capital Account Contribution.* In the event that any Participant's capital account balance is a negative amount after all allocations to such account in accordance with Section 10.01 hereof and distributions in accordance with Section 9.03 hereof, such Participant shall have no obligation to contribute any amount to the Joint Venture as a result of such negative capital account balance; provided that the foregoing shall not relieve any Participant of any obligations to make a capital contribution under Article 4 hereof.

(d) *Termination of Joint Venture.* Upon completion of the distribution of Joint Venture assets as provided in Section 9.03 hereof, the Joint Venture shall be terminated, and the Liquidator (or the Participants, if necessary) shall take such other actions as may be necessary to terminate the Joint Venture.

(e) *Governmental Approvals.* If the CON and any other licenses and permits necessary to own and operate the Project have been obtained, the Joint Venture shall take all action required by law to notify the appropriate governmental bodies to transfer or terminate the CON and any other licenses and permits obtained for the Project.

ARTICLE 10
PROFITS, LOSSES AND DISTRIBUTIONS

10.01 *ALLOCATION OF PROFITS AND LOSSES.* For purposes of this Agreement, profits and losses shall mean the net profits or losses of the Joint Venture as finally determined for each fiscal year of the Joint Venture by the Joint Venture's auditors. Except as otherwise provided in this Agreement, profits and losses shall be allocated as follows: fifty percent (50%) to HCE and fifty percent (50%) to Developer.

10.02 *DISTRIBUTIONS.*

(a) *Available Funds.* "Available funds" shall mean all cash funds of the Joint Venture in excess of reasonable reserves deemed necessary by the Joint Venture acting through its Management Committee to meet the expected future cash flow needs of the Joint Venture.

(b) *Distribution of Available Funds.* Available funds of the Joint Venture shall be distributed fifty percent (50%) to HCE and fifty percent (50%) to Developer.

10.03 *ALLOCATION IN THE EVENT PROPERTY IS CONTRIBUTED.* If a Participant on formation of the Joint Venture, or any time thereafter, contributes to the Joint Venture any property (other than United States Dollars) with an adjusted income tax basis different from the fair market value at which the Property is accepted and credited to the Participant's account by the Joint Venture, any depreciation, depletion, gain or loss with respect to that property shall be allocated in accordance with Federal and State tax laws so as to take account of the variation between the basis of such property to the Joint Venture and its fair market value at the time of contribution.

ARTICLE 11
ACCOUNTING AND RECORDS MATTERS

11.01 *METHOD OF ACCOUNTING.* The Joint Venture books shall be kept on an accrual basis.

11.02 *FISCAL YEAR.* The fiscal year of the Joint Venture shall be the calendar year, unless amended by the mutual agreement of the Participants.

11.03 *JOINT VENTURE BOOKS AND RECORDS.* Developer, as the Managing Participant, shall keep, or cause to be kept, such full and true books of account of the Joint Venture as are deemed necessary. All of such books and records shall at all times be maintained at the principal office of Developer, and shall be open to the inspection, examination, copying and duplicating at reasonable times by either of the Participants or their respective agents. The Managing Participant shall, within three (3) months after the termination of each fiscal year, furnish to each Participant an annual report of budgetary expenditures for the year. The fiscal year of the Joint Venture shall end on the last day of December of each year. Additionally, Developer, as the Managing Participant, shall maintain such books, records, and financial statements.

The U.S. Partnership Income Tax Return (and any applicable State Income Tax Returns) shall be prepared by the Joint Venture's auditors, and appropriate tax information shall be submitted to the Joint Venture, together with the annual unaudited financial statements.

To the extent that any Participant, or individual or entity related to a Participant, is performing professional services, the Joint Venture shall provide such information to any third-party payor, government agency, or licensing or accreditation authority, as is reasonably necessary for securing compensation for services rendered or for meeting any professional or legal requirements.

ARTICLE 12
GENERAL PROVISIONS

12.01 *WARRANTIES.* Each Participant hereby warrants that it is legally constituted and authorized to enter into this Agreement, and that it has not knowingly made any misrepresentation or omitted any material fact to induce the other Participant to enter into this Agreement.

12.02 *AMENDMENTS.* This Agreement may be amended only upon mutual written consent of both Participants.

12.03 *NOTICES.* Whenever a provision is made in this Agreement for the giving, service, or delivery of any notice, such notice shall be deemed to have been duly given, served and delivered on the occurrence of any of the following: (a) immediately upon receipt, if delivered on a business day by personal delivery, telex, telefax, telecopy or other facsimile service, (b) the next business day after deposit with a recognized overnight courier service (such as Federal Express) or (c) three business days after being mailed by registered or certified United States mail, in each case addressed to the party entitled to receive the same at Participant's address specified in this Agreement. Any Participant may change its mailing address by giving to the Management Committee written notice specifying the Participant's new address.

12.04 *COUNTERPARTS.* This Agreement may be executed in any number of counterparts and when so executed, all of such counterparts shall constitute a single instrument binding upon all parties hereto notwithstanding the fact that all parties are not signatory to the original or to the same counterpart.

12.05 *SURVIVAL OF RIGHTS.* Subject to the restrictions against unauthorized transfer hereinbefore set forth, the provisions of this Agreement shall inure to the benefit of and be binding upon the parties hereto and their respective heirs, devisees, legatees, personal representatives, successors and assigns.

12.06 *ADDITIONAL DOCUMENTS.* Each Participant agrees to execute and deliver to the other Participant such additional documents and instruments as Developer, in its sole and absolute discretion, deems necessary or desirable to carry out or more effectively implement the provisions of this Agreement or the business or purposes of the Joint Venture.

12.07 *ENTIRE AGREEMENT.* This Agreement contains the entire understanding among the Participants and supersedes any prior written or oral agreements between them respecting the subject matter contained herein. There are no representations, agreements, arrangements, or understandings, oral or written between and among the Participants relating to the subject matter of this Agreement which are not fully expressed herein.

12.08 *CROSS-REFERENCE.* All cross-references in this Agreement, unless specifically directed to another agreement or document, refer to the provisions in this Agreement as set forth in the cross-referenced section or subsection and shall not be deemed to be references to the overall transaction or to any other agreement or document.

12.09 *GOVERNING LAW.* All questions with respect to the construction of this Agreement and the rights and liabilities of the parties hereto shall be governed by the laws of the State of ____________. On all matters not covered by this Agreement, the Act shall apply.

12.10 *SEVERABILITY.* In the event any of the provisions of this Agreement are determined to be invalid or unenforceable, the same shall be deemed severable from the remainder of this Agreement and shall not cause the invalidity or unenforceability of the remainder of this Agreement.

12.11 *INCORPORATION OF SCHEDULES OR EXHIBITS.* All exhibits, schedules, and other documents attached to this Agreement and specified herein are incorporated herein by reference the same as if set forth in full herein.

12.12 *PARTIES IN INTEREST.* Nothing in this Agreement, whether expressed or implied, is intended to confer any rights or remedies under or by reason of this Agreement on any persons other than the parties to it and their respective successors and assigns, nor is anything in this Agreement intended to relieve or discharge the obligation or liability of any third persons to any party to this Agreement, nor shall any provision give any third persons any rights of subrogation or action over against any party to this Agreement.

IN WITNESS WHEREOF, the parties hereto have executed, acknowledged and delivered this Agreement as of the date first above written.

HEALTHCARE CORPORATION ENTERPRISES, INC.	ADDRESSES FOR NOTICES
By: ____________________	____________________
	____________________
ATTEST: ________________	____________________
DEVELOPMENT COMPANY, INC.	
By: ____________________	____________________
	____________________
ATTEST: ________________	____________________

EXHIBIT A
PROPERTY

EXHIBIT B
PROJECT'S PRIMARY MARKET AREA

CHAPTER 11

HAZARDOUS WASTE AND CLEANUP PROJECTS

Steven J. Comen
Evan Slavitt

Steven J. Comen is a partner in the law firm of Hinckley, Allen, Snyder & Comen in Boston, Massachusetts. A graduate of Brown University, Mr. Comen received his J.D. from the University of Michigan Law School. He has been involved in both environmental and privatization matters for over 20 years and handled some of the earliest environmental regulatory matters and waste management projects in this country. Mr. Comen devotes a substantial portion of his practice to the full range of environmental matters and Superfund projects. A frequent lecturer to both legal and trade groups, he represents clients in state and federal courts, arbitration proceedings, boards of contract appeals, and before administrative agencies.

Evan Slavitt is a partner in the law firm Hinckley, Allen, Snyder & Comen in Boston, Massachusetts, where he concentrates in the fields of environmental litigation and criminal defense. A graduate of Yale University and Harvard Law School, Mr. Slavitt spent two years in the Antitrust Division of the United States Department of Justice before serving as an Assistant United States Attorney in Massachusetts. Mr. Slavitt is a frequent lecturer and author in the field of environmental law.

§ 11.1 Introduction

The United States Environmental Protection Agency (EPA) has in its computerized inventory over 30,000 potentially abandoned or uncontrolled hazardous waste sites. Many states, including Massachusetts, New Jersey, New York, and California, maintain separate inventories of hazardous waste sites not on the EPA's list that will be cleaned up within the next 10 years. Cleanups under the Comprehensive Environmental Response, Compensation, and Liability Act[1] (CERCLA or Superfund) and state cleanups under parallel state laws are done primarily via private contractors. Thus, during the first 10 years of the EPA's Superfund activities, contractors have received between 80 to 90 percent of the available funds each year. In recent years, notwithstanding criticism of excessive spending, this cleanup budget has been approximately $1 billion per year.

The EPA effort is only the tip of the iceberg, however. Many sites, both federally controlled and state controlled, are under the control of private entities who are under orders from the federal or state government to clean up the site. This spending, which does not show up on the EPA budget, has grown geometrically in the last 10 years and is likely to continue to be a strong source of contracting work in the foreseeable future.

The aggregate assessment of cleanup costs, both public and private, varies dramatically. Nonetheless, recent estimates placed the costs at $500 billion over the next 50 years, exclusive of Department of Energy cleanup costs, which are estimated to be approximately $100 billion. Further, new enforcement efforts under CERCLA's parallel statute, the Resource Conservation and Recovery Act[2] (RCRA), will add substantially to the potential cleanup expenditures in the next decade. Similarly, there will be an increasing effort to remove underground storage tanks and to control emissions both into water and the air. In short, under current statutory and regulatory conditions, it can be anticipated that spending on the environment will be in excess of $1.5 trillion over the next 50 years.

§ 11.2 Unique Joint Venturing Considerations

As the market for environmental contracting services has increased, firms have taken two divergent approaches to maintaining competitiveness. For instance, a

---

[1] 42 U.S.C. §§ 9601–9675 (1988).

[2] *Id.* §§ 6901–6992k.

few enterprises have continued to present themselves as full-service environmental firms; that is, they perform all testing, design the remediation, and then build the structures or remove the material as required. These companies are typically extremely large because they must maintain the capabilities to bring a project from engineering through testing and full implementation, both in construction and operations. The strength of this approach is that it permits strong, coordinated bidding for entire projects, with a flexible emphasis on the most profitable aspects of each project and the ability to cross-sell services.

This approach does, however, have several serious drawbacks. First, for many government projects, the Federal Acquisition Regulation prohibits the same firm from performing both the engineering and design function and the construction and operation function. To avoid the possibility that design decisions will be influenced to favor one particular firm, the government separates the two activities. As a result, firms frequently must decide whether to bid on the design portion of a contract—which may be small but profitable—and forgo the construction aspect, or to pass up the design and go for the larger but less certain construction activity.

Second, the resources necessary to maintain a full-service environmental company are extensive. Not only are the financial demands enormous but the difficulties in maintaining a staff large enough to respond to all possible issues can be quite significant.

Finally, the economics of a full-service environmental company preclude bidding on many small but profitable projects because the company's overhead is so high. In essence, many full-service companies have priced themselves out of the small project market.

The second and more common approach involves specialization. Enterprises focus either on particular media—air, groundwater, rivers and estuaries, and so on—or on particular technologies such as polychlorinated biphenyl (PCB) removal, volatile organic compound (VOC) removal, or asbestos abatement. Such specialization has advantages both economically and in the development of expertise. It does, however, require increasingly sophisticated joint venture arrangements in order to respond to each particular project. These joint ventures typically join two or more participants to provide unified services for one or more projects. The participants may bid as individual but related companies or as a unified entity. In either case, they must take into account a variety of joint venture issues.

What then are the specific joint venturing considerations in the hazardous waste and cleanup field? Perhaps the most important for the next decade is identification and definition of each joint venturer's scope of activities. Unlike traditional construction, in which the boundaries between specialties are so well known that they barely need discussion, the boundaries between activities in the environmental field are still quite fluid and developing. One of the most difficult portions of any joint venture is ensuring minimal duplication of effort. In order to become competitive and to serve the customer, duplication of effort is not economical and, in the long run, will cause substantial problems. In the same way, ongoing intra-venturer disputes over the proper allocation of work benefit no one.

There is no easy solution to the problem of allocating responsibility. One typical approach is to set the joint venture up as a general contractor/subcontractor format. The theory behind this approach is that the general contractor will make all the decisions as to who performs work and will delegate appropriate tasks to the subcontractor. At least in theory, most of the definitional issues are resolved because they are in the hands of one enterprise.

In fact, however, this approach rarely meets those expectations. For example, on a project involving both construction of a groundwater remediation system and of a soil remediation system, both the general contractor and the special groundwater subcontractor are interested in groundwater levels and directions of flow. The subcontractor, who must meet certain specified deadlines and success criteria, will often be reluctant to rely on the general contractor's groundwater mapping. First, the subcontractor may (often correctly) consider itself better able to perform such work with the appropriate level of accuracy and detail it needs. Second, because accuracy is much more important to its work than to soil remediation, when it comes time to make the appropriate performance guarantees and warranties, it may be unwilling to depend on work performed by another party. This type of potential dispute is often multiplied, especially when cleanup projects require substantial investigation and design before the final shape of the design is specified.

Accordingly, one of the most important aspects of any joint venture, whether it takes the form of a general contractor/subcontractor approach or an equal partner approach, is to define not only spheres of activities but methods of dispute resolution for the entire project. It is not enough to rely on the customer to make the decision nor is it enough to rely on general goodwill between the parties. Ultimately, decisions on the scope of activities are subject to the customer's approval. Even at the bidding stage, customers are increasingly looking to joint venturers to demonstrate that there will be minimal duplication of effort and cost as the project develops.

A second issue specific to cleanup joint ventures is the possibility that the joint venture may be liable for substantial fines and penalties from the EPA. Typical agreements between the EPA and private entities that must clean up a site require the private entities to subject themselves to substantial fines for failure to meet deadlines imposed by the EPA. Such fines can be as high as \$5000 per violation per day. Increasingly, private entities that contract with environmental cleanup firms require those firms to indemnify the private entities for such fines in the event they result in whole or in part from the joint venture's failures. Consequently, joint venture participants must determine how such fines are to be allocated among the various participating entities. This can be a particularly difficult issue when a delay penalty is imposed and there is no single cause for the delay. Many delays are caused by failures of more than one joint venture party. For example, if one entity's maps are late, that may cause another to have difficulties with design and also delay construction. When the private parties contracting with the joint venture seek indemnification for fines, the joint venture will be much better off if it has predetermined the allocation of responsibilities, thus avoiding some potential disputes.

A final concern for any joint venturer dealing with the government arises from the suspension/debarment policies of the EPA. The EPA has the power to suspend or debar contractors from performing any work on any government cleanup contract because of either a conviction for a felony or for other egregious violations of the environmental statutes. As a result, a joint venture must face the possibility that although one of its parties may be prohibited from government work, the other parties may wish to continue performing on other government contracts. If the joint venture agreement does not permit substitution for bidding or for performance of governmental contracts, then all the participants may be unable to work on government contracts for a substantial period of time. Even if the agreement makes such substitution difficult, it may prevent the performance or award of several contracts.

§ 11.3 Funding Issues

Both government and nongovernment cleanups are driven in large part by a structured set of deadlines for the entire project. Accordingly, there will be deadlines for various levels of predesign work, final design work, implementation, and postimplementation testing and verification. These deadlines are often tied to payments to cleanup contractors. Thus, for example, a contractor may not receive any payment until one or more of the thresholds has been successfully reached. This means that the contractor may need to finance the cleanup work for a substantial period of time before seeing any cash flow. In a project in New England, the contractor has expended over $1 million of its own funds because of certain delays in reaching the first important payment threshold. Fortunately for that contractor, it had the resources to fund the work. Otherwise, it would have defaulted on its contract, received no payments for a substantial amount of work, and become liable for substantial penalties.

For many joint venturers, therefore, particularly those bidding on more than one project at the time, financing issues must be a primary consideration for any project proposal. If the joint venture takes the general contractor/subcontractor approach, the parties must determine whether the general contractor may be a necessary source of financing for the subcontractor's work. If not, each venturer must be assured that it will not suffer if another coventurer runs into financial difficulty. On some occasions, the entire joint venture may seek a uniform credit or financing line from a financial institution or from an affiliated entity of one of the participants. On other occasions, each joint venturer must provide evidence of financial soundness so that the customer can be assured of adequate financial resources.

One ray of sunshine in this area is that rarely are joint venturers concerned about the financial default of the customer. The EPA is able to pay out of its Superfund with comparatively little difficulty, providing that the billing is in the appropriate format and is documented correctly. With respect to private contracts, the EPA generally requires that the private entities have on hand adequate funds for at least 90 days of payments. As a result, the payments for the contractors are generally provided in immediately available funds. Further, because private parties are jointly and severally liable for cleanup, rarely does the default of any single private party affect the payments to the cleanup contractor.

§ 11.4 Organizational Issues

There are essentially three key organizational issues in a hazardous waste joint venture:

1. Liaison with the customer
2. Product quality control
3. Site control.

Failure to address the implications of each of these areas is the most likely cause of the joint venture's failure.

§ 11.5 —Liaison with Customers

Whether the customer is a federal agency or is a group of private entities, there is continued and substantial need for communication between the customer and the joint venture. The customer's needs, because of the potential for penalties and substantial cost, will usually focus on performance and budgeting issues. In general, the customer will want not only historical information but also the estimated time to complete each aspect of the project, the budget and budget projections, and all the important pieces of information that may need to be reported to EPA or to the public.

This type of approach may designate one joint venturer as liaison with the customer. In other words, the customer talks to one entity (perhaps the general contractor) and that entity is responsible for gathering data and presenting information to the customer. The advantage of this model is simplicity; the disadvantage is that it rarely works well.

As a practical matter, because even component portions of an environmental subcontract are very complicated, it is very difficult to anticipate all the questions and concerns the customer may have as the project develops. With only a single source of information, the customer will often experience frustration and delays in obtaining information and responses. Thus, except in the most straightforward and well-defined projects, the single liaison approach is unlikely to work well over the long haul.

A second, and probably more useful, approach is to create a joint venture team that will act as liaison to the customer. Each substantial component of the joint venture will have a representative on the team. That team will meet frequently to ensure that each component understands what issues are likely to arise. When the customer desires information, although one person may be designated as the primary contact, the customer is encouraged to call any member of the team to get information. As a result, the customer has some burden in deciding what type of information it needs. On the other hand, once the customer accurately identifies the team member having the necessary information, the communication is both more accurate and more rapid.

The team approach does, however, require from the joint venturers a heightened level of coordination and interchange of information. It is embarrassing and sometimes devastating if two joint venturers are giving different information to the customer at the same time. In particular, when the joint venture deals with the almost inevitable change order, it must have a unified approach and theory as to the necessity for the change order. Otherwise, one joint venturer will be set off against the other under the threat of sanctions or penalties.

The third, and still a common, approach to liaison with the customer is for the joint venture to abdicate that responsibility. In other words, although the joint venture presents itself as a team to the customer for bidding purposes, it delegates entirely to the customer the task of gaining information. This model of communication works best only if the activities of the joint venture can be very clearly segregated either by scope or by time. Thus, if one portion of the joint venture is entirely completed before the second portion begins, there is little need for a coordinated liaison with the customer.

§ 11.6 —Product Control

One characteristic that distinguishes most environmental cleanups from other types of construction projects is that the participants not only must perform the work, but also write about it extensively. Thus, before the project can begin, an extensive and detailed report is usually submitted to the customer and through the customer to the EPA. After the project is complete, another report must be submitted. During the course of the project, various reports are frequently required. These reports are not simply afterthoughts or minor components of the activity. Given the highly technical nature of most cleanups and the standards for testing, submitting a report that inaccurately characterizes a site or the quality of work may result in some or all of the work be entirely repeated, frequently with the imposition of penalties. Put another way, work that is not well documented is often work that must be repeated.

As a result, it is imperative that all the work product of the joint venture meet the appropriate standard of quality and be well documented with good quality assurance and quality control procedures. Thus, if all the participants in a joint venture contribute to one report to be submitted to the EPA, the customer should not act as the coordinator or the final quality control on the report. Similarly, it is not and should not be the customer's job to ensure that all portions of the report are prepared in a timely fashion. The joint venture must determine how to coordinate the documentation and who will be responsible for ensuring that the report meets all appropriate criteria and that the underlying data is accurate.

To take a rather dramatic example, if one portion of the report contains data that is incorrect, at least in theory that report could be classified as a false statement, and all signatories to the report could be equally liable (potentially criminally liable) for the submission of incorrect and false data. Thus, it is incumbent on all members of the joint venture to come up with a system to ensure each other and themselves that all documentation is done properly.

§ 11.7 —Site Control

A typical hazardous waste site is usually an empty or partially empty area that cannot be entered without appropriate environmental control equipment and rarely has all of the utilities necessary for the ultimate cleanup. For example, even if there are sewer hookups at the site, contaminated groundwater can rarely be discharged to the sewer. Thus, whenever groundwater is pulled out of the ground there must be some mechanism to store and ultimately dispose of that groundwater. Because projects often require more than one joint venture participant to be present at the site at one time and because of the interaction of various joint venture activities, site control is an absolute essential. Joint ventures may encounter problems by allowing more than one participant to undertake groundwater treatment and disposal; they may be setting themselves up for an enormous lawsuit by the parties paying for the cleanup if the groundwater treatment portion of the joint venture so disturbs the soil that the soil remediation portion of the project processes twice as much soil as originally estimated.

Thus, each joint venture agreement must contain a provision defining site control and the ultimate chain of authority for site activities. Frequently, the customer will require that a construction manager be designated to oversee site control. Site control requires attention to each aspect of the job and to the potential for interaction, both beneficial and detrimental. Even if the joint venture agreement itself does not address these areas, there must be a mechanism for coordination and for conflict resolution.

A second aspect of site control relates to the responsibility for hazardous materials at the site. Often, one or more entities must be identified as the "generator" of hazardous materials that are shipped from the site to other locations.

At all costs, the joint venturer does not want to become the generator because that designation can lead to substantial future liability in the event of mishandling of hazardous materials. Accordingly, one essential aspect of site control is to identify the customer's representative who will be signing all required RCRA hazardous waste manifests and will be ultimately charged with responsibility for the site. Thus, any joint venture agreement must specify how that status is to be determined and how responsibility is to be allocated.

§ 11.8 Tax Issues

The most significant issue relating both to tax and planning considerations is the question of ownership of materials brought to the site. On the one hand, only the owner can take advantage of the depreciation benefits of material or equipment brought to the site and ultimately used there for some substantial period of time. On the other hand, equipment brought to the site must usually be decontaminated prior to reuse. Thus, the cost of decontamination or disposal of material from the site often far outweighs the salvage value. For example, many sites with substantial groundwater require the installation of sheet piling, which can frequently be reused. On the other hand, the unit cost of new sheet piling can be lower than the cost of decontaminating used sheet piling. Thus, the joint venture must ensure that ownership issues and liabilities be resolved among the joint venturers and between the joint venturer and the customer well before material is brought to the site. Not only do such decisions affect financing and cost issues, they may ultimately affect liability issues as well.

§ 11.9 Indemnification Issues

Indemnification has traditionally been a major concern for contractors in the hazardous waste business. When Superfund first began, contractors were given fairly broad indemnification. That indemnification policy changed when CERCLA was amended. Currently, the EPA is authorized to indemnify contractors against hazardous-waste-related risks only to the extent that adequate pollution insurance is not available.

The statutory framework for indemnification of hazardous waste cleanup contractors was established by both the CERCLA amendments and the Superfund Amendments and Reauthorization Act (SARA).[3] Specifically, that provision authorizes the EPA to indemnify contractors against risks from hazardous waste to the extent that insurance is not available at a fair and reasonable price. That indemnity is available only for the negligent acts of the contractors; grossly negligent or intentional misconduct is excluded from indemnification provisions.

---

[3] 42 U.S.C. § 9619 (1989).

In order to remain eligible for indemnification, contractors must engage in "diligent efforts" to obtain pollution insurance from private sources.

Since the passage of SARA, the EPA has developed various guidelines.[4] Notwithstanding all the related provisions, private pollution insurance is rarely a possibility for contractors. As a practical matter, even if it were available, the cost of such insurance would be prohibitive and would probably not fall within the fair and reasonable price standard established by the law. As a result, contractors are forced to deal either with the EPA or, in private cleanup projects, with those private parties to require indemnification.

In practice indemnification is still a substantial issue. When joint venturers are performing directly for the EPA on an emergency basis and with a limited scope, indemnification can be obtained. Thus, those engaged in barrel removal and initial stabilizations of sites can often get a relatively reasonable indemnification. In contrast, contractors seeking to perform comprehensive cleanups, particularly on a fixed-fee basis for private parties, may not only fail to get indemnification from the private parties but may wind up indemnifying the private parties. Private parties are often willing to pay a substantial premium to shift the risk of failure or unforeseen circumstances to the private contractor. Indeed, private parties often make such risk allocation a prerequisite to any cleanup contract. Although it is beyond the scope of this chapter to define all the possible indemnity outcomes, there are three essentials.

First, the conditions of indemnification must be defined. Simply providing indemnification either to the joint venture or from the joint venture does not necessarily mean it occurs under all circumstances. Is it triggered by the imposition of a fine or only by the payment of such fine? Does it occur when there are changed circumstances or only unforeseen changed circumstances? Knowing exactly when the indemnification provision kicks in is essential.

Second, what is the scope of indemnification? Does it cover only direct costs or is there an additional allocation for overhead and lost profits? Does the indemnification have a ceiling or should it be unlimited in time and in scope? In the event indemnification is limited, are there any occasions when there should be exceptions to such limits?

Third, how are disputes about the indemnification to be resolved? The more detailed and complicated the indemnification procedure and the more it replicates the complexity of the typical hazardous waste site, the more likely it is that there will be a dispute as to its applicability or scope. As a result, dispute resolution is an essential term of any indemnification agreement even if it simply ties in to an already established dispute resolution mechanism.

The situation is very different for contractors involved in cleanups relating to nuclear materials. A prescribed contract provision that governs indemnification must be inserted in every contract or subcontract. Speaking generally, the

---

[4] EPA, Interim Guidance on Indemnification of Superfund Response Action Contractors under § 119 of SARA, OSWER directive no. 9835.5.

indemnification gives very broad coverage, but subjects the contractor to civil or criminal penalties for violations of safety and handling regulations.

§ 11.10 Guarantee/Warranty Issues

In an underlying contract with a customer, a cleanup contractor may be required to make three types of guarantees:

1. The contractor may be required to meet certain standards, for example, to clean up the soil or groundwater to a particular level or concentration of contamination
2. The contractor may be required to meet certain time guarantees
3. The contractor may be required to meet certain performance guarantees; for example, that the equipment will take out a certain percentage of the contamination, will generate only a certain amount of by-product, or will cost only a certain amount to operate.

These guarantees are not part of the joint venture agreement between the participants but must be recognized if they appear in the agreement between the joint venture and the parties paying for the cleanup. For example, if meeting such guarantees is within the power and control of only one of the venturers, the other venturer may choose to seek indemnification or other protection in the event the guarantee or warranty is not met. Conversely, if the venture is a design/build enterprise, there must be some mechanism to determine the basis for any failure to meet a required guarantee. In short, a joint venture agreement must correspond and coordinate with the basic cleanup contract that is the purpose of the enterprise.

§ 11.11 Dispute Resolution Issues

As with many construction contracts, one essential requirement of most cleanup contracts is that the contractor must proceed even if there is a substantial dispute between the contractor and the customer. Obviously, this mandate is universal if the dispute is not between the contractor and the customer but between two or more parties to a joint venture. As a result, any dispute resolution mechanism must meet two fundamental criteria: it must resolve the dispute in a timely fashion, and it must resolve the dispute in a way that permits the parties to proceed.

Accordingly, unlike the standard format arbitration clause, which simply transfer a dispute to the American Arbitration Association or other similar body without criteria for resolution, a joint venture dispute resolution mechanism should include time deadlines, procedures, and mandates for the arbitration panel, and a clear description of precisely how the arbitration panel is to reach its decision and what such decision means. The most common mistakes in drafting arbitration clauses in this context are failing to make sure that all disputes go to dispute resolution and leaving the potential for litigation, or giving the arbitration panel too much latitude in hearing extraneous claims or matters not within the contemplation of the contract.

§ 11.12 Sample Selected Joint Venture Agreement Provisions

In many respects, joint venture agreements for hazardous waste and cleanup projects are very similar to other construction joint venture agreements. Thus, issues as to financing, in-progress recapitalization, control, and operation must be resolved before the agreement can be signed. Because this book contains a variety of such agreements, the reader should consult other chapters to get the flavor of such archetypal provisions, although joint venture agreement forms should be tailored to any specific venture. The following provisions are of particular importance to venturers in the environmental field.

SAMPLE JOINT VENTURE AGREEMENT PROVISIONS

TABLE OF CONTENTS

1. SCOPE OF ACTIVITIES

1. The Joint Venturers acknowledge the potential for possible overlap in their respective tasks. Accordingly, the provisions in this section shall govern the resolution of such conflict in order to avoid to the extent possible unnecessary duplication of effort.

(a) In the first instance, tasks shall be assigned as governed by the following documents, listed in order of precedence:

1. Any Change Orders or Work Amendments to the extent they have been properly approved in accordance with the Contract;
2. The Contract with the Customer;
3. Any plan, program, or other document submitted for approval to a governmental entity or which has been approved by a governmental entity;
4. This Joint Venture Agreement as it may be modified or amended.

(b) To the extent that the division of the Work cannot be determined in accordance with ¶ 1(a) above, the Project Managers for each of the Joint Venturers shall meet to coordinate the division of the Work. The Project Managers shall take into account the following factors: minimization of cost to the Customer, expertise in accomplishing the task(s), equitable allocation of costs, and profit opportunities as between the Joint Venturers. In the event such resolution is not achieved, either party may invoke the provisions of the [expedited] dispute resolution provisions.

2. For the purposes of ¶ 1(a) of this section, the following division of the Work shall apply in addition to the general description in Appendix A:

(a) *Reports:* Each Joint Venturer shall be responsible for preparing all draft and final reports concerning its portion of the Work. Overall supervision of such reports shall be the responsibility of ____________, who shall perform such final editing and production as is necessary.

(b) *Laboratory Work:* Each Joint Venturer shall be responsible for performing the laboratory work or obtaining the laboratory work for its portion of the Work. Such laboratory work shall be performed in accordance with the standards set forth in any governing document or guideline, and the entity performing such work or arranging for its performance shall be solely and exclusively responsible for any costs of quality assurance/quality control, reporting, and retesting.

(c) *Interface Design:*

(d) *Survey/Sampling:*

(e) *Accounting/Scheduling:*

(f) ____________ [Insert other specific task allocations]:

2. FINANCIAL LIABILITY FOR FINES, PENALTIES, AND DELAYS

1. The parties specifically acknowledge and agree that the costs of any fines, penalties, and delays are not to be considered as Joint Venture Costs as defined in ¶ ____. The financial responsibility for such fines, penalties, and delays shall be determined in accordance with this provision.

2. (a) In the event that fines, penalties, or delay costs result from improperly performed Work, the Joint Venturer responsible for such Work shall bear the full costs. If the Work is common Work, or if responsibility cannot be determined, then costs shall be apportioned on the basis of total revenues paid to that point to each Joint Venturer.

(b) In the event that fines, penalties, or delay costs result from failure to perform Work in a timely manner, then the Joint Venturer responsible for such failure shall bear the full costs. If the failure results from more than one cause, costs shall be allocated as follows:

> [A variety of allocation systems are common in the construction industry; joint venturers should choose the system most appropriate to their circumstances.]

(c) In the event the parties to this Agreement are not able to allocate the costs of fines, penalties, or delays, either party may invoke the dispute resolution provisions of this Agreement. Until final resolution of such dispute, the parties shall pay the costs in proportion to the revenues each has received to the date such payment becomes due.

3. In the event that a party responsible for the payment of the costs of fines, penalties, or delay fails to pay such costs and such costs are advanced by one or

more other parties, or in the event that the provisions of ¶ 2 of this section are invoked, monies shall bear interest from the time they should have been paid until they are paid or reimbursed at a rate of ____% per annum.

4. In the event a Joint Venturer is suspended or debarred from contracting with a state government or the federal government (the "Sanctioned Venturer"), the Joint Venturers will seek a prompt determination from the Customer as to any potential effect on the Contract. If such suspension or debarment will cause the Contract to become voidable or otherwise subject to cancellation, the Sanctioned Venturer may be replaced by the other Joint Venturer(s), and the other Joint Venturer(s) are hereby irrevocably appointed with durable power of attorney to do all things necessary for such substitution and to execute such documents as are necessary for such substitution with the full power and authority as if the Sanctioned Joint Venturer had acted. The Sanctioned Joint Venturer shall not be entitled to any return of capital or to any profits until the Contract is completed and all payments and expenses shall have been met. The Sanctioned Joint Venturer shall be entitled to such profits only as they were earned prior to the date of replacement.

3. LIAISON WITH THE CUSTOMER

1. Pursuant to § ______ [the management provision], the Joint Venturers shall designate one person to act as the liaison with the Customer. Such person shall receive all correspondence between the Customer and the Joint Venturers, shall approve all communications relating to bills, interpretation of [documents between Customer and Joint Venture], and the Contract and this Agreement, and shall participate in any negotiations with the Customer or on behalf of the Joint Venture with any third party. It shall be the duty of such liaison to report all communications promptly to the Joint Venturers and to act on their joint behalf without favoring any Joint Venturer.

[OR]

1. All correspondence between the Customer and the Joint Venturers and all communications relating to bills, interpretation of [documents between Customer and Joint Venture], and the Contract and this Agreement, and all negotiations with the Customer or on behalf of the Joint Venture with any third party shall be the responsibility of the Liaison Team. Each Joint Venturer shall designate a person to act as a member of the Liaison Team. The Liaison Team shall implement such arrangements as will ensure coordination of complete and efficient communications between the Customer and the Joint Venture and between the Joint Venturers. As a general principle, it shall be the presumption that each Joint Venturer shall take the lead in communications or negotiations that relate to its portion of the Work. The Liaison Team's arrangements shall be subject to review and approval from time to time by the Management Board of the Joint Venture.

4. SITE CONTROL

1. Prior to entry on the Site, the Management Board shall designate a Site Manager. In the event that more than one Joint Venturer is operating at the site at any time, the Site Manager or his or her designee shall have ultimate on-site authority to control scheduling and to resolve any conflicts between any entities

operating on the Site. All subcontracts executed by any Joint Venturer shall contain provisions necessary to ensure that such authority is recognized by all subcontractors. Decisions of the Site Manager or his or her designee shall be subject to appeal to the Management Board but shall be effective until such time as the Management Board issues other instructions.

5. DISPUTE RESOLUTION

1. There shall be two forms of dispute resolution that will be the sole and exclusive remedies for disputes between the Joint Venturers. Expedited Dispute Resolution may be invoked where specified or by mutual agreement. Full Disputes Resolution shall be implemented in all other cases.

2. Expedited Dispute Resolution Procedures shall be as follows. Demand may be made by writing or telephonic communication to all Joint Venturers. In the event of telephonic invocation, confirmation in writing shall be made as soon as practicable. The Project Managers for the Joint Venturers shall meet either in person or by telephone and shall attempt to resolve the dispute informally. There shall be no procedural requirements for such resolution. In the event resolution is not achieved within 48 hours of the first meeting of the Project Managers or within 96 hours of invocation of the process, whichever is shorter, each disputant shall submit its position in a writing not to exceed ten typewritten, double-spaced pages to a neutral third party designated by the Project Managers. In the event the Project Managers are unable to designate such person, or otherwise fail to do so, the dispute shall be resolved by ___________, or in his or her absence, by a partner in the law firm of ___________ [identify such person] or by such other person as may be designated by unanimous vote of the Management Board from time to time (the "Failsafe Third Party"). The decision of the Failsafe Third Party shall be final, conclusive, and unappealable and unreviewable except upon verified allegation of fraud or corruption. Each party shall bear the costs of this dispute resolution procedure.

3. The procedures for Full Dispute Resolution are as follows.

(a) A party with the right to initiate Full Dispute Resolution must do so in writing, with notice given to each of the joint venturers. Such notice shall contain a brief statement of the nature of the dispute, shall identify the provision(s) of this Agreement which govern the dispute, and shall state a nonbinding estimate of the amount in controversy, if applicable.

(b) Within five business days of actual receipt of such notice, the Project Managers of the parties involved in the dispute, or all of the Project Managers if the issue arises under §§ ______, ______, or ______, shall meet to attempt to resolve the dispute in good faith. Unless otherwise agreed, if after ten business days of the first meeting thereof, (1) the request for full dispute resolution is not withdrawn by written notice, or (2) a settlement is not reached in writing and executed by all involved parties, then the dispute shall be referred to the chief executive officer or his or her designee for each involved party.

(c) In the event a dispute is referred to the chief executive officer or his or her designee for each involved party (the "Senior Executive"), such Senior Executives shall meet in person or by telephone within ten business days of such referral to attempt to resolve the dispute in good faith. Unless otherwise agreed, if after ten business days of the first meeting thereof, (1) the request for Full Dispute Resolution is not withdrawn by written notice, or (2) a settlement is not reached in writing and executed by all involved parties, then the dispute shall be referred to arbitration in accordance with this Agreement.

4. In the event a matter is referred to arbitration pursuant to this provision, the following procedures shall apply.

(a) If the dispute is monetary and the amount in dispute is less than $______ or by agreement, all involved parties shall designate a neutral arbitrator to determine the dispute pursuant to this section. If the parties are unable to agree on an arbitrator within ten business days of referral to arbitration, then the Failsafe Third Party shall designate, in his sole and exclusive discretion, a neutral arbitrator.

(b) Once the neutral arbitrator is selected, the following pre-arbitration schedule shall apply in the absence of agreement by the parties otherwise:

> No later than FIVE business days after the arbitrator is designated all parties making claims, counterclaims, crossclaims, setoff claims or defenses, or recoupment claims or defenses shall file with the arbitrator and with each involved party a statement describing the nature of the claim, the provision(s) of this Agreement relevant to the dispute, all calculations of the amount in dispute, and any legal authorities that may be relevant or useful to the arbitrator.
>
> No later than TEN business days after the arbitrator is designated there shall be an initial meeting with representatives of the parties and their counsel. At such meeting, the arbitrator should attempt to define the issues in dispute and confirm the schedule contained herein, and each party shall identify their lead representative for the arbitration and each witness it intends to call with a summary of their expected testimony. This initial meeting may be in person or by telephone.
>
> No later than THIRTY business days after the initial meeting of the arbitrator, each party shall produce all documents relevant to the dispute without further need for request. Each party may also request the production of documents or categories of documents in the form prescribed by Fed. R. Civ. P. 34. The only basis for declining to produce documents shall be a good faith assertion of attorney/client or attorney work product privilege. All documents produced shall be used only for the purposes of the arbitration and must be returned or destroyed at the conclusion of arbitration. Issues of relevance shall *not* be a basis to withhold production of documents. In the event, however, that a request for production of documents calls for the production of more than 1,000 documents or more than 10 hours of an attorney's time, the requesting party shall be notified. If the requesting party does not withdraw or modify the request to below such threshold, the requesting party shall pay for all costs, expenses, and attorneys' fees associated with such production within ten days of the production of documents. Any relevant or responsive document not produced except by inadvertence or mistake may not be introduced by the party having the obligation to produce it, and, in the case of intentional or bad faith withholding, the arbitrator may impose sanctions including attorneys' fees, forfeiture of part or whole of a claim or defense, or allowance of part or whole of a claim or defense.

No later than FORTY-FIVE days after the initial meeting of the arbitrator, all depositions must be completed. Each involved party may notice no more than ten depositions, and each party shall have no more than thirty hours of examination, excluding breaks. Depositions of experts (witnesses who shall offer opinions) shall not be taken. Depositions of witnesses who are both fact and opinion witnesses shall be limited to the facts about which they will testify.

No later than SIXTY days after the initial meeting of the arbitrator, the arbitration hearing shall commence. The only bases for postponement of such hearing are (1) the illness or death of a party's lead representative or of a member of his or her immediate family, (2) the unavailability of a central witness necessary for the arbitrator's consideration, (3) a trial for which a party's lead representative has been designated lead counsel, or (4) such other reason as may be deemed appropriate.

(c) The arbitrator shall conduct its hearings in a fair and impartial manner. From the time the arbitrator begins the hearing until the time he or she renders a decision, no party or representative of a party may have any contact or communication with the arbitrator and the arbitrator must report any attempted contact or communication immediately to all parties. The arbitrator shall hear all testimony, direct and cross, through live witnesses except that the arbitrator may accept in writing (1) stipulations agreed to by both parties, (2) accounting and damage calculations, provided that the person or persons making such calculations are available for cross-examination, and (3) testimony authenticating or laying the foundation for documents to be introduced. The arbitrator shall not be bound by rules of evidence, but shall take into consideration the Federal Rules of Evidence and cases discussing them. Each party shall, in the absence of agreement to the contrary, have a maximum of thirty hours to put on its direct case and forty hours for cross-examination, excluding breaks. Notwithstanding such time allowances, the arbitrator may exclude irrelevant or duplicative evidence. Once the parties have rested or have exhausted their time allotments, the arbitrator shall declare the evidence closed. Within THIRTY days after the evidence has been closed, each party shall submit final briefs to the arbitrator. The arbitrator may choose to hear oral argument, and, if so, such argument shall be within TWENTY days of the date briefs are submitted to the arbitrator. The arbitrator shall render its decision within SIXTY days after the date briefs are submitted. If necessary, the arbitrator may award prospective relief, may issue such collateral orders as are necessary to effectuate its relief, and may award costs and attorneys' fees if he or she determines that a party was not acting in good faith or if he or she finds that the claim or the opposition was without colorable justification. The arbitrator *shall* award simple interest on all sums as of the date such sums became due at the average prime rate established by the ____________ Bank. All sums due as a result of the decision of the arbitrator must be paid within thirty days. After such time, such sums shall accrue interest at the rate of 18% per annum, compounded daily. The decision of the arbitrator shall be final and non-appealable except upon verified allegation of fraud or corruption.

INDEX